Perl for System Administration

Perl for System Administration

David N. Blank-Edelman

O'REILLY®

Beijing · Cambridge · Farnham · Köln · Paris · Sebastopol · Taipei · Tokyo

Perl for System Administration
by David N. Blank-Edelman

Copyright © 2000 O'Reilly & Associates, Inc. All rights reserved.
Printed in the United States of America.

Published by O'Reilly & Associates, Inc., 101 Morris Street, Sebastopol, CA 95472.

Editor: Linda Mui

Production Editor: Colleen Gorman

Cover Designer: Hanna Dyer

Printing History:

　　　　July 2000:　　　　　　　　First Edition.

Library of Congress Cataloging-in-Publication Data

Blank-Edelman, David N.
　　Perl for system administration / David N. Blank-Edelman. p. cm.
　　ISBN 1-56592-609-9
　　1. Perl (Computer program language) I. Title.

QA76.73.P22 B43 2000
005.13'3--dc21   00-055770

ISBN: 1-56592-609-9   [10/00]
[M]

Table of Contents

Preface

Perl is a powerful programming language that grew out of the traditional system administration toolbox. Over the years it has adapted and expanded to meet the challenges of new operating systems and new tasks. Until now, however, no book has recognized this deep history by concentrating solely on using Perl for system administration.

If you know a little Perl, and you need to perform system administration tasks, this is the right book for you. Readers with varying levels of both Perl programming experience and system administration experience will all find something of use within these pages.

How This Book Is Structured

Each chapter in this book addresses a different system administration domain and ends with a list of the Perl modules used in that chapter and references to facilitate deeper exploration of the information presented. The chapters are as follows:

Chapter 1, *Introduction*

> The introduction describes the material covered by the book in more detail, how it will serve you, and what you need to get the most from it. The material in this book is powerful and meant to be used by powerful people (e.g., Unix superusers and NT/2000 administrators). The introduction provides some important guidelines to help you write more secure Perl programs.

Chapter 2, *Filesystems*

> This chapter is about keeping multiplatform filesystems tidy and properly used. We start by looking at the salient differences between the native filesystems for each operating system. We then explore the process of walking or

traversing filesystems from Perl and how that can be useful. Finally, we look at manipulating disk quotas from Perl.

Chapter 3, *User Accounts*

This chapter discusses how these user accounts manifest themselves on two different operating systems. The crux of this chapter is a rudimentary account system written in Perl. In the process of building this system, we examine the mechanisms necessary for recording accounts in a simple XML-based database, creating these accounts, and deleting them.

Chapter 4, *User Activity*

Chapter 4 explores different process control mechanisms for all three operating systems. These range from the simple (e.g., MacOS processes) to the more complex (e.g., WinNT/2000 Windows Management Instrumentation). We put these mechanisms to work with administration helper scripts. Finally, we look at how to track file and network operations from Perl.

Chapter 5, *TCP/IP Name Services*

Name services allow hosts on a TCP/IP network to communicate with each other amicably. This chapter takes a historical perspective by starting with host files, moving to Network Information Service, and finally to the glue of the Internet, Domain Name Service. Each step of the way we show how Perl can make professional management of these services easier.

Chapter 6, *Directory Services*

As the complexity of the information we deal with increases over time, so does the importance of the directory services we use to access this information. System administrators are increasingly being called upon to not only use these services, but to build tools for their management. This chapter discusses some of the more popular directory service frameworks such as LDAP and ADSI, and shows you how to work with them from Perl.

Chapter 7, *SQL Database Administration*

Over time, more uses for relational databases are being found in the system administration realm. As a result, system administrators need to become familiar with SQL database administration. This chapter explains two SQL database frameworks, DBI and ODBC, and provides examples of them in action.

Chapter 8, *Electronic Mail*

This chapter demonstrates how Perl can make better use of email as a system administration tool. After discussing the basics of sending and parsing email via Perl, we look at several interesting applications, including Unsolicited Commercial Email (a.k.a. spam) analysis and managing tech support email.

Chapter 9, *Log Files*

System administrators are often awash in a sea of log files. Every machine, operating system, and program can (and often does) log information. This chapter looks at the logging systems offered by Unix and NT/2000. We discuss approaches for analyzing all of this information so it can work for you.

Chapter 10, *Security and Network Monitoring*

The final chapter heads right into the maelstrom called "security." We demonstrate how Perl can make hosts and networks more secure. In addition, we discuss several network monitoring techniques, including use of the Simple Network Management Protocol (SNMP) and network sniffing.

Appendixes

Some of the chapters assume some basic knowledge about a topic that you may not already have. For those who are new to these topics, this book includes several mini-tutorials to bring you up to speed quickly. These include introductions to the Revision Control System (RCS), Lightweight Directory Access Protocol (LDAP), Structured Query Language (SQL), eXstensible Markup Language (XML), and the Simple Network Management Protocol (SNMP).

Typographical Conventions

Italic

Used for filenames, usernames, directories, commands, hostnames, URLs, and terms when they are first introduced.

`Constant width`

Used for Perl module and function names, and when showing code and computer output.

`Constant width bold`

Used to indicate user input in examples.

`Constant width bold italic`

Used for parts of a command line that are user replaceable, or code annotations.

How to Contact Us

We have tested and verified the information in this book to the best of our ability, but you may find that features have changed (or even that we have made mistakes!). Please let us know of any errors you find, as well as your suggestions for future editions, by writing to:

O'Reilly & Associates, Inc.
101 Morris Street
Sebastopol, CA 95472
(800) 998-9938 (in the U.S. or Canada)
(707) 829-0515 (international/local)
(707) 829-0104 (FAX)

You can also send us messages electronically. To be put on the mailing list or request a catalog, send email to:

info@oreilly.com

To ask technical questions or comment on the book, send email to:

bookquestions@oreilly.com

We have a web site for the book, where we'll list examples, errata, and any plans for future editions. You can access this page at:

http://www.oreilly.com/catalog/perlsysadmin/

For more information about this book and others, see the O'Reilly web site:

http://www.oreilly.com

Acknowledgments

Writing a book turned out to be a lot like building one of those classical arches. It started with two pillars in my life that leaned towards each other, one technical, and the other personal.

On the technical side, I have the greatest appreciation for Larry Wall, who not only created Perl but imbued it and the Perl community with the spirit. I am thankful to the great Perl teachers, Tom Christiansen and Randal L. Schwartz, who have helped me and countless others learn all the twisty little passages of the language. Further up on this pillar are the kerjillions of programmers and hackers who poured countless hours and energy into the language and then chose to share their work with me and the rest of the Perl community. Wherever possible in this book I have tried to give these folks credit, but my thanks go to all of the named and unnamed folks who enrich the Perl culture with their efforts.

Moving further up the tech column past the Perl section, we come to the system administration section. Here we find another vibrant community that has helped to shape me, this book, and the whole computing field. The members of Usenix, SAGE, and the people who have contributed to the LISA conferences over the years deserve our thanks for cultivating and sharing the best the system administration field has to offer. In particular I'd like to acknowledge and thank Rémy Evard for being such a great influence on my professional and personal understanding of this field as a friend, mentor, and role model. He is one of the system administrators I want to be when I grow up.

Towards the top of the professional column are those directly responsible for the creation of this book. I'd first like to thank my reviewers and other commentators who sacrificed many hours on the alter of this text (in alphabetical order): Jerry Carter, Toby Everett, Æleen Frisch, Joe Johnston, Tom Limoncelli, John A. Montgomery, Jr., Chris Nandor, Michael Peppler, Michael Stok, and Nathan Torkington. Even towards the end of this process, they continued to teach me the finer points of Perl. I am grateful to Rhon Porter for his illustrations, to Hanna Dyer and Lorrie LeJeune for the most amazing cover animal, and to the O'Reilly production staff listed in the colophon. And finally, I am barely worthy to thank Linda Mui, my editor, whose incredible skill, finesse, and care allowed me to birth this book and raise it in a good home. She's the greatest.

Just as an arch is not built from a single column, so too did this book arise from another, more personal base. I need to thank all of the people in my spiritual community, Havurat Shalom in Somerville, Massachusetts, for their constant support during this whole process. They have taught me the meaning of community. Thank you, *M'kor HaChayim*, for this book and all of the many blessings in my life.

On a separate spiritual front, I am indebted to the Shona people of Zimbabwe for their incredible *mbira* music, the playing of which kept me sane during the writing process. I am thankful in particular to the many people who shared this music with me, some as teachers, some as students learning/playing beside me. Erica Azim, Stuart Carduner, Tute Chigamba, Wiri Chigonga, Musekiwa Chingodza, Forward Kwenda, Cosmas Magaya, Naomi Moland, Solomon Murungu, Paul Novitsky, and Nina Rubin have all had a special role in this process.

I am grateful to my friends Avner, Ellen, and Phil Shapiro, and Alex Skovronek for their encouragement. A special thank you goes to Jon Orwant and Joel Segel, two friends whose sage council and support gave me the opportunity and courage to wordwrestle. My thanks to the faculty and staff at the Northeastern University College of Computer Science. I'm extremely grateful to the folks in the CCS Systems group, who gave me the space, time, and patience I needed while dealing with this book. Larry Finkelstein, the Dean of the College of Computer Science, also deserves special recognition. I have never met a person outside of the system administration field who better understands system administrators, their needs, and the field in general. Dean Finkelstein continues to teach me, especially by example, what it means to be a true leader.

Let's return to the arch metaphor, because we're almost at the top. Here we find my extended and immediate family. I'm thankful to them all. My nuclear family, Myra, Jason, and Steven Blank, are the folks whose nature and nurture (and love) over the years allow me to be here today. My thanks to Shimmer and Bendir, my two late night/early morning companions during many a writing jag. Thanks also to my TCM pit crew, Kristen Porter and Thom Donovan.

If you're familiar with arches, you've probably noticed that I left out one key part: the capstone. The capstone is the stone at the top of the arch that keeps the whole thing together. Cindy Blank-Edelman was that capstone for me in the writing of this book. If there is anyone who sacrificed more for this book than I did, it is she. Without her love, support, care, humor, teaching, and inspiration, I could not be the same person, never mind write a book.

This book is dedicated to Cindy, love of my life.

1

Introduction

System Administration Is a Craft

In my town, several of our local bus lines are powered by cables strung high above the street. One day, when going to an unfamiliar destination, I asked the driver to let me know when a particular street was approaching. He said, "I'm sorry, I can't. I just follow the wires."

These are words you will never hear good system administrators use to describe their job. System and network administration is about deciding what wires to put in place, where to put them, getting them deployed, keeping watch over them, and then eventually ripping them out and starting all over again. Good system administration is hardly ever rote, especially in multiplatform environments where the challenges come fast and furious. Like any other craft, there are better and worse ways to meet these challenges. This book is for the people who face those challenges, either as full-time system administrators or part-time tinkerers. I'll try to show you how Perl can help.

How Perl Can Help

System administration work should use any and every computer language available when appropriate. So why single out Perl for a book?

The answer to this question harkens back the to the very nature of system administration. Rémy Evard, a colleague and friend, once described the job of a system administrator like this: "On one side, you have a set of resources: computers, networks, software, etc. On the other side, you have a set of users with needs and projects—people who want to get work done. Our job is to bring these two sets together in the most optimal way possible, translating between the world of vague human needs and the technical world when necessary."

System administration is often a *glue* job; Perl is one of the best glue languages. Perl was being used for system administration work well before the World Wide Web came along with its voracious need for glue mechanisms.

Perl has several other things going for it from a system administration perspective:

- It is clearly an offspring of the various Unix shells and the C language, tools many system administrators are comfortable using.

- It is available on almost all modern operating systems. It does its best to present a consistent interface on each. This is important for multiplatform system administration.

- It has excellent tools for text manipulation, database access, and network programming, three of the mainstays of the profession.

- The core language can easily be extended through a carefully constructed module mechanism.

- A large and dedicated community of users has poured countless hours into creating modules for virtually every task. Most of these modules are collected in an organized fashion (more on these collections in a moment). This community support can be very empowering.

- It is just plain fun to program.

In the interest of full disclosure, it is important to note that Perl is not the answer to all of the world's problems. Sometimes it is not even the appropriate tool for system administration programming because:

- Perl has a somewhat dicey object-oriented programming mechanism grafted on top of it. Python is much better in this regard.

- Perl is not ubiquitous. You are more likely to find the Bourne shell than Perl on a system as it comes off the shelf.

- Perl is not always simple or internally self-consistent and is chock full of arcania. Tcl has far fewer surprises.

- Perl has enough power and esoterica to shoot you in the foot.

The moral here is *choose the appropriate tool.* More often than not, Perl has been that tool for me, and hence this book.

This Book Will Show You How

In the 1966–68 "Batman" television show, the dynamic duo wore utility belts. If Batman and Robin had to scale a building, Batman would say, "Quick Robin, the Bat Grappling Hook!" Or Batman would say, "Quick Robin, the Bat Knockout Gas!" and they'd both have the right tool at hand to subdue the bad guys. This book aims to give you the utility belt you need to do good system administration work.

Every chapter attempts to provide you with three things.

Clear and concise information about a system administration domain.

In each chapter we discuss in depth one domain of the system administration world. The number of possible domains in multiplatform system administration is huge, far too many to be included in a single book. The best survey books on just Unix system administration, *Essential System Administration,* by Æleen Frisch (O'Reilly & Associates), and *Unix System Administration Handbook,* by Evi Nemeth, Garth Snyder, and Trent R. Hein (Prentice-Hall), are two and three times, respectively, the size of this book. We'll be looking at topics from three different operating systems: Unix, Windows NT, Windows 2000, and MacOS.

As a result, some hard choices were made on what to include and what to exclude. In general the topics that I believe will become even more important over the next five years made the cut. Important technologies like XML are explored because they are likely to have a significant impact on the field as time goes by. Unfortunately, these guidelines meant that some system administration stalwarts like backup and printing are edged out by newer topics like LDAP and SNMP. The skills and tools provided by this book can help with the domains I omit, but a direct treatment will have to be found elsewhere.

I've tried to put together a good stew of system and network administration information for people with varying levels of experience in the field. Seasoned veterans and new recruits may come away from this book having learned completely different material, but everyone should find something of interest to chew on. Each chapter ends with a list of references which can help you get deeper into a topic should you so choose.

For each domain or topic, especially the ones that have a considerable learning curve, I include appendixes with all of the information you need to come up to speed quickly. Even if you're familiar with a topic, you may find these appendixes can round out your knowledge about that matter (e.g., how something is implemented on a different operating system).

Perl techniques and approaches that can be used in system administration.

To get the most out of this book, you'll need some initial Perl background. Every chapter is full of Perl code that ranges in complexity from beginner to advanced levels of Perl knowledge. Whenever we encounter an intermediate-to-advanced technique, data structure, or idiom, I'll take the time to carefully step us through it, piece by piece. In the process, you should be able to pick up some interesting Perl techniques to add to your programming repertoire. The hope is that Perl programmers of all levels will be able to find something to learn from the examples presented in this book. And as your Perl skills improve over time, you should be able to come back to this book, learning new things each time.

To further enhance this learning experience, I will often present more than one way to accomplish the same task using Perl rather than showing a single limited answer. Remember the Perl motto, "There's More Than One Way To Do It." These multiple-approach examples are designed to better equip your Perl utility belt: the more tools you have at hand, the better the choices you can make when approaching a new task.

Sometimes it will be obvious that one technique is superior to the others. But this book only addresses a certain subset of situations you may find yourself in, and a solution that is woefully crude for one problem may be just the ticket for another. So bear with me. For each example I'll try to show you both the advantages and drawbacks of each approach (and often tell you which method I prefer).

System administration best practices and deep principles.

As I mentioned at the start of this chapter, there are better and worse ways to do system administration. I've been a system and network administrator for the last 15 years in some pretty demanding multiplatform environments. In each chapter I try to bring this experience to bear as I offer you some of the best practices I've learned and the deeper principles behind them. Occasionally I'll use a personal "war story from the front lines" as the starting point for these discussions. Hopefully the depth of the craft in system administration will become apparent as you read along.

What You Need

To get the most of this book, you will need some technical background and some resources at hand. Let's start with the background first:

You'll need to know some Perl

There isn't enough room in this book to provide the basics of the Perl language, so you need to seek that elsewhere before working through this material. Once you have learned the material in a book like *Learning Perl,* by Randal L. Schwartz and Tom Christiansen (O'Reilly), or *Learning Perl on Win32 Systems,* by Randal L. Schwartz, Erik Olson, and Tom Christiansen (O'Reilly), you should be in good shape to approach the code in this book.

You'll need to know the basics of your operating system(s)

This book assumes that you have some facility with the operating system or systems you plan to administer. You'll need to know how to get around in that OS, run commands, find documentation, etc. Background information on the more complex frameworks built into the OS (e.g., WMI on Windows 2000 or SNMP) is provided.

You may need to know the specifics of your operating system(s)

I make an attempt to describe the differences between the major operating systems as we encounter them, but I can't cover all of the intra-OS differences. In particular, every variant of Unix is a little different from all of the others. As a result, you may need to find OS-specific information and roll with the punches should the information be different than what is described here.

For technical resources, you will need just two things:

Perl

You will need a copy of Perl installed on or available to every system you wish to administer. The downloads section of *http://www.perl.com* will help you find either the source code or binary distributions for your particular operating system. The examples in this book use Perl Version 5.005 (the latest stable version as of this writing). On Unix we use the core Perl distribution compiled from source, on Win32 platforms we use the version provided by ActiveState (build 522) and on MacOS we use the MacPerl distribution (5.2.0r4).

The ability to find and install Perl modules

The next section of this chapter is devoted to the location and installation of Perl modules because this skill is extremely important. This book assumes you have the knowledge and necessary permission to install any modules you need.

At the end of each chapter is a list of the version numbers for all of the modules used by the code in that chapter. The version information is provided because modules are updated all the time. Not all updates retain backwards compatibility, so if you run into problems, this information can help you determine if there has been a module change since this book was published.

Locating and Installing Modules

Much of the benefit of using Perl for system administration work comes from all of the free code available in module form. The modules mentioned in this book can be found in one of three places:

Comprehensive Perl Archive Network (CPAN)

CPAN is a huge archive of Perl source code, documentation, scripts, and modules that is replicated at over a hundred sites around the world. Information on CPAN can be found at *http://www.cpan.org*. The easiest way to find the modules on CPAN is to use the search engine developed and maintained by Elaine Ashton, Graham Barr, and Clifton Posey at *http://search.cpan.org*. The "CPAN Search:" box makes it simple to find the right modules for the job.

Individual repositories for pre-built packages

In a moment we'll encounter the Perl Package Manager (PPM), an especially important tool for Win32 Perl users. This tool connects to *repositories* (the most famous one is housed at ActiveState) to retrieve pre-built module packages. A good list of these repositories can be found in the PPM Frequently Asked Questions list at *http://www.activestate.com/Products/ActivePerl//docs/faq/ActivePerl-faq2.html*. If a Win32 package we use does come from a repository other than ActiveState's, I'll be sure to point you at it. For MacOS modules, the canonical place to look is the MacPerl Module Porters site at *http://pudge.net/mmp/*.

Individual web sites

Some modules are not published to CPAN or any of the PPM repositories. I'll always tell you where to get modules if they are found off the beaten path.

How do you install one of these modules when you find it? The answer depends on the operating system you are running. Perl now ships with documentation on this process in a file called *perlmodinstall.pod* (type *perldoc perlmodinstall* to read it). The next sections provide brief summaries of the steps required for each operating system used in this book.

Installing Modules on Unix

In most cases, the process goes like this:

1. Download the module and unpack it.

2. Run *perl Makefile.PL* to create the necessary *Makefile*.

3. Run *make* to build the package.

4. Run *make test* to run any test suites included with the module by the author.

5. Run *make install* to install it in the usual place for modules on your system.

If you want to save yourself the trouble of performing these steps all by hand, you can use the CPAN module by Andreas J. König (shipped with Perl). This module allows you to perform all of those steps by typing:

```
% perl -MCPAN -e shell
cpan> install modulename
```

The CPAN module is smart enough to handle module dependencies (i.e., if one module requires another module to run, it will install both modules for you automatically). CPAN also has a built-in search function for finding related modules and packages. I recommend typing *perldoc CPAN* on your system to see all of the handy features of this module.

Installing Modules on Win32

The process for installing modules on Win32 platforms mirrors that for Unix with one additional step, *ppm*. If you plan to install modules by hand using the Unix instructions above, you can use programs like WinZip (*http://www.winzip.com*) to unpack a distribution and *nmake* (found at *ftp://ftp.microsoft.com/Softlib/MSLFILES/ nmake15.exe*) instead of *make* to build and install a module.

Some modules require compilation of C files as part of their build process. A large portion of the Perl users in the Win32 world do not have the necessary software installed on their computers for this compilation, so ActiveState created the Perl Package Manager to handle pre-built module distribution.

The PPM system is similar to that of the CPAN module. It uses a Perl program called *ppm.pl* to handle the download and installation of special archive files from PPM repositories. You can either start this program by typing *ppm* or by running *perl ppm.pl* from within the Perl *bin* directory:

```
C:\Perl\bin>perl ppm.pl
PPM interactive shell (1.1.1) - type 'help' for available commands.
PPM> install module-name
```

ppm, like CPAN, can also search the list of available and installed modules for you. Type *help* at the *ppm* command prompt for more information on how to use these commands.

Installing Modules on MacOS

Installing modules on MacOS is a strange hybrid of the methods we've seen so far. Chris Nandor has put together a distribution called *cpan-mac* (found either at CPAN or *http://pudge.net/macperl*) that includes ports of CPAN and a whole slew of other important modules to the Mac.

Once the *cpan-mac* distribution is installed, it is possible to download most Perl-only modules from CPAN and install them. Nandor makes this task easy by providing an MacPerl droplet called *installme*. Archive files (i.e., *.tar.gz* files) dropped on top of *installme* will be de-archived and installed in a CPAN-like fashion.

For more information on MacOS module installation, be sure to see an expanded version of the *perlmodinstall.pod* document mentioned earlier called *macperl modinstall.pod*. This can also be found at *http://pudge.net/macperl*.

It's Not Easy Being Omnipotent

Before we continue with the book, let's take a few minutes for some cautionary words. Programs written for system administration have a twist that makes them different from most other programs. On Unix and NT/2000 they are often run with elevated privileges, i.e., as *root* or *Administrator*. With this power comes responsibility. There is an extra onus on us as programmers to write secure code. We write code that can and will bypass the security restrictions placed on mere mortals. If we are not careful, less "ethical" users may use flaws in our code for nefarious purposes. Here are some of the issues you should consider when you use Perl under these circumstances.

Don't Do It

By all means, use Perl. But if you can, avoid having your code run in a privileged context. Most tasks do not require *root* or *Administrator* privileges. For example, your log analysis program probably does not need to run as *root*. Create another, less privileged user for this sort of automation. Have a small, dedicated, privileged program hand the data to that user if necessary, and then use that user to perform the analysis.

Drop Your Privileges as Soon as Possible

Sometimes you can't avoid running a script as *root* or *Administrator*. For instance, a mail delivery program you create may need to be able to write to a file as any user on the system. Programs like these should shed their omnipotence as soon as possible during their run.

Perl programs running under Unix and Linux can set the $< and $> variables:

```
# permanently drops privs
($<,$>) = (getpwnam('nobody'),getpwnam('nobody'));
```

This sets the real and effective user IDs to that of *nobody,* hopefully an underprivileged user. To be even more thorough, you may wish to use $(and $)to change the real and effective group IDs as well.

Windows NT and Windows 2000 do not have user IDs per se, but there are similar processes for dropping privileges. Windows 2000 has a feature called "RunAs" which can be used to run processes as a different user. Under both Windows NT and Windows 2000, users with the user right of Act as part of the operating system can impersonate other users. This user right can be set using the *User Manager* or *User Manager for Domains* program:

1. Under the "Policies" menu, choose "User Rights."

2. Select the "Show Advanced User Rights" check box.

3. Choose "Act as part of the operating system" from the drop-down selector.

4. Select "Add..." and choose the users or groups who should receive this right. You may need to choose "Show Users" if you will be adding this right to a specific user.

5. If this is an interactive user, that user must log out and back in again to make use of this new user right.

You will also need to add the rights Replace a process level token and in some cases Bypass traverse checking (see the Win32::AdminMisc documentation). Once you have assigned these rights to a user, that user can run Perl scripts with LogonAsUser() from David Roth's Win32::AdminMisc module found at *http://www.roth.net*:

```
use Win32::AdminMisc;
die "Unable to impersonate $user\n"
    if (!Win32::AdminMisc::LogonAsUser('',$user,$userpw);
```

Note: there is some danger here, because unlike the previous example, you must pass the password of the user to the LogonAsUser() call.

Be Careful When Reading Data

When reading important data like configuration files, test for unsafe conditions first. For instance, you may wish to check that the file and all of the directories that hold the file are not writeable (since that means someone could have tampered with them). There's a good recipe for testing this in Chapter 8 of the *Perl Cookbook,* by Tom Christiansen and Nathan Torkington (O'Reilly).

The other concern is user input. Never trust that input from a user is palatable. Even if you explicitly print Please answer Y or N:, there is nothing preventing the user from answering with 2049 random characters (either out of spite, malice, or because they stepped away from the keyboard and a two-year-old came over to the keyboard instead).

User input can be the cause of even more subtle trouble. My favorite example is the "Poison NULL Byte" exploit as reported in an article on Perl CGI problems.

Be sure to see the whole article (cited in the References section at the end of this chapter). This particular exploit takes advantage of the difference between Perl's handling of a NULL (\000) byte in a string and the handling done by the C libraries on a system. To Perl, there is nothing special about this character. To the libraries, this character is used to indicate the end of a string.

In practical terms, this means that it is possible for a user to evade simple security tests. One example given in the article is that of a password-changing program whose code looks like this:

```
if ($user ne "root"){ <call the necessary C library routine>}
```

If $user is set to root\000 (i.e., root followed by a NULL byte) then the above test will succeed. When that string is passed to the underlying library, the string will be treated as just *root*, and someone will have just walked right past the security check. If not caught, this same exploit will allow access to random files and other resources. The easiest way to avoid being caught by this exploit is to sanitize your input with something like:

```
$input =~ tr /\000//d;
```

This is just one example of how user input can get our programs in trouble. Because user input can be so problematic, Perl has a security precaution called "taint mode." See the *perlsec* manpage that ships with Perl for an excellent discussion of "taintedness" and other security precautions.

Be Careful When Writing Data

If your program can write or append to every single file on the local filesystem, you need to take special care with the how, where, and when it writes data. On Unix systems, this is especially important because symbolic links make file switching and redirection easy. Unless your program is diligent, it may find itself writing to the wrong file or device. There are two classes of programs where this concern comes especially into play.

Programs that append data to a file fall into the first class. The steps your program should take in sequence *before* appending to a file are:

1. Check the file's attributes before opening it using stat() and the normal file test operators. Make sure it is not a hard or soft link, that it has the appropriate permissions and ownership, etc.

2. Open the file for appending.

3. stat() the open filehandle.

4. Compare the values from steps 1 and 3 to be sure that you have an open file handle to the file you intended.

You can see the *bigbuffy* program in Chapter 9, *Log Files*, for sample code that uses this procedure.

Programs that use temporary files or directories are in the second class. You've often seen code like this:

```
open(TEMPFILE,">/tmp/temp.$$") or die "unable to write /tmp/temp.$$:$!\n";
```

Unfortunately, that's not sufficiently secure on a multiuser machine. The process ID ($$) sequence on most machines is easily predictable, which means the next temporary filename your script will use is equally predictable. If someone can predict that name, they may be able to get there first and that's usually bad news.

Some operating systems have library calls that will produce a temporary filename using a decent randomization algorithm. To test your operating system, you can run the following code. If the printed names look reasonably random to you, POSIX::tmpnam() is a safe bet. If not, you may have to roll your own random filename generation function:

```
use POSIX qw(tmpnam);
for (1..20){ print POSIX::tmpnam(),"\n"; }
```

Once you have a filename that cannot be guessed, you will need to open it securely:

```
sysopen(TEMPFILE,$tmpname,O_RDWR|O_CREAT|O_EXCL,0666);
```

There is a second, easier way to perform these two steps (getting and opening a temporary file). The IO::File->new_tmpfile() method from the IO::File module will not only pick a good name (if the system libraries support this), but it will also open the file for you for reading and writing.

Examples of POSIX::tmpnam() and IO::File->new_tmpfile() along with other information about this topic can be found in Chapter 7 of the *Perl Cookbook*. Tim Jenness' File::Temp module also attempts to provide secure temporary file operations.

Avoid Race Conditions

Whenever possible, avoid writing code that is susceptible to race condition exploits. The traditional race condition starts with the assumption that the following sequence is valid:

1. Your program will amass some data.

2. Your program can then act on that data.

If users can break into this sequence, let's say at step 1.5, and make some key substitutions, they may cause trouble. If they can get your program in step 2 to naively act upon different data than it found in step 1, they have effectively exploited a race condition (i.e., their program won the race to get at the data in question). Other race conditions occur if you do not handle file locking properly.

Race conditions often show up in system administration programs that scan the filesystem as a first pass and then change things in a second pass. Nefarious users may be able to make changes to the filesystem right after the scanner pass so that changes are made to the wrong file. Make sure your code does not leave gaps like this open.

Enjoy

It is important to remember that system administration is fun. Not all the time, and not when you have to deal with the most frustrating of problems, but there's a definite enjoyment to be found. There is a real pleasure in supporting other people and building the infrastructures that make other people's lives better. When the collection of Perl programs you've just written brings other people together for a common purpose, there is joy.

Now that you are ready, let's get to work on those wires.

References for More Information

http://dwheeler.com/secure-programs/Secure-Programs-HOWTO.html is a HOWTO document for secure programming under Linux, but the concepts and techniques are applicable to other situations as well.

http://www.cs.ucdavis.edu/~bishop/secprog.html contains more good secure programming resources from security expert Matt Bishop.

http://www.homeport.org/~adam/review.html lists security code review guidelines by Adam Shostack.

http://www.dnaco.net/~kragen/security-holes.html is a good paper on how to find security holes (especially in your own code) by Kragen Sitaker.

http://www.shmoo.com/securecode/ offers an excellent collection of articles on how to write secure code.

Perl CGI Problems, by Rain Forest Puppy (Phrack Magazine, 1999) can be found online at *http://www.insecure.org/news/P55-07.txt* or from the Phrack archives at *http://www.phrack.com/archive.html*.

Perl Cookbook, by Tom Christiansen and Nathan Torkington (O'Reilly, 1998) contains many good tips on coding securely.

2

Filesystems

Perl to the Rescue

Laptops fall in slow motion. Or at least that's the way it looked when the laptop I was using to write this book fell off a table onto a hardwood floor. The machine was still in one piece and running when I picked it up. As I checked the laptop to see if anything was damaged, I noticed it started to run slower and slower. Not only that, but the laptop began to make sporadic and disturbing humming-buzzing sounds during disk access. Figuring the software slowdown was caused by a software problem, I shut the laptop down. It did not go gently into the night, refusing to shut down cleanly. This was a bad sign.

Even worse was its reluctance to boot again. It would begin the Windows NT booting process and then fail with a "file not found" error. By now it was clear that the fall had caused some serious physical damage to the hard drive. The heads had probably skidded over the hard drive platter surface, destroying files and directory entries in their wake. Now the question was, "Did any of my files survive? Did the files for *this book* survive?"

I first tried booting to Linux, the other operating system installed on the laptop. Linux booted fine, an encouraging sign. The files for this book, however, resided on the Windows NT NTFS partition that did not boot. Using Martin von Löwis's Linux NTFS driver, available at *http://www.informatik.hu-berlin.de/~loewis/ntfs/*

(now shipping with the Linux 2.2 kernels), I mounted the partition and was greeted with what *looked* like all of my files intact.

My attempts to copy these files off that partition would proceed fine for a while until I reached a certain file. At that point the drive would make those ominous sounds again and the backup would fail. It was clear that if I wanted to rescue my data I was going to have to skip all the damaged files on the disk. The program I was using (*gnutar*) had the ability to skip a list of files, but here was the problem: which files? There were over *sixteen thousand* files on this filesystem at time of impact. How was I going to figure out which files were damaged and which were fine? Clearly running *gnutar* again and again was not a reasonable strategy. This was a job for Perl!

I'll show you the code I used to solve this problem a little later on in this chapter. For that code to make sense, we'll first need to place it into context by looking at filesystems in general and how we operate on them using Perl.

Filesystem Differences

We'll start with a quick review of the native filesystems for each of our target operating systems. Some of this may be old news to you, especially if you have significant experience with a particular operating system. Still, it is worth your while to pay careful attention to the differences between the filesystems (especially the ones you don't know) if you intend to write Perl code that works on multiple platforms.

Unix

All modern Unix variants ship with a native filesystem with semantics that resemble those of their common ancestor, the Berkeley Fast File System. Different vendors have extended their filesystem implementations in different ways (e.g., Solaris adds Access Control Lists for better security, Digital Unix ships a spiffy transaction-based filesystem called *advfs*, etc.). We'll be writing code aimed at the lowest common denominator to allow it to work across different Unix platforms.

The top, or root, of a Unix filesystem is indicated by a forward slash (/). To uniquely identify a file or directory in a Unix filesystem, we construct a path starting with a slash and then add directories, separating them with forward slashes, as we descend deeper into the filesystem. The final component of this path is the desired directory or filename. Directory and filenames in modern Unix variants are case sensitive. Almost all ASCII characters can be used in these names if you are crafty enough, but sticking to alphanumeric characters and some limited punctuation will save you hassle later.

Microsoft Windows NT/2000

Windows NT (Version 4.0 as of this writing) ships with two supported filesystems: File Allocation Table (FAT) and NT FileSystem (NTFS). Windows 2000 adds FAT32, an improved version of FAT that allows for larger partitions and smaller cluster sizes to the NT family.

Windows NT uses an extended version of the basic FAT filesystems found in DOS. Before we look at the extended version, it is important to understand the foibles of the basic FAT filesystem. In basic or real-mode FAT filesystems, filenames conform to the 8.3 specification. This means that file and directory names can start with no more than eight characters, must have a period (or *dot* as it is spoken), and are followed by a suffix of up to three characters in length. Unlike Unix, where a period in a filename has no special meaning, basic FAT filesystems can only use a single period as an enforced separator between the filename and its extension or suffix.

Real-mode FAT was later enhanced in a version called VFAT or protected-mode FAT. This is roughly the version that Windows NT and Windows 2000 support. VFAT hides all of the name restrictions from the user. Longer filenames without separators are provided by a very creative hack. VFAT uses a chain of standard file/directory name slots to transparently shoehorn extended filename support into the basic FAT filesystem structure. For compatibility, every file and directory name can still be accessed using a special 8.3-conforming DOS alias. For instance, the directory called *Downloaded Program Files* is also available as *DOWNLO~1*.

There are four key differences between a VFAT and a Unix filesystem:

1. FAT filesystems are case-insensitive. In Unix, an attempt to open a file using the wrong case (i.e., *MYFAVORITEFILE* versus *myfavoritefile*) will fail. With FAT or VFAT, this will succeed with no problem.

2. The second difference is the choice of characters used to separate path components and root designations. Instead of forward slash, FAT uses the backward slash (\) as its path separator. This has a direct ramification for the Perl programmer. The backslash is a quoting character in Perl. Paths written in single quotes with only single separators (i.e., `$path='\dir\dir\filename'`) are just fine. However, situations in which you need to place multiple backslashes next to each other (i.e., *server**dir**file*) are potential trouble. In those cases, you have to be vigilant in doubling any multiple backslashes. Some Perl functions and some Perl modules will accept paths with forward slashes, but this convention should not be counted upon when programming. It is better to bite the bullet and write `\\\\winnt\\temp\\` than to learn that your code breaks because the conversion hasn't been done for you.

3. FAT files and directories have special flags associated with them that are called *attributes*. Example attributes include "Read-only" and "System."

4. Finally, the last difference is in the root directory specification. The root of a FAT filesystem is specified starting at the drive letter that filesystem lives on. For instance, the absolute path for a file might be specified as *c:\home\cindy\ docs\resume\current.doc*.

FAT32 and NTFS filesystems have the same semantics as VFAT. They share the same support for long filenames and use the same root designator. NTFS is slightly more sophisticated in its name support because it allows these names to be specified using Unicode. Unicode is a multibyte character encoding scheme that can be used to represent all of the characters of all of the written languages on the planet.

NTFS also has some functional differences that distinguish it from the other Windows NT/2000 and basic Unix filesystems. NTFS supports the notion of an Access Control List (ACL). ACLs provide a fine-grained permission mechanism for file and directory access. Later on in this chapter we will write some code to take advantage of some of these differences.

Before we move on to another operating system, it is important to at least mention the Universal Naming Convention. UNC is a convention for locating things (files and directories in our case) in a networked environment. Instead of the drive letter and a colon preceding an absolute path, the *drive letter:* part is replaced with *\\server\sharename*. This convention suffers from the same Perl backslash syntax clash we saw a moment ago. As a result, it is not uncommon to see a set of leaning toothpicks like this:

```
$path = "\\\\server\\sharename\\directory\\file"
```

MacOS

Despite its GUI-centrist approach, the MacOS Hierarchical File System (HFS) also lets users specify textual pathnames, albeit with a few twists. Absolute pathnames are specified using the following form: *Drive/Volume Name:Folder:Folder:Folder: FileName*. A specification with no colons refers to a file in the current directory.

Unlike the two previous operating systems, HFS paths are considered absolute if they do *not* begin with their path separator (:). An HFS path that begins with a colon is a relative path. One subtle difference that sets MacOS paths apart from the other operating systems is the number of separators you need to use when pointing to objects higher up in the directory hierarchy. For instance, under Unix, you would use *../../../FileName* to get to a file three levels higher than the current directory. Under MacOS, you would use four separators (i.e., *::::FileName*), because you must include a reference to the current directory in addition to the three previous levels.

File and directory names are limited to 31 characters under HFS. As of MacOS Version 8.1, an alternative volume format called MacOS Extended Format or HFS+ was introduced to allow for 255 Unicode character filenames. Although the HFS+ filesystem allows these long names, MacOS does not yet support them as of this writing.

A more significant departure from the previous two operating systems (at least from a Perl programming point of view) is MacOS's use of the "fork" idiom for its file storage. Each file is said to have a *data fork* and a *resource fork*. The former holds the data part of the file, while the latter contains a variety of different *resources*. These resources can include executable code (in the case of a program), user interface specifications (dialog boxes, fonts, etc.), or any other components a programmer wishes to define. Though we won't be dealing with forks per se this chapter, MacPerl does have facilities for reading and writing to both forks.

> The core Perl operators and functions operate on the data fork only in MacPerl. For example, the *−s* operator returns only the data fork's size of a file. You will need to use some of the bundled Macintosh Toolbox modules if you wish to access a file's resource fork.

Each file in the HFS filesystem also has two special tags, *creator* and *type,* that allow the OS to identify which application created that file and what kind of file it is purported to be. These tags play the same role as extensions used in the FAT filesystem (e.g., *.doc* or *.exe*). Later in this chapter we'll briefly show how to use the type/creator tags to your advantage.

Filesystem Differences Summary

Table 2-1 summarizes all of the differences we just discussed along with a few more items of interest.

Table 2-1. Filesystem Comparison

OS and Filesystem	Path separator	Case-Sensitive?	Filename Specification Length	Absolute Path Format	Relative Path Format	Unique Features
Unix (Berkeley Fast File System and others)	/	Y	OS-dependent number of chars	*/dir/file*	*dir/file*	OS-variant-dependent additions

Table 2-1. Filesystem Comparison (continued)

OS and Filesystem	Path separator	Case-Sensitive?	Filename Specification Length	Absolute Path Format	Relative Path Format	Unique Features
MacOS (HFS)	:	Y	31 chars (or 255 if using HFS+)	*volume: dir:file*	*:dir:file*	Data/ resource forks, creator/ type attributes
WinNT/ 2000 (NTFS)	\	N	255 chars	*Drive:\ dir\file*	*dir\file*	ACLs, attributes, Unicode names
DOS (BASIC FAT)	\	N	8.3	*Drive:\ dir\file*	*dir\file*	Attributes

Dealing with Filesystem Differences from Perl

Perl can help you write code that takes most of these filesystem quirks into account. It ships with a module called `File::Spec` to hide some of the differences between the filesystems. For instance, if we pass in the components of a path to the `catfile` method like so:

```
use File::Spec;

$path = File::Spec->catfile("home","cindy","docs","resume.doc");
```

then `$path` is set to home\cindy\docs\resume.doc on a Windows NT/2000 system, while on a Unix system it becomes home/cindy/docs/resume.doc, and so on. `File::Spec` also has methods like `curdir` and `updir` that return the punctuation necessary to describe the current and parent directories (e.g., "." and ".."). The methods in this module give you an abstract way to construct and manipulate your path specifications. If you'd prefer not to have to write your code using an object-oriented syntax, the module `File::Spec::Functions` provides a more direct route to the methods found in `File::Spec`.

Walking or Traversing the Filesystem

By now you are probably itching to get to some practical applications of Perl. We'll begin by examining the process of "walking the filesystem," one of the most common system administration tasks associated with filesystems. Typically this entails searching an entire set of directory trees and taking action based on the files or directories we find. Each OS provides a tool for this task. Under Unix it is the *find* command, under NT and Windows 2000 it is *Find Files or Folders* or

Search For Files or Folders, and in MacOS it is *Find File* or *Sherlock.* All of these commands are useful for searching, but they lack the power by themselves to perform arbitrary and complex operations as they encounter their desired search targets. We're going to see how Perl allows us to write more sophisticated file walking code beginning with the very basics and ratcheting up the complexity as we go on.

To get started, let's take a common scenario that provides a clear problem for us to solve. In this scenario, we're a Unix system administrator with overflowing user filesystems and an empty budget. (Unix is being picked on first, but the other operating systems will get their turns in a moment.)

We can't add more disk space without any money, so we've got to make better use of our existing resources. Our first step is to remove all the files on our filesystems that can be eliminated. Under Unix, good candidates for elimination are the core files left around by programs that have died nasty deaths. Most users either do not notice that these files are created, or just ignore them in their directory, leaving large amounts of disk space claimed for no reason. We need something to search through a filesystem and delete these varmints.

To walk a filesystem, we start by reading the contents of a single directory and work our way down from there. Let's ease into the process and begin with code that examines the contents of the current directory and reports on either a core file or another directory to be searched.

We start by opening the directory using roughly the same syntax used for opening a file. If the open fails, we exit the program and print the error message set by the `opendir()` call (`$!`):

```
opendir(DIR,".") or die "Can't open the current directory: $!\n";
```

This provides us with a directory handle, `DIR` in this case, which we can pass to `readdir()` to get a list of all of the files and directories in the current directory. If `readdir()` can't read that directory, our code prints an error message (which hopefully explains why it failed) and the program exits:

```
# read file/directory names in that directory into @names
@names = readdir(DIR) or die "Unable to read current dir:$!\n";
```

We then close the open directory handle:

```
closedir(DIR);
```

Now we can work with those names:

```
foreach $name (@names) {
    next if ($name eq ".");    # skip the current directory entry
    next if ($name eq "..");   # skip the parent  directory entry
```

```
    if (-d $name){            # is this a directory?
      print "found a directory: $name\n";
      next;                   # can skip to the next name in the for loop
    }
    if ($name eq "core") {    # is this a file named "core"?
      print "found one!\n";
    }
  }
```

Now we have some very simple code that scans a single directory. This isn't even "crawling" a filesystem, never mind walking it. To walk the filesystem we'll have enter all of the directories we find as we scan and look at their contents as well. If these subdirectories have subdirectories, we'll need to check them out also.

Whenever you have a hierarchy of containers and an operation that gets performed the exact same way on every container and subcontainer in that hierarchy, this calls out for a recursive solution (at least to computer science majors). As long as the hierarchy is not too deep and doesn't loop back upon itself (i.e., all containers hold only their immediate children and do not reference some other part of the hierarchy), recursive solutions tend to make the most sense. This is the case with our example; we're going to be scanning a directory, all of its subdirectories, all of their subdirectories, and so on.

If you've never seen recursive code (i.e., code that calls itself), you may find it a bit strange at first. Recursive code is a bit like the process of painting a set of the *Matreskha* nesting Russian dolls. These are the dolls that contain another smaller doll of the exact same shape, that contains another doll, and so on until you get to a very small doll in the center.

A recipe for painting these dolls might go something like this:

1. Examine the doll in front of you. Does it contain a smaller doll? If so, remove the contents and set aside the outer doll.

2. Repeat step 1 with the contents you just removed until you reach the center.

3. Paint the center doll. When it is dry, put it back in its container and repeat step 3 with the next container.

The process is the same every step of the way. If the thing in your hand has sub-things, put off dealing with what you have in hand and deal with the sub-things first. If the thing you have in your hand doesn't have sub-things, do something with it, and then return to the last thing you put off.

In coding terms, this typically consists of a subroutine that deals with containers. It first looks to see if the current container has subcontainers. If it does, it calls *itself* to deal with the subcontainer. If it doesn't, it performs some operation and returns back from whoever called it. If you haven't seen code that calls itself, I recommend sitting down with a paper and a pencil and tracing the program flow until you are convinced it actually works.

Let's see some recursive code. To make our code recursive, we first encapsulate the operation of scanning a directory and acting upon its contents in a subroutine called `ScanDirectory()`. `ScanDirectory()` takes a single argument, the directory it is supposed to scan. It figures out its current directory, enters the requested directory, and scans it. When it has completed this scan, it returns to the directory it was called from. Here's the new code:

```perl
#!/usr/bin/perl -s

# note the use of -s for switch processing. Under NT/2000, you will need to
# call this script explicitly with -s (i.e., perl -s script) if you do not
# have perl file associations in place.
#
# -s is also considered 'retro', many programmers prefer to load
# a separate module (from the Getopt:: family) for switch parsing.

use Cwd; # module for finding the current working directory

# This subroutine takes the name of a directory and recursively scans
# down the filesystem from that point looking for files named "core"
sub ScanDirectory{
    my ($workdir) = shift;

    my ($startdir) = &cwd; # keep track of where we began

    chdir($workdir) or die "Unable to enter dir $workdir:$!\n";
    opendir(DIR, ".") or die "Unable to open $workdir:$!\n";
    my @names = readdir(DIR) or die "Unable to read $workdir:$!\n";
    closedir(DIR);

    foreach my $name (@names){
        next if ($name eq ".");
        next if ($name eq "..");

        if (-d $name){                  # is this a directory?
            &ScanDirectory($name);
            next;
        }
        if ($name eq "core") {          # is this a file named "core"?
            # if -r specified on command line, actually delete the file
            if (defined $r){
                unlink($name) or die "Unable to delete $name:$!\n";
            }
            else {
                print "found one in $workdir!\n";
            }
        }
    }
    chdir($startdir) or
        die "Unable to change to dir $startdir:$!\n";
}

&ScanDirectory(".");
```

The most important change from the previous example is our code's behavior when it finds a subdirectory in the directory it has been requested to scan. If it finds a directory, instead of printing "found a directory!" as our previous sample did, it recursively calls itself to examine that directory first. Once that entire subdirectory has been scanned (i.e., the call to `ScanDirectory()` returns), it returns to looking at the rest of the contents of the current directory.

To make our code fully functional as a core file-destroyer, we've also added file deletion functionality to it. Pay attention to how that code is written: it will only delete files if the script is started with a certain command-line switch, *−r* (for *remove*).

We're using Perl's built-in *-s* switch for automatic option parsing as part of the invocation line (`#!/usr/bin/perl  -s`). This is the simplest way to parse command-line options; for more sophistication, we'd probably use something from the `Getopt` module family. If a command-line switch is present (e.g., *−r*) then a global scalar variable with the same name (e.g., `$r`) is set when the script is run. In our code, if Perl is not invoked with *−r*, we revert to the past behavior of just announcing that we found a core file.

 When you write automatic tools, make destructive actions harder to perform. Take heed: Perl, like most powerful languages, allows you to nuke your filesystem without breaking a sweat.

Now, lest the NT/2000-focused readers think the previous example didn't apply to them, let me point out this code could be useful for them as well. A single line change from:

```
if ($name eq "core") {
```

to:

```
if ($name eq "MSCREATE.DIR") {
```

will create a program that deletes the annoying hidden zero-length files certain Microsoft program installers leave behind.

With this code under our belt, let's return to the quandary that started this chapter. After my laptop kissed the floor, I found myself in desperate need of a way to determine which files could be read off the disk and which files were damaged.

Here's the actual code I used:

```
use Cwd; # module for finding the current working directory
$|=1;    # turn off I/O buffering

sub ScanDirectory {
```

```
    my ($workdir) = shift;

    my($startdir) = &cwd; # keep track of where we began

    chdir($workdir) or die "Unable to enter dir $workdir:$!\n";

    opendir(DIR, ".") or die "Unable to open $workdir:$!\n";
    my @names = readdir(DIR);
    closedir(DIR);

    foreach my $name (@names){
        next if ($name eq ".");
        next if ($name eq "..");

        if (-d $name){                        # is this a directory?
            &ScanDirectory($name);
            next;
        }
        unless (&CheckFile($name)){
            print &cwd."/".$name."\n"; # print the bad filename
        }
    }
    chdir($startdir) or die "Unable to change to dir $startdir:$!\n";
}

sub CheckFile{
    my($name) = shift;

    print STDERR "Scanning ". &cwd."/".$name."\n";
    # attempt to read the directory entry for this file
    my @stat = stat($name);
    if (!$stat[4] && !$stat[5] && !$stat[6] && !$stat[7] && !$stat[8]){
        return 0;
    }
    # attempt to open this file
    unless (open(T,"$name")){
        return 0;
    }
    # read the file one byte at a time
    for (my $i=0;$i< $stat[7];$i++){
        my $r=sysread(T,$i,1);
        if ($r !=1) {
            close(T);
            return 0;
        }
    }
    close(T);
    return 1;
}

&ScanDirectory(".");
```

The difference between this code and our last example is the addition of a subroutine to check each file encountered. For every file, we use the **stat** function to see if we can read that file's directory information (e.g., its size). If we can't, we know the file is damaged. If we can read the directory information, we attempt to open the file. And for a final test, we attempt to read every single byte of the file. This doesn't guarantee that the file hasn't been damaged (the contents could have been modified) but it does at least show that the file is readable.

You may wonder why we use an esoteric function like `sysread()` to read the file instead of using `<>` or `read()`, Perl's usual file reading operator and function. `sysread()` gives us the ability to read the file byte-by-byte without any of the usual buffering. If a file is damaged at location X, we don't want to waste time waiting for the standard library routines to attempt to read the bytes at location X+1, X+2, X+3, etc., as part of their usual pre-fetch. We want the code to quit trying to read the file immediately. In general, you really want file reads to fetch whole chunks at a time for performance sake, but here that's undesirable because it means the laptop would spend long prolonged periods of time making awful noises every time it found a damaged file.

Now that you've seen the code I used, let me offer some closure to this story. After the script you just saw ran all night long (literally), it found 95 bad files out of 16,000 total. Fortunately, none of those files were files from the book you are now reading; I backed up the good files and moved them. Perl saved the day.

Walking the Filesystem Using the File::Find Module

Now that we've seen the basics of filesystem walking, here's a faster and spiffier way to do it. Perl comes with a module called `File::Find` that allows Perl to emulate the Unix *find* command. The easiest way to begin using this module is to use the *find2perl* command to generate prototypical Perl code for you.

---

find2perl is not always easy to use on non-Unix Perl ports. For example, MacOS users either will need Macintosh Programmer's Workshop (MPW) to run it, or should modify the code to take @ARGV from a dialog box. Here's a code snippet from Chris Nandor, co-author of *MacPerl: Power and Ease*, to do this:

```
@ARGV = @ARGV ? @ARGV :
split "\s", MacPerl::Ask("Arguments?");
```

All ports do have the `File::Find` module that *find2perl* and *find.pl* use, so this should not be a real problem. We'll show you how to call it directly later in this chapter.

For instance, let's say you need some code to search the */home* directory for files named *beesknees*. The command line that uses the Unix *find* command is:

```
% find /home -name beesknees -print
```

Feed the same options to *find2perl*:

```
% find2perl /home -name beesknees -print
```

and it produces:

```
#!/usr/bin/perl
    eval 'exec /usr/bin/perl -S $0 ${1+"$@"}'
        if $running_under_some_shell;

require "find.pl";

# Traverse desired filesystems

&find('/home');

exit;

sub wanted {
    /^beesknees$/ && print("$name\n");
}
```

The *find2perl*-generated code is fairly straightforward. It loads in the necessary *find.pl* library with a **require** statement, then calls the subroutine &find() with the name of the starting directory. We'll discuss the purpose of the &wanted() subroutine in a moment, since that's where all of the interesting modifications we're about to explore will live.

Before we begin our modifications of this code, it's important to note a few things that may not be obvious just by looking at the sample output above:

- The folks who have worked on the **File::Find** module have gone to considerable trouble to make this module portable across platforms. **File::Find**'s internal routines work behind the scenes so the same Perl code for filesystem walking works for Unix, MacOS, NT, VMS, and so on.

- Though the code *find2perl* generates looks like Perl Version 4 code on the surface (for example, it uses **require** to load a *.pl* file), *find.pl* actually sets up some Perl Version 5 aliases for the user. In general, it is useful to look under the hood whenever you use a module in your code. If you need to find the Perl source for a module already installed on your system, running either *perl -V* or the following code will show you the standard library directories for your installation:

```
% perl -e 'print join("\n",@INC,"")'
```

Let's talk about the `&wanted()` subroutine that we will modify for our own purposes. The `&wanted()` subroutine gets called with the current file or directory name by `&find()` (`&File::Find::find()` to be precise) once for every file or directory encountered during its filesystem walk. It's up to the code in `&wanted()` to select the "interesting" files or directories and operate on them accordingly. In the sample output above, it first checks to see if the file or directory name matches the string `beesknees`. If it matches, the `&&` operator causes Perl to execute the `print` statement to print the name of the file that was found.

We'll have to address two practical concerns when we create our own `&wanted()` subroutines. Since `&wanted()` is called once per file or directory name, it is important to make the code in this subroutine short and sweet. The sooner we can exit the `&wanted()` subroutine, the faster the `find` routine can proceed with the next file or directory, and the speedier the overall program will run. It is also important to keep in mind the behind-the-scenes portability concerns we mentioned a moment ago. It would be a shame to have a portable `&find()` call an OS-specific `&wanted()` subroutine unless this is unavoidable. Looking at the source code for the `File::Find` module may offer some hints on how to avoid this situation.

For our first use of `File::Find`, let's rewrite our previous core-destroyer example and then extend it a bit. First we type:

```
% find2perl -name core -print
```

which gives us:

```
require "find.pl";

# Traverse desired filesystems

&find('.');

exit;

sub wanted {
    /^core$/ && print("$name\n");
}
```

Then we add *−s* to the Perl invocation line and modify the `&wanted()` subroutine:

```
sub wanted {
    /^core$/ && print("$name\n") && defined $r && unlink($name);
}
```

This gives us the desired deletion functionality when the user invokes the program with *−r*. Here's a tweak that adds another measure of protection to our potentially destructive code:

```
sub wanted {
    /^core$/ && -s $name && print("$name\n") &&
              defined $r && unlink($name);
}
```

It checks any file called *core* to see if it is a non-zero length file before printing the name or contemplating deletion. Sophisticated users sometimes create a link to */dev/null* named *core* in their home directory to prevent inadvertent core dumps from being stored in that directory. The –*s* test makes sure we don't delete links or zero-length files by mistake. If we wanted to be even more diligent, we should probably make two additional checks:

1. Open and examine the file to confirm that it is an actual core file, either from within Perl or by calling the Unix *file* command. Determining whether a file is an authentic core dump file can be tricky when you have filesystems remotely mounted over a network by machines of different architectures, all with different core file formats.

2. Look at the modification date of the file. If someone is actively debugging a program that has core dumped, she may not be happy if you delete the core file out from under her.

Let's take a break from the Unix world for a bit and look at Mac- and NT/2000-specific examples. Earlier in this chapter I mentioned that every file in a MacOS HFS filesystem has two attributes, *creator* and *type*, that allow the OS to determine which application created it and what kind of file it is. These attributes are stored as four-character strings. For instance, a text document created by Simple-Text would be listed with creator **ttxt** and type **TEXT**. From Perl (MacPerl only) we can get at this information through the **MacPerl::GetFileInfo()** function. The syntax is:

```
$type = MacPerl::GetFileInfo(filename);
```

or:

```
($creator,$type) = MacPerl::GetFileInfo(filename);
```

To find all of the text files in a MacOS filesystem, we can do the following:

```
use File::Find;

&File::Find::find(\&wanted,"Macintosh HD:");

sub wanted{
    -f $_ && MacPerl::GetFileInfo($_) eq "TEXT" &&
          print "$Find::File::name\n";
}
```

You might notice it looks a little different from our previous examples. However, it is functionally equivalent. We're just calling the **File::Find** routines directly without the *find.pl* shim. We're also using the variable `$name` defined in the `File::Find` namespace to print the absolute path of the file, rather than just printing the filename itself. Table 2-2 shows the complete list of variables defined by `File::Find` as it walks a filesystem.

Table 2-2. File::Find Variables

Variable Name	Meaning
`$_`	Current filename
`$File::Find::dir`	Current directory name
`$File::Find::name`	Full path of current filename (i.e., `$File::Find::dir/$_`)

Here's a similar NT/2000-specific example:

```
use File::Find;
use Win32::File;

&File::Find::find(\&wanted,"\\");

sub wanted{
  -f $_ &&
    # attr will be populated by Win32::File::GetAttributes function
    (Win32::File::GetAttributes($_,$attr)) &&
    ($attr & HIDDEN) &&
     print "$File::Find::name\n";
}
```

This example searches the entire filesystem of the current drive for hidden files (i.e., those with the **HIDDEN** attribute set). This example works on both NTFS and FAT filesystems.

Here's an NTFS-specific example that will look for all files that have Full Access enabled for the special group **Everyone** and print their names:

```
use File::Find;
use Win32::FileSecurity;

# determine the DACL mask for Full Access
$fullmask = Win32::FileSecurity::MakeMask(FULL);

&find(\&wanted,"\\");

sub wanted {
    # Win32::FileSecurity::Get does not like the paging file, skip it
    next if ($_ eq "pagefile.sys");
    (-f $_) &&
        Win32::FileSecurity::Get($_, \%users) &&
        (defined $users{"Everyone"}) &&
        ($users{"Everyone"} == $fullmask) &&
         print "$File::Find::name\n";
}
```

In the above code, we query the Access Control List for all files (except for the Windows NT paging file). We then check if that list includes an entry for the group `Everyone`. If it does, we compare the `Everyone` entry to the value for Full Access (computed by `MakeMask()`), printing the absolute path of the file when we find a match.

Here is another real life example of how useful even simple code can be. I recently attempted to defragment the (newly rebuilt) NT partition on my laptop when the software reported `Metadata Corruption Error`. Perusing the web site of the vendor who makes the defragmentation software, I encountered a tech support note that suggested, "This situation can be caused by a long filename which contains more characters than is legal under Windows NT." It then suggested locating this file by copying each folder to a new location, comparing the number of files in the copy to the original, and if the copied folder has fewer files, then identifying which file in the original folder did not get copied to the new location.

This seemed like a ridiculous suggestion given the number of folders on my NT partition and the amount of time it would take. Instead, I whipped up the following in about a minute using the methods we've been discussing:

```
require "find.pl";

# Traverse desired filesystems

&find('.');
print "max:$max\n";

exit;

sub wanted {
    return unless -f $_;
    if (length($_) > $maxlength){
        $max = $name;
        $maxlength = length($_);
    }
    if (length($name) > 200) { print $name,"\n";}
}
```

This printed out the name of all the files with names larger than 200 characters, followed by the name of the largest file found. Job done, thanks to Perl.

Let's return to Unix to close this section with a moderately complex example. One idea that seems to get short shrift in many systems administration contexts, but can yield tremendous benefit in the end, is the notion of empowering the user. If your users can fix their own problems with tools you provide, everybody wins.

Much of this chapter is devoted to dealing with problems that arise from filesystems being filled. Often this occurs because users do not know enough about their environment, or because it is too cumbersome to perform any basic disk space

---

When Not to Use the File::Find Module

When is the `File::Find` method we've been discussing *not* appropriate? Four situations come to mind:

1. If the filesystem you are traversing does not follow the normal semantics, you can't use it. For instance, in the bouncing laptop scenario which began the chapter, the Linux NTFS filesystem driver I was using had the strange property of not listing "." or ".." in empty directories. This broke `File::Find` badly.

2. If you need to change the names of the directories in the filesystem you are traversing *while you are traversing it*, `File::Find` gets very unhappy and behaves in an unpredictable way.

3. If you need your (Unix-based) code to chase symbolic links to directories, `File::Find` will skip them.

4. If you need to walk a non-native filesystem mounted on your machine (for example, an NFS mount of a Unix filesystem on a Win32 machine), `File::Find` will attempt to use the native operating systems's filesystem semantics.

It is unlikely that you'll encounter these situations, but if you do, see the first filesystem-walking section of this chapter for information on how to traverse filesystems by hand.

---

management. Many a support request starts with "I'm out of disk space in my home directory and I don't know why." Here's a bare-bones version of a script called *needspace* that can help users with this problem. A user simply types *needspace* and the script attempts to locate items in the user's home directory that could be deleted. It looks for two kinds of files: known backup files and those that can be recreated automatically. Let's dive into the code:

```perl
use File::Find;
use File::Basename;

# array of fname extensions and the extensions they can be derived from
% derivations = (".dvi" => ".tex",
                 ".aux" => ".tex",
                 ".toc" => ".tex",
                 ".o"   => ".c",
                 );
```

We start by loading the libraries we need: our friend `File::Find` and another useful library called `File::Basename`. `File::Basename` will come in handy for parsing pathnames. We then initialize a hash table with known derivations; for instance, we know that running the command *TeX* or *LaTeX* on the file *happy.tex* can generate the file *happy.dvi,* and that *happy.o* could possibly be created by running a C compiler on *happy.c*. The word "possibly" is used because sometimes multiple source files are needed to generate a single derived file. We can only make simple guesses based on file extensions. Generalized dependency analysis is a complex problem we won't attempt to touch here.

Next we locate the user's home directory by finding the user ID of the person running the script ($<) and feeding it to getpwuid(). getpwuid() returns password information in list form (more on this in the next chapter), from which an array index ([7]) selects the home directory element. There are shell-specific ways to retrieve this information (e.g., querying the $HOME environment variable), but the code as written is more portable.

Once we have the home directory, we enter it and begin scanning using a &find() call just like the ones we've seen before:

```
$homedir=(getpwuid($<))[7]; # find the user's home directory

chdir($homedir) or
   die "Unable to change to your homedir $homedir:$!\n";

$|=1; # print to STDOUT in an unbuffered way
print "Scanning";
find(\&wanted, "."); # chew through dirs, &wanted does the work
```

Here's the &wanted() subroutine we call. It starts by looking for *core* files and *emacs* backup and autosave files. We assume these files can be deleted without checking for their source file (perhaps not a safe assumption). If one of these files is found, its size and location is stored in a hash whose key is the path to the file and whose value is the size of that file.

The remaining checks for derivable files are very similar. They call a routine &BaseFileExists() to check if a particular file can be derived from another file in that directory. If this routine returns true, we store filename and size info for later retrieval:

```
sub wanted {
    # print a dot for every dir so the user knows we're doing something
    print "." if (-d $_);

    # we're only checking files
    return unless (-f $_);

    # check for core files, store them in the %core table, then return
    $_ eq "core" && ($core{$File::Find::name} = (stat(_))[7]) && return;

    # check for emacs backup and autosave files
    (/^#.*#$/ || /~$/) &&
      ($emacs{$File::Find::name}=(stat(_))[7]) &&
      return;

    # check for derivable tex files
```

```
    (/\.dvi$/ || /\.aux$/ || /\.toc$/) &&
      &BaseFileExists($File::Find::name) &&
      ($tex{$File::Find::name} = (stat(_))[7]) &&
      return;

    # check for derivable .o files
     /\.o$/ &&
      &BaseFileExists($File::Find::name) &&
      ($doto{$File::Find::name} = (stat(_))[7]) &&
      return;
}
```

Here's the routine which checks if a particular file can be derived from another
"base" file in the same directory (i.e., does *happy.o* exist if we find *happy.c*):

```
sub BaseFileExists {
    my($name,$path,$suffix) =
     &File::Basename::fileparse($_[0],'\..*');

    # if we don't know how to derive this type of file
    return 0 unless (defined $derivations{$suffix});

    # easy, we've seen the base file before
    return 1 if (defined $baseseen{$path.$name.$derivations{$suffix}});

    # if file (or file link points to) exists and has non-zero size
    return 1 if (-s $name.$derivations{$suffix} &&
                    ++$baseseen{$path.$name.$derivations{$suffix}});
}

print "done.\n";
```

Here's how this code works:

1. `&File::Basename::fileparse()` is used to separate the path into a filename, its leading path, and its suffix (e.g., *resume.dvi, /home/cindy/docs/, .dvi*).

2. This file's suffix is checked to determine if it is one we recognize as being
   derivable. If not, we return 0 (false in a scalar context).

3. We check if we've already seen a "base file" for this particular file, and if so
   return `true`. In some situations (*TeX/LaTeX* in particular), a single base file
   can yield many derived files. This check speeds things up considerably
   because it saves us a trip to the filesystem.

4. If we haven't seen a base file for this file before, we check to see if one exists
   and that it is non-zero length. If so, we cache the base file information and
   return 1 (true in a scalar context).

All that's left for us to do now is to print out the information we gathered as we
walked the filesystem:

```
foreach my $path (keys %core){
    print "Found a core file taking up ".&BytesToMeg($core{$path}).
```

```
                "MB in ".&File::Basename::dirname($path).".\n";
    }

    if (keys %emacs){
        print "The following are most likely emacs backup files:\n";

        foreach my $path (keys %emacs){
            $tempsize += $emacs{$path};
            $path =~ s/^$homedir/~/;     # change the path for prettier output
            print "$path ($emacs{$path} bytes)\n";
        }
        print "\nThese files take up ".&BytesToMeg($tempsize)."MB total.\n";
        $tempsize=0;
    }

    if (keys %tex){
        print "The following are most likely files that can be recreated by
               running La/TeX:\n";
        foreach my $path (keys %tex){
            $tempsize += $tex{$path};
            $path =~ s/^$homedir/~/;     # change the path for prettier output
            print "$path ($tex{$path} bytes)\n";
        }
        print "\nThese files take up ".&BytesToMeg($tempsize)."MB total.\n";
        $tempsize=0;
    }

    if (keys %doto){
        print "The following are most likely files that can be recreated by
               recompiling source:\n";
        foreach my $path (keys %doto){
            $tempsize += $doto{$path};
            $path =~ s/^$homedir/~/;     # change the path for prettier output
            print "$path ($doto{$path} bytes)\n";
        }
        print "\nThese files take up ".&BytesToMeg($tempsize)."MB total.\n";
        $tempsize=0;
    }

sub BytesToMeg{ # convert bytes to X.XXMB
    return sprintf("%.2f",($_[0]/1024000));
}
```

Before we close this section, it should be noted that the previous example could be extended in many ways. The sky's really the limit on this sort of program. Here are a few ideas:

- Use a more complex data structure to hold derivations and found files. The above code was written to be easy to read without much knowledge of Perl data structures. It repeats itself in several places and is harder to extend than it needs to be. Ideally, you'd like a way to represent all of the derivations without having special case hashes (e.g., %tex) in the code.

- Search for web browser cache directories (a common source of missing disk space).

- Offer to delete files that are found. The operator `unlink()` and the subroutine `rmpath` from the `File::Path` module would be used to perform the deletion step.

- Perform more analysis on files instead of making guesses based on filenames.

Manipulating Disk Quotas

Perl scripts like our core-killers from the last section can offer a way to deal with junk files that cause unnecessary disk full situations. But even when run on a regular basis, they are still a reactive approach; the administrator deals with these files only after they've come into existence and cluttered the filesystem.

There's another, more proactive approach: filesystem quotas. Filesystem quotas, operating system permitting, allow you to constrain the amount of disk space a particular user can consume on a filesystem. Windows 2000 and all modern Unix variants offer quotas. NT4 requires a third-party product, and MacOS users are S.O.L. (Simply or Sore Out of Luck).

Though proactive, this approach is considerably more heavy-handed than cleanup scripts because it applies to all files, not just spurious ones like core dumps. Most system administrators find using a combination of the automated cleanup scripts and quotas to be the best strategy. The former helps prevent the latter from being necessary.

In this section, we'll deal with manipulating Unix quotas from Perl. Before we get to that subject, we should take a moment to understand how quotas are set and queried "by hand." To enable quotas on a filesystem, a Unix system administrator usually adds an entry to the filesystem mount table (e.g., */etc/fstab* or */etc/vfstab*) and then reboots the system or manually invokes the quota enable command (usually *quotaon*). Here's an example */etc/vfstab* from a Solaris box:

```
#device              device          mount  FS    fsck  mount     mount
#to mount            to fsck         point  type  pass  at boot   options
/dev/dsk/c0t0d0s7 /dev/dsk/c0d0t0d0s7 /home  ufs   2     yes       rq
```

The *rq* option in the last column enables quotas on this filesystem. They are stored on a per-user basis. To view the quota entries for a user on all of the mounted filesystems that have quotas enabled, one can invoke the *quota* command like so:

```
$ quota -v sabrams
```

to produce output similar to this:

```
Disk quotas for sabrams (uid 670):
Filesystem    usage quota   limit    timeleft  files  quota  limit timeleft
/home/users   228731 250000  253000              0      0      0
```

For our next few examples, we're only interested in the first three columns of this output. The first number is the current amount of disk space being used by the user *sabrams* on the filesystem mounted at */home/users*. The second is that user's "soft quota." The soft quota is the amount after which the OS begins complaining for a set period of time, but does not restrict space allocation. The final number is the "hard quota," the absolute upper bound for this user's space usage. If a program attempts to request more storage space on behalf of the user after this limit has been reached, the OS will deny this request and return an error message like `disk quota exceeded`.

If we wanted to change these quota limits by hand, we'd use the *edquota* command. *edquota* pops you into your editor of choice preloaded with a small temporary text file that contains the pertinent quota information. Setting the EDITOR environment variable in your shell specifies the editor. Here's an example buffer that shows a user's limits on each of the four quota-enabled filesystems. This user most likely has her home directory on */exprt/server2* since that's the only filesystem where she has quotas in place:

```
fs /exprt/server1 blocks (soft = 0, hard = 0) inodes (soft = 0, hard = 0)
fs /exprt/server2 blocks (soft = 250000, hard = 253000) inodes (soft = 0,
hard = 0)
fs /exprt/server3 blocks (soft = 0, hard = 0) inodes (soft = 0, hard = 0)
fs /exprt/server4 blocks (soft = 0, hard = 0) inodes (soft = 0, hard = 0)
```

Using *edquota* by hand may be a comfy way to edit a single user's quota limits, but it is not a viable way to deal with tens, hundreds, or thousands of user accounts. One of Unix's flaws is its lack of command-line tools for editing quota entries. Most Unix variants have C library routines for this task, but no command-line tools that allow for higher-level scripting. True to the Perl motto "There's More Than One Way To Do It" (TMTOWTDI, pronounced "tim-toady"), we are going to look at two very different ways of setting quotas from Perl.

Editing Quotas with edquota Trickery

The first method involves a little trickery on our part. A moment ago we mentioned the process for manually setting a user's quota: *edquota* invokes an editor to allow a user to edit a small text file and then uses any changes to update the quota entries. There's nothing in this scenario mandating that an actual human has to type at a keyboard to make changes in the editor invoked by *edquota*. In fact, there's not even a constraint on which editor has to be used. All *edquota* needs is a program it can launch that will properly change a small text file. Any valid path (as specified in the EDITOR environment variable) to such a program will do. Why not point *edquota* at a Perl script? Let's look at just such a script for our next example.

Our example script will need to do double duty: first, it has to get some command-line arguments from the user, set EDITOR appropriately, and call *edquota*. *edquota* will then run another copy of our program to do the real work of editing this temporary file. Figure 2-1 shows a diagram of the action.

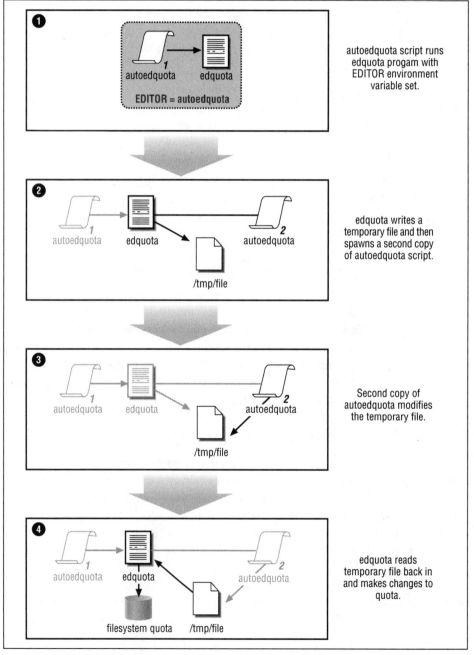

Figure 2-1. Changing quotas using a "sleight-of-hand" approach

The second copy must be told what to change by the initial program invocation. How it gets this information from the copy that called *edquota* is less straightforward than one might hope. The manual page for *edquota* says: "The editor invoked is *vi(1)* unless the EDITOR environment variable specifies otherwise." The idea of passing command-line arguments via EDITOR or another environment variable is a dicey prospect at best because we don't know how *edquota* will react. Instead, we'll have to rely on one of the other types of interprocess communication methods available from Perl. For instance, the two processes could:

- Pass a temporary file between them

- Create a named pipe and talk over that

- Pass AppleEvents (under MacOS)

- Use mutexes or mutually agreed upon registry keys (under NT/2000)

- Rendezvous at network socket

- Use a shared memory section

And so on. It's up to you as the programmer to choose the appropriate communication method, though often the data will dictate this for you. When looking at this data, you'll want to consider:

- Direction of communication (one- or two-way?)

- Frequency of communication (is this a single message or are there multiple chunks of information that need to be passed?)

- Size of data (is it a 10MB file or 20 characters?)

- Format of data (is it a binary file or just text characters, fixed width, or character separated?)

Finally, be conscious of how complicated you want to make your script.

In our case, we're going to choose a simple but powerful method to exchange information. Since the first process only has to provide the second one with a single set of change instructions (what quotas need to be changed and their new values), we're going to set up a standard Unix pipe between the two of them.* The first process will print a change request to its output and the copy spawned by *edquota* will read this info as its standard input.

Let's write the program. The first thing the program has to do when it starts up is decide what role it's been asked to play. We can assume that the first invocation receives several command-line arguments (i.e., what to change) while the second,

---

* Actually, the pipe will be to the *edquota* program, which is kind enough to hook up its input and output streams to the Perl script being spawned.

called by *edquota*, receives only one (i.e., the name of the temporary file). The program forces a set of command flags to be present if it is called with more than one argument, so we're pretty safe in using this assumption as the basis of our role selection. Here's the role selection code:

```
$edquota = "/usr/etc/edquota";     # edquota path
$autoedq = "/usr/adm/autoedquota"; # full path for this script

# are we the first or second invocation?

# if there is more than one argument, we're the first invocation
if ($#ARGV > 0) {
    &ParseArgs;
    &CallEdquota;
}
# else - we're the second invocation and will have to perform the edits
else {
    &EdQuota();
}
```

Let's look at the code called by the first invocation to parse arguments and call *edquota* over a pipe:

```
sub ParseArgs{
    use Getopt::Std; # for switch processing

    # This sets $opt_u to the user ID, $opt_f to the filesystem name,
    # $opt_s to the soft quota amount, and $opt_h to the hard quota
    # amount
    getopt("u:f:s:h:"); # colon (:) means this flag takes an argument
    die "USAGE: $0 -u uid -f <fsystem> -s <softq> -h <hardq>\n"
      if (!$opt_u || !$opt_f || !$opt_s || !$opt_h);
}

sub CallEdquota{
    $ENV{"EDITOR"} = $autoedq; # set the EDITOR variable to point to us

    open(EPROCESS, "|$edquota $opt_u") or
      die "Unable to start edquota:$!\n";

    # send the changes line to the second script invocation
    print EPROCESS "$opt_f|$opt_s|$opt_h\n";

    close(EPROCESS);
}
```

Here's the second part of the action:

```
sub EdQuota {
    $tfile = $ARGV[0]; # get the name of edquota's temp file

    open(TEMPFILE, $tfile) or
      die "Unable to open temp file $tfile:$!\n";
```

```
# open a scratch file, could use IO::File → new_tmpfile() instead
open(NEWTEMP, ">$tfile.$$") or
    die "Unable to open scratch file $tfile.$$:$!\n";

# receive line of input from first invocation and lop off the newline
chomp($change = <STDIN>);
my($fs,$soft,$hard) = split(/\|/,$change); # parse the communique

# read in a line from the temp file.  If it contains the
# filesystem we wish to modify, change its values. Write the input
# line (possibly changed) to the scratch file.
while (<TEMPFILE>){
    if (/^fs $fs\s+/){
        s/(soft\s*=\s*)\d+(, hard\s*=\s*)\d+/$1$soft$2$hard/;
        print NEWTEMP;
    }
}
close(TEMPFILE);
close(NEWTEMP);

# overwrite the temp file with our modified scratch file so
# edquota will get the changes
rename("$tfile.$$",$tfile)
    or die "Unable to rename $tfile.$$ to $tfile:$!\n";
}
```

The above code is bare bones, but it still offers a way to make automated quota changes. If you've ever had to change many quotas by hand, this should be good news. Before putting something like this into production, considerable error checking and a mechanism that prevents multiple concurrent changes should be added. In any case, you may find this sort of sleight-of-hand technique useful in other situations besides quota manipulation.

Editing Quotas Using the Quota Module

Once upon a time, the previous method (or, to be honest, the previous hack) was the only way to automate quota changes unless you wanted to get into the gnarly business of hacking the C quota library routine calls into the Perl interpreter itself. Now that Perl's extension mechanism makes gluing library calls into Perl much easier, it was only an amount of time before someone produced a Quota module for Perl. Thanks to Tom Zoerner and some other porting help, setting quotas from Perl is now much more straightforward if this module supports your variant of Unix. If it doesn't, the previous method should work fine.

Here's some sample code that takes the same arguments as our last quota-editing example:

```
use Getopt::Std;
use Quota:;
```

```
getopt("u:f:s:h:");
die "USAGE: $0 -u uid -f <filesystem> -s <softquota> -h <hard quota>\n"
    if (!$opt_u || !$opt_f || !$opt_s || !$opt_h);

$dev = Quota::getcarg($opt_f) or die "Unable to translate path $opt_f:$!\n";

($curblock,$soft,$hard,$curinode,$btimeout,$curinode,$isoft,$ihard,$itimeout)=
    Quota::query($dev,$uid) or die "Unable to query quota for $uid:$!\n";

Quota::setqlim($dev,$opt_u,$opt_s,$opt_h,$isoft,$ihard,1) or
    die "Unable to set quotas:$!\n";
```

After we parse the arguments, there are three simple steps: first, we use `Quota::getcarg()` to get the correct device identifier to feed to the other quota routines. Next, we feed this identifier and the user ID to `Quota::query()` to get the current quota settings. We need these settings to avoid perturbing the quota limits we are not interested in changing (like number of files). Finally, we set the quota. That's all it takes, three lines of Perl code.

Remember, the Perl slogan TMTOWTDI means "there's more than one way to do it," not necessarily "several equally good ways."

Querying Filesystem Usage

Given the methods of controlling filesystem usage we've just explored, it is only natural to want to keep track of how well they work. To end this chapter, let's look at a method for querying the filesystem usage on each of the operating systems found in this book.

MacOS is the operating system for which this task is hardest. MacOS does have a Macintosh Toolbox routine (`PBHGetVInfo`) to retrieve volume information, but at the current time there is no MacPerl module available to make calling this function easy. Instead, we have to take a roundabout approach and ask the *Finder* to query this information for us. This is easy in practice thanks to a glue module, but the setup needed for this method makes MacOS the more difficult operating system to deal with.

All the materials for the following involve work by Chris Nandor and can be found at *http://pudge.net* or on CPAN. Bear with me as we go over this setup step by step:

1. Install the *cpan-mac* bundle. *cpan-mac* includes the `CPAN.pm` module by Andreas J. König and other handy modules we mentioned in Chapter 1, *Introduction*. Even if you don't want to query filesystem usage from MacOS, you'll still be well served by installing this bundle. When you install this bundle, be sure to follow all of the directions found in the *README* file.

2. Install the latest `Mac::AppleEvents::Simple` module by dropping the distribution file on top of the *installme* droplet.

3. Install the `Mac::Glue` module. The *installme* droplet decompresses and unpacks the contents of the `Mac::Glue` distribution file into a new folder as part of the installation process. Be sure to run the *gluedialect* and *gluescriptadds* setup scripts from the *scripts* subfolder of the unpacked distribution.

4. Create the finder glue file. Open your *System Folder* and drag the *Finder* file on top of the *gluemac* droplet to create the necessary glue file (and, in a particularly nice touch by Nandor, to create pod documentation for the glue).

This complex setup process allows us to write the following simple-looking code:

```
use Mac::Glue qw(:all);

$fobj   = new Mac::Glue 'Finder';

$volumename = "Macintosh HD"; # the name of one of our mounted disks
$total = $fobj->get($fobj->prop('capacity',
                    disk => $volumename),
               as => 'doub');
$free   = $fobj->get($fobj->prop('free_space',
                    disk => $volumename),
               as => 'doub');

print "$free bytes of $total bytes free\n";
```

Let's move to easier territory. If we wanted to query the same information from a Win32 machine, we could use Dave Roth's `Win32::AdminMisc` module:

```
use Win32::AdminMisc;

($total,$free) = Win32::AdminMisc::GetDriveSpace("c:\\");

print "$free bytes of $total bytes free\n";
```

Finally, let's end this chapter by looking at the Unix equivalent. There are several Unix modules available, including **Filesys::DiskSpace** by Fabien Tassin, **Filesys::Df** by Ian Guthrie, and **Filesys::DiskFree** by Alan R. Barclay. The first two of these make use of the Unix system call `statvfs()` while the last one actually parses the output of the Unix command *df* on all of the systems it supports. Choosing between these modules is mostly a matter of personal preference and operating system support. I prefer **Filesys::Df** because it offers a rich feature set and does not spawn another process (a potential security risk, as discussed in Chapter 1) as part of a query. Here's one way to write code equivalent to the previous two examples:

```
use Filesys::Df;

$fobj = df("/");
```

```
print $fobj->{su_bavail}*1024." bytes of ".
      $fobj->{su_blocks}*1024." bytes free\n";
```

We have to do a little bit of arithmetic (i.e., `*1024`) because `Filesys::Df` returns values in terms of blocks, and each block is 1024 bytes on our system. The `df()` function for this module can be passed a second optional argument for block size if necessary. Also worth noting about this code are the two hash values we've requested. `su_bavail` and `su_blocks` are the values returned by this module for the "real" size and disk usage information. On most Unix filesystems, the *df* command would show a value that hides the standard 10% of a disk set aside for superuser overflow. If we wanted to see the total amount of space available and the current amount free from a normal user's perspective, we would have used `user_blocks` and `user_bavail` instead.

With the key pieces of Perl code we've just seen, it is possible to build more sophisticated disk monitoring and management systems. These filesystem watchdogs will help you deal with space problems before they occur.

Module Information for This Chapter

Name	CPAN ID	Version
`File::Find` (ships with Perl)		
`File::Spec` (ships with Perl)		
`Cwd` (ships with Perl)		
`Win32::File::GetAttributes` (ships with ActiveState Perl)		
`Win32::FileSecurity` (ships with ActiveState Perl)		
`File::Basename` (ships with Perl)		
`Getopt::Std` (ships with Perl)		
`Quota`	TOMZO	1.2.3
cpan-mac (bundle)	CNANDOR	0.40
`Mac::AppleEvents::Simple`	CNANDOR	0.81
`Mac::Glue`	CNANDOR	0.58

References for More Information

For good information on platform differences for Perl programmers, the *perlport* manual page is invaluable. Chris Nandor and Gurasamy Sarathy presented a talk based on an early version of this manual page at the Perl Conference 2.0; Nandor has posted the slides from this talk at *http://pudge.net/macperl/tpc/98*.

3

User Accounts

Here's a short pop quiz. If it wasn't for users, system administration would be:

    a) More pleasant.
    b) Nonexistent.

Despite the comments from system administrators on their most beleaguered days, b) is the best answer to this question. As I mentioned in the first chapter, ultimately system administration is about making it possible for people to use the available technology.

Why all the grumbling then? Users introduce two things into the systems and networks we administer that make them significantly more complex: nondeterminism and individuality. We'll address the nondeterminism issues when we discuss user activity in the next chapter, but for now let's focus on individuality.

In most cases, users want to retain their own separate identities. Not only do they want a unique name, but they want unique "stuff" too. They want to be able to say, "These are *my* files. I keep them in *my* directories. I print them with *my* print quota. I make them available from *my* home page on the Web." Modern operating systems keep an account of all of these details for each user.

But who keeps track of all of the accounts on a system or network of systems? Who is ultimately responsible for creating, protecting, and disposing of these little shells for individuals? I'd hazard a guess and say "*you*, dear reader"—or if not you personally, then tools you'll build to act as your proxy. This chapter is designed to help you with that responsibility.

Let's begin our discussion of users by addressing some of the pieces of information that form their identity and how it is stored on a system. We'll start by looking at Unix and Unix-variant users, and then address the same issues for Windows

NT/Windows 2000. For current-generation MacOS systems, this is a non-issue, so we'll skip MacOS in this chapter. Once we address identity information for both operating systems, we'll construct a basic account system.

Unix User Identity

When discussing this topic, we have to putter around in a few key files because they store the persistent definition of a user's identity. By persistent definition, I mean those attributes of a user that exist during the entire lifespan of that user, persisting even while that user is not actively using a computer. Another word that we'll use for this persistent identity is *account*. If you have an account on a system, you can log in and become a user of that system.

Users come into being on a system at the point when their information is first added to the password file (or the directory service which offers the same information). A user's subsequent departure from the scene occurs when this entry is removed. We'll dive right in and look at how the user identity is stored.

The Classic Unix Password File

Let's start off with the "classic" password file format and then get more sophisticated from there. I call this format classic because it is the parent for all of the other Unix password file formats currently in use. It is still in use today in many Unix variants, including SunOS, Digital Unix, and Linux. Usually found on the system as */etc/passwd*, this file consists of lines of ASCII text, each line representing a different account on the system or a link to another directory service. A line in this file is composed of several colon-separated fields. We'll take a close look at all of these fields as soon as we see how to retrieve them.

Here's an example line from */etc/passwd*:

```
dnb:fMP.olmno4jGA6:6700:520:David N. Blank-Edelman:/home/dnb:/bin/zsh
```

There are at least two ways to go about accessing this information from Perl:

1. If we access it "by hand," we can treat this file like any random text file and parse it accordingly:

```
$passwd = "/etc/passwd";
open(PW,$passwd) or die "Can't open $passwd:$!\n";
while (<PW>){
    ($name,$passwd,$uid,$gid,$gcos,$dir,$shell) = split(/:/);
    <your code here>
}
close(PW);
```

2. Or we can "let the system do it," in which case Perl makes available some of the Unix system library calls that parse this file for us. For instance, another way to write that last code snippet is:

```
while(($name,$passwd,$uid,$gid,$gcos,$dir,$shell) = getpwent()){
        <your code here>
}
endpwent();
```

Using these calls has the added advantage of automatically tying in to any OS-level name service being used (e.g., Network Information Service, or NIS). We'll see more of these library call functions in a moment (including an easier way to use `getpwent()`), but for now let's look at the fields our code returns:[*]

Name

The login name field holds the short (usually eight characters or less), unique, *nomme de machine* for each account on the system. The Perl function `getpwent()`, which we saw earlier being used in a list context, will return the name field if we call it in a scalar context:

```
$name = getpwent();
```

User ID (UID)

On Unix systems, the user ID (UID) is actually more important than the login name for most things. All of the files on a system are owned by a UID, not a login name. If we change the login name associated with UID 2397 in */etc/passwd* from *danielr* to *drinehart,* these files instantly show up as be owned by *drinehart* instead. The UID is the persistent part of a user's identity internal to the operating system. The Unix kernel and filesystems keep track of UIDs, not login names, for ownership and resource allocation. A login name can be considered to be the part of a user's identity that is *external* to the core OS; it exists to make things easier for humans.

Here's some simple code to find the next available unique UID in a password file. This code looks for the highest UID in use and produces the next number:

```
$passwd = "/etc/passwd";
open(PW,$passwd) or die "Can't open $passwd:$!\n";
while (<PW>){
    @fields = split(/:/);
    $highestuid = ($highestuid < $fields[2]) ? $fields[2] : $highestuid;
}
close(PW);
print "The next available UID is " . ++$highestuid . "\n";
```

Table 3-1 lists other useful name- and UID-related Perl functions and variables.

---

[*] The values returned by `getpwent()` changed between Perl 5.004 and 5.005; this is the 5.004 list of values. As of 5.005, two additional fields, `$quota` and `$comment` appear right before `$gcos`.

Table 3-1. Login Name- and UID-Related Variables and Functions

Function/Variable	How Used
getpwnam($name)	In a scalar context returns the UID for that login name; in a list context returns all of the fields of a password entry
getpwuid($uid)	In a scalar context returns the login name for that UID; in a list context returns all of the fields of a password entry
$>	Holds the effective UID of the currently running Perl program
$<	Holds the real UID of the currently running Perl program

The primary group ID (GID)

On multiuser systems, users often want to share files and other resources with a select set of other users. Unix provides a user grouping mechanism to assist in this process. An account on a Unix system can be part of several groups, but it must be assigned to one primary group. The primary group ID (GID) field in the password file lists the primary group for that account.

Group names, GIDs, and group members are usually stored in the */etc/group* file. To make an account part of several groups, you just list that account in several places in the file. Some OSes have a hard limit on the number of groups an account can join (eight used to be a common restriction). Here's a couple of lines from an */etc/group* file:

```
bin::2:root,bin,daemon
sys::3:root,bin,sys,adm
```

The first field is the group name, the second is the password (some systems allow people to join a group by entering a password), the third is the GID of the group, and the last field is a list of the users in this group.

Schemes for group ID assignment are site-specific because each site has its own particular administrative and project boundaries. Groups can be created to model certain populations (students, salespeople, etc.), roles (backup operators, network administrators, etc.), or account purposes (backup accounts, batch processing accounts, etc.).

Dealing with group files via Perl files is a very similar process to the *passwd* parsing we did above. We can either treat it as a standard text file or use special Perl functions to perform the task. Table 3-2 lists the group-related Perl functions and variables.

Table 3-2. Group Name- and GID-Related Variables and Functions

Function/Variable	How Used
getgrent()	In a scalar context returns the group name; in a list context returns these fields: $name, $passwd, $gid, $members
getgrnam($name)	In a scalar context returns the group ID; in a list context returns the same fields mentioned for getgrent()

Table 3-2. Group Name- and GID-Related Variables and Functions (continued)

Function/Variable	How Used
`getgrgid($gid)`	In a scalar context returns the group name; in a list context returns the same fields mentioned for `getgrent()`
`$)`	Holds the effective GID of the currently running Perl program
`$(`	Holds the real GID of the currently running Perl program

The "encrypted" password

So far we've seen three key parts of how a user's identity is stored on a Unix machine. The next field is not part of this identity, but is used to verify that someone should be allowed to assume all of the rights, responsibilities, and privileges bestowed upon a particular user ID. This is how the computer knows that someone presenting her or himself as *mguerre* should be allowed to assume a particular UID. There are other, better forms of authentication that now exist in the world (e.g., public key cryptographic), but this is the one that has been inherited from the early Unix days.

It is common to see a line in a password file with just an asterisk (*) for a password. This convention is usually used when an administrator wants to disable the user from logging into an account without removing it altogether.

Dealing with user passwords is a topic unto itself. We deal with it later in this book in Chapter 10, *Security and Network Monitoring.*

GCOS field

The GCOS* field is the least important field (from the computer's point of view). This field usually contains the full name of the user (e.g., "Roy G. Biv"). Often, people put their title and/or phone extension in this field as well.

System administrators who are concerned about privacy issues on behalf of their users (as all should be) need to watch the contents of this field. It is a standard source for account-name-to-real-name mappings. On most Unix systems, this field is available as part of a world-readable */etc/passwd* file or directory service, and hence the information is available to everyone on the system. Many Unix programs, mailers and finger daemons also consult this field when they attach a user's login name to some piece of information. If you have any need to withhold a user's real name from other people (e.g., if that user is a political dissident, federal witness, or a famous person), this is one of the places you must monitor.

---

* For some amusing details on the origin of the name of this field, see the GCOS entry at the Jargon Dictionary: *http://www.jargon.org.*

As a side note, if you maintain a site with a less mature user base, it is often a good idea to disable mechanisms that allow users to change their GCOS field to any random string (for the same reasons that user-selected login names can be problematic). You may not want your password file to contain expletives or other unprofessional information.

Home directory

The next field contains the name of the user's *home directory*. This is the directory where the user begins her or his time on the system. Typically this is also where the files that configure that user's environment live.

It is important for security purposes that an account's home directory be owned and writable by that account only. World-writable home directories allow trivial account hacking. There are cases, however, where even a *user*-writable home directory is problematic. For example, in restricted shell scenarios (accounts that can only log in to perform a specific task without permission to change anything on the system), a user-writable home directory is a big no-no.

Here's some Perl code to make sure that every user's home directory is owned by that user and is not world writable:

```
use User::pwent;
use File::stat;

# note: this code will beat heavily upon any machine using
# automounted homedirs
while($pwent = getpwent()){
    # make sure we stat the actual dir, even through layers of symlink
    # indirection
    $dirinfo = stat($pwent->dir."/.");
    unless (defined $dirinfo){
        warn "Unable to stat ".$pwent->dir.": $!\n";
        next;
    }
    warn $pwent->name."'s homedir is not owned by the correct uid (".
        $dirinfo->uid." instead ".$pwent->uid.")!\n"
        if ($dirinfo->uid != $pwent->uid);

    # world writable is fine if dir is set "sticky" (i.e., 01000),
    # see the manual page for chmod for more information
    warn $pwent->name."'s homedir is world-writable!\n"
        if ($dirinfo->mode & 022 and (!$stat->mode & 01000));
}
endpwent();
```

This code looks a bit different than our previous parsing code because it uses two magic modules by Tom Christiansen: `User::pwent` and `File::stat`. These modules override the normal `getpwent()` and `stat()` functions, causing them to return something different than the values mentioned before. When `User::pwent` and `File::stat` are loaded, these functions return objects instead of lists or scalars. Each object has a method named after a field that normally would be returned in a list context. So code like:

```
$gid = (stat("filename"))[5];
```

can be written more legibly as:

```
use File::stat;
$stat = stat("filename");
$gid = $stat->gid;
```

or even:

```
use File::stat;
$gid = stat("filename")->gid;
```

User shell

The final field in the classic password file format is the user shell field. This field usually contains one of a set of standard interactive programs (e.g., *sh*, *csh*, *tcsh*, *ksh*, *zsh*) but it can actually be set to the path of any executable program or script. From time to time, people have joked (half-seriously) about setting their shell to be the Perl interpreter. For at least one shell (*zsh*), people have actually contemplated embedding a Perl interpreter in the shell itself, but this has yet to happen. There is, however, some serious work that has been done to create a Perl shell (*http://www.focusresearch.com/gregor/psh/*) and to embed Perl into Emacs, an editor that could easily pass for an operating system (*http://john-edwin-tobey.org/perlmacs/*).

On occasion, you might have reason to list nonstandard interactive programs in this field. For instance, if you wanted to create a menu-driven account, you could place the menu program's name here. In these cases some care has to be taken to prevent someone using that account from reaching a real shell or they may wreak havoc. A common mistake made is including a mail program in the menu that allows the user to launch an editor or pager for mail composition and mail reading. Either the editor or pager could have a shell-escape function built in.

A list of standard, acceptable shells on a system is often kept in */etc/shells* for the FTP daemon's benefit. Most FTP daemons will not allow a normal user to connect to a machine if their shell in */etc/passwd* (or networked password file) is not one of a list kept in */etc/shells*. Here's some Perl code to report accounts that do not have approved shells:

```
use User::pwent;

$shells = "/etc/shells";
open (SHELLS,$shells) or die "Unable to open $shells:$!\n";
while(<SHELLS>){
    chomp;
    $okshell{$_}++;
}
```

```
close(SHELLS);

while($pwent = getpwent()){
    warn $pwent->name." has a bad shell (".$pwent->shell.")!\n"
        unless (exists $okshell{$pwent->shell});
}
endpwent();
```

Extra Fields in BSD 4.4 passwd Files

At the BSD (Berkeley Software Distribution) 4.3 to 4.4 upgrade point, the BSD variants added two twists to the classic password file format: additional fields, and the introduction of a binary database format used to store account information.

BSD 4.4 systems add some fields to the password file in between the GID and GCOS fields. The first field they added was the *class* field. This allows a system administrator to partition the accounts on a system into separate classes (e.g., different login classes might be given different resource limits like CPU time restrictions). BSD variants also add *change* and *expire* fields to hold an indication of when a password must be changed and when the account will expire. We'll see fields like these when we get to the next Unix password file format as well.

When compiled under an operating system that supports these extra fields, Perl includes the contents of these fields in the return value of functions like getpwent(). This is one good reason to use getpwent() in your programs instead of split()ing the password file entries by hand.

Binary Database Format in BSD 4.4

The second twist added to the password mechanisms by BSD is their use of a database format, rather than plain text, for primary storage of password file information. BSD machines keep their password file information in DB format, a greatly updated version of the older (Unix database) DBM (Database Management) libraries. This change allows the system to do speedy lookups of password information.

The program *pwd_mkdb* takes the name of a password text file as its argument, creates and moves two database files into place, and then moves this text file into */etc/master.passwd*. The two databases are used to provide a shadow password scheme, differing in their read permissions and encrypted password field contents. We'll talk more about this in the next section.

Perl has the ability to directly work with DB files (we'll work with this format later in Chapter 9, *Log Files*), but in general I would not recommend directly editing the databases while the system is in use. The issue here is one of locking: it's very important not to change a crucial database like your password file without making sure other programs are not similarly trying to write to it or read from it. Standard operating system programs like *chpasswd* handle this locking for you.* The sleight-of-hand approach we saw for quotas in Chapter 2, *Filesystems*, which used the EDITOR variable, can be used with *chpasswd* as well.

Shadow Passwords

Earlier I emphasized the importance of protecting the contents of the GCOS field, since this information is publicly available through a number of different mechanisms. Another fairly public, yet rather sensitive piece of information is the list of encrypted passwords for all of the users on the system. Even though the password information is cryptologically hidden, having it exposed in a world-readable file still provides some measure of vulnerability. Parts of the password file need to be world-readable (e.g., the UID and login name mappings), but not all of it. There's no need to provide a list of encrypted passwords to users who may be tempted to run password-cracking programs.

One alterative is to banish the encrypted password string for each user to a special file that is only readable by *root*. This second file is known as a "shadow password" file, since it contains lines that shadow the entries in the real password file.

Here's how it all works: the original password file is left intact with one small change. The encrypted password field contains a special character or characters to indicate password shadowing is in effect. Placing an **x** in this field is common, though the insecure copy of the BSD database uses a *****.

I've heard of some shadow password suites that insert a special, normal-looking string of characters in this field. If your password file goes awanderin', this provides a lovely time for the recipient who will attempt to crack a password file of random strings that bear no relation to the real passwords.

Most operating systems take advantage of this second shadow password file to store more information about the account. This additional information resembles the surplus fields we saw in the BSD files, storing account expiration data and information on password changing and aging.

In most cases Perl's normal password functions like `getpwent()` can handle shadow password files. As long as the C libraries shipped with the OS do the right thing, so will Perl. Here's what "do the right thing" means: when your Perl script is run with the appropriate privileges (as *root*), these routines will return the encrypted password. Under all other conditions that password will not be accessible to those routines.

---

* *pwd_mkdb* may or may not perform this locking for you (depending on the BSD flavor and version), however, so caveat implemptor.

Unfortunately, it is dicier if you want to retrieve the additional fields found in the shadow file. Perl may not return them for you. Eric Estabrooks has written a `Passwd::Solaris` module, but that only helps if you are running Solaris. If these fields are important to you, or you want to play it safe, the sad truth (in conflict with my recommendation to use `getpwent()` above) is that it is often simpler to open the *shadow* file by hand and parse it manually.

Windows NT/2000 User Identity

Now that we've explored the pieces of information that Unix systems cobble together to form a user's identity, let's take a look at the same topic for NT/2000 users. Much of this info is conceptually similar, so we'll dwell mostly on the differences between the two operating systems.

NT/2000 User Identity Storage and Access

NT/2000 stores the persistent identity information for a user in a database called the *SAM* (Security Accounts Manager), or *directory*, database. The SAM database is part of the NT/2000 registry living in *%SYSTEMROOT%/system32/config*. The files that make up the registry are all stored in a binary format, meaning normal Perl text manipulation idioms cannot be used to read or write changes to this database. It is theoretically possible to use Perl's binary data operators (i.e., `pack()` and `unpack()`) with the SAM, providing you do so when NT/2000 is not running, but this way lies madness and misery.

Luckily, there are better ways to access and manipulate this information via Perl.

One approach is to call an external binary to interact with the OS for you. Every NT/2000 machine has a feature-bloated command called *net* that can add, delete, and view users. *net* is quirky and limited, and probably the method of last resort.

For example, here's the *net* command in action on a machine with two accounts:

```
C:\>net users

User accounts for \\HOTDIGGITYDOG
----------------------------------
Administrator            Guest
The command completed successfully.
```

It would be easy to parse the output of this program from Perl if we needed to. Besides *net*, there are other commercial packages that offer a command-line executable to perform similar tasks.

Another approach is to use the Perl module `Win32::NetAdmin` (bundled with the ActiveState Perl distribution) or one of the modules created to fill in the gaps in the functionality of `Win32::NetAdmins`. These modules include David Roth's `Win32::AdminMisc` (from *http://www.roth.net*), or `Win32::UserAdmin` (described in Ashley Meggitt and Timothy Ritchey's O'Reilly book, *Windows NT User Administration*, module found at *ftp://ftp.oreilly.com/pub/examples/windows/winuser/*).

I prefer Roth's `Win32::AdminMisc` for most user operations because it offers the largest grab-bag of system administration tools and Roth actively supports it in a number of online forums. Though the online documentation for this module is good, the best documentation for this module is the author's book, *Win32 Perl Programming: The Standard Extensions* (Macmillan Technical Publishing). It's a good book to have on hand in any case if you plan to write Win32-specific Perl programs.

Here's some example code that shows the users on the local machine and some details about them. It prints out lines that look similar to */etc/passwd* under Unix:

```
use Win32::AdminMisc

# retrieve all of the local users
Win32::AdminMisc::GetUsers('','',\@users) or
    die "Unable to get users: $!\n";

# get their attributes and print them
foreach $user (@users){
  Win32::AdminMisc::UserGetMiscAttributes('',$user,\%attribs) or
    warn "Unable to get attrib: $!\n";
  print join(":",$user,
                 '*',
                 $attribs{USER_USER_ID},
                 $attribs{USER_PRIMARY_GROUP_ID},
                 '',
                 $attribs{USER_COMMENT},
                 $attribs{USER_FULL_NAME},
                 $attribs{USER_HOME_DIR_DRIVE}."\\".
                 $attribs{USER_HOME_DIR},
                 ''),"\n";
}
```

Finally, you can use the `Win32::OLE` module to access the Active Directory Service Interfaces (ADSI) functionality built in to Windows 2000 and installable on Windows NT 4.0. We'll go into this topic in great detail in Chapter 6, *Directory Services*, so we won't look at an example here.

We'll see more Perl code to access and manipulate NT/2000 users later on, but for the time being let's return to our exploration of the differences between Unix and NT/2000 users.

NT/2000 User ID Numbers

User IDs in NT/2000 are not created by mortals, and they cannot be reused. Unlike Unix, where we simply picked a UID number out of the air, the OS uniquely generates the equivalent identifier in NT/2000 every time a user is created. A unique user identifier (which NT/2000 calls a *Relative ID,* or RID) is combined with machine and domain IDs to create a large ID number called a SID, or *Security Identifier,* which acts as a users UID. An example RID is 500, part of a longer SID which looks like this:

```
S-1-5-21-2046255566-1111630368-2110791508-500
```

The RID is a number we get back as part of the `UserGetMiscAttributes()` call we saw in our last code snippet. Here's the code necessary to print the RID for a particular user:

```
use Win32::AdminMisc;

Win32::AdminMisc::UserGetMiscAttributes('',$user,\%attribs);
print $attribs{USER_USER_ID},"\n";
```

You can't (by normal means) recreate a user after she/he/it is deleted. Even if you create a new user with the same name as the deleted user, the SID will not be the same. The new user will not have access to its predecessor's files and resources.

This is why some NT books recommend renaming accounts that are due to be inherited by another person. If a new employee is supposed to receive all of the files and privileges of a departing employee, they suggest renaming the existing account to preserve the SID rather than creating a new account, transferring files, and then deleting the old account. I personally find this method for account hand-offs to be a little uncouth because it means the new employee will inherit all of the corrupted and useless registry settings of her or his predecessor. But it is the most expedient method, and sometimes that is important.

Part of this recommendation comes from the pain associated with transferring ownership of files. In Unix, a privileged user can say, "Change the ownership of all of these files so that they are now owned by the new user." In NT, however, there's no giving of ownership, only taking. Luckily there are two ways to get around this restriction and pretend we're using Unix's semantics. From Perl we can:

- Call a separate binary, including:
  - The *chown* binaries from either the Microsoft NT Resource kit (commercial; we'll hear more about this product later in this chapter) or the Cygwin distribution found at *http://www.cygnus.com* (free).
  - The *setowner* binary, part of the NTSEC utilities sold by Pedestal Software at *http://www.pedestalsoftware.com.* I prefer this binary because it is the most flexible while still requiring the least amount of overhead.

- The `Win32::Perms` module written by Dave Roth, located at *http://www.roth. net/perl/perms*. Here's some sample code that will change the owner of a directory and its contents including subdirectories:

```
use Win32::Perms;

$acl  = new Win32::Perms();
$acl->Owner($NewAccountName);
$result = $acl->SetRecurse($dir);
$acl->Close();
```

NT/2000 Passwords

The algorithms used to obscure the passwords that protect access to a user's identity in NT/2000 and Unix are cryptologically incompatible. Once encrypted, you cannot transfer the encrypted password information from one OS to the other and expect to use it for password changes or account creations. As a result, two separate sets of passwords have to be used and/or kept in sync. This difference is the bane of every system administrator who has to administer a mixed Unix–NT/2000 environment. Some administrators get around this by using custom authentication modules, commercial or otherwise.

As a Perl programmer, the only thing you can do if you are not using custom authentication mechanisms is to create a system whereby the user provides her or his password in plain text. This plain text password then gets used to perform two separate password-related operations (changes, etc.), one for each OS.

NT Groups

So far in our discussion of user identity for both operating systems, I've been able to gloss over any distinction between storage of a user's identity on a local machine and storage in some network service like NIS. For the information we've encountered, it hasn't really mattered if that information was used on a single system or all of the systems in a network or workgroup. In order to talk cogently about NT/2000 user groups and their intersection with Perl, we unfortunately have to break from this convention. We'll concentrate primarily on Windows NT 4.0 groups. For Windows 2000, another layer of complication was added, so information about Windows 2000 groups has been banished to the sidebar called "Windows 2000 Group Changes," later in this chapter.

On NT systems, a user's identity can be stored in one of two places: the SAM of a specific machine or the SAM of a domain controller. This is the distinction between a *local user*, who can only log into a single machine, and a *domain user*, who can log into any of the permitted machines that participate in that domain.

NT groups also come in two flavors, *global* and *local*. The difference between these two is not precisely what the name would lead you to expect. One is *not* just composed of domain users while the other of local users. Nor, as people with Unix backgrounds might expect, is one type effective on only one machine while the other is in effect globally on a network. Both of these descriptions are partially correct, but let's look at the full story.

If we start with the goals behind this mechanism's naming scheme and implementation it may make a little more sense. Here's what we're trying to accomplish:

- User accounts for an entire domain should be centrally managed. Administrators should be able to define arbitrary subsets of these user permissions and privileges can be assigned to whole groups at a time for administrative ease.

- All of the machines in a domain should be able to take advantage of this centralized management if they so choose. The administrator of an individual machine should also be able to create users that live only on that machine.

- The administrator of an individual machine should be able to decide which users are granted access to that machine. The administrator should be able to do this using the domain-wide user groups rather than having to specify each user by name.

- The members of these groups and certain local users should be able to be treated exactly the same from an administrative perspective (permissions, etc.).

Global and local groups allow us to do all of the above. The two sentence explanation is: global groups hold domain users only. Local groups hold local users and hold/import (the users of) global groups.

We'll use a simple example to help show how this works. Say you have an NT domain for a university department that already has domain users created for all of the students, faculty, and staff. When a new research project called Omphaloskepsis is started up, the central system administration staff creates a new global group called `Global-Omph People`. This global group contains all of the domain users working on this project. As staff members and students join and leave the project, they are added or removed from the group.

A computer lab is set aside for the exclusive use of this research project. Local guest accounts are created on the machines in this lab for a couple of faculty members who are not part of the department (and hence not domain users). The system administrator for this lab does the following (via Perl, of course) to prevent all but project members from using these machines:

1. Creates a *local* group on each machine called `Local-Authorized Omphies`.

2. Adds the local guest accounts to this local group.

3. Adds the *global* group `Global-Omph People` to this local group.

4. Adds the user right (we'll discuss user rights in the next section) `Log on Locally` to the local group `Local-Authorized Omphies`.

5. Removes the user right `Log on Locally` from all other unauthorized groups.

The result is that only the authorized local users and the users in the authorized global group can log on to the machines in this exclusive computer lab. A new user placed in the `Global-Omph People` group will instantly be granted permission to log on to these machines and nothing has to be changed on any of the machines themselves. Once you get a handle on the local/global group concepts, it's a pretty handy scheme.*

Windows 2000 Group Changes

Almost everything we've described about NT global and local groups is still true in Windows 2000, but there are few new twists that need to be mentioned:

1. Windows 2000 uses Active Directory (more details of which can be found in Chapter 6) to store its user data. This means that global group information is now stored in an Active Directory *store* on a domain controller, not in its SAM.

2. Local groups are now called *domain local* groups.

3. A third group, *scope* (as the distinction is now called), has been added. In addition to global and domain local groups, Windows 2000 adds *universal* groups. Universal groups essentially cut across domain boundaries. They can hold accounts, global groups, and universal groups from anywhere in the directory. Just as domain local groups can contain global groups, now they hold universal groups as well.

As of this writing, the standard Perl user administration modules haven't caught up with these changes. The modules can still be used because the NT4 SAM interfaces are still operational, but they won't be able to access any of the new functionality. Because of this lag, this sidebar is the only mention we'll make of these Windows 2000 changes. For further access and information, you will need to turn to the Active Directory Service Interfaces (ADSI) framework we discuss in Chapter 6.

This scheme would be even handier if it didn't complicate our Perl programming. All the Perl modules we mentioned before follow the Win32 API lead by providing

---

* For any Unix folks still reading along, a similar scheme can be set up by using NIS netgroups and special */etc/passwd* entries on each machine in an NIS domain. See your machine's *netgroup* manual page for more details.

completely separate functions for local and global groups. For instance, with `Win32::NetAdmin`, we have:

`GroupCreate()`	`LocalGroupCreate()`
`GroupDelete()`	`LocalGroupDelete()`
`GroupGetAttributes()`	`LocalGroupGetAttributes()`
`GroupSetAttributes()`	`LocalGroupSetAttributes()`
`GroupAddUsers()`	`LocalGroupAddUsers()`
`GroupDeleteUsers()`	`LocalGroupDeleteUsers()`
`GroupIsMember()`	`LocalGroupIsMember()`
`GroupGetMembers()`	`LocalGroupGetMembers()`

This duality means your code may have to call two functions for the same operation. For example, if you need to obtain all of the groups a user may be in, you may have to call two functions, one for local groups and the other for global groups. The group functions above are pretty self-explanatory. See the online documentation and Roth's book for more details.

 A quick tip found in Roth's book: your program must run with administrative privileges to access the list of local groups, but global group names are available to all users.

NT/2000 User Rights

The last different between Unix and NT/2000 user identity that we're going to address is the concept of a "user right." In Unix, the actions a user can take are either constrained by file permissions or by the superuser/non-superuser distinction. Under NT/2000, the permission scheme is more like superheroes. Users (and groups) can be imbued with special powers that become part of their identity. For instance, one can attach the user right `Change the System Time` to an ordinary user and that user will be able to effect the setting of the system clock on that machine.

Some people find the user rights concept confusing because they have attempted to use NT 4.0's heinous *User Rights* dialog in the *User Manager* or *User Manager for Domains* application. This dialog presents the information in exactly the opposite manner most people expect to see it. It shows a list of the possible user rights and expects you to add groups or users to a list of entities that already have this right. Figure 3-1 shows a screenshot of this UI example in action.

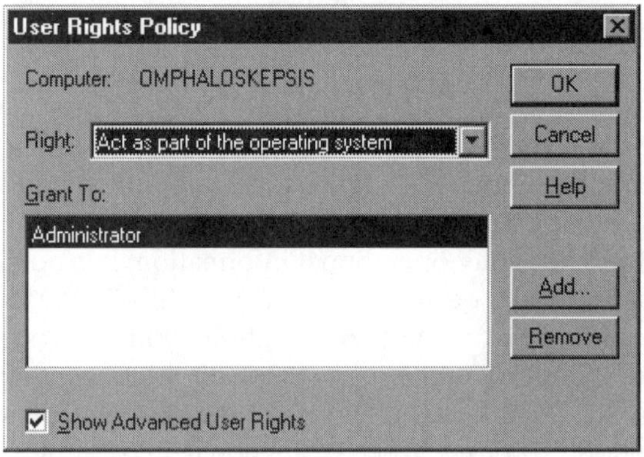

Figure 3-1. The User Rights Policy dialog box from the NT4 User Manager

A more user-centric UI would offer a way to add or remove user rights to and from users, instead of the other way around. This is in fact how we will operate on rights using Perl.

One approach is to call the program *ntrights.exe* from the Microsoft *NT Resource Kit.* If you haven't heard of the resource kit, be sure to read the upcoming sidebar about it.

Using *ntrights.exe* is straightforward; we call the program from Perl like any other (i.e., using backticks or the **system()** function). In this case, we call *ntrights.exe* with a command line of the form:

```
C:\>ntrights.exe +r <right name> +u <user or group name> [-m \\machinename]
```

to give a right to a user or group (on an optional machine named *machinename*). To take that right away:

```
C:\>ntrights.exe -r <right name> +u <user or group name> [-m \\machinename]
```

Unix users will be familiar with the use of the + and – characters (as in *chmod*), in this case used with the *–r* switch, to give and take away privileges. The list of right names like **SetSystemtimePrivilege** (can set the system time) can be found in the Microsoft *NT Resource Kit* documentation for the *ntrights* command.

A second, pure-Perl approach entails using the **Win32::Lanman** module by Jens Helberg, found at either *ftp://ftp.roth.net/pub/ntperl/Others/Lanman/* or at *http://jenda.krynicky.cz.* Let's start off by looking at the process of retrieving an account's user rights. This is a multiple-step process; let's go over it step by step.

The Microsoft Windows NT/ Windows 2000 Resource Kits

"You must have the *NT 4.0 Server* and/or *Workstation Resource Kit*" is the general consensus among serious NT administrators and the media that covers this field. Microsoft Press publishes two large tomes, one for each of the NT/2000 OS versions, full of nitty-gritty operational information. It is not this information that makes these books so desirable; rather, it is the CD-ROMs included with the books that makes them worth their weight in zlotniks. The CD-ROMs contain a grab bag of crucial utilities for NT/2000 administration. The utilities shipped with the NT/2000 Server editions are a superset of those shipped with the NT Workstation/Windows 2000 Professional version, so if you have to choose one of the two to buy, you may wish to get the Server edition.

Many of the utilities were contributed by the NT/2000 development group who wrote their own code because they couldn't find the tools they needed anywhere else. For example, there are utilities which add users, change filesystem security information, show installed printer drivers, work with roaming profiles, help with debugging domain and network browser services, and so on.

The tools in the Resource Kit are provided "as is," meaning there is virtually no support available for them. This no-support policy may sound harsh, but it serves the important purpose of allowing Microsoft to put a variety of useful code in the hands of administrators without having to pay prohibitive support costs. The utilities in the Resource Kits have a few small bugs, but on the whole they work great. Updates that fix bugs in some of these utilities have been posted to Microsoft's web site.

First, we need to load the module:

```
use Win32::Lanman;
```

Then, we need to retrieve the actual SID for the account we wish to query or modify. In the following sample, we'll get the *Guest* account's SID:

```
unless(Win32::Lanman::LsaLookupNames($server, ['Guest'], \@info)
    die "Unable to lookup SID: ".Win32::Lanman::GetLastError()."\n";
```

@info now contains an array of references to anonymous hashes, one element for each account we query (in this case, it is just a single element for *Guest*). Each hash contains the following keys: **domain**, **domainsid**, **relativeid**, **sid**, and **use**. We only care about **sid** for our next step. Now we can query the rights:

```
unless (Win32::Lanman::LsaEnumerateAccountRights($server, ${$info[0]}{sid},
                                                 \@rights);
    die "Unable to query rights: ".Win32::Lanman::GetLastError()."\n";
```

@rights now contains a set of names describing the rights apportioned to *Guest*.

Knowing the API (Application Program Interface) name of a user right and what it represents is tricky. The easiest way to learn which names correspond to which rights and what each right offers is to look at the SDK (Software Developement Kit) documentation found on *http://msdn.microsoft.com*. This documentation is easy to find because Helberg has kept the standard SDK function names for his Perl function names. To find the names of the available rights, we search the MSDN (Microsoft's Developer News) site for "LsaEnumerateAccountRights" and we'll find pointers to them quickly.

This information also comes in handy for the modification of user rights. For instance, if we want to add a user right to allow our *Guest* account to shut down the system, we could use:

```
use Win32::Lanman;

unless (Win32::Lanman::LsaLookupNames($server, ['Guest'], \@info))
  die "Unable to lookup SID: ".Win32::Lanman::GetLastError()."\n";


unless (Win32::Lanman::LsaAddAccountRights($server, ${$info[0]}{sid},
                          [&SE_SHUTDOWN_NAME]))
    die "Unable to change rights: ".Win32::Lanman::GetLastError()."\n"
```

In this case we found the **SE_SHUTDOWN_NAME** right in the SDK doc and used **&SE_SHUTDOWN_NAME** (a subroutine defined by `Win32::Lanman`), which returns the value for this SDK constant.

`Win32::Lanman::LsaRemoveAccountRights()`, a function that takes similar arguments to those we used to add rights, is used to remove user rights.

Before we move on to other topics, it is worth mentioning that `Win32::Lanman` also provides a function that works just like *User Manager*'s broken interface described earlier. Instead of matching users to rights, we can match rights to users. If we use `Win32::Lanman::LsaEnumerateAccountsWithUserRight()` we can retrieve a list of SIDs that has a specific user right. This could be useful in certain select situations.

Building an Account System to Manage Users

Now that we've had a good look at user identity, we can begin to address the administration aspect of user accounts. Rather than just show you the select Perl subroutines or function calls you need for user addition and deletion, we're going to take this topic to the next level by showing these operations in a larger context. In the remainder of this chapter, we're going to work towards writing a bare-bones account system that starts to really manage both NT and Unix users.

Our account system will be constructed in four parts: user interface, data storage, process scripts (Microsoft would call them the "business logic"), and low-level library routines. From a process perspective they work together (see Figure 3-2).

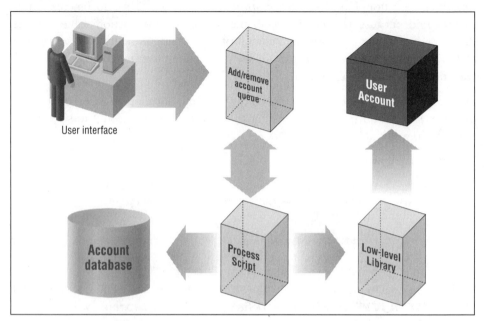

Figure 3-2. The structure of a basic account system

Requests come into the system through a user interface and get placed into an "add account queue" file for processing. We'll just call this an "add queue" from here on in. A process script reads this queue, performs the required account creations, and stores information about the created accounts in a separate database. That takes care of adding the users to our system.

For removing a user, the process is similar. A user interface is used to create a "remove queue." A second process script reads this queue and deletes the users from our system and updates the central database.

We isolate these operations into separate conceptual parts because it gives us the maximum possible flexibility should we decide to change things later. For instance, if some day we decide to change our database backend, we only need to modify the low-level library routines. Similarly, if we want our user addition process to include additional steps (perhaps cross-checking against another database in Human Resources), we will only need to change the process script in question. Let's start by looking at the first component: the user interface used to create the initial account queue. For the bare-bones purposes of this book, we'll use a simple text-based user interface to query for account parameters:

```perl
sub CollectInformation{
    # list of fields init'd here for demo purposes, this should
    # really be kept in a central configuration file
    my @fields = qw{login fullname id type password};
    my %record;

    foreach my $field (@fields){
        print "Please enter $field: ";
        chomp($record{$field} = <STDIN>);
    }
    $record{status}="to_be_created";
    return \%record;
}
```

This routine creates a list and populates it with the different fields of an account record. As the comment mentions, this list is in-lined in the code here only for brevity's sake. Good software design suggests the field name list really should be read from an additional configuration file.

Once the list has been created, the routine iterates through it and requests the value for each field. Each value is then stored back into the record hash. At the end of the question and answer session, a reference to this hash is returned for further processing. Our next step will be to write the information to the add queue. Before we see this code, we should talk about data storage and data formats for our account system.

The Backend Database

The center of any account system is a database. Some administrators use their */etc/passwd* file or SAM database as the only record of the users on their system, but this practice is often shortsighted. In addition to the pieces of user identity we've discussed, a separate database can be used to store metadata about each account, like its creation and expiration date, account sponsor (if it is a guest account), user's phone numbers, etc. Once a database is in place, it can be used for more than just basic account management. It can be useful for all sorts of niceties, such as automatic mailing list creation, LDAP services, and personal web page indexes.

Mentioning the creation of a separate database makes some people nervous. They think "Now I have to buy a really expensive commercial database, another machine for it to run on, and hire a database administrator." If you have thousands or tens of thousands of user accounts to manage, yes, you do need all of those things (though you may be able to get by with some of the noncommercial SQL databases like Postgres and MySQL). If this is the case for you, you may want

Why the Really Good System Administrators Create Account Systems

System administrators fall into roughly two categories: mechanics and architects. Mechanics spend most of their time in the trenches dealing with details. They know amazing amounts of arcania about the hardware and software they administer. If something breaks, they know just the command, file, or spanner wrench to wield. Talented mechanics can scare you with their ability to diagnose and fix problems even while standing clear across the room from the problem machine.

Architects spend their time surveying the computing landscape from above. They think more abstractly about how individual pieces can be put together to form larger and more complex systems. Architects are concerned about issues of scalability, extensibility, and reusability.

Both types bring important skills to the system administration field. The system administrators I respect the most are those who can function as a mechanic but whose preferred mindset is closely aligned to that of an architect. They fix a problem and then spend time after the repair determining which systemic changes can be made to prevent it from occurring again. They think about how even small efforts on their part can be leveraged for future benefit.

Well-run computing environments require both architects and mechanics working in a symbiotic relationship. A mechanic is most useful while working in a solid framework constructed by an architect. In the automobile world we need mechanics to fix cars. But mechanics rely on the car designers to engineer slow-to-break, easy-to-repair vehicles. They need infrastructure like assembly lines, service manuals, and spare-part channels to do their job well. If an architect performs her or his job well, the mechanic's job is made easier.

How do these roles play out in the context of our discussion? Well, a mechanic will probably use the built-in OS tools for user management. She or he might even go so far as to write small scripts to help make individual management tasks like adding users easier. An architect looking at the same tasks will immediately start to construct an account system. An architect will think about issues like:

- The repetitive nature of user management and how to automate as much of the process as possible.

- The sorts of information an account system collects, and how a properly built account system can be leveraged as a foundation for other functionality. For instance, Lightweight Directory Access Protocol (LDAP) directory services and automatic web site generation tools could be built on top of an account system.

—Continued—

- Protecting the data in an account system (i.e., security).
- Creating a system that will scale if the number of users increases.
- Creating a system that other sites might be able to use.
- How other system administration architects have dealt with the problems.

---

to turn to Chapter 7, *SQL Database Administration*, for more information on dealing with databases like this in Perl.

But in this chapter when I say *database*, I'm using the term in the broadest sense. A flat-file, plain text database will work fine for smaller installations. Win32 users could even use an access database file (e.g., *database.mdb*). For portability, we'll use plain text databases in this section for the different components we're going to build. To make things more interesting, our databases will be in XML format. If you have never encountered XML before, please take a moment to read Appendix C, *The Eight-Minute XML Tutorial.*

Why XML? XML has a few properties that make it a good choice for files like this and other system administration configuration files:

- XML is a plain text format, which means we can use our usual Perl bag o' tricks to deal with it easily.

- XML is self-describing and practically self-documenting. With a character-delimited file like */etc/passwd*, it is not always easy to determine which part of a line represents which field. With XML, this is never a problem because an obvious tag can surround each field.

- With the right parser, XML can also be self-validating. If you use a validating parser, mistakes in an entry's format will be caught right away, since the file will not parse correctly according to its document type definition or schema. The Perl modules we'll be using in this chapter are based on a nonvalidating parser, but there is considerable work afoot (both within this framework and in other modules) to provide XML validation functionality. One step in this direction is **XML::Checker**, part of Enno Derksen's *libxml-enno*. Even without a validating parser, any XML parser that checks for well-formedness will catch many errors.

- XML is flexible enough to describe virtually any set of text information you would ever desire to keep. This flexibility means you could use one parser library to get at all of your data, rather than having to write a new parser for each different format.

We'll use XML-formatted plain text files for the main user account storage file and the add/delete queues.

As we actually implement the XML portions of our account system, you'll find that the TMTOWTDI police are out in force. For each XML operation we require, we'll explore or at least mention several ways to perform it. Ordinarily when putting together a system like this, it would be better to limit our implementation options, but this way you will get a sense of the programming palette available when doing XML work in Perl.

Writing XML from Perl

Let's start by returning to the cliffhanger we left off with earlier in "NT 2000 User Rights." It mentioned we needed to write the account information we collected with `CollectInformation()` to our add queue file, but we didn't actually see code to perform this task. Let's look at how that XML-formatted file is written.

Using ordinary `print` statements to write an XML-compliant text would be the simplest method, but we can do better. Perl modules like `XML::Generator` by Benjamin Holzman and `XML::Writer` by David Megginson can make the process easier and less error-prone. They can handle details like start/end tag matching and escaping special characters (<, >, &, etc.) for us. Here's the XML writing code from our account system which makes use of `XML::Writer`:

```perl
sub AppendAccountXML {
    # receive the full path to the file
    my $filename = shift;
    # receive a reference to an anonymous record hash
    my $record = shift;

    # XML::Writer uses IO::File objects for output control
    use IO::File;

    # append to that file
    $fh = new IO::File(">>$filename") or
        die "Unable to append to file:$!\n";

    # initialize the XML::Writer module and tell it to write to
    # filehandle $fh
    use XML::Writer;
    my $w = new XML::Writer(OUTPUT => $fh);

    # write the opening tag for each <account> record
    $w->startTag("account");

    # write all of the <account> data start/end sub-tags & contents
    foreach my $field (keys %{$record}){
        print $fh "\n\t";
        $w->startTag($field);
        $w->characters($$record{$field});
```

```
        $w->endTag;
    }
    print $fh "\n";

    # write the closing tag for each <account> record
    $w->endTag;
    $w->end;
    $fh->close();
}
```

Now we can use just one line to collect data and write it to our add queue file:

```
&AppendAccountXML($addqueue,&CollectInformation);
```

Here's some sample output from this routine:[*]

```
<account>
    <login>bobf</login>
    <fullname>Bob Fate</fullname>
    <id>24-9057</id>
    <type>staff</type>
    <password>password</password>
    <status>to_be_created</status>
</account>
```

Yes, we are storing passwords in clear text. This is an exceptionally bad idea for anything but a demonstration system and even then you should think twice. A real account system would probably pre-encrypt the password before adding it to the add queue or not keep this info in a queue at all.

`AppendAccountXML()` will make another appearance later when we want to write data to the end of our delete queue and our main account database.

The use of `XML::Writer` in our `AppendAccountXML()` subroutine gives us a few perks:

- The code is quite legible; anyone with a little bit of markup language experience will instantly understand the names `startTag()`, `characters()`, and `endTag()`.

- Though our data didn't need this, `characters()` is silently performing a bit of protective magic for us by properly escaping reserved entities like the greater-than symbol (>).

- Our code doesn't have to remember the last start tag we opened for later closing. `XML::Writer` handles this matching for us, allowing us to call `endTag()` without specifying *which* end tag we need. Keeping track of tag pairs is less

---

[*] As a quick side note: the XML specification recommends that every XML file begin with a declaration (e.g., `<?xml version="1.0"?>`). It is not mandatory, but if we want to comply, `XML::Writer` offers the `xmlDecl()` method to create one for us.

of an issue with our account system because our data uses shallowly nesting tags, but this functionality becomes more important in other situations where our elements are more complex.

Reading XML using XML::Parser

We'll see one more way of writing XML from Perl in a moment, but before we do, let's turn our attention to the process of reading all of the great XML we've just learned how to write. We need code that will parse the account addition and deletion queues and the main database.

It would be possible to cobble together an XML parser in Perl for our limited data set out of regular expressions, but that gets trickier as the XML data gets more complicated.[*] For general parsing, it is easier to use the **XML::Parser** module initially written by Larry Wall and now significantly enhanced and maintained by Clark Cooper.

XML::Parser is an event-based module. Event-based modules work like stock market brokers. Before trading begins, you leave a set of instructions with them for actions they should take should certain triggers occur (e.g., sell a thousand shares should the price drop below $3\frac{1}{4}$, buy this stock at the beginning of the trading day, and so on). With event-based programs, the triggers are called *events* and the instruction lists for what to do when an event happens are called *event handlers*. Handlers are usually just special subroutines designed to deal with a particular event. Some people call them *callback routines*, since they are run when the main program "calls us back" after a certain condition is established. With the **XML::Parser** module, our events will be things like "started parsing the data stream," "found a start tag," and "found an XML comment," and our handlers will do things like "print the contents of the element you just found."[†]

Before we begin to parse our data, we need to create an **XML::Parser** object. When we create this object, we'll specify which parsing mode, or *style*, to use. **XML::Parser** provides several styles, each of which behaves a little different during the parsing of data. The style of a parse will determine which event handlers are called by default and the way data returned by the parser (if any) is structured.

Certain styles require that we specify an association between each event we wish to manually process and its handler. No special actions are taken for events we haven't chosen to explicitly handle. This association is stored in a simple hash table with keys that are the names of the events we want to handle, and values

---

[*] But it is doable; for instance, see Eric Prud'hommeaux's module at *http://www.w3.org/1999/02/26-modules/W3C-SAX-XmlParser-**.

[†] Though we don't use it here, Chang Liu's **XML::Node** module allows the programmer to easily request callbacks for only certain elements, further simplifying the process we're about to discuss.

that are references to our handler subroutines. For the styles that require this association, we pass the hash in using a named parameter called `Handlers` (e.g., `Handlers => {Start => \&start_handler})` when we create a parser object.

We'll be using the `stream` style that does not require this initialization step. It simply calls a set of predefined event handlers if certain subroutines are found in the program's namespace. The `stream` event handlers we'll be using are simple: `StartTag`, `EndTag`, and `Text`. All but `Text` should be self-explanatory. `Text`, according to the `XML::Parser` documentation, is "called just before start or end tags with accumulated non-markup text in the `$_` variable." We'll use it when we need to know the contents of a particular element.

Here's the initialization code we're going to use for our application:

```
use XML::Parser;
use Data::Dumper; # used for debugging output, not needed for XML parse
$p = new XML::Parser(ErrorContext => 3,
                     Style       => 'Stream',
                     Pkg         => 'Account::Parse');
```

This code returns a parser object after passing in three named parameters. The first, `ErrorContext`, tells the parser to return three lines of context from the parsed data if an error should occur while parsing. The second sets the parse style as we just discussed. `Pkg`, the final parameter, instructs the parser to look in a different namespace than the current one for the event handler subroutines it expects to see. By setting this parameter, we've instructed the parser to look for `&Account::Parse::StartTag()`, `&Account::Parse::EndTag()`, and so on, instead of just `&StartTag()`, `&EndTag()`, etc. This doesn't have any operational impact, but it does allow us to sidestep any concerns that our parser might inadvertently call someone else's function called `StartTag()`. Instead of using the `Pkg` parameter, we could have put an explicit `package Account::Parse;` line before the above code.

Now let's look at the subroutines that perform the event handling functions. We'll go over them one at a time:

```
package Account::Parse;

sub StartTag {
    undef %record if ($_[1] eq "account");
}
```

`&StartTag()` is called each time we hit a start tag in our data. It is invoked with two parameters: a reference to the parser object and the name of the tag encountered. We'll want to construct a new record hash for each new account record we encounter, so we can use `StartTag()` in order to let us know when we've hit the beginning of a new record (e.g., an `<account>` start tag). In that case, we obliterate any existing record hash. In all other cases we return without doing anything:

```
sub Text {
    my $ce = $_[0]->current_element();
    $record{$ce}=$_ unless ($ce eq "account");
}
```

Here we use `&Text()` to populate the `%record` hash. Like the previous function, it too receives two parameters upon invocation: a reference to the parser object and the "accumulated nonmarkup text" the parser has collected between the last start and end tag. We determine which element we're in by calling the parser object's `current_element()` method. According to the `XML::Parser::Expat` documentation, this method "returns the name of the innermost currently opened element." As long as the current element name is not "account," we're sure to be within one of the subelements of `<account>`, so we record the element name and its contents:

```
sub EndTag {
    print Data::Dumper->Dump([\%record],["account"])
        if ($_[1] eq "account");
    # here's where we'd actually do something, instead of just
    # printing the record
}
```

Our last handler, `&EndTag()`, is just like our first, `&StartTag()`, except it gets called when we encounter an end tag. If we reach the end of an account record, we do the mundane thing and print that record out. Here's some example output:

```
$account = {
             'login' => 'bobf',
             'type' => 'staff',
             'password' => 'password',
             'fullname' => 'Bob Fate',
             'id' => '24-9057'
           };
$account = {
             'login' => 'wendyf',
             'type' => 'faculty',
             'password' => 'password',
             'fullname' => 'Wendy Fate',
             'id' => '50-9057'
           };
```

If we were really going to use this parse code in our account system we would probably call some function like `CreateAccount(\%record)` rather than printing the record using `Data::Dumper`.

Now that we've seen the `XML::Parser` initialization and handler subroutines, we need to include the piece of code that actually initiates the parse:

```
# handle multiple account records in a single XML queue file
open(FILE,$addqueue) or die "Unable to open $addqueue:$!\n";
```

```
# this clever idiom courtesy of Jeff Pinyan
read(FILE, $queuecontents, -s FILE);
$p->parse("<queue>".$queuecontents."</queue>");
```

This code has probably caused you to raise an eyebrow, maybe even two. The first two lines open our add queue file and read its contents into a single scalar variable called $queuecontents. The third line would probably be easily comprehensible, except for the funny argument being passed to **parse()**. Why are we bothering to read in the contents of the actual queue file and then bracket it with more XML before actually parsing it?

Because it is a hack. As hacks go, it's not so bad. Here's why these convolutions are necessary to parse the multiple <account> elements in our queue file.

Every XML document, by definition (in the very first production rule of the XML specification), must have a *root* or *document element.* This element is the container element for the rest of the document; all other elements are subelements of it. An XML parser expects the first start tag it sees to be the start tag for the root element of that document and the last end tag it sees to be the end tag for that that element. XML documents that do not conform to this structure are not considered to be well-formed.

This puts us in a bit of a bind when we attempt to model a queue in XML. If we do nothing, <account> will be found as the first tag in the file. Everything will work fine until the parser hits the end </account> tag for that record. At that point it will cease to parse any further, even if there are more records to be found, because it believes it has found the end of the document.

We can easily put a start tag (<queue>) at the beginning of our queue, but how do we handle end tags (</queue>)? We always need the root element's end tag at the bottom of the file (and only there), a difficult task given that we're planning to repeatedly append records to this file.

A plausible but fairly heinous hack would be to **seek()** to the end of the file, and then **seek()** backwards until we backed up just before the last end tag. We could then write our new record over this tag, leaving an end tag at the end of the data we were writing. Just the risk of data corruption (what if you back up too far?) should dissuade you from this method. Also, this method gets tricky in cases where there is no clear end of file, e.g., if you were reading XML data from a network connection. In those cases you would probably need to do some extra shadow buffering of the data stream so it would be possible to back up from the end of transmission.

The method we demonstrated in the code above of prepending and appending a root element tag pair to the existing data may be a hack, but it comes out looking almost elegant compared to other solutions. Let's return to more pleasant topics.

Reading XML using XML::Simple

We've seen one method for bare bones XML parsing using the `XML::Parser` module. To be true to our TMTOWTDI warning, let's revisit the task, taking an even easier tack. Several authors have written modules built upon `XML::Parser` to parse XML documents and return the data in easy-to-manipulate Perl object/data structure form, including `XML::DOM` by Enno Derksen, Ken MacLeod's `XML::Grove` and `ToObjects` (part of the *libxml-perl* package), `XML::DT` by Jose Joao Dias de Almeida, and `XML::Simple` by Grant McLean. Of these, `XML::Simple` is perhaps the easiest to use. It was designed to handle smallish XML configuration files, perfect for the task at hand.

`XML::Simple` provides exactly two functions. Here's the first (in context):

```
use XML::Simple;
use Data::Dumper;  # just needed to show contents of our data structures

$queuefile = "addqueue.xml";
open(FILE,$queuefile) or die "Unable to open $queuefile:$!\n";
read(FILE, $queuecontents, -s FILE);
$queue = XMLin("<queue>".$queuecontents."</queue>");
```

We dump the contents of `$queue`, like so:

```
print Data::Dumper->Dump([$queue],["queue"]);
```

It is now a reference to the data found in our add queue file, stored as a hash of a hash keyed on our `<id>` elements. Figure 3-3 shows this data structure.

```
$queue = {
          'account' => {
                '24-9057' => {
                               'login' => 'bobf',
                               'type' => 'staff',
                               'password' => 'password',
                               'fullname' => 'Bob Fate',
                               'status' =>'to_be_created'
                }
                '50-9057' => {
                               'login' => 'wendyf',
                               'type' => 'faculty',
                               'password' => 'password',
                               'fullname' => 'Wendy Fate',
                               'status' =>'to_be_created'
                }
          }
        };
```

Figure 3-3. The data structure created by XMLin() with no special arguments

The data structure is keyed this way because **XML::Simple** has a feature that recognizes certain tags in the data, favoring them over the others during the conversion process. When we turn this feature off:

```
$queue = XMLin("<queue>".$queuecontents."</queue>",keyattr=>[]);
```

we get a reference to a hash with the sole value of a reference to an anonymous array. The anonymous array holds our data as seen in Figure 3-4.

```
$queue = {
          'account' => [
                  {
                    'login' => 'bobf',
                    'type' => 'staff',
                    'password' => 'password',
                    'status' => 'to_be_created',
                    'fullname' => 'Bob Fate',
                    'id' => '24-9057'
                  },
                  {
                    'login' => 'wendyf',
                    'type' => 'faculty',
                    'password' => 'password',
                    'status' => 'to_be_created',
                    'fullname' => 'Wendy Fate',
                    'id' => '50-9057'
                  }
                ]
        };
```

Figure 3-4. The data structure created by XMLin( ) with keyattr turned off

That's not a particularly helpful data structure. We can tune the same feature in our favor:

```
$queue = XMLin("<queue>".$queuecontents."</queue>",keyattr => ["login"]);
```

Now we have a reference to a data structure (a hash of a hash keyed on the login name), perfect for our needs as seen in Figure 3-5.

How perfect? We can now remove items from our in-memory add queue after we process them with just one line:

```
# e.g. $login = "bobf";
delete $queue->{account}{$login};
```

If we want to change a value before writing it back to disk (let's say we were manipulating our main database), that's easy too:

```
# e.g. $login="wendyf"; $field="status";
$queue->{account}{$login}{$field}="created";
```

```
$queue = {
        'account' => {
                'bobf' =>      {
                                'type' => 'staff',
                                'password' => 'password',
                                'fullname' => 'Bob Fate',
                                'status' => 'to_be_created',
                                'id' => '24-9057'
                               },
                'wendyf' =>    {
                                'type' => 'faculty',
                                'password' => 'password',
                                'fullname' => 'Wendy Fate',
                                'status' => 'to_be_created',
                                'id' => '50-9057'
                               }
                      }
        };
```

Figure 3-5. The same data structure with a user-specified keyattr

Writing XML using XML::Simple

The mention of "writing it back to disk" brings us to back the method of writing
XML promised earlier. **XML::Simple**'s second function takes a reference to a data
structure and generates XML:

```
# rootname sets the root element's name, we could also use
# xmldecl to add an XML declaration
print XMLout($queue, rootname =>"queue");
```

This yields (indented for readability):

```
<queue>
  <account name="bobf" type="staff"
          password="password" status="to_be_created"
          fullname="Bob Fate" id="24-9057" />
  <account name="wendyf" type="faculty"
          password="password" status="to_be_created"
          fullname="Wendy Fate" id="50-9057" />
</queue>
```

This is perfectly good XML, but it's not in the same format as our data files. The
data for each account is being represented as attributes of a singleelement, not as nested elements. **XML::Simple** has a set of rules for
how it translates data structures. Two of these rules (the rest can be found in the
documentation) can be stated as "single values are translated into XML attributes"
and "references to anonymous arrays are translated as nested XML elements."

We need a data structure in memory that looks like Figure 3-6 to produce the "correct" XML output (correct means "in the same style and format as our data files").

```
        $queue = {
                'account' => {
                        {
                                'login' => ['bobf'],
                                'type' => ['staff'],
                                'password' => ['password'],
                                'status' => ['to_be_created'],
                                'fullname' => ['Bob Fate'],
                                'id' => ['24-9057']
                        },
                        {
                                'login' => ['wendyf'],
                                'type' => ['faculty'],
                                'password' => ['password'],
                                'status' => ['to_be_created'],
                                'fullname' => ['Wendy Fate'],
                                'id' => ['50-9057']
                        }
                }
        };
```

Figure 3-6. The data structure needed to output our XML queue file

Ugly, isn't it? We have a few choices at this point, including:

1. Changing the format of our data files. This seems a bit extreme.

2. Changing the way we ask `XML::Simple` to parse our file. To get an in-memory data structure like the one in Figure 3-6 we could use:

```
$queue = XMLin("<queue>".$queuecontents."</queue>",forcearray=>1,
                                              keyattr => [""]);
```

   But when we tailor the way we read in the data to make for easy writing, we lose our easy hash semantics for data lookup and manipulation.

3. Performing some data manipulation after reading but before writing. We could read the data into a structure we like (just like we did before), manipulate the data to our heart's contents, and then transform the data structure into one `XML::Simple` "likes" before writing it out.

Option number three appears to be the most reasonable, so let's pursue it. Here's a subroutine that takes the data structure in Figure 3-5 and transforms it into the data structure found in Figure 3-6. An explanation of this code will follow:

```
sub TransformForWrite{
  my $queueref = shift;
  my $toplevel = scalar each %$queueref;

  foreach my $user (keys %{$queueref->{$toplevel}}){
    my %innerhash =
      map {$_,[$queueref->{$toplevel}{$user}{$_}] }
          keys %{$queueref->{$toplevel}{$user}};
    $innerhash{'login'} = [$user];
```

```
        push @outputarray, \%innerhash;
    }

    $outputref = { $toplevel => \@outputarray};
    return $outputref;
}
```

Let's walk through the `TransformForWrite()` subroutine one step at a time.

If you compare Figures 3-5 and 3-6, you'll notice one common feature between these two structures: there is an outermost hash keyed with the same key (account). The following retrieves that key name by requesting the first key in the hash pointed to by `$queueref`:

```
my $toplevel = scalar each %$queueref;
```

Let's see how this data structure is created from the inside out:

```
my %innerhash =
    map {$_, [$queueref->{$toplevel}{$user}{$_}] }
        keys %{$queueref->{$toplevel}{$user}};
```

This piece of code uses `map()` to iterate over the keys found in the innermost hash for each entry (i.e., login, type, password, status). The keys are returned by:

```
keys %{$queueref->{$toplevel}{$user}};
```

As we iterate over each key, we ask `map` to return two values for each key: the key itself, and the reference to an anonymous array that contains the value of this key:

```
map {$_, [$queueref->{$toplevel}{$user}{$_}] }
```

The list returned by `map()` looks like this:

```
(login,[bobf], type,[staff], password,[password]...)
```

It has a key-value format, where the values are stored as elements in anonymous arrays. We can simply assign this list to `%innerhash` to populate the inner hash table for our resulting data structure (`my %innerhash =`). We also add a `login` key to that hash based on the current user being processed:

```
$innerhash{'login'} = [$user];
```

The data structure we are trying to create is a list of hashes like these, so after we create and populate our inner hash, we add a reference to it on to the end of our output structure list:

```
push @outputarray, \%innerhash;
```

We repeat this procedure once for every `login` key found in our original data structure (once per account record). When we are done, we have a list of references to hashes in the form we need. We create an anonymous hash with a key that is the same as the outermost key for the original data structure and a value that is our list of hashes. We return a reference to this anonymous hash back to the caller of our subroutine, and we're done:

```
$outputref = { $toplevel => \@outputarray};
return $outputref;
```

With `&TransformForWrite()`, we can now write code to read in, manipulate, and then write out our data:

```
$queue = XMLin("<queue>".$queuecontents."</queue>",keyattr => ["login"]);
manipulate the data...
print OUTPUTFILE XMLout(TransformForWrite($queue),rootname => "queue");
```

The data written will be in the same format as the data read.

Before we move on from the subject of reading and writing data, let's tie up some loose ends:

1. Eagle-eyed readers may notice that using `XML::Writer` and `XML::Simple` in the same program to write to our account queue could be problematic. If we write with `XML::Simple`, our data will be nested in a root element by default. If we write using `XML::Writer` (or with just print statements), that's not necessarily the case, meaning we need to resort to the `"<queue>".$queuecontents."</queue>"` hack. We have an undesirable level of reader-writer synchronization between our XML parsing and writing code.

   To get around this, we will have to use an advanced feature of `XML::Simple`: if `XMLout()` is passed a `rootname` parameter with a value that is empty or `undef`, it will produce XML code that does not have a root element. In most cases this is a dangerous thing to do because it means the XML being produced is not well-formed and will not be parseable. Our queue-parsing hack allows us to get away with it, but in general this is not a feature you want to invoke lightly

2. Though we didn't do this in our sample code, we should be ready to deal with parsing errors. If the data file contains non-well-formed data, then your parser will sputter and die (as per the XML specification), taking your whole program with it unless you are careful. The most common way to deal with this in Perl is to wrap your parse statement in `eval()` and then check the contents of `$@` after the parse completes.* For example:

   ```
   eval {$p->parse("<queue>".$queuecontents."</queue>")};
   if ($@) { do something graceful to handle the error before quitting... };
   ```

   Another solution would be to use something like the `XML::Checker` module mentioned before, since it handles parse errors with more grace.

---

* Daniel Burckhardt pointed out on the Perl-XML list that this method has its drawbacks. In a multithreaded Perl program, checking the global `$@` may not be safe without taking other precautions. Threading issues like this were still under discussion among the Perl developers at the time of this publishing.

The Low-Level Component Library

Now that we have all of the data under control, including how it is acquired, written, read, and stored, let's look at how it is actually used deep in the bowels of our account system. We're going to explore the code that actually creates and deletes users. The key to this section is the notion that we are building a library of reusable components. The better you are able to compartmentalize your account system routines, the easier it will be to change only small pieces when it comes time to migrate your system to some other operating system or make changes. This may seem like unnecessary caution on our part, but the one constant in system administration work is constant change.

Unix account creation and deletion routines

Let's begin with the code that handles Unix account creation. Most of this code will be pretty trivial because we're going to take the easy way out. Our account creation and deletion routines will call vendor-supplied "add user," "delete user," and "change password" executables with the right arguments.

Why the apparent cop-out? We are using this method because we know the OS-specific executable will play nice with the other system components. Specifically, this method:

- Handles the locking issues for us (i.e., avoids the data corruption problems, that two programs simultaneously trying to write to the password file can cause).

- Handles the variations in password file formats (including password encoding) we discussed earlier.

- Is likely to be able to handle any OS-specific authentication schemes or password distribution mechanisms. For instance, under Digital Unix, the external "add user" executable can add directly add a user to the NIS maps on a master server.

Drawbacks of using an external binary to create and remove accounts include:

OS variations
Each OS has a different set of binaries, located at a different place on the system, which take slightly different arguments. In a rare show of compatibility, almost all of the major Unix variants (Linux included, BSD variants excluded) have mostly compatible add and remove account binaries called *useradd* and *userdel*. The BSD variants use *adduser* and *rmuser*, two programs with similar purpose but very different argument names. Variations like this tend to increase the complexity of our code.

Security concerns are introduced

The program we call and the arguments passed to it will be exposed to users wielding the *ps* command. If accounts are only created on a secure machine (like a master server), this reduces the data leakage risk considerably.

Added dependency

If the executable changes for some reason or is moved, our account system is kaput.

Loss of control

We have to treat a portion of the account creation process as being *atomic*; in other words, once we run the executable we can't intervene or interleave any of our own operations. Error detection and recovery becomes more difficult.

These programs rarely do it all

It's likely these programs will not perform all of the steps necessary to instantiate an account at your site. Perhaps you need to add specific user types to specific auxiliary groups, place users on a site-wide mailing list, or add users to a license file for a commercial package. You'll have to add some more code to handle these specifities. This isn't a problem with the approach itself, it's more of a heads up that any account system you build will probably require more work on your part than just calling another executable. This will not surprise most system administrators, since system administration is very rarely a walk in the park.

For the purposes of our demonstration account system, the positives of this approach outweigh the negatives, so let's see some code that uses external executables. To keep things simple, we're going to show code that works under Solaris and Linux on a local machine only, ignoring complexities like NIS and BSD variations. If you'd like to see a more complex example of this method in action, you may find the `CfgTie` family of modules by Randy Maas instructive.

Here's our basic account creation routine:

```
# these variables should really be set in a central configuration file
$useraddex    = "/usr/sbin/useradd";  # location of useradd executable
$passwdex     = "/bin/passwd";        # location of passwd executable
$homeUnixdirs = "/home";              # home directory root dir
$skeldir      = "/home/skel";         # prototypical home directory
$defshell     = "/bin/zsh";           # default shell

sub CreateUnixAccount{

    my ($account,$record) = @_;

    ### construct the command line, using:
    # -c = comment field
    # -d = home dir
```

```
# -g = group (assume same as user type)
# -m = create home dir
# -k = and copy in files from this skeleton dir
# (could also use -G group, group, group to add to auxiliary groups)
my @cmd = ($useraddex,
           "-c", $record->{"fullname"},
           "-d", "$homeUnixdirs/$account",
           "-g", $record->{"type"},
           "-m",
           "-k", $skeldir,
           "-s", $defshell,
           $account);

print STDERR "Creating account...";
my $result = 0xff & system @cmd;
# the return code is 0 for success, non-0 for failure, so we invert
if ($result){
    print STDERR "failed.\n";
    return "$useraddex failed";
}
else {
    print STDERR "succeeded.\n";
}

print STDERR "Changing passwd...";
unless ($result = &InitUnixPasswd($account,$record->{"password"})){
    print STDERR "succeeded.\n";
    return "";
}
else {
    print STDERR "failed.\n";
    return $result;
}
}
```

This adds the appropriate entry to our password file, creates a home directory for
the account, and copies over some default environment files (*.profile*, *.tcshrc*, *.zshrc*,
etc.) from a skeleton directory.

Notice we make a separate subroutine call to handle setting a password for the
account. The *useradd* command on some operating systems (like Solaris) will
leave an account in a locked state until the *passwd* command is run for that
account. This process requires a little sleight of hand, so we encapsulate that step
in a separate subroutine to keep the details out of our way. We'll see that subroutine in just a moment, but first for symmetry's sake here's the simpler account
deletion code:

```
# these variables should really be set in a central configuration file
$userdelex = "/usr/sbin/userdel";  # location of userdel executable

sub DeleteUnixAccount{
```

```
    my ($account,$record) = @_;

    ### construct the command line, using:
    # -r = remove the account's home directory for us
    my @cmd = ($userdelex, "-r", $account);

    print STDERR "Deleting account...";
    my $result = 0xffff & system @cmd;
    # the return code is 0 for success, non-0 for failure, so we invert
    if (!$result){
        print STDERR "succeeded.\n";
        return "";
    }
    else {
        print STDERR "failed.\n";
        return "$userdelex failed";
    }
}
```

Before we move on to NT account operations, let's deal with the
`InitUnixPasswd()` routine we mentioned earlier. To finish creating an account
(under Solaris, at least), we need to change that account's password using the
standard *passwd* command. *passwd <accountname>* will change that account's
password.

Sounds simple, but there's a problem lurking here. The *passwd* command expects
to prompt the user for the password. It takes great pains to make sure it is talking
to a real user by interacting directly with the user's terminal device. As a result, the
following will *not* work:

```
# this code DOES NOT WORK
open(PW,"|passwd $account");
print PW $oldpasswd,"\n";
print PW $newpasswd,"\n";
```

We have to be craftier than usual; somehow faking the *passwd* program into thinking it is dealing with a human rather than our Perl code. We can achieve this level
of duplicity by using *Expect.pm*, a Perl module by Austin Schutz that sets up a
pseudo-terminal (pty) within which another program will run. *Expect.pm* is heavily
based on the famous Tcl program *Expect* by Don Libes. This module is part of the
family of bidirectional program interaction modules. We'll see its close relative, Jay
Rogers's `Net::Telnet`, in Chapter 6.

These modules function using the same basic conversational model: wait for output from a program, send it some input, wait for a response, send some data, and
so on. The code below starts up *passwd* in a pty and waits for it to prompt for the
password. The discussion we have with *passwd* should be easy to follow:

```
use Expect;

sub InitUnixPasswd {
```

```
my ($account,$passwd) = @_;

# return a process object
my $pobj = Expect->spawn($passwdex, $account);
die "Unable to spawn $passwdex:$!\n" unless (defined $pobj);

# do not log to stdout (i.e. be silent)
$pobj->log_stdout(0);

# wait for password & password re-enter prompts,
# answering appropriately
$pobj->expect(10,"New password: ");
# Linux sometimes prompts before it is ready for input, so we pause
sleep 1;
print $pobj "$passwd\r";
$pobj->expect(10, "Re-enter new password: ");
print $pobj "$passwd\r";

# did it work?
$result = (defined ($pobj->expect(10, "successfully changed")) ?
                            "" : "password change failed");

# close the process object, waiting up to 15 secs for
# the process to exit
$pobj->soft_close();

return $result;
}
```

The *Expect.pm* module meets our meager needs well in this routine, but it is worth noting that the module is capable of much more complex operations. See the documentation and tutorial included with the *Expect.pm* module for more information.

Windows NT/2000 account creation and deletion routines

The process of creating and deleting an account under Windows NT/2000 is slightly easier than the process under Unix because standard API calls for the operation exist under NT. Like Unix, we could call an external executable to handle the job (e.g., the ubiquitous *net* command with its USERS/ADD switch), but it is easy to use the native API calls from a handful of different modules, some we've mentioned earlier. Account creation functions exist in `Win32::NetAdmin`, `Win32::UserAdmin`, `Win32API::Net`, and `Win32::Lanman`, just to start. Windows 2000 users will find the ADSI material in Chapter 6 to be their best route.

Picking among these NT4-centric modules is mostly a matter of personal preference. In order to understand the differences between them, we'll take a quick look behind the scenes at the native user creation API calls. These calls are documented in the Network Management SDK documentation on *http://msdn.microsoft. com* (search for "NetUserAdd" if you have a hard time finding it). `NetUserAdd()` and the other calls take a parameter that specifies the information level of the data being submitted. For instance, with information level 1, the C structure that is passed in to the user creation call looks like this:

```
typedef struct _USER_INFO_1 {
   LPWSTR     usri1_name;
   LPWSTR     usri1_password;
   DWORD      usri1_password_age;
   DWORD      usri1_priv;
   LPWSTR     usri1_home_dir;
   LPWSTR     usri1_comment;
   DWORD      usri1_flags;
   LPWSTR     usri1_script_path;
}
```

If information level 2 is used, the structure expected is expanded considerably:

```
typedef struct _USER_INFO_2 {
   LPWSTR     usri2_name;
   LPWSTR     usri2_password;
   DWORD      usri2_password_age;
   DWORD      usri2_priv;
   LPWSTR     usri2_home_dir;
   LPWSTR     usri2_comment;
   DWORD      usri2_flags;
   LPWSTR     usri2_script_path;
   DWORD      usri2_auth_flags;
   LPWSTR     usri2_full_name;
   LPWSTR     usri2_usr_comment;
   LPWSTR     usri2_parms;
   LPWSTR     usri2_workstations;
   DWORD      usri2_last_logon;
   DWORD      usri2_last_logoff;
   DWORD      usri2_acct_expires;
   DWORD      usri2_max_storage;
   DWORD      usri2_units_per_week;
   PBYTE      usri2_logon_hours;
   DWORD      usri2_bad_pw_count;
   DWORD      usri2_num_logons;
   LPWSTR     usri2_logon_server;
   DWORD      usri2_country_code;
   DWORD      usri2_code_page;
}
```

Without having to know anything about these parameters, or even much about C at all, we can still tell that a change in level increases the amount of information that can be specified as part of the user creation. Also, each subsequent information level is a superset of the previous one.

What does this have to do with Perl? Each module mentioned makes two decisions:

1. Should the notion of "information level" be exposed to the Perl programmer?

2. Which information level (i.e., how many parameters) can the programmer use?

Win32API::Net and Win32::UserAdmin both allow the programmer to choose
an information level. Win32::NetAdmin and Win32::Lanman do not. Of the modules, Win32::NetAdmin exposes the least number of parameters; for example,
you cannot set the full_name field as part of the user creation call. If you choose
to use Win32::NetAdmin, you will probably have to supplement it with calls from
another module to set the additional parameters it does not expose. If you do go
with a combination like Win32::NetAdmin and Win32::AdminMisc, you'll want
to consult the Roth book mentioned earlier, because it is an excellent reference
for the documentation-impoverished Win32::NetAdmin module.

Now you have some idea why the module choice really boils down to personal
preference. A good strategy might be to first decide which parameters are important to you, and then find a comfortable module that supports them. For our demonstration subroutines below, we're going to arbitrarily pick Win32::Lanman.
Here's the user creation and deletion code for our account system:

```
use Win32::Lanman;    # for account creation
use Win32::Perms;     # to set the permissions on the home directory

$homeNTdirs = "\\\\homeserver\\home";        # home directory root dir


sub CreateNTAccount{

    my ($account,$record) = @_;

    # create this account on the local machine
    # (i.e., empty first parameter)
    $result = Win32::Lanman::NetUserAdd("",
                        {'name' => $account,
                         'password'  => $record->{password},
                         'home_dir'  => "$homeNTdirs\\$account",
                         'full_name' => $record->{fullname}});
    return Win32::Lanman::GetLastError() unless ($result);

    # add to appropriate LOCAL group (first get the SID of the account)
    # we assume the group name is the same as the account type
    die "SID lookup error: ".Win32::Lanman::GetLastError()."\n" unless
        (Win32::Lanman::LsaLookupNames("", [$account], \@info));
    $result = Win32::Lanman::NetLocalGroupAddMember("",$record->{type},
                                            ${$info[0]}{sid});
    return Win32::Lanman::GetLastError() unless ($result);

    # create home directory
    mkdir "$homeNTdirs\\$account",0777 or
        return "Unable to make homedir:$!";

    # now set the ACL and owner of the directory
    $acl = new Win32::Perms("$homeNTdirs\\$account");
    $acl->Owner($account);
```

```
    # we give the user full control of the directory and all of the
    # files that will be created within it (hence the two separate calls)
    $acl->Allow($account, FULL, DIRECTORY|CONTAINER_INHERIT_ACE);
    $acl->Allow($account, FULL,
                          FILE|OBJECT_INHERIT_ACE|INHERIT_ONLY_ACE);
    $result = $acl->Set();
    $acl->Close();

    return($result ? "" : $result);
}
```

The user deletion code looks like this:

```
use Win32::Lanman;    # for account deletion
use File::Path;       # for recursive directory deletion

sub DeleteNTAccount{

    my($account,$record) = @_;

    # remove user from LOCAL groups only. If we wanted to also
    # remove from global groups we could remove the word "Local" from
    # the two Win32::Lanman::NetUser* calls (e.g., NetUserGetGroups)
    die "SID lookup error: ".Win32::Lanman::GetLastError()."\n" unless
        (Win32::Lanman::LsaLookupNames("", [$account], \@info));
    Win32::Lanman::NetUserGetLocalGroups($server, $account,'', \@groups);
    foreach $group (@groups){
        print "Removing user from local group ".$group->{name}."...";
        print(Win32::Lanman::NetLocalGroupDelMember("",
                          $group->{name},
                          ${$info[0]}{sid}) ?
                          "succeeded\n" : "FAILED\n");
    }

    # delete this account on the local machine
    # (i.e., empty first parameter)
    $result = Win32::Lanman::NetUserDel("", $account);

    return Win32::Lanman::GetLastError() if ($result);

    # delete the home directory and its contents
    $result = rmtree("$homeNTdirs\\$account",0,1);

    # rmtree returns the number of items deleted,
    # so if we deleted more than 0,it is likely that we succeeded
    return $result;
```

As a quick aside, the above code uses the portable `File::Path` module to remove an account's home directory. If we wanted to do something Win32-specific, like move the home directory to the Recycle Bin instead, we could use a module called `Win32::FileOp` by Jenda Krynicky, at *http://jenda.krynicky.cz/*. In this case, we'd use `Win32::FileOp` and change the `rmtree()` line to:

```
# will move directory to the Recycle Bin, potentially confirming
# the action with the user if our account is set to confirm
# Recycle Bin actions
$result = Recycle("$homeNTdirs\\$account");
```

This same module also has a `Delete()` function that will perform the same operation as the `rmtree()` call above in a less portable (although quicker) fashion.

The Process Scripts

Once we have a backend database, we'll want to write scripts that encapsulate the day-to-day and periodic processes that take place for user administration. These scripts are based on a low-level component library (*Account.pm*) we created by concatenating all of the subroutines we just wrote together into one file. To make sure all of the modules we need are loaded, we'll add this subroutine:

```
sub InitAccount{

    use XML::Writer;

    $record   = { fields => [login,fullname,id,type,password]};
    $addqueue = "addqueue"; # name of add account queue file
    $delqueue = "delqueue"; # name of del account queue file
    $maindata = "accountdb"; # name of main account database file

    if ($^O eq "MSWin32"){
        require Win32::Lanman;
        require Win32::Perms;
        require File::Path;

        # location of account files
        $accountdir = "\\\\server\\accountsystem\\";
        # mail lists, example follows
        $maillists = "$accountdir\\maillists\\";
        # home directory root
        $homeNTdirs = "\\\\homeserver\\home";
        # name of account add subroutine
        $accountadd = "CreateNTAccount";
        # name of account del subroutine
        $accountdel = "DeleteNTAccount";
    }
    else {
        require Expect;
        # location of account files
        $accountdir  = "/usr/accountsystem/";
        # mail lists, example follows
        $maillists   = "$accountdir/maillists/";
        # location of useradd executable
        $useraddex   = "/usr/sbin/useradd";
```

```
          # location of userdel executable
          $userdelex    = "/usr/sbin/userdel";
          # location of passwd executable
          $passwdex     = "/bin/passwd";
          # home directory root dir
          $homeUnixdirs = "/home";
          # prototypical home directory
          $skeldir      = "/home/skel";
          # default shell
          $defshell     = "/bin/zsh";
          # name of account add subroutine
          $accountadd   = "CreateUnixAccount";
          # name of account del subroutine
          $accountdel   = "DeleteUnixAccount";
     }
}
```

Let's see some sample scripts. Here's the script that processes the add queue:

```
use Account;
use XML::Simple;

&InitAccount;      # read in our low level routines
&ReadAddQueue;     # read and parse the add account queue
&ProcessAddQueue;  # attempt to create all accounts in the queue
&DisposeAddQueue;  # write account record either to main database or back
                   # to queue if there is a problem

# read in the add account queue to the $queue data structure
sub ReadAddQueue{
    open(ADD,$accountdir.$addqueue) or
      die "Unable to open ".$accountdir.$addqueue.":$!\n";
    read(ADD, $queuecontents, -s ADD);
    close(ADD);
    $queue = XMLin("<queue>".$queuecontents."</queue>",
                   keyattr => ["login"]);
}

# iterate through the queue structure, attempting to create an account
# for each request (i.e., each key) in the structure
sub ProcessAddQueue{
    foreach my $login (keys %{$queue->{account}}){
        $result = &$accountadd($login,$queue->{account}->{$login});
        if (!$result){
            $queue->{account}->{$login}{status} = "created";
        }
        else {
            $queue->{account}->{$login}{status} = "error:$result";
        }
    }
}

# now iterate through the queue structure again. For each account with
# a status of "created," append to main database. All others get written
# back to the add queue file, overwriting it.
```

```perl
sub DisposeAddQueue{
    foreach my $login (keys %{$queue->{account}}){
        if ($queue->{account}->{$login}{status} eq "created"){
            $queue->{account}->{$login}{login} = $login;
            $queue->{account}->{$login}{creation_date} = time;
            &AppendAccountXML($accountdir.$maindata,
                              $queue->{account}->{$login});
            delete $queue->{account}->{$login};
            next;
        }
    }

    # all we have left in $queue at this point are the accounts that
    # could not be created

    # overwrite the queue file
    open(ADD,">".$accountdir.$addqueue) or
      die "Unable to open ".$accountdir.$addqueue.":$!\n";
    # if there are accounts that could not be created write them
    if (scalar keys %{$queue->{account}}){
        print ADD XMLout(&TransformForWrite($queue),rootname => undef);
    }
    close(ADD);
}
```

Our "process the delete user queue file" script is similar:

```perl
use Account;
use XML::Simple;

&InitAccount;       # read in our low level routines
&ReadDelQueue;      # read and parse the add account queue
&ProcessDelQueue;   # attempt to delete all accounts in the queue
&DisposeDelQueue;   # write account record either to main database or back
                    # to queue if there is a problem

# read in the del user queue to the $queue data structure
sub ReadDelQueue{
    open(DEL,$accountdir.$delqueue) or
      die "Unable to open ${accountdir}${delqueue}:$!\n";
    read(DEL, $queuecontents, -s DEL);
    close(DEL);
    $queue = XMLin("<queue>".$queuecontents."</queue>",
                   keyattr => ["login"]);
}

# iterate through the queue structure, attempting to delete an account for
# each request (i.e. each key) in the structure
sub ProcessDelQueue{
    foreach my $login (keys %{$queue->{account}}){
        $result = &$accountdel($login,$queue->{account}->{$login});
        if (!$result){
```

```
                $queue->{account}->{$login}{status} = "deleted";
            }
            else {
                $queue->{account}->{$login}{status} = "error:$result";
            }
        }
    }
}


# read in the main database and then iterate through the queue
# structure again. For each account with a status of "deleted," change
# the main database information. Then write the main database out again.
# All that could not be deleted are written back to the del queue
# file, overwriting it.
sub DisposeDelQueue{
    &ReadMainDatabase;

    foreach my $login (keys %{$queue->{account}}){
        if ($queue->{account}->{$login}{status} eq "deleted"){
            unless (exists $maindb->{account}->{$login}){
                warn "Could not find $login in $maindata\n";
                next;
            }
            $maindb->{account}->{$login}{status} = "deleted";
            $maindb->{account}->{$login}{deletion_date} = time;
            delete $queue->{account}->{$login};
            next;
        }
    }

    &WriteMainDatabase;

    # all we have left in $queue at this point are the accounts that
    # could not be deleted
    open(DEL,">".$accountdir.$delqueue) or
        die "Unable to open ".$accountdir.$addqueue.":$!\n";
    # if there are accounts that could not be created, else truncate
    if (scalar keys %{$queue->{account}}){
        print DEL XMLout(&TransformForWrite($queue),rootname => undef);
    }
    close(DEL);
}


sub ReadMainDatabase{
    open(MAIN,$accountdir.$maindata) or
        die "Unable to open ".$accountdir.$maindata.":$!\n";
    read (MAIN, $dbcontents, -s MAIN);
    close(MAIN);
    $maindb = XMLin("<maindb>".$dbcontents."</maindb>",
                    keyattr => ["login"]);
}


sub WriteMainDatabase{
    # note: it would be *much, much safer* to write to a temp file
    # first and then swap it in if the data was written successfully
```

```
open(MAIN,">".$accountdir.$maindata) or
   die "Unable to open ".$accountdir.$maindata.":$!\n";
print MAIN XMLout(&TransformForWrite($maindb),rootname => undef);
close(MAIN);
}
```

There are many other process scripts you could imagine writing. For example, we could certainly use scripts that perform data export and consistency checking (e.g., does the user's home directory match up with the main databases account type? Is that user in the appropriate group?). We don't have space to cover this wide range of programs, so let's end this section with a single example of the data export variety. Earlier we mentioned that a site might want a separate mailing list for each type of user on the system. The following code reads our main database and creates a set of files that contain user names, one file per user type:

```
use Account;          # just to get the file locations
use XML::Simple;

&InitAccount;
&ReadMainDatabase;
&WriteFiles;

# read the main database into a hash of lists of hashes
sub ReadMainDatabase{
    open(MAIN,$accountdir.$maindata) or
      die "Unable to open ".$accountdir.$maindata.":$!\n";
    read (MAIN, $dbcontents, -s MAIN);
    close(MAIN);
    $maindb = XMLin("<maindb>".$dbcontents."</maindb>",keyattr => [""]);
}

# iterate through the lists, compile the list of accounts of a certain
# type and store them in a hash of lists. Then write out the contents of
# each key to a different file.
sub WriteFiles {
    foreach my $account (@{$maindb->{account}}){
        next if $account->{status} eq "deleted";
        push(@{$types{$account->{type}}},$account->{login});
    }

    foreach $type (keys %types){
        open(OUT,">".$maillists.$type) or
          die "Unable to write to ".$accountdir.$maillists.$type.": $!\n";
        print OUT join("\n",sort @{$types{$type}})."\n";
        close(OUT);
    }
}
```

If we look at the mailing list directory, we see:

```
> dir
faculty staff
```

And each one of those files contains the appropriate list of user accounts.

Account System Wrap-Up

Now that we've seen four components of an account system, let's wrap up this section by talking about what's missing (besides oodles of functionality):

Error checking

Our demonstration code has only a modicum of error checking. Any self-respecting account system would grow another 40–50% in code size because it would check for data and system interaction problems every step of the way.

Scalability

Our code could probably work in a small-to mid-sized environment. But any time you see "read the entire file into memory," it should set off warning bells. To scale we would need to change our data storage and retrieval techniques at the very least. The module XML::Twig by Michel Rodriguez may help with this problem, since it works with large, well-formed XML documents without reading them into memory all at once.

Security

This is related to the very first item on error checking. Besides truck-sized security holes like the storage of plain text passwords, we also do not perform any security checks in our code. We do not confirm that the data sources we use like the queue files are trustworthy. Add another 20–30% to the code size to take care of this issue.

Multiuser

We make no provision for multiple users or even multiple scripts running at once, perhaps the largest flaw in our code as written. If the "add account" process script is being run at the same time as the "add to the queue" script, the potential for data loss or corruption is very high. This is such an important issue that we should take a few moments to discuss it before concluding this section.

One way to help with the multiuser deficiency is to carefully introduce file locking. File locking allows the different scripts to cooperate. If a script plans to read or write to a file, it can attempt to lock the file first. If it can obtain a lock, then it knows it is safe to manipulate the file. If it cannot lock the file (because another script is using it), it knows not to proceed with an operation that could corrupt data. There's considerably more complexity involved with locking and multiuser access in general than just this simple description reveals; consult any fundamental Operating or Distributed Systems text. It gets especially tricky when dealing with files residing on network filesystems, where there may not be a good locking mechanism. Here are a few hints that may help you when you approach this topic using Perl.

- There are smart ways to cheat. My favorite method is to use the *lockfile* program distributed with the popular mail filtering program *procmail* found at *http://www.procmail.org*. The *procmail* installation procedure takes great pains to determine safe locking strategies for the filesystems you are using. *lockfile* does just what its name suggests, hiding most of the complexity in the process.

- If you don't want to use an external executable, there are a plethora of locking modules available. For example, `File::Flock` by David Muir Sharnoff, `File::LockDir` from the *Perl Cookbook* by Tom Christiansen and Nathan Torkington (O'Reilly), and a Win95/98 version of it by William Herrera called `File::FlockDir`, `File::Lock` by Kenneth Albanowski, `File::Lockf` by Paul Henson, and `Lockfile::Simple` by Raphael Manfredi. They differ mostly in interface, though `File::FlockDir` and `Lockfile::Simple` attempt to perform locking without using Perl's `flock()` function. This is useful for platforms like MacOS that don't support that function. Shop around and pick the best one for your needs.

- Locking is easier to get right if you remember to lock before attempting to change data (or read data that could change) and only unlock *after* making sure that data has been written (e.g., after the file has been closed). For more information on this, see the previously mentioned *Perl Cookbook*, the Perl Frequently Asked Questions list, and the documentation that comes with Perl on the `flock()` function and the `DB_File` module.

This ends our look at user account administration and how it can be taken to the next level using a bit of an architectural mindset. In this chapter we've concentrated on the beginning and the end of an account's lifecycle. In the next chapter, we'll examine what users do in between these two points.

Module Information for This Chapter

Name	CPAN ID	Version
`User::pwent` (ships with Perl)		
`File::stat` (ships with Perl)		
`Win32::AdminMisc` (found at *http://www.roth.net*)		20000117
`Win32::Perms` (found at *http://www.roth.net*)		20000216
`Win32::Lanman` (found at *ftp://ftp.roth.net/pub/ntperl/Others/Lanman/*)		1.05
`IO::File` (ships with Perl)	GBARR	1.20
`XML::Writer`	DMEGG	0.30
`XML::Parser`	COOPERCL	2.27

Name	CPAN ID	Version
Data::Dumper	GSAR	2.101
XML::Simple	GRANTM	1.01
Expect.pm	AUSCHUTZ	1.07
File::Path (ships with Perl)		1.0401
Win32::FileOp	JENDA	0.10.4

References for More Information

Unix Password Files

http://www.freebsd.org/cgi/man.cgi is where the FreeBSD Project provides access to the online manual pages for *BSD and other Unix variants. This is a handy way to compare the file formats and user administration commands (*useradd*, et al.) for several operating systems.

Practical Unix & Internet Security, 2nd Edition, by Simson Garfinkel and Gene Spafford (O'Reilly, 1999), is an excellent place to start for information about password files.

NT User Administration

http://Jenda.Krynicky.cz is another site with useful Win32 modules applicable to user administration.

http://windows.microsoft.com/windows2000/en/server/help/, from the Windows 2000 online help. (Navigate to the Active Directory→Concepts→Understanding Active Directory→Understanding Groups section.) This is a good overview of the new Windows 2000 group mechanisms.

http://www.activestate.com/support/mailing_lists.htm hosts the Perl-Win32-Admin and Perl-Win32-Users mailing lists. Both lists and their archives are invaluable resources for Win32 programmers.

Win32 Perl Programming: The Standard Extensions, by Dave Roth (Macmillan Technical Publishing, 1999) is currently the best reference for Win32 Perl module programming.

Windows NT User Administration, by Ashley J. Meggitt and Timothy D. Ritchey (O'Reilly, 1997).

http://www.mspress.com are the publishers of the Microsoft NT Resource kit. They also offer a subscription services that provides access to the latest RK utilities.

http://www.roth.net is the home of Win32::AdminMisc, Win32::Perms, and other modules the Win32 community relies upon for user administration.

XML

There's been a tremendous explosion of material covering XML in the last two years. The following are some of the best references I know of for people interested in learning about XML. There haven't been any XML for Perl books released as of this publication, but I know of several projects in the works.

http://msdn.microsoft.com/xml and *http://www.ibm.com/developer/xml* both contain copious information at their respective sites. Microsoft and IBM are very serious about XML.

http://www.activestate.com/support/mailing_lists.htm hosts the Perl-XML mailing list. It (and its archive) is one of the best sources on this topic.

http://www.w3.org/TR/1998/REC-xml-19980210 is the actual XML 1.0 specification. Anyone who does anything with XML eventually winds up reading the spec. For anything but quick reference checks, I recommend reading an annotated version like those mentioned in the next two citations.

http://www.xml.com is a good reference for articles and XML links. Also contains an excellent annotated version of the specification created by Tim Bray, one of its authors.

XML: The Annotated Specification, by Bob DuCharme (Prentice Hall, 1998), is another excellent annotated version of the specification, chock full of XML code examples.

XML Pocket Reference, by Robert Eckstein (O'Reilly, 1999), a concise but surprisingly comprehensive introduction to XML for the impatient.

Other

http://www.mcs.anl.gov/~evard is Rémy Evard's home page. Using a set of central databases from which configuration files are automatically generated is a best practice that shows up in a number of places in this book; credit for my exposure to this methodology goes to Evard. Though it is now in use at many sites, I first encountered it when I inherited the Tenwen computing environment he built (as described in the Tenwen paper linked off of Evard's home page). See the section "Implemented the Hosts Database" for one example of this methodology in action.

http://www.rpi.edu/~finkej/ contains a number of Jon Finke's published papers on the use of relational databases for system administration.

4

User Activity

In the previous chapter, we explored the identity of a user and how this identity is managed and stored. Now let's talk about how to manage users while they are active on our systems and network.

The significant actions of users fall into four domains:

Processes

Users can spawn, kill, pause, and resume processes on our machines. These processes compete for a computer's finite processing power, adding resource issues to the list of problems a system administrator needs to mediate.

File operations

Most of the time, operations like writing, reading, creating, deleting, etc., take place when some user process interacts with files in a filesystem. But under Unix, there's more to this picture. Unix uses the filesystem as a gateway to more than just file storage. Device control, input/output channels, and even some process control and network access are file operations. We dealt with filesystem administration in Chapter 2, *Filesystems*, but in this chapter we'll approach this topic from a user administration perspective.

Network

Users can send and receive data over network interfaces on our machine. There is material elsewhere in this book on networking, but we'll address this issue here from a different perspective.

OS-specific activities

This last domain is a catchall for the OS-specific features that users can access via different APIs. Included in this list are things like GUI element controls, shared memory usage, file sharing APIs, sound, etc. This category is so diverse that there's no way to discuss it well in our current context. I recommend tracking down the OS-specific web sites like *http://www.macperl.com* for information on these topics.

Let's look at ways to deal with the first three of these domains using Perl. Each of the operating systems in this book treats this topic differently, so we're going to have to address them on an individual basis. The closest thing to common ground they share is the Perl kill() function, and even that is not implemented under MacOS. We will take each OS in turn, beginning with the least complicated (from a Perl perspective). Because we're interested in user administration, the focus here will be on dealing with processes started by other users.

MacOS Process Control

"Control" might be too strong a word for the functionality offered under MacOS, since MacOS is not multiuser and is just barely multitasking. Using the module Mac::Processes, we can interact with the Macintosh Process Manager using the MacOS Toolbox API for process control. If you are going to delve any deeper than surface level with this module, you'll want to seek out a copy of the *Inside Macintosh:Processes* volume that deals with the Process Manager.

When we load Mac::Processes via the standard use Mac::Processes directive, it initializes a special hash called %Process. This hash is magical because it always contains a representation of the *current* process state of the machine thanks to Perl's tied variable functionality. Each time the contents of %Process are accessed, information about the machine's current running processes are returned. To see a list of the current process serial numbers (the MacOS term for process ID, often abbreviated as PSN), we can simply query the list of keys in this hash:

```
use Mac::Processes;
print map{"$_\n"} keys %Process;
```

For more information on the individual processes, we need to work with the values returned for each key. Each hash entry contains an object representing a ProcessInfo structure. To get at the individual fields of this structure, you call object methods with their names. For more information on each field and what it represents, see the canonical reference book *Inside Macintosh:Processes*. The currently available method names are processName(), processNumber(), processType(), processSignature(), processSize(), processMode(), processLocation(), processLauncher(), processLaunchDate(), processActiveTime(), and processAppSpec().

To get a list of the running processes and their names, we could write:

```
use Mac::Processes;
while(($psn, $psi) = each (%Process)){
  $name = $psi->processName();
```

```
  write;
}

format STDOUT_TOP =
Process Serial Number       Process Name
=====================       =========================================

.

format STDOUT =
@<<<<<<                     @<<<<<<<<<<<<<<<<<<<<<<<<<<<<<<<
$psn,                       $name
.
```

which would yield output that looked like this:

```
Process Serial Number       Process Name
=====================       =========================
8192                        FaxMonitor
8193                        Queue Watcher
8194                        Finder
8195                        Serial Port Monitor
8198                        MacPerl
```

Once you know the processes running on a machine, it is natural to want to control them. Unfortunately, our abilities in this realm are negligible. The most exciting thing we can do is bring a process to the foreground using `SetFrontProcess($psn)`. We don't even have the ability to directly kill a process (the Perl `kill()` function is not implemented). The best we can do is send an AppleEvent to a running application or the finder to request that this process shut itself down. The easiest way to perform this task is to use Chris Nandor's `Mac::Apps::Launch` module. It offers a function called `QuitApps()` that can quit an application given its creator ID. `Mac::Apps::Launch` also provides some useful functions for launching applications and bringing them to and away from the foreground similar to those we mentioned in `Mac::Processes`.

Let's move on to an operating system that is much less limited in the process control realm.

NT/2000 Process Control

We're going to briefly look at four different ways to deal with process control on NT/2000 because each of these approaches opens up a door to interesting functionality outside the scope of our discussion. We're primarily going to concentrate on two tasks: finding all of the running processes and killing select processes.

Using the Microsoft Resource Kit Binaries

As we've mentioned in Chapter 3, *User Accounts*, the NT Resource Kit is a wonderful source of scripts and information. The two programs we are going to use from the resource kit are *pulist.exe* and *kill.exe*. The former lists processes, the second nukes them. There is another utility in the resource kit similar to *pulist.exe* called *tlist.exe* that can list processes in a pleasant tree format, but it but lacks some features of *pulist.exe*. For instance, *pulist.exe* can list processes on other machines besides the current one.

Here's an excerpt from some *pulist* output:

```
Process          PID  User
TAPISRV.EXE      119  NT AUTHORITY\SYSTEM
TpChrSrv.exe     125  NT AUTHORITY\SYSTEM
RASMAN.EXE       131  NT AUTHORITY\SYSTEM
mstask.exe       137  NT AUTHORITY\SYSTEM
mxserver.exe     147  NT AUTHORITY\SYSTEM
PSTORES.EXE      154  NT AUTHORITY\SYSTEM
NDDEAGNT.EXE     46   OMPHALOSKEPSIS\Administrator
explorer.exe     179  OMPHALOSKEPSIS\Administrator
SYSTRAY.EXE      74   OMPHALOSKEPSIS\Administrator
cardview.exe     184  OMPHALOSKEPSIS\Administrator
ltmsg.exe        167  OMPHALOSKEPSIS\Administrator
daemon.exe       185  OMPHALOSKEPSIS\Administrator
```

Using *pulist.exe* from Perl is trivial. Here's one way to do it:

```
$pulistexe = "\\bin\\PULIST.EXE"; # location of the executable
open(PULIST,"$pulistexe|") or die "Can't execute $pulistexe:$!\n";

scalar <PULIST>; # drop the first title line
while(defined($_=<PULIST>)){
    ($pname,$pid,$puser) = /^(\S+)\s*(\d+)\s*(.+)/;
    print "$pname:$pid:$puser\n";

close(PULIST);
```

The other program we mentioned, *kill.exe,* is equally easy to use. It takes as an argument either a process ID or part of a task name. I recommend the process ID format, to err on the safe side, since it is very easy to kill the wrong process if you use task names.

kill.exe offers two different ways to shoot down processes. The first is the polite death: *kill.exe <process id>* will ask that process to shut itself down. But if we add */f* to the command line, *kill.exe /f <process id>* works more like the native Perl function and kills the process with extreme prejudice.

Using the Win32::IProc Module

Our second approach uses the `Win32::IProc` module by Amine Moulay Ramdane. Though you wouldn't know it from the name, `Win32::IProc` is actually more useful for our purposes than `Win32::Process`, the more obviously named choice. `Win32::Process` has one significant drawback that takes it out of the running: it is designed to control processes that are started by the module itself. We're more interested in the processes *other* users have started. If you have trouble installing `Win32::IProc`, see the section "Module Information for This Chapter" at the end of the chapter for installation hints.

First, create a process object like so:

```
use Win32::IProc;

# note case of object is important, must be "IProc"
$pobj = new Win32::IProc or die "Unable to create proccess object: $!\n";
```

This object is mostly used as a springboard from which to launch the module's object methods. For instance, to find the list of all of the running processes on a machine, we would use:

```
$pobj-> EnumProccesses(\@processlist) or
    die "Unable to get process list:$!\n";
```

`@processlist` is now an array of references to anonymous hashes. Each anonymous hash has two keys, `ProcessName` and `ProcessId`, with their expected values. To display this info nicely, we could use the following code:

```
use Win32::IProc;

$pobj=new Win32::IProc or die "Unable to create process object: $!\n";

$pobj->EnumProcesses(\@processlist) or
    die "Unable to get process list:$!\n";

foreach $process (@processlist){
  $pid  = $process->{ProcessId};
  $name = $process->{ProcessName};
  write;
}

format STDOUT_TOP =
Process ID      Process Name
==========      ==============================

.
format STDOUT =
@<<<<<<<        @<<<<<<<<<<<<<<<<<<<<<<<<<<<<<<
$pid,           $name

.
```

We get output like this:

```
Process ID        Process Name
==========        ==================================
0                 System-Idle
2                 System
25                smss.exe
39                winlogon.exe
41                services.exe
48                lsass.exe
78                spoolss.exe
82                DKSERVICE.EXE
...
```

One difference between this approach and our use of *pulist.exe* earlier is that `Win32::IProc` does not have the ability to tell you the user context for a given process. If this information is important to you, you will need to use *pulist.exe*.

pulist.exe can only produce one kind of output, but the fun with `Win32::IProc` is just beginning. Let's say you were curious about not only which processes were running, but also which executable and dynamically loaded libraries (*.dlls*) each process was using. Finding this information is simple:

```
# imports the FULLPATH constant to show the path for the dlls, could be NOPATH
use Win32::IProc "FULLPATH";
$pobj = new Win32::IProc;

$pobj->EnumProcesses(\@processlist) or
    die "Unable to get process list:$!\n";

foreach $process (@processlist){
  print "\n",$process->{ProcessName},
        "\n",('=' x length($process->{ProcessName})),"\n";

  $pobj->GetProcessModules($process->{ProcessId},\@modules,FULLPATH);
  print join("\n",map {lc $_->{ModuleName}} @modules),"\n";

}
```

`GetProcessModules()` takes a process ID, an array reference, and a flag that indicates whether the full directory path of the module will be returned. The array we reference is populated with references to anonymous hashes that contain information about each module used for that process. In our code we gather the names of all of the modules. `map()` is used to iterate over the array of references, dereferencing each anonymous hash and looking up the `ModuleName` key as we go.

Here's an excerpt from some sample output:

```
smss.exe
========
\systemroot\system32\smss.exe
c:\winnt\system32\ntdll.dll

winlogon.exe
```

```
============
\??\c:\winnt\system32\winlogon.exe
c:\winnt\system32\ntdll.dll
c:\winnt\system32\msvcrt.dll
c:\winnt\system32\kernel32.dll
c:\winnt\system32\advapi32.dll
c:\winnt\system32\user32.dll
c:\winnt\system32\gdi32.dll
c:\winnt\system32\rpcrt4.dll
c:\winnt\system32\userenv.dll
c:\winnt\system32\shell32.dll
c:\winnt\system32\shlwapi.dll
c:\winnt\system32\comctl32.dll
c:\winnt\system32\netapi32.dll
c:\winnt\system32\netrap.dll
c:\winnt\system32\samlib.dll
c:\winnt\system32\winmm.dll
c:\winnt\system32\cwcmmsys.dll
c:\winnt\system32\cwcfm3.dll
c:\winnt\system32\msgina.dll
c:\winnt\system32\rpclts1.dll
c:\winnt\system32\rpcltc1.dll...
```

Let's take this train of thought one stop further. We can find out *even more* about a running process with just a little bit of effort. To get the information we need about a process, we first have to get a handle for that process.

A process handle can be thought of as an open connection to a particular process. To illuminate the difference between a process handle and a process ID, let's take the analogy of a trailer park. If each trailer in the park is a process, then you can think of the process ID as the address of a trailer. It is a way of finding that specific trailer. A process handle is like the power/water/phone lines that run from the park itself into a specific trailer. Once these lines are in place, not only can you find a particular trailer, but you can also begin to communicate and exchange information with it from the outside.

To get the process handle from a process if we have its ID, we use `Win32::IProc`'s `Open()` method. `Open()` takes a process ID, an access flag, an inheritance flag, and a reference to the scalar that will store the handle. The access flags we'll be using in the following example request just enough access to query a process for information. For more information on these flags, see the `Win32::IProc` documentation and the "Processes and Threads" section of the Win32 SDK base services documentation found on *http://msdn.microsoft.com*. Process handles that are `Open()`'d need to be closed using `CloseHandle()`.

With process handle in hand, we can use the `Kill()` method to kill this process:

```
# kill process and make it exit with that code
$pobj->Kill($handle,$exitcode);
```

But killing processes is not the only use for process handles. For instance, we can use methods like `GetStatus()` to learn more about the process. Here's sample code that dumps out timing information about a given process ID:

```
use Win32::IProc qw(PROCESS_QUERY_INFORMATION INHERITED DIGITAL);

$pobj = new Win32::IProc;

$pobj->Open($ARGV[0],PROCESS_QUERY_INFORMATION,INHERITED,\$handle) or
  warn "Can't get handle:".$pobj->LastError()."\n";

# DIGITAL = pretty-printed times
$pobj->GetStatus($handle,\$statusinfo,DIGITAL);

$pobj->CloseHandle($handle);

while (($procname,$value)=each %$statusinfo){
  print "$procname: $value\n";
}
```

Its output looks something like this:

```
KernelTime: 00:00:22:442:270
ExitDate:
ExitTime:
CreationDate: 29/7/1999
CreationTime: 17:09:28:100
UserTime: 00:00:11:566:632
```

Now we know when this process was started and how much system time it has taken up. The `ExitDate` and `ExitTime` fields are blank because the process is still running. You may be wondering how these fields could ever get filled in, given that one has to use the process ID of a running process to get a process handle. There are two answers to this question. First, it is possible to get a process handle for a running process and have that process die before you've closed the handle. A `GetStatus()` at that point will yield exit information for the deceased process. The second possibility involves a method we haven't seen yet called `Create()`.

`Create()` allows you to launch processes from `Win32::IProc`, similar to the `Win32::Process` functionality mentioned earlier. If you do launch processes from the module, then the process object (`$pobj`) we've mostly ignored so far will contain process and thread information for the created process. With this information, you can do fun things like manipulate thread priorities and the windows of that process. We're not going to look at this functionality, but its mention does offer us a good segue to the next process module approach.

Using the Win32::Setupsup Module

If last section's mention of manipulating the windows of a process piqued your interest, you will like our next approach. For this approach, we'll be looking at a module by Jens Helberg called `Win32::Setupsup`. It's called "Setupsup" because it is primarily designed to be used to supplement software installation (which often uses a program called *Setup.exe*).

Some installers can be run in so-called "silent mode" for totally automated installation. In this mode they ask no questions and require no "OK" buttons to be pushed, freeing the administrator from having to babysit the install. Software installation mechanisms that do not offer this mode (and there are far too many of them) make a system administrator's life difficult. `Win32::Setupsup` helps deal with these deficiencies. It can find information on running processes and manipulate them (or manipulate them dead if you so choose).

To get and install `Win32::Setupsup`, you should refer to the section "Module Information for This Chapter" later for hints on getting it installed.

With `Win32::Setupsup`, getting the list of running processes is easy. Here's a slightly different version of the first full code sample we saw in the last section:

```perl
use Win32::Setupsup;

$machine = ""; # query the list on the current machine

Win32::Setupsup::GetProcessList($machine, \@processlist, \@threadlist) or
  die "process list error: ".Win32::Setupsup::GetLastError()."\n";

pop(@processlist); # remove the bogus entry always appended to the list
foreach $processlist (@processlist){
  $pid  = $processlist->{pid};
  $name = $processlist->{name};
  write;
}

format STDOUT_TOP =
Process ID      Process Name
==========      ==============================

.
format STDOUT =
@<<<<<<<        @<<<<<<<<<<<<<<<<<<<<<<<<<<<<<<
$pid,           $name
.
```

Killing processes is equally easy:

```perl
KillProcess($pid, $exitvalule, $systemprocessflag) or
  die "Unable to kill process: ".Win32::Setupsup::GetLastError()."\n";
```

The last two arguments are optional. The first kills the process and sets its exit value accordingly (by default it is set to 0). The second argument allows you to kill system-run processes (providing you have the **Debug Programs** user right).

That's the boring stuff. We can take process manipulation to yet another level by interacting with the windows a running process may have open. To list all of the windows available on the desktop, we use:

```
Win32::Setupsup::EnumWindows(\@windowlist) or
    die "process list error: ".Win32::Setupsup::GetLastError()."\n";
```

@windowlist now contains a list of window handles that just look like normal numbers when you print them. To learn more about each window, you can use a few different functions. For instance, to find the titles of each window, you can use **GetWindowText()** like so:

```
use Win32::Setupsup;

Win32::Setupsup::EnumWindows(\@windowlist) or
    die "process list error: ".Win32::Setupsup::GetLastError()."\n";

foreach $whandle (@windowlist){
    if (Win32::Setupsup::GetWindowText($whandle,\$text)){
      print "$whandle: $text","\n";
    }
    else {
      warn "Can't get text for $whandle" .
           Win32::Setupsup::GetLastError()."\n";
    }
}
```

Here's a little bit of sample output:

```
66130: chapter02 - Microsoft Word
66184: Style
194905150:
66634: setupsup - WordPad
65716: Fuel
328754: DDE Server Window
66652:
66646:
66632: OleMainThreadWndName
```

As you can see, some windows have titles, while others do not. Observant readers might notice something else interesting about this output. Window **66130** belongs to a Microsoft Word session that is currently running (it is actually the one this chapter was composed into). Window **66184** looks vaguely like the name of another window that might be connected to Microsoft Word. How can we tell if they are related?

Win32::Setupsup also has an EnumChildWindows() function that can show us the children of any given window. Let's use it to write something that will show us a basic tree of the current window hierarchy:

```perl
use Win32::Setupsup;

# get the list of windows
Win32::Setupsup::EnumWindows(\@windowlist) or
  die "process list error: ".Win32::Setupsup::GetLastError()."\n";

# turn window handle list into a hash
# NOTE: this conversion populates the hash with plain numbers and
# not actual window handles as keys. Some functions, like
# GetWindowProperties (which we'll see in a moment), can't use these
# converted numbers. Caveat implementor.
for (@windowlist){$windowlist{$_}++;}

# check each window for children
foreach $whandle (@windowlist){
    if (Win32::Setupsup::EnumChildWindows($whandle,\@children)){
        # keep a sorted list of children for each window
        $children{$whandle} = [sort {$a <=>$b} @children];

        # remove all children from the hash, we won't directly
        # iterate over them
        foreach $child (@children){
          delete $windowlist{$child};
        }
    }
}

# iterate through the list of parent or childless windows and
# recursively print each window handle and its children (if any)
foreach my $window (sort {$a <=> $b} keys %windowlist){
 &printfamily($window,0);
}

# print a given window handle number and its children (recursively)
sub printfamily {
  # starting window, how deep in a tree are we?
  my($startwindow,$level) = @_;

  # print the window handle number at the appropriate indentation
  print(("  " x $level)."$startwindow\n");

  return unless (exists $children{$startwindow}); # no children, done.

  # otherwise, we have to recurse for each child
  $level++;
  foreach $childwindow (@{$children{$startwindow}}){
      &printfamily($childwindow,$level);
  }
}
```

There's one last window property function we should look at before moving on: `GetWindowProperties()`. `GetWindowProperties()` is basically a catchall for the rest of the window properties we haven't seen yet. For instance, using `GetWindowProperties()` we can query the process ID for the process that created a specific window. This could be combined with some of the functionality we just saw for the `Win32::IProc` module.

The `Win32::Setupsup` documentation contains a list of the available properties that can be queried. Let's use one of them to write a very simple program that will print the dimensions of the rectangle of a window on the desktop. `GetWindowProperties()` takes three arguments: a window handle, a reference to an array that contains the names of the properties to query, and a reference to a hash where the query results will be stored. Here's the code we need for our task:

```
Win32::Setupsup::GetWindowProperties($ARGV[0],[rect,id],\%info);

print "\t" . $info{rect}{top} . "\n";
print $info{rect}{left} . " -" . $ARGV[0] .
      "- " . $info{rect}{right} . "\n";
print "\t" . $info{rect}{bottom} . "\n";
```

The output is a bit cutesy. Here's a sample showing the top, left, right, and bottom dimensions of the window with handle `66180`:

```
    154
272 -66180- 903
    595
```

`GetWindowProperties()` returns a special data structure for only one property, `rect`. All of the others will simply show up in the referenced hash as normal keys and values. If you are uncertain about the properties being returned by Perl for a specific window, the *windowse* utility found at *http://greatis.virtualave.net/ products.htm* is often helpful.

Now that we've seen how to determine various window properties, wouldn't it be spiffy if we could make changes to some of these properties? For instance, it might be useful to change the title of a particular window. With this capability, we could create scripts that used the window title as a status indicator:

```
"Prestidigitation In Progress ... 32% complete"
```

Making this change to a window is a single function call:

```
Win32::Setupsup::SetWindowText($handle,$text);
```

We can also set the `rect` property we just saw. This code makes the specified window jump to the position we've specified:

```
use Win32::Setupsup;

$info{rect}{left}  = 0;
$info{rect}{right} = 600;
```

```
$info{rect}{top}   = 10;
$info{rect}{bottom}= 500;
Win32::Setupsup::SetWindowProperties($ARGV[0],\%info);
```

I've saved the most impressive function for last. With **SendKeys()** it is possible to send arbitrary keystrokes to any window on the desktop. For example:

```
use Win32::Setupsup;

$texttosend = "\\DN\\Low in the gums";
Win32::Setupsup::SendKeys($ARGV[0],$texttosend,'',0);
```

This will send a "down cursor key" followed by some text to the specified window. The arguments to **SendKeys()** are pretty simple: window handle, text to send, a flag to determine if a window should be activated for each keystroke, and an optional time between keystrokes. Special key codes like the "down cursor" are surrounded by backslashes. The list of available keycodes can be found in the module's documentation.

With the help of this module, we've taken process control to an entirely new level. Now it is possible to remotely control applications (and parts of the OS) without requiring the explicit cooperation of those applications. We don't need them to offer command line support or a special API. We have the ability to essentially script a GUI, useful in a myriad of system administration contexts.*

Using Window Management Instrumentation (WMI)

Let's look at one final approach to NT/2000 process control before we switch to another operating system. This approach might be subtitled "Futureland" because it involves a technology which isn't widely available now, but is right on the horizon. Window Management Instrumentation (WMI) is available in Windows 2000 (and NT4.0SP4+ if explicitly installed).† Over time, when Windows 2000 is widely deployed, this has the potential to become an important part of the NT/2000 administration landscape.

Unfortunately WMI is one of those not-for-the-faint-of-heart technologies that gets very complex, very quickly. It is based on an object-oriented model that has the power to represent not only data, but relationships between objects as well. For instance, it is possible to create an association between a web server and the Redundant Arrays of Independent Disks (RAID) that holds the data for this server,

---

* Another module for GUI scripting you may find useful is Ernesto Guisado's Win32Guitest. It offers similar functionality to Win32::Setupsup.

† The "Download SDK" page linked off of the WMI section at *http://msdn.microsoft.com/developer/sdk* lets you download the core WMI libraries needed to run WMI on an NT4.0SP4 (or higher) machine.

so if the RAID device should fail, a problem for the web server will be reported as well. To deal with this complexity, we're just going to skim the very surface of WMI by providing a small and simple introduction, followed by a few code samples.

If you want to get a deeper look at this technology, I recommend downloading the WMI white papers, LearnWBM tutorial, and WMI SDK from the WMI section found at *http://msdn.microsoft.com/developer/sdk*. You should also have a look at the information found provided at the Distributed Management Task Force's web site, *http://www.dtmf.org*. In the meantime, here is a brief synopsis to get you started.

WMI is the Microsoft implementation and extension of an unfortunately named initiative called the *Web-Based Enterprise Management* initiative, or WBEM for short. Though the name conjures up visions of something that requires a browser, it has virtually nothing to do with the World Wide Web. The companies that were part of the Distributed Management Task Force (DMTF) wanted to create something that could make it easier to perform management tasks using browsers. Putting the name aside, it is clearer to say that WBEM defines a data model for management and instrumentation information. It provides specifications for organizing, accessing, and moving this data around. WBEM is also meant to offer a cohesive frontend for accessing data provided by the other management protocols like Simple Network Management Protocol (SNMP) (discussed in Chapter 10, *Security and Network Monitoring*) and Common Management Information Protocol (CMIP).

Data in the WBEM world is organized using the *Common Information Model* (CIM). CIM is the source of the power and complexity in WBEM/WMI. It provides an extensible data model that contains objects and object classes for any physical or logical entity one might want to manage. For instance, there are object classes for entire networks, and objects for a single slot in a specific machine. There are objects for hardware settings and objects for software application settings. On top of this, CIM allows us to define object classes that describe relationships between other objects.

This data model is documented in two parts: the CIM *Specification* and the CIM *Schema*. The former describes the *how* of CIM (how the data will be specified, its connection to prior management standards, etc.); the latter provides the *what* of CIM (the actual objects). This division may remind you of the SNMP SMI and MIB relationship (see Chapter 10).

In practice, you'll be consulting the CIM Schema more than the CIM Specification once you get the hang of how the data is represented. The schema format (called MOF for *Managed Object Format*) is fairly easy to read.

The CIM Schema has two layers:

- The *core model* for objects and classes useful in all types of WBEM interaction.

- The *common model* for generic objects that are vendor- and operating-system independent. Within the common model there are currently five specific areas defined: Systems, Devices, Applications, Networks, and Physical.

Built on top of these two layers can be any number of *Extension schema* that define objects and classes for vendor- and OS-specific information.

A crucial part of WMI that distinguishes it from generic WBEM implementations is the Win32 Schema, an extension schema for Win32-specific information built on the core and common models. WMI also adds to the generic WBEM framework by providing Win32-specific access mechanisms to the CIM data.* Using this schema extension and set of data access methods, we can explore how to perform process control using WMI in Perl.

Two of these access methods, Open Database Connectivity (ODBC) and Compnent Object Model/Distributed Component Object Model (COM/DCOM), will receive a more complete treatment in other places in this book. We're going to use the latter for these examples because ODBC only allows us to query information from WMI (albeit in a simple, database-like manner). COM/DCOM allows us to both query management information and interact with it, crucial for the "control" part of process control.

The Perl code that follows does not appear to be particularly complex, so you may wonder about the "gets very complex, very quickly" description. The code below looks simple because:

- We're only scratching the surface of WMI. We're not even going to touch subjects like "associations" (i.e., relationships between objects and object classes).

- The management operations we are performing are simple. Process control in this context will consist of querying the running processes and being able to terminate them at will. These operations are easy in WMI using the Win32 Schema extension.

- Our samples are hiding the complexity of translating WMI documentation and code samples in VBscript/JScript to Perl code.

- Our samples are hiding the opaqueness of the debugging process. When WMI-related Perl code fails, it does so with very little information that would help debug the problem. You may receive error messages, but they never say `ERROR: YOUR EXACT PROBLEM IS....` You're more likely to get back

---

* As much as Microsoft would like to see these data access mechanisms become ubiquitous, the likelihood of finding them in a non-Win32 environment is slight. This is why I refer to them as "Win32-specific."

`wbemErrFailed` `0x8004100` or just an empty data structure. To be fair to Perl, most of this opaqueness comes from Perl's role in this process. It is acting as a frontend to a set of fairly complex multilayered operations that don't concern themselves with passing back useful feedback when something fails.

I know this sounds pretty grim, so let me offer some potentially helpful advice before we actually get into the code itself:

- Look at all of the `Win32::OLE` sample code you can lay your hands on. The ActiveState *Win32-Users* mailing list archives found at *http://www.activestate. com* are a good source for this. If you compare this sample code to equivalent VBscript examples, you'll start to understand the translation idioms necessary. "ADSI (Active Directory Service Interfaces)" in Chapter 6, *Directory Services*, may also help.

- Make friends with the Perl debugger, and use it to try out code snippets as part of this learning process. Another way to test out Perl snippets on Win32 platforms is to combine the TurboPerl program by William P. Smith (found at *http://users.erols.com/turboperl/*) with the *dumpvar.pl* or `Data::Dumper` modules. It has some bugs (I recommend you save your code often), but in general it can make prototyping Perl code easier. Other Integrated Development Environment tools may also offer this functionality.

- Keep a copy of the WMI SDK handy. The documentation and the VBscript code examples are very helpful.

- Use the WMI object browser in the WMI SDK frequently. It helps you get the lay of the land.

Let's get to the Perl part of this section. Our initial task will be to determine the information we can retrieve about Win32 processes and how we can interact with that information.

First we need to establish a connection to a WMI *namespace*. A namespace is defined in the WMI SDK as "a unit for grouping classes and instances to control their scope and visibility." In our case we're interested in connecting to the root of the standard `cimv2` namespace, which contains all of the data that is interesting to us.

We will also have to set up a connection with the appropriate security privileges and impersonation level. Our program will need to be given the privilege to debug a process and to impersonate us; in other words, run as the user calling the script. After we get this connection, we will retrieve a `Win32_Process` object (as defined in the Win32 Schema).

There is a hard way and an easy way to create this connection and get the object. We'll look at both in the first example, so you get an idea of what the methods entail. Here's the hard way, with explanation to follow.

```
use Win32::OLE('in');

$server = ''; # connect to local machine

# get a SWbemLocator object
$lobj = Win32::OLE->new('WbemScripting.SWbemLocator') or
  die "can't create locator object: ".Win32::OLE->LastError()."\n";

# set the impersonate level to "impersonate"
$lobj->{Security_}->{impersonationlevel} = 3;

# use it to get a an SWbemServices object
$sobj = $lobj->ConnectServer($server, 'root\cimv2') or
  die "can't create server object: ".Win32::OLE->LastError()."\n";

# get the schema object
$procschm = $sobj->Get('Win32_Process');
```

The hard way involves:

- Getting a locator object, used to find a connection to a server object

- Setting the impersonation so our program will run with our privileges

- Using this locator object to get a server connection to the cimv2 WMI namespace

- Using this connection to retrieve a Win32_Process object

We can do this all in one step using a COM *moniker's display name*. According to the WMI SDK, "in Common Object Model (COM), a moniker is standard mechanism for encapsulating the location and binding of another COM object. The textual representation of a moniker is called a display name." Here's an easy way to do the same thing as the previous code snippet:

```
use Win32::OLE('in');

$procschm = Win32::OLE->GetObject(
  'winmgmts:{impersonationLevel=impersonate}!Win32_Process')
    or die "can't create server object: ".Win32::OLE->LastError()."\n";
```

Now that we have a Win32_Process object in hand, we can use it to show us the relevant parts of the schema that represents processes under Win32. This includes all of the available Win32_Process properties and methods we can use. The code to do this is fairly simple; the only magic in the following code is the use of the Win32::OLE in operator. To explain this, we need a quick digression.

Our $procschm object has two special properties, Properties_ and Methods_. Each holds a special child object, known as a *collection object* in COM parlance. A collection object is just a parent container for other objects; in this case, they are holding the schema's property method description objects. The in operator just returns an array with references to each child object of a container object. Once we have this array, we can iterate through it, returning the **Name** property of each child object as we go. See the section on "ADSI (Active Directory Service Interfaces)" in Chapter 6 for another prominent use of **in**. Here's what the code looks like:

```
use Win32::OLE('in');

# connect to namespace, set the impersonate level, and retrieve the
# Win32_process object just by using a display name
$procschm = Win32::OLE->GetObject(
            'winmgmts:{impersonationLevel=impersonate}!Win32_Process')
      or die "can't create server object: ".Win32::OLE->LastError()."\n";

print "--- Properties ---\n";
print join("\n",map {$_->{Name}}(in $procschm->{Properties_}));
print "\n--- Methods ---\n";
print join("\n",map {$_->{Name}}(in $procschm->{Methods_}));
```

The output (on an NT4.0 machine) looks like this:

```
--- Properties ---
Caption
CreationClassName
CreationDate
CSCreationClassName
CSName
Description
ExecutablePath
ExecutionState
Handle
InstallDate
KernelModeTime
MaximumWorkingSetSize
MinimumWorkingSetSize
Name
OSCreationClassName
OSName
PageFaults
PageFileUsage
PeakPageFileUsage
PeakWorkingSetSize
Priority
ProcessId
QuotaNonPagedPoolUsage
QuotaPagedPoolUsage
QuotaPeakNonPagedPoolUsage
QuotaPeakPagedPoolUsage
Status
TerminationDate
UserModeTime
WindowsVersion
WorkingSetSize
--- Methods ---
Create
Terminate
GetOwner
GetOwnerSid
```

Let's get down to the business at hand. To retrieve a list of running processes, we need to ask for all instances of **Win32_Process** objects:

```
use Win32::OLE('in');

# perform all of the initial steps in one swell foop

$sobj = Win32::OLE->GetObject(
                    'winmgmts:{impersonationLevel=impersonate}')
    or die "can't create server object: ".Win32::OLE->LastError()."\n";

foreach $process (in $sobj->InstancesOf("Win32_Process")){
  print $process->{Name}." is pid #".$process->{ProcessId},"\n";
}
```

Our initial display name did not include a path to a specific object (i.e., we left off **!Win32_Process**). As a result, we receive a server connection object. When we call the **InstancesOf()** method, it returns a collection object that holds all of the instances of that particular object. Our code visits each object in turn and prints its **Name** and **ProcessId** property. This yields a list of all the running processes.

If we want to be a little less beneficent when iterating over each process, we could instead use one of the methods we saw listed above:

```
foreach $process (in $sobj->InstancesOf("Win32_Process")){
  $process->Terminate(1);
}
```

This will terminate every process running. I do not recommend you run this code as is; customize it for your specific needs by making it more selective.

Now you have the knowledge necessary to begin using WMI for process control. WMI has Win32 extensions for many other parts of the operating system, including the registry and event log facility.

This is as far as we're going to delve into process control on WinNT/2000. Let's turn our attention to one last operating system.

Unix Process Control

Strategies for Unix process control offer another multiple-choice situation. Luckily, these choices aren't nearly as complex to introduce as those offered by NT. When we speak of process control under Unix, we're referring to three operations:

1. Enumerating the list of running processes on a machine

2. Changing their priority or process group

3. Terminating the processes

For the final two of these operations, there are Perl functions to do the job: `setpriority()`, `setpgrp()`, and `kill()`. The first one offers us a few options. To list running processes, you can:

- Call an external program like *ps*

- Take a crack at deciphering */dev/kmem*

- Look through the */proc* filesystem

- Use the `Proc::ProcessTable` module

Let's discuss each of these approaches. For the impatient reader, I'll reveal right now that `Proc::ProcessTable` is my preferred technique, and you might just skip directly to the discussion of that module. But I recommend reading about the other techniques anyway, since they may come in handy in the future.

Calling an External Program

Common to all modern Unix variants is a program called *ps*, used to list running processes. However, *ps* is found different places in the filesystem on different Unix variants and the command-line switches it takes are also not consistent across variants. Therein lies one problem with this option: it lacks portability.

An even more annoying problem is the difficulty in parsing the output (which also varies from variant to variant). Here's a snippet of output from *ps* on a SunOS machine:

```
USER       PID %CPU %MEM   SZ  RSS TT STAT START   TIME COMMAND
dnb        385  0.0  0.0  268    0 p4 IW   Jul  2  0:00 /bin/zsh
dnb      24103  0.0  2.610504 1092 p3 S    Aug 10 35:49 emacs
dnb        389  0.0  2.5 3604 1044 p4 S    Jul  2 60:16 emacs
remy     15396  0.0  0.0  252    0 p9 IW   Jul  7  0:01 -zsh (zsh)
sys        393  0.0  0.0   28    0 ?  IW   Jul  2  0:02 in.identd
dnb      29488  0.0  0.0   68    0 p5 IW   20:15   0:00 screen
dnb      29544  0.0  0.4   24  148 p7 R    20:39   0:00 less
dnb       5707  0.0  0.0  260    0 p6 IW   Jul 24  0:00 -zsh (zsh)
root     28766  0.0  0.0  244    0 ?  IW   13:20   0:00 -:0 (xdm)
```

Notice the third line. Two of the columns have run together, making the parsing of this output an annoying task. It's not impossible, just annoying. Some Unix variants are kinder than others in this regard, but it is something you may have to take into account.

The Perl code required for this option is straightforward: `open()` to run *ps*, `while(<FH>){...}` to read the output, and `split()`, `unpack()`, or `substr()` to parse it. A recipe for this can be found in the *Perl Cookbook* by Tom Christiansen and Nathan Torkington (O'Reilly).

Examining the Kernel Process Structures

I only mention this option for completeness' sake. It is possible to write code that opens up a device like */dev/kmem* and accesses the current running kernel's memory structures. With this access, you can track down the current process table in memory and read it. Given the pain involved (taking apart complex binary structures by hand), and its extreme non-portability (just a version difference within the same operating system is likely to break your program), I'd strongly recommend against using this option.

If you decide not to heed this advice, you should begin by memorizing the Perl documentation for `pack()`, `unpack()`, and the header files for your kernel. Open the kernel memory file (often */dev/kmem*), then `read()` and `unpack()` to your heart's content. You may find it instructive to look at the source for programs like *top* (found at *ftp://ftp.groupsys.com/pub/top*) that perform this task using a great deal of C code. Our next option offers a slightly better version of this method.

Using the /proc Filesystem

One of the more interesting additions to Unix found in most of the current variants is the */proc* filesystem. This is a magical filesystem that has nothing to do with data storage. It provides a file-based interface for the running process table of a machine. A "directory" named after the process ID appears in this filesystem for each running process. In this directory are a set of "files" that provide information about that process. One of these files can be written to, thus allowing control of this process.

It is a really clever concept, and that's the good news. The bad news is that each Unix vendor/developer team decided to take this clever concept and run with it in a different direction. As a result, the files found in a */proc* directory are often variant-specific, both in name and format. For a description of which files are available and what they contain, you will need to see the manual pages (usually found in sections 4, 5, or 8) for *procfs* or *mount_procfs* on your system.

The one fairly portable use of the */proc* filesystem is the enumeration of running processes. If we want to list just the process IDs and their owners, we can use Perl's directory and `lstat()` operators:

```
opendir(PROC,"/proc") or die "Unable to open /proc:$!\n";
while (defined($_= readdir(PROC))){
    next if ($_ eq "." or $_ eq "..");
    next unless /^\d+$/; # filter out any random non-pid files
    print "$_\t". getpwuid((lstat "/proc/$_")[4])."\n";
}
closedir(PROC);
```

If you are interested in more information about a process, you will have to open and unpack() the appropriate binary file in the */proc* directories. Common names for this file are *status* and *psinfo*. The manual pages cited a moment ago should provide details about the C structure found in this file or at least a pointer to a C include file that documents this structure. Because these are operating system- (and OS version-) specific formats, you are still going to run into the program fragility mentioned in our previous option.

You may be feeling discouraged at this point because all of our options so far look like they require code with lots of special cases, one for each version of each operating system we wish to support. Luckily, we have one more option up our sleeve that may help in this regard.

Using the Proc::ProcessTable Module

Daniel J. Urist (with the help of some volunteers) has been kind enough to write a module called Proc::ProcessTable that offers a consistent interface to the process table for the major Unix variants. It hides the vagaries of the different */proc* or *kmem* implementations for you, allowing you to write relatively portable code.

Simply load the module, create a Proc::ProcessTable::Process object, and run methods from that object:

```
use Proc::ProcessTable;

$tobj = new Proc::ProcessTable;
```

This object uses Perl's tied variable functionality to present a real-time view of the system. You do not need to call a special function to refresh the object; each time you access it, it re-reads the process table. This is similar to the %Process hash we saw in our Mac::Processes discussion earlier in this chapter.

To get at this information, you call the object method table():

```
$proctable = $tobj->table();
```

table() returns a reference to an array with members that are references to individual process objects. Each of these objects has its own set of methods that returns information about that process. For instance, here's how you would get a listing of the process IDs and owners:

```
use Proc::ProcessTable;

$tobj = new Proc::ProcessTable;
$proctable = $tobj->table();
for (@$proctable){
    print $_->pid."\t". getpwuid($_->uid)."\n";
}
```

If you want to know which process methods are available on your Unix variant, the `fields()` method of your `Proc::ProcessTable` object (`$tobj` above) will return a list for you.

`Proc::ProcessTable` also adds three other methods to each process object, `kill()`, `priority()`, and `pgrp()`, which are just frontends to the built-in Perl function we mentioned at the beginning of this section.

To bring us back to the big picture, let's look at some of the uses of these process control techniques. We started to examine process control in the context of user actions, so let's look at a few teeny scripts that focus on these actions. We'll use the `Proc::ProcessTable` on Unix for these examples, but these ideas are not operating system specific.

The first example is from the documentation for `Proc::ProcessTable`:

```
use Proc::ProcessTable;

$t = new Proc::ProcessTable;
foreach $p (@{$t->table}){
  if ($p->pctmem > 95){
    $p->kill(9);
  }
}
```

This code will shoot down any processes consuming 95% of that machine's memory when run on the Unix variants that provide the `pctmem()` method (most do). As it stands, this code is probably too ruthless to be used in real life. It would be much more reasonable to add something like this before the `kill()` command:

```
print "about to nuke ".$p->pid."\t". getpwuid($p->uid)."\n";
print "proceed? (yes/no) ";
chomp($ans = <>);
next unless ($ans eq "yes");
```

There's a bit of a race condition here: it is possible that the system state will change during delay induced by prompting the user. Given that we are only prompting for huge processes, and huge processes are those least likely to change state in a short amount of time, we're probably fine coding this way. If you wanted to be pedantic you would probably collect the list of processes to be killed first, prompt for input, and then recheck the state of the process table before actually killing the desired processes.

There are times when death is too good for a process. Sometimes it is important to notice a process is running while it is running so real life action (like "user attitude correction") can be taken. For example, at our site we have a policy against the use of Internet Relay Chat *bots*. *Bots* are daemon processes that connect to an IRC network of chat servers and perform automated actions. Though *bots* can be used for constructive purposes, these days they play a mostly antisocial role on

IRC. We've also had security breaches come to our attention because the first (and often only) thing the intruder has done is put up an IRC *bot* of some sort. As a result, noting their presence on our system without killing them is important to us.

The most common *bot* by far is called *eggdrop*. If we wanted to look for this process name being run on our system, we could use code like this:

```
use Proc::ProcessTable;

open(LOG,">>$logfile") or die "Can't open logfile for append:$!\n";

$t = new Proc::ProcessTable;
foreach $p (@{$t->table}){
  if ($p->fname() =~ /eggdrop/i){
    print LOG time."\t".getpwuid($p->uid)."\t".$p->fname()."\n";
  }
}
close(LOG);
```

If you are thinking, "This code is not good enough! All someone has to do is rename the eggdrop executable to evade its check," you're absolutely right. We'll take a stab at writing less naïve *bot*-check code in the very last section of this chapter.

In the meantime, let's see one more example where Perl assists us in managing user processes. So far all of our examples have been fairly negative. We've seen code that deals with resource-hungry and naughty processes. Let's look at something with a sunnier disposition.

There are times when a system administrator needs to know which (legitimate) programs are being used by users on a system. Sometimes this is necessary in the context of software metering where there are legal concerns about the number of users running a program concurrently. In those cases there is usually a licensing mechanism in place to handle the bean counting. Another situation where this knowledge comes in handy is that of machine migration. If you are migrating a user population from one architecture to another, you'll want to make sure all the programs used on the previous architecture are available on the new one.

One approach to solving this problem involves replacing every non-OS binary available to users with a wrapper that first records that a particular binary has been run and then actually runs it. This can be difficult to implement if there are a large number of binaries. It also has the unpleasant side effect of slowing down every program invocation.

If precision is not important and a rough estimate of which binaries are in use will suffice, then we can use `Proc::ProcessTable` to solve this problem as well. Here's some code that wakes up every five minutes and surveys the current process landscape. It keeps a simple count of all of the process names it finds, and is smart enough not to count processes it already saw during its last period of wake-fulness twice. Every hour it prints its findings and starts collecting again. We wait five minutes between each run because walking the process table is usually a resource-intensive operation and we'd prefer this program add as little load to the system as possible:

```perl
use Proc::ProcessTable;

$interval    = 600; # sleep interval of 5 minutes
$partofhour  =   0; # keep track of where in hour we are

$tobj = new Proc::ProcessTable; # create new process object

# forever loop, collecting stats every $intervar secs
# and dumping them once an hour
while(1){
    &collectstats;
    &dumpandreset if ($partofhour >= 3600);
    sleep($interval);
}

# collect the process statistics
sub collectstats {
    my($process);
    foreach $process (@{$tobj->table}){

        # we should ignore ourselves
        next if ($process->pid() == $$);

        # save this process info for our next run
        push(@last,$process->pid(),$process->fname());

        # ignore this process if we saw it last iteration
        next if ($last{$process->pid()} eq $process->fname());

        # else, remember it
        $collection{$process->fname()}++;
    }
    # set the last hash using the current table for our next run
    %last = @last;
    $partofhour += $interval;
}

# dump out the results and reset our counters
sub dumpandreset{
    print scalar localtime(time).("-"x50)."\n";
    for (sort reverse_value_sort keys %collection){
        write;
    }

    undef %collection;
    $partofhour = 0;
}
}
```

```
# (reverse) sort by values in %collection and by key name
sub reverse_value_sort{
    return $collection{$b} <=> $collection{$a} || $a cmp $b;
}

format STDOUT =
@<<<<<<<<<<<<<<  @>>>>
$_,             $collection{$_}
.


format STDOUT_TOP =
Name           Count
-------------- -----
.
```

There are many ways this program could be enhanced. It could track processes on a per-user basis (i.e., only recording one instance of a program launch per user), collect daily stats, present its information as a nice bar graph, and so on. It's just a matter of where you want to take it.

Tracking File and Network Operations

For our last section of this chapter, we're going to lump two of the user action domains together. The processes we've just spent so much time controlling do more than just suck up CPU and memory. They also perform operations on filesystems and communicate on a network on behalf of a user. User administration requires that we deal with these second-order effects as well.

Our focus is going to be fairly narrow. We're only interested in looking at file and network operations that *other* users are performing on a system. We're also only going to focus on those operations that we can track back to a specific user (or a specific process run by a specific user). With these blinders in mind, let's go forth.

Tracking Operations on Windows NT/2000

If we want to track other users' open files, the closest we can come involves using a third-party command-line program called *nthandle* by Mark Russinovich, found at *http://www.sysinternals.com*. It can show us all of the open handles on a particular system. Here's some sample output:

```
System pid: 2
      10: File      C:\WINNT\SYSTEM32\CONFIG\SECURITY
      84: File      C:\WINNT\SYSTEM32\CONFIG\SAM.LOG
      cc: File      C:\WINNT\SYSTEM32\CONFIG\SYSTEM
      d0: File      C:\WINNT\SYSTEM32\CONFIG\SECURITY.LOG
      d4: File      C:\WINNT\SYSTEM32\CONFIG\DEFAULT
      e8: File      C:\WINNT\SYSTEM32\CONFIG\SYSTEM.ALT
      fc: File      C:\WINNT\SYSTEM32\CONFIG\SOFTWARE.LOG
     118: File      C:\WINNT\SYSTEM32\CONFIG\SAM
```

```
      128: File          C:\pagefile.sys
      134: File          C:\WINNT\SYSTEM32\CONFIG\DEFAULT.LOG
      154: File          C:\WINNT\SYSTEM32\CONFIG\SOFTWARE
      1b0: File          \Device\NamedPipe\
      294: File          C:\WINNT\PROFILES\Administrator\ntuser.dat.LOG
      2a4: File          C:\WINNT\PROFILES\Administrator\NTUSER.DAT
-------------------------------------------------------------------------
 SMSS.EXE pid: 27 (NT AUTHORITY:SYSTEM)
        4: Section       C:\WINNT\SYSTEM32\SMSS.EXE
        c: File          C:\WINNT
       28: File          C:\WINNT\SYSTEM32
```

Information on specific files or directories can also be requested:

```
> nthandle c:\temp
Handle V1.11
Copyright (C) 1997 Mark Russinovich
http://www.sysinternals.com

WINWORD.EXE          pid: 652     C:\TEMP\~DFF2B3.tmp
WINWORD.EXE          pid: 652     C:\TEMP\~DFA773.tmp
WINWORD.EXE          pid: 652     C:\TEMP\~DF913E.tmp
```

nthandle can provide this information for a specific process using the $-p$ switch.

Using this executable from Perl is straightforward, so we won't provide any sample code. Instead, let's look at a related and more interesting operation: auditing.

NT/2000 allows us to efficiently watch a file, directory, or hierarchy of directories for changes. You could imagine repeatedly performing `stat()`s on the desired object or objects, but that would be highly CPU intensive. Under NT/2000, we can ask the operating system to keep watch for us.

There are two specialized Perl modules that make this job relatively painless for us: `Win32::ChangeNotify` by Christopher J. Madsen and `Win32::AdvNotify` by Amine Moulay Ramdane. The latter is a bit more flexible, so we'll use it for our example in this section.

Using `Win32::AdvNotify` is a multiple-step process. First, you load the module and create a new `AdvNotify` object:

```
# also import two constants we'll use in a moment
use Win32::AdvNotify qw(All %ActionName);
use Data::Dumper;

$aobj = new Win32::AdvNotify() or die "Can't make a new object\n";
```

The next step is to create a monitoring thread for the directory in question. `Win32::AdvNotify` allows you to watch multiple directories at once simply by creating multiple threads. We'll stick to monitoring a single directory:

```
$thread = $aobj->StartThread(Directory => 'C:\temp',
                             Filter => All,
```

```
                                    WatchSubtree => 0)
      or die "Unable to start thread\n";
```

The first parameter of this method is self-explanatory; let's look at the others.

We can look for many types of changes by setting `Filter` to one or a combination
(`SETTING1 | SETTING2 | SETTING3...`) of the constants listed in Table 4-1.

Table 4-1. Win32::AdvNotify Filter Parameters

Parameter	Notices
FILE_NAME	Creating, deleting, renaming of a file or files
DIR_NAME	Creating or deleting a directory or directories
ATTRIBUTES	Change in any directory attribute
SIZE	Change in any file size
LAST_WRITE	Change in the modification date of a file or files
CREATION	Change in the creation date of a file or files
SECURITY	Change in the security info (ACL, etc.) of a file or files

The `All` setting you see in our code above is just a constant that includes a combination of the choices. Leaving the `Filter` parameter out of the method call will
also select `All`. The `WatchSubtree` parameter determines if the thread will watch
just the directory specified, or it and all of its subdirectories.

`StartThread()` creates a monitoring thread, but that thread doesn't actually
begin monitoring until we ask it to:

```
    $thread->EnableWatch() or die "Can't start watching\n";
```

There is also a `DisableWatch()` call, should you choose to turn off monitoring at
any point in your program.

Now that we're monitoring our desired object, how do we know when something
changes? We need some way for our thread to report back to us when the change
we're looking for takes place. The process is similar to one we'll see in Chapter 9,
Log Files, when we discuss network sockets. Basically, we call a function that
blocks, or hangs, until a change occurs:

```
    while($thread->Wait(INFINITE)){
        print "Something changed!\n";
        last if ($changes++ == 5);
    }
```

This `while()` loop will call the `Wait()` method for our thread. This call will block
until the thread has something to report. `Wait()` normally takes a parameter that
dictates the number of milliseconds it should wait until giving up, though here
we've given it a special value that says "wait forever." Once `Wait()` returns, we

print a message and go back to waiting unless we've already noticed five other changes. We now clean up:

```
$thread->Terminate();
undef $aobj;
```

Our program isn't all that useful as written. All we know is *something* changed, but we don't know what changed or how it changed. To improve the situation, let's replace the contents of the while() loop and add a Perl format specification:

```
while($thread->Wait(INFINITE)){
    while ($thread->Read(\@status)){
        foreach $event (@status){
            $filename = $event->{FileName};
            $time     = $event->{DateTime};
            $action   = $ActionName{$event->{Action}};
            write;
        }
    }
}

format STDOUT =
@<<<<<<<<<<<<<<<<<< @<<<<<<<<<<<<<<<<<<< @<<<<<<<<<<<<<<<<<<<
$filename,$time,$action
.


format STDOUT_TOP =
File Name           Date                 Action
------------------  -------------------- ----------------------
.
```

The key change here is the addition of the Read() method. Read() gets information about the change event and populates the @status list above with a set of hash references. Each reference points to an anonymous hash that looks something like this:

```
{'FileName' => '~GLF2425.TMP',
 'DateTime' => '11/08/1999 06:23:25p',
 'Directory' => 'C:\temp',
 'Action' => 3 }
```

Multiple sets of event changes can queue up for every change, hence our need to call Read() in the while() loop until it runs out of steam. When we de-reference the contents of those hash references appropriately and pass them through a Perl format, we get handy output that like this:

```
File Name           Date                 Action
------------------  -------------------- ----------------------
~DF40DE.tmp         11/08/1999 07:29:56p FILE_ACTION_REMOVED
~DF6E5C.tmp         11/08/1999 07:29:56p FILE_ACTION_ADDED
~DF6E66.tmp         11/08/1999 07:29:56p FILE_ACTION_ADDED
~DF6E5C.tmp         11/08/1999 07:29:56p FILE_ACTION_REMOVED
```

Unfortunately, the tracking of network operations under NT/2000 is not nearly as impressive. Ideally, as an administrator you'd like to know which process (and therefore which user) has opened a network port. Unfortunately, I know of no Perl module or free third-party command-line tool that can provide this information. There does exist a single commercial command-line tool called *TCPVstat* that can show us the network-connection-to-process mapping. *TCPVstat* is found in the TCPView Professional Edition package available at *http://www.winternals.com*.

If we are only able to use free tools, then we'll have to make do with a simple listing of the currently open network ports on our system. For that, we'll use another module by Ramdane called `Win32::IpHelp`. Here's code to print this information:

```perl
use Win32::IpHelp;

# note: the case of "IpHelp" is signficant in this call
my $iobj = new Win32::IpHelp;

# populates list of hash of hashes
$iobj->GetTcpTable(\@table,1);

foreach $entry (@table){
    print $entry->{LocalIP}->{Value} . ":" .
        $entry->{LocalPort}->{Value}. " -> ";
    print $entry->{RemoteIP}->{Value} . ":" .
        $entry->{RemotePort}->{Value}."\n";
}
```

Let's see how we'd perform the same tasks from within the Unix world.

Tracking Operations in Unix

To handle the tracking of both file and network operations in Unix, we can use a single approach. This is one of few times in this book where calling a separate executable is clearly the superior method. Vic Abell has given an amazing gift to the system administration world by writing and maintaining a program called *lsof* (LiSt Open Files) that can be found at *ftp://vic.cc.purdue.edu/pub/tools/unix/lsof*. *lsof* can show in detail all of the currently open files and network connections on a Unix machine. One of the things that make it truly amazing is its portability. The latest version as of this writing runs on at least 18 flavors of Unix and supports several OS versions for each flavor.

Here's a snippet of *lsof*'s output showing one of the processes I am running. *lsof* tends to output very long lines, so I've inserted a blank line between each line of output to make the distinctions clear:

```
COMMAND    PID USER   FD   TYPE    DEVICE  SIZE/OFF    NODE NAME
netscape 21065  dnb   cwd   VDIR   172,2891     8192   12129 /home/dnb
```

```
netscape 21065  dnb  txt   VREG   172,1246  14382364    656749 /net/arch-solaris
(fileserver:/vol/systems/arch-solaris)

netscape 21065  dnb  txt   VREG    32,6       54656      35172 /usr (/dev/dsk/
c0t0d0s6)

netscape 21065  dnb  txt   VREG    32,6      146740       6321 /usr/lib/libelf.
so.1

netscape 21065  dnb  txt   VREG    32,6       69292     102611 /usr (/dev/dsk/
c0t0d0s6)

netscape 21065  dnb  txt   VREG    32,6       21376      79751 /usr/lib/locale/
en_US/en_US.so.1

netscape 21065  dnb  txt   VREG    32,6       19304       5804 /usr/lib/libmp.so.
2

netscape 21065  dnb  txt   VREG    32,6       98284      22860 /usr/openwin/lib/
libICE.so.6

netscape 21065  dnb  txt   VREG    32,6       46576      22891 /usr/openwin/lib/
libSM.so.6

netscape 21065  dnb  txt   VREG    32,6     1014020       5810 /usr/lib/libc.so.1

netscape 21065  dnb  txt   VREG    32,6      105788       5849 /usr/lib/libm.so.1

netscape 21065  dnb  txt   VREG    32,6      721924       5806 /usr/lib/libnsl.
so.1

netscape 21065  dnb  txt   VREG    32,6      166196       5774 /usr/lib/ld.so.1

netscape 21065  dnb    0u  VCHR    24,3        0t73       5863 /devices/pseudo/
pts@0:3-> ttcompat->ldterm->ptem->pts

netscape 21065  dnb    3u  VCHR    13,12        0t0       5821 /devices/pseudo/
mm@0:zero

netscape 21065  dnb    7u  FIFO 0x6034d264      0t1      47151 PIPE->0x6034d1e0

netscape 21065  dnb    8u  inet 0x6084cb68 0xfb210ec       TCP host.ccs.neu.edu:
46575-> host2.ccs.neu.edu:6000 (ESTABLISHED)

netscape 21065  dnb   29u  inet 0x60642848  0t215868       TCP host.ccs.neu.edu:
46758-> www.mindbright.se:80 (CLOSE_WAIT)
```

In the previous output you can see some of the power this command provides. We can see the current working directory (VDIR), regular files (VREG), character devices (VCHR), pipes (FIFO), and network connections (inet) opened by this process.

The easiest way to use *lsof* from Perl is to invoke its special "field" mode (*–F*). In this mode, its output is broken up into specially labeled and delimited fields, instead of the *ps*-like columns show above. This makes parsing the output a cinch.

There is one quirk to the output. It is organized into what the author calls "process sets" and "file sets." A process set is a set of field entries referring to a single process; a file set is a similar set for a file. This all makes more sense if we turn on field mode with the 0 option. Fields are then delimited with NUL (ASCII 0) characters and sets with NL (ASCII 12). Here's the same group of lines as those above, this time in field mode (NUL is represented as ^@):

```
p21065^@cnetscape^@u6700^@Ldnb^@

fcwd^@a ^@l ^@tVDIR^@D0x2b00b4b^@s8192^@i12129^@n/home/dnb^@

ftxt^@a ^@l ^@tVREG^@D0x2b004de^@s14382364^@i656749^@n/net/arch-solaris
(fileserver:/vol/systems/arch-solaris)^@

ftxt^@a ^@l ^@tVREG^@D0x800006^@s54656^@i35172^@n/usr (/dev/dsk/c0t0d0s6)^@

ftxt^@a ^@l ^@tVREG^@D0x800006^@s146740^@i6321^@n/usr/lib/libelf.so.1^@

ftxt^@a ^@l ^@tVREG^@D0x800006^@s40184^@i6089^@n/usr (/dev/dsk/c0t0d0s6)^@

ftxt^@a ^@l ^@tVREG^@D0x800006^@s69292^@i102611^@n/usr (/dev/dsk/c0t0d0s6)^@

ftxt^@a ^@l ^@tVREG^@D0x800006^@s21376^@i79751^@n/usr/lib/locale/en_US/en_US.so.
1^@

ftxt^@a ^@l ^@tVREG^@D0x800006^@s19304^@i5804^@n/usr/lib/libmp.so.2^@

ftxt^@a ^@l ^@tVREG^@D0x800006^@s98284^@i22860^@n/usr/openwin/lib/libICE.so.6^@

ftxt^@a ^@l ^@tVREG^@D0x800006^@s46576^@i22891^@n/usr/openwin/lib/libSM.so.6^@

ftxt^@a ^@l ^@tVREG^@D0x800006^@s1014020^@i5810^@n/usr/lib/libc.so.1^@

ftxt^@a ^@l ^@tVREG^@D0x800006^@s105788^@i5849^@n/usr/lib/libm.so.1^@

ftxt^@a ^@l ^@tVREG^@D0x800006^@s721924^@i5806^@n/usr/lib/libnsl.so.1^@

ftxt^@a ^@l ^@tVREG^@D0x800006^@s166196^@i5774^@n/usr/lib/ld.so.1^@
f0^@au^@l ^@tVCHR^@D0x600003^@o73^@i5863^@n/devices/pseudo/pts@0:3->ttcompat->
ldterm->ptem->pts^@

f3^@au^@l ^@tVCHR^@D0x34000c^@o0^@i5821^@n/devices/pseudo/mm@0:zero^@

f7^@au^@l ^@tFIFO^@d0x6034d264^@o1^@i47151^@nPIPE->0x6034d1e0^@

f8^@au^@l ^@tinet^@d0x6084cb68^@o270380692^@PTCP^@nhost.ccs.neu.edu:46575-> host2.
ccs.neu.edu:6000^@TST=ESTABLISHED^@
```

```
f29^@au^@1 ^@tinet^@d0x60642848^@o215868^@PTCP^@nhost.ccs.neu.edu:46758-> www.
mindbright.se:80^@TST=CLOSE_WAIT^@
```

Let's take this output apart. The first line is a process set (we can tell because it begins with the letter p):

```
p21065^@cnetscape^@u6700^@Ldnb^@
```

Each field begins with a letter identifying the field's contents (p for **pid**, c for **command**, u for **uid**, and L for **login**) and ends with a delimiter character. Together the fields on this line make up a process set. All of the lines that follow, up until the next process set, describe the open files/network connections of the process described by this process set.

Let's put this mode to use. If we wanted to show all of the open files on a system and the pids that are using them, we could use code like this:

```perl
use Text::Wrap;

$lsofexec = "/usr/local/bin/lsof"; # location of lsof executable

# (F)ield mode, NUL (0) delim, show (L)ogin, file (t)ype and file (n)ame
$lsofflag = "-FL0tn";
open(LSOF,"$lsofexec $lsofflag|") or  die "Unable to start $lsof:$!\n";

while(<LSOF>){
    # deal with a process set
    if (substr($_,0,1) eq "p"){
        ($pid,$login) = split(/\0/);
        $pid = substr($pid,1,length($pid));
    }

    # deal with a file set, note: we are only interested
    # in "regular" files
    if (substr($_,0,5) eq "tVREG"){
        ($type,$pathname) = split(/\0/);

        # a process may have the same path name open twice,
        # these two lines make sure we only record it once
        next if ($seen{$pathname} eq $pid);
        $seen{$pathname} = $pid;

        $pathname = substr($pathname,1,length($pathname));
        push(@{$paths{$pathname}},$pid);
    }
}

close(LSOF);

for (sort keys %paths){
    print "$_:\n";
    print wrap("\t","\t",join(" ",@{$paths{$_}})),"\n";
}
```

This code instructs *lsof* to show only a few of its possible fields. We iterate through its output, collecting filenames and pids in a hash of lists. When we've received all of the output, we print the filenames in a nicely formatted pid list (thanks to David Muir Sharnoff's `Text::Wrap` module):

```
/usr (/dev/dsk/c0t0d0s6):
        115 117 128 145 150 152 167 171 184 191 200 222 232 238 247 251 276
        285 286 292 293 296 297 298 4244 4709 4991 4993 14697 20946 21065
        24530 25080 27266 27603
/usr/bin/tcsh:
        4246 4249 5159 14699 20949
/usr/bin/zsh:
        24532 25082 27292 27564
/usr/dt/lib/libXm.so.3:
        21065 21080
/usr/lib/ld.so.1:
        115 117 128 145 150 152 167 171 184 191 200 222 232 238 247 251 267
        276 285 286 292 293 296 297 298 4244 4246 4249 4709 4991 4993 5159
        14697 14699 20946 20949 21065 21080 24530 24532 25080 25082 25947
        27266 27273 27291 27292 27306 27307 27308 27563 27564 27603
/usr/lib/libc.so.1:
        267 4244 4246 4249 4991 4993 5159 14697 14699 20949 21065 21080
        24530 24532 25080 25082 25947 27273 27291 27292 27306 27307 27308
        27563 27564 27603
...
```

For our last example of tracking Unix file and network operations, let's return to an earlier example, where we attempted to find IRC *bots* running on a system. There are more reliable ways to find network daemons like *bots* than looking at the process table. A user may be able to hide the name of a *bot* by renaming the executable, but she or he will have to work a lot harder to hide the open network connection. More often than not, this connection is to a server running on TCP ports 6660–7000. *lsof* makes looking for these processes easy:

```
$lsofexec = "/usr/local/bin/lsof";
$lsofflag = "-FL0c -iTCP:6660-7000";

# this is a hash slice being used to preload a hash table, the
# existence of whose keys we'll check later. Usually this gets written
# like this:
#     %approvedclients = ("ircII" => undef, "xirc" => undef, ...);
# (but this is a cool idiom popularized by Mark-Jason Dominus)
@approvedclients{"ircII","xirc","pirc"} = ();

open(LSOF,"$lsofexec $lsofflag|") or
  die "Unable to start $lsof:$!\n";

while(<LSOF>){
    ($pid,$command,$login) = /p(\d+)\000
                             c(.+)\000
                             L(\w+)\000/x;
```

```
    warn "$login using an unapproved client called $command (pid $pid)!\n"
        unless (exists $approvedclients{$command});
}

close(LSOF);
```

This is the simplest check we can make. It will catch users who rename *eggdrop* to *pine* or *–tcsh*, and it will catch those users who don't even attempt to hide their *bot*, but it suffers from a similar flaw to our other approach. If a user is smart enough, she or he may rename their *bot* to something on our "approved clients" list. To continue the cat-and-mouse game we could take at least two more steps:

- Use *lsof* to check that the file opened for that executable really is the file we expect it to be, and not some random binary in a user filesystem.

- Use our process control methods to check that the user is running this program from an existing shell. If this is the only process running for a user (i.e., they've logged off but still left it running), it is probably a daemon and hence a *bot*.

This cat-and-mouse game brings us to a point that will help wrap up the chapter. In Chapter 3, we mentioned that users are fundamentally unpredictable. They do things systems administrators don't anticipate. There is an old saying: "Nothing is foolproof because fools are so ingenious." It is important to come to grips with this fact as you program Perl for user administration. You'll write more robust programs as a result. When one of your programs goes "blooey" because a user did something unexpected, you'll be able to sit back calmly and admire the ingenuity.

Module Information for This Chapter

Module	CPAN ID	Version
`Mac::Processes` (ships with MacPerl; a modified version is available in the Mac-Glue package)	CNANDOR	1.01
`Win32::API`		0.011
`Win32::ISync` (found at *http://www.generation.net/~aminer/Perl/*)		1.11
`Win32::IProc` (found at *http://www.generation.net/~aminer/Perl/*)		1.32
`Win32::Setupsup` (found at *ftp://ftp.roth.net/pub/NTPerl/Others/SetupSup/* or *http://Jenda.Krynicky.cz*)		980320
`Win32::Lanman` (found at *ftp://ftp.roth.net/pub/ntperl/Others/Lanman/*)		1.05
`Win32::OLE` (ships with ActiveState Perl)	JDB	1.11
`Proc::ProcessTable`	DURIST	0.26
`Win32::AdvNotify` (found at *http://www.generation.net/~aminer/Perl/*)		1.01

Module	CPAN ID	Version
`Data::Dumper`	GSAR	2.101
`Win32::IpHelp` (found at *http://www.generation. net/~aminer/Perl/*)		1.02
`Text::Wrap` (ships with Perl)	MUIR	98.112902

Installing Win32::IProc

Getting and installing `Win32::IProc` is a little less straightforward than with other modules. The module itself can be found along with Ramdane's other modules at *http://www.generation.net/~aminer/Perl/*. To make use of `Win32::IProc`, you will also need to get two other modules: Ramdane's `Win32::ISync`, and `Win32::API` by Aldo Calpini. The former can be found at Ramdane's site, the latter in the ActiveState module repository or at *http://dada.perl.it/*.

Some of Ramdane's modules are installed by hand, without the help of the *ppm* command, and require some minor source code edits. Here's a complete recipe for installation, assuming you have unzipped the distributions and are installing into an ActiveState build that lives in *C:\Perl*:

1. *ppm install Win32-API*

2. *md c:\Perl\site\lib\auto\Win32\Sync* and *C:\Perl\site\lib\auto\Win32\Iproc*

3. Copy *timer.dll* and *sync.dll* to *c:\Perl\site\lib\auto\Win32\Sync*

4. Copy *iprocnt.dll, psapi.dll* and *iproc.dll* to *C:\Perl\site\lib\auto\Win32\Iproc*

5. Copy *iproc.pm, iipc.pm* and *isync.pm* to *C:\Perl\site\lib\Win32*

6. Change the `DLLPath` lines in *iproc.pm* to look like this:

   ```
   my($DLLPath) ="C:\\Perl\\site\\lib\\auto\\Win32\\Iproc\\IProc.dll";
   my($DLLPath1)="C:\\Perl\\site\\lib\\auto\\Win32\\Iproc\\IprocNT.dll";
   my($DLLPath2)="C:\\Perl\\site\\lib\\auto\\Win32\\Sync\\Sync.dll";
   ```

7. Change the `DLLPath` line in *iipc.pm* to:

   ```
   my($DLLPath)="C:\\Perl\\site\\lib\\auto\\Win32\\Sync\\sync.dll";
   ```

8. Change the `DLLPath` lines in *isync.pm* to:

   ```
   my($DLLPath) ="C:\\Perl\\site\\lib\\auto\\Win32\\Sync\\sync.dll";
   my($DLLPath1)="C:\\Perl\\site\\lib\\auto\\Win32\\Sync\\timer.dll";
   ```

Installing Win32::Setupsup

If you want to install `Win32::Setupsup` by hand and/or gaze at the source code, you can find a ZIP archive of the module at *ftp://ftp.roth.net/pub/NTPerl/Others/ SetupSup/*. If you'd prefer to install it the easy way on an ActiveState installation, you can connect to Jenda Krynicky's module archive and install it using the usual *ppm* method. For instructions on how to do this, see the instructions (and other useful modules) at *http://Jenda.Krynicky.cz.*

The tricky part is that the pod documentation does not format its information correctly when it is processed by *perldoc* or when installed as HTML. The documentation at the end of *setupsup.pm* (most likely found in *<your Perl directory>\site\ lib\Win32*) is much more legible. If you are trying to learn how to use this module, I would recommend opening this file up in an editor and then scanning for the documentation portions.

References for More Information

http://pudget.net/macperl is the home of Chris Nandor's Perl modules. Nandor is one of the most active developers of MacPerl modules (and co-author of the book cited below).

http://www.activestate.com/support/mailing_lists.htm hosts the *Perl-Win32-Admin and Perl-Win32-Users* mailing lists. Both lists and their archives are invaluable resources for Win32 programmers.

http://www.microsoft.com/management is the home for all of Microsoft's management technologies, including WMI.

http://www.sysinternals.com is home of the *nthandle* program (called just *Handle* on that site) and many other valuable NT/2000 utilities. It has a sister site, *http://www.winternals.com,* which sells excellent commercial utilities.

MacPerl:Power and Ease, by Vicki Brown and Chris Nandor (Prime Time Freeware, 1998) is the best book for information on MacPerl modules. The publisher also has a web site at *http://www.macperl.com* that is very useful.

http://www.dmtf.org is the home of the Distributed Management Task Force and a good source for WBEM information.

http://www.mspress.com are the publishers of the Microsoft NT Resource kit. They also offer a subscription services that provides access to the latest RK utilities.

5

TCP/IP Name Services

The majority of the conversations between computers these days take place using a protocol called *Transmission Control Protocol* running over a lower layer called *Internet Protocol.** These two protocols are commonly lumped together into the acronym TCP/IP. Every machine that participates on a TCP/IP network must be assigned at least one unique numeric identifier, called an *IP address.* IP addresses are usually written using the form *NNN.NNN.N.N*, e.g., 192.168.1.9.

While machines are content to call each other by strings of dot-separated numbers, most people are less enamored by this idea. TCP/IP would have fallen flat on its face as a protocol if users had to remember a unique 12-digit sequence for every machine they wanted to contact. Mechanisms had to be invented to manage and distribute an IP address to human-friendly name mappings.

This chapter describes the evolution of the network name services that allow us to access data at *www.oog.org* instead of at 192.168.1.9, and what takes place behind the scenes. Along the way we combine a dash of history with a healthy serving of practical advice on how Perl can help to manage this crucial part of any networking infrastructure.

Host Files

The first approach used to solve the problem of mapping IP addresses to names was the most obvious and simple one: a standard file was created to hold a table of IP addresses and their corresponding computer names. This file can be found as */etc/hosts* on Unix systems, *Macintosh HD:System Folder:Preferences:hosts* on Macs,

---

* This chapter will be discussing IPv4, the current (deployed) standard. IPv6 (the next generation of IP) will probably replace it in due course.

and \$*systemroot*$*System32**Drivers**Etc**hosts* on NT/2000 machines. On NT/2000 there is also an *lmhosts* file that serves a slightly different purpose, which we'll talk about later. Here's an example Unix-style host file:

```
127.0.0.1     localhost
192.168.1.1   everest.oog.org     everest
192.168.1.2   rivendell.oog.org   rivendell
```

The limitations of this approach become clear very quickly. If *oog.org*'s network manager has two machines on a TCP/IP network that communicate with each other, and she wants to add a third which will be addressed by name, she's got to edit the correct file on all of her machines. If *oog.org* buys yet another machine, there are now four separate host files to be maintained (one on each machine).

As untenable as this may seem, this is what actually happened during the early days of the Internet/ARPAnet. As new sites were connected, every site on the net that wished to talk with the new site needed to update their host files. The central host repository, known as the Network Information Center (NIC) (or more precisely the SRI-NIC, since it was housed at SRI at the time), updated and published a host file for the entire network called *HOSTS.TXT*. System administrators would anonymously FTP this file from SRI-NIC's NETINFO directory on a regular basis.

Host files are still in use today, despite their limitations and the replacements we'll be talking about later in this chapter. There are some situations where host files are even mandatory. For example, under SunOS, a machine consults its */etc/hosts* file to determine its own IP address. Host files also solve the "chicken and egg" problem encountered while a machine boots. If the network name servers that machine will be using are specified by name, there must be some way to determine their IP addresses. But if the network name service isn't operational yet, there's no way (unless it broadcasts for help) to receive this information. The usual solution is to place a stub file (with just a few hosts) in place for booting purposes.

On a small network, having an up-to-date host file that includes all of the hosts on that network is useful. It doesn't even have to reside on each machine in that network to be helpful (since the other mechanisms we'll describe later do a much better job of distributing this information). Just having one around that can be consulted is handy for quick manual lookups and address allocation purposes.

Since these files are still a part of everyday administration, let's look at better ways to manage them. Perl and host files are a natural match, given Perl's predilection for text file processing. Given their affinity for each other, we're going to use the simple host file as a springboard for a number of different explorations.

Let's look at the parsing of host files. Parsing a host file can be a simple as this:

```perl
open(HOSTS, "/etc/hosts") or die "Unable to open host file:$!\n";
while (defined ($_ = <HOSTS>)) {
```

```
        next if /^#/;  # skip comments lines
        next if /^$/;  # skip empty lines
        s/\s*#.*$//;  # delete in-line comments and preceding whitespace
        ($ip, @names) = split;
        die "The IP address $ip already seen!\n" if (exists $addrs{$ip});
        $addrs{$ip} = [@names];
        for (@names){
            die "The host name $_ already seen!\n" if (exists $names{$_});
            $names{$_} = $ip;
        }
    }
    close(HOSTS);
```

The previous code walks through an */etc/hosts* file (skipping blank lines and comments), creating two data structures for later use. The first data structure is a hash of lists of hostnames keyed by the IP address. For the host file above, the data structure created would look like this:

```
$addrs{'127.0.0.1'} = ['localhost'];
$addrs{'192.168.1.2'} = ['rivendell.oog.org','rivendell'];
$addrs{'192.168.1.1'} = ['everest.oog.org','everest'];
```

The second is a hash table of host names, keyed by the name. For the same file, the **%names** hash would look like this:

```
$names{'localhost'}='127.0.0.1'
$names{'everest'}='192.168.1.1'
$names{'everest.oog.org'}='192.168.1.1'
$names{'rivendell'}='192.168.1.2'
$names{'rivendell.oog.org'}='192.168.1.2'
```

Note that in the simple process of parsing this file, we've also added some additional functionality. Our code checks for duplicate host names and IP addresses (both bad news on a TCP/IP network). When dealing with network-related data, use every opportunity possible to check for errors and bad information. It is always better to catch problems early in the game than to be bitten by them once the data has been propagated to your entire network. Because it is so important, I'll return to this topic later in the chapter

Generating Host Files

Now we turn to the more interesting topic of generating host files. Let's assume we have the following host database file for the hosts on our network:

```
name: shimmer
address: 192.168.1.11
aliases: shim shimmy shimmydoodles
owner: David Davis
department: software
building: main
room: 909
manufacturer: Sun
```

```
model: Ultra60
-=-
name: bendir
address: 192.168.1.3
aliases: ben bendoodles
owner: Cindy Coltrane
department: IT
building: west
room: 143
manufacturer: Apple
model: 7500/100
-=-
name: sulawesi
address: 192.168.1.12
aliases: sula su-lee
owner: Ellen Monk
department: design
building: main
room: 1116
manufacturer: Apple
model: 7500/100
-=-
name: sander
address: 192.168.1.55
aliases: sandy micky mickydoo
owner: Alex Rollins
department: IT
building: main
room: 1101
manufacturer: Intergraph
model: TD-325
-=-
```

The format is simple: *fieldname: value* with -=- used as a separator between records. You might find you need other fields than those listed above, or have too many records to make it practical to keep in a single flat file. Though we are using a single flat file, the concepts we'll show in this chapter are not backend-specific.

Here's some code that will parse a file like this to generate a host file:

```
$datafile ="./database";
$recordsep = "-=-\n";

open(DATA,$datafile) or die "Unable to open datafile:$!\n";

$/=$recordsep; # prepare to read in database file one record at a time

print "#\n\# host file - GENERATED BY $0\n# DO NOT EDIT BY HAND!\n#\n";
while (<DATA>) {
    chomp;                          # remove the record separator
    # split into key1,value1,...bingo, hash of record
    %record = split /:\s*|\n/m;
    print "$record{address}\t$record{name} $record{aliases}\n";
}
close(DATA);
```

Here's the output:

```
#
# host file - GENERATED BY createhosts
# DO NOT EDIT BY HAND!
#
192.168.1.11      shimmer shim shimmy shimmydoodles
192.168.1.3       bendir ben bendoodles
192.168.1.12      sulawesi sula su-lee
192.168.1.55      sander sandy micky mickydoo.
```

Got "System Administration Database" Religion Yet?

In Chapter 3, *User Accounts*, I made an impassioned plea for the use of a separate administrative database to track account information. The same arguments are doubly true for network host data. In this chapter we're going to demonstrate how even a simple flat-file host database can be manipulated to produce impressive output that drives each of the services we'll be discussing. For larger sites, a "real" database would serve well. If you'd like to see an example of this output, take a quick glance ahead at the output at the end of the "Improving the Host File Output" section, later in this chapter.

The host database approach is beautiful for a number of reasons. Changes need to be made only to a single file or data source. Make the changes, run some scripts, and *presto!*, we've generated the configuration files needed for a number of services. These configuration files are significantly less likely to contain small syntax errors (like missing semicolons or comment characters) because they won't be touched by human hands. If we write our code correctly, we can catch most of the other possible errors during the parse stage.

If you haven't seen the wisdom of this "best practice" yet, you will by the end of the chapter.

Let's look at a few of the more interesting Perl techniques in this small code sample. The first unusual thing we do is set $/. From that point on, Perl treats chunks of text that end in -=-\n as a single record. This means the while statement will read in an entire record at a time and assign it to $_.

The second interesting tidbit is the split assign technique. Our goal is to get each record into a hash with a key as the field name and its value as the field value. You'll see why we go to this trouble later as we develop this example further. The first step is to break $_ into component parts using split(). The array we get back from split() is shown in Table 5-1.

Table 5-1. The Array Returned by split( )

Element	Value
$record[0]	name
$record[1]	shimmer
$record[2]	address
$record[3]	192.168.1.11
$record[4]	aliases
$record[5]	shim shimmy shimmydoodles
$record[6]	owner
$record[7]	David Davis
$record[8]	department
$record[9]	software
$record[10]	building
$record[11]	main
$record[12]	room
$record[13]	909
$record[14]	manufacturer
$record[15]	Sun
$record[16]	model
$record[17]	Ultra60

Now take a good look at the contents of the list. Starting at $record[0], we have a key-value pair list (i.e., key=Name, value=shimmer\n, key=Address, value=192. 168.1.11\n...) which we can just assign to populate a hash. Once this hash is created, we can print the parts we need.

Error Checking the Host File Generation Process

Printing the parts we need is just the beginning of what we can do. One very large benefit of using a separate database that gets converted into another form is the ability to insert error checking into the conversion process. As we mentioned before, this can prevent simple typos from becoming a problem *before* they get a chance to propagate or be put into production use. Here's the previous code with some simple additions to check for typos:

```
$datafile ="./database";
$recordsep = "-=-\n";

open(DATA,$datafile) or die "Unable to open datafile:$!\n";

$/=$recordsep; # prepare to read in database file one record at a time
```

```
print "#\n\# host file - GENERATED BY $0\n# DO NOT EDIT BY HAND!\n#\n";
while (<DATA>) {
    chomp;  # remove the record separator
    # split into key1,value1,...bingo, hash of record
    %record = split /:\s*|\n/m;

        # check for bad hostnames
        if ($record{name} =~ /[^-.a-zA-Z0-9]/) {
            warn "!!!! $record{name} has illegal host name characters,
                    skipping...\n";
            next;
        }

        # check for bad aliases
        if ($record{aliases} =~ /[^-.a-zA-Z0-9\s]/) {
            warn "!!!! $record{name} has illegal alias name characters,
                    skipping...\n";
            next;
        }

        # check for missing address
        if (!$record{address}) {
            warn "!!!! $record{name} does not have an IP address,
                    skipping...\n";
            next;
        }

        # check for duplicate address
        if (defined $addrs{$record{address}}) {
            warn "!!!! Duplicate IP addr: $record{name} &
                    $addrs{$record{address}}, skipping...\n";
            next;
        }
        else {
            $addrs{$record{address}} = $record{name};
        }

    print "$record{address}\t$record{name} $record{aliases}\n";
}
close(DATA);
```

Improving the Host File Output

Let's borrow from Chapter 9, *Log Files*, and add some analysis to the conversion process. We can automatically add useful headers, comments, and separators to the data. Here's an example output using the exact same database:

```
#
# host file - GENERATED BY createhosts3
# DO NOT EDIT BY HAND!
#
# Converted by David N. Blank-Edelman (dnb) on Sun Jun  7 00:43:24 1998
#
```

```
# number of hosts in the design department: 1.
# number of hosts in the software department: 1.
# number of hosts in the IT department: 2.
# total number of hosts: 4
#

# Owned by Cindy Coltrane (IT): west/143
192.168.1.3      bendir ben bendoodles

# Owned by Alex Rollins (IT): main/1101
192.168.1.55     sander sandy micky mickydoo

# Owned by Ellen Monk (design): main/1116
192.168.1.12     sulawesi sula su-lee

# Owned by David Davis (software): main/909
192.168.1.11     shimmer shim shimmy shimmydoodles
```

Here's the code that produced that output, followed by some commentary:

```perl
$datafile ="./database";

# get username on either WinNT/2000 or Unix
$user = ($^O eq "MSWin32")? $ENV{USERNAME} :
                       (getpwuid($<))[6]." (".(getpwuid($<))[0].")";

open(DATA,$datafile) or die "Unable to open datafile:$!\n";

$/=$recordsep; # read in database file one record at a time

while (<DATA>) {
    chomp;                           # remove the record separator
    # split into key1,value1
    @record = split /:\s*|\n/m;

    $record ={};                     # create a reference to empty hash
    %{$record} = @record;            # populate that hash with @record

    # check for bad hostname
    if ($record->{name} =~ /[^-.a-zA-Z0-9]/) {
        warn "!!!! ".$record->{name} .
            " has illegal host name characters, skipping...\n";
        next;
    }

    # check for bad aliases
    if ($record->{aliases} =~ /[^-.a-zA-Z0-9\s]/) {
        warn "!!!! ".$record->{name} .
            " has illegal alias name characters, skipping...\n";
        next;
    }

    # check for missing address
    if (!$record->{address}) {
        warn "!!!! ".$record->{name} .
```

```
                         " does not have an IP address, skipping...\n";
              next;
        }

        # check for duplicate address
        if (defined $addrs{$record->{address}}) {
            warn "!!!! Duplicate IP addr:".$record->{name}.
                  " & ".$addrs{$record->{address}}.", skipping...\n";
            next;
        }
        else {
            $addrs{$record->{address}} = $record->{name};
        }

        $entries{$record->{name}} = $record; # add this to a hash of hashes
}
close(DATA);

# print a nice header
print "#\n\# host file - GENERATED BY $0\n# DO NOT EDIT BY HAND!\n#\n";
print "# Converted by $user on ".scalar(localtime)."\n#\n";

# count the number of entries in each department and then report on it
foreach my $entry (keys %entries){
    $depts{$entries{$entry}->{department}}++;
}
foreach my $dept (keys %depts) {
    print "# number of hosts in the $dept department: $depts{$dept}.\n";
}
print "# total number of hosts: ".scalar(keys %entries)."\n#\n\n";

# iterate through the hosts, printing a nice comment and the entry itself
foreach my $entry (keys %entries) {
    print "# Owned by ",$entries{$entry}->{owner}," (",
            $entries{$entry}->{department},"): ",
            $entries{$entry}->{building},"/",
            $entries{$entry}->{room},"\n";
    print $entries{$entry}->{address},"\t",
            $entries{$entry}->{name}," ",
            $entries{$entry}->{aliases},"\n\n";
}
```

The most significant difference between this code example and the previous one is
the data representation. Because there was no need in the previous example to
retain the information from a record after it had been printed, we could use the
single hash %record. But for this code, we chose to read the file into a slightly
more complex data structure (a hash of hashes) so we could do some simple analysis of the data before printing it.

We could have kept a separate hash table for each field (similar to our *needspace*
example in Chapter 2, *Filesystems*), but the beauty of this approach is its maintain-
ability. If we decide later on to add a **serial_number** field to the database, we do

not need to change our program's parsing code; it will just magically appear as $record->{serial_number}. The downside is that Perl's syntax probably makes our code look more complex than it is.

Here's an easy way to look at it: we're parsing the file in precisely the same way we did in the last example. The difference is this time we are storing each record in a newly-created anonymous hash. Anonymous hashes are just like normal hash variables except they are accessed through a reference, instead of a name.

To create our larger data structure (a hash of hashes), we link this new anonymous hash back into the main hash table %entries. We created a key with an associated value that is the reference to the anonymous hash we've just populated. Once we are done, %entries has a key for each machine's name and a value that is a reference to a hash table containing all of the fields associated with that machine name (IP address, room, etc.).

Perhaps you'd prefer to see the output sorted by IP address? No problem, just include a custom sort routine by changing:

```
foreach my $entry (keys %entries) {
```

to:

```
foreach my $entry (sort byaddress keys %entries) {
```

and adding:

```
sub byaddress {
   @a = split(/\./,$entries{$a}->{address});
   @b = split(/\./,$entries{$b}->{address});
   ($a[0]<=>$b[0]) ||
   ($a[1]<=>$b[1]) ||
   ($a[2]<=>$b[2]) ||
   ($a[3]<=>$b[3]);
}
```

Here's the relevant portion of the output, now nicely sorted:

```
# Owned by Cindy Coltrane (IT): west/143
192.168.1.3     bendir ben bendoodles

# Owned by David Davis (software): main/909
192.168.1.11    shimmer shim shimmy shimmydoodles

# Owned by Ellen Monk (design): main/1116
192.168.1.12    sulawesi sula su-lee

# Owned by Alex Rollins (IT): main/1101
192.168.1.55    sander sandy micky mickydoo
```

Make the output look good to you. Let Perl support your professional *and* aesthetic endeavors.

Incorporating a Source Code Control System

In a moment we're going to move on to the next approach to the IP Address-to-Name mapping problem. Before we do, we'll want to add another twist to our host file creation process, because a single file suddenly takes on network-wide importance. A mistake in this file will affect an entire network of machines. To give us a safety net, we'll want a way to back out of bad changes, essentially going back in time to a prior configuration state.

The most elegant way to build a time machine like this is to add a source control system to the process. Source control systems are typically used by developers to:

*   Keep a record of all changes to important files

*   Prevent multiple people from changing the same file at the same time, inadvertently undoing each other's efforts

*   Allow them to revert back to a previous version of a file, thus backing out of problems

This functionality is extremely useful to a system administrator. The error-checking code we added to the conversion process earlier, in "Error Checking the Host File Generation Process," can help with certain kinds of typo and syntax errors, but it does not offer any protection against semantic errors (e.g., deleting an important hostname, assigning the wrong IP address to a host, misspelling a hostname). You could add semantic error checks into the conversion process, but you probably won't catch all of the possible errors. As we've quoted before, nothing is foolproof, since fools are so ingenious.

You might think it would be better to apply source control system functionality to the initial database editing process, but there are two good reasons why it is also important to apply it to the resultant output:

Time

>   For large data sets, the conversion process might take some time. If your network is flaking out and you need to revert to a previous revision, it's discouraging to have to stare at a Perl process chugging away to generate the file you need (presuming you can get at Perl in the first place at that point).

Database

>   If you choose to use a real database engine for your data storage (and often this is the right choice), there may not be a convenient way to apply a source control mechanism like this. You'll probably have to write your own change control mechanisms for the database editing process.

My source control system of choice is the Revision Control System (RCS). RCS has some Perl- and system administration-friendly features:

- It is multiplatform. There are ports of GNU RCS 5.7 to most Unix systems, Windows NT, MacOS, etc.

- It has a well-defined command-line interface. All functions can be performed from the command line, even on GUI-heavy operating systems

- It is easy to use. There's a small command set for basic operations that can be learned in five minutes (see Appendix A, *The Five-Minute RCS Tutorial*).

- It has keywords. Magic strings can be embedded in the text of files under RCS that are automatically expanded. For instance, any occurrence of `$Date:$` in a file will be replaced with the date the file was last entered into the RCS system.

- It's free. The source code for the GNU version of RCS is freely redistributable, and binaries for most systems are also available. A copy of the source can be found at *ftp://ftp.gnu.org/gnu/rcs*.

If you've never dealt with RCS before, please take a moment to read Appendix A. The rest of this section assumes a cursory knowledge of the RCS command set.

Craig Freter has written an object-oriented module called `Rcs` which makes using RCS from Perl easy. The steps are:

1. Load the module.

2. Tell the module where your RCS command-line binaries are located.

3. Create a new `Rcs` object; configure it with the name of the file you are using.

4. Call the necessary object methods (named after their corresponding RCS commands).

Let's add this to our host file generation code so you can see how the module works. Besides the `Rcs` module code, we've also changed things so the output is sent to a specific file and not **STDOUT** as in our previous versions. Only the code that has changed is shown. Refer to the previous example for the omitted lines represented by "...":

```
$outputfile="hosts.$$"; # temporary output file
$target="hosts";         # where we want the converted data stored
...
open(OUTPUT,"> $outputfile") or
  die "Unable to write to $outputfile:$!\n";

print OUTPUT "#\n\# host file - GENERATED BY $0\n
              # DO NOT EDIT BY HAND!\n#\n";
print OUTPUT "# Converted by $user on ".scalar(localtime)."\n#\n";

...
foreach my $dept (keys %depts) {
    print OUTPUT "# number of hosts in the $dept department:
                  $depts{$dept}.\n";
}
```

```
print OUTPUT "# total number of hosts: ".scalar(keys %entries)."\n#\n\n";
# iterate through the hosts, printing a nice comment and the entry
foreach my $entry (sort byaddress keys %entries) {
    print OUTPUT
            "# Owned by ",$entries{$entry}->{owner}," (",
            $entries{$entry}->{department},"): ",
            $entries{$entry}->{building},"/",
            $entries{$entry}->{room},"\n";
    print OUTPUT
            $entries{$entry}->{address},"\t",
            $entries{$entry}->{name}," ",
            $entries{$entry}->{aliases},"\n\n";
}

close(OUTPUT);
```

```
    use Rcs;
    # where our RCS binaries are stored
    Rcs->bindir('/usr/local/bin');
    # create a new RCS object
    my $rcsobj = Rcs->new;
    # configure it with the name of our target file
    $rcsobj->file($target);
    # check it out of RCS (must be checked in already)
    $rcsobj->co('-l');
    # rename our newly created file into place
    rename($outputfile,$target) or
        die "Unable to rename $outputfile to $target:$!\n";
    # check it in
    $rcsobj->ci("-u","-m"."Converted by $user on ".scalar(localtime));
```

This code assumes the target file has been checked in at least once already.

To see the effect of this code addition, we can look at three entries excerpted from the output of *rlog hosts*:

```
revision 1.5
date: 1998/05/19 23:34:16;  author: dnb;  state: Exp;  lines: +1 -1
Converted by David N. Blank-Edelman (dnb) on Tue May 19 19:34:16 1998
----------------------------
revision 1.4
date: 1998/05/19 23:34:05;  author: eviltwin;  state: Exp;  lines: +1 -1
Converted by Divad Knalb-Namlede (eviltwin) on Tue May 19 19:34:05 1998
----------------------------
revision 1.3
date: 1998/05/19 23:33:35;  author: dnb;  state: Exp;  lines: +20 -0
Converted by David N. Blank-Edelman (dnb) on Tue May 19 19:33:16 1998
```

The previous example doesn't show much of a difference between file versions (see the `lines:` part of the entries), but you can see that we are tracking the changes every time the file gets created. If we needed to, we could use the *rcsdiff* command to see exactly what changed. Under dire circumstances, we would be able to revert to previous versions if one of these changes had wreaked unexpected havoc on the network.

NIS, NIS+, and WINS

Developers at Sun Microsystems realized that the "edit one file per machine" approach endemic to host files didn't scale, so they invented something called *Yellow Pages* (YP). Yellow Pages was designed to distribute all the network-wide configuration file information found in files like */etc/hosts, /etc/passwd, /etc/services,* etc. In this chapter, we'll concentrate on its use as a network name service to distribute the machine name-to-IP address mapping information.

YP was renamed *Network Information Service,* or NIS, in 1990, shortly after British Telecom asserted (with lawyers) that it held the trademark for "Yellow Pages" in the U.K. The ghost of the name "Yellow Pages" still haunts many a Unix box today in the names used for NIS commands and library calls (e.g., *ypcat, ypmatch, yppush*). All modern Unix variants support NIS. NT machines can be made to use NIS for authentication through the use of special home-brewed authentication libraries,* but I know of no NT-based NIS servers. I do not know of any Mac ports of NIS.

In NIS, an administrator designates one or more machines as servers from which other machines will receive client services. One server is the *master* server, the others *slave* servers. The master server holds the master copies of the actual text files (e.g., */etc/hosts* or */etc/passwd*) all machines normally use. Changes to these files take place on the master and are then propagated to the slave servers.

Any machine on the network that needs hostname-to-IP address mapping information can query a server instead of keeping a local copy of the information. A client can request this information from either the master or any of the slave servers. Client queries are looked up in the *NIS maps,* another name for the master's data files after they've been converted to the Unix DBM database format and propagated to the slave servers. The details of this conversion process (which involves *makedbm* and some other random munging) can be found in the *Makefile* located in */var/yp* on most machines. A collection of NIS servers and clients that share the same maps is called an *NIS domain.*

With NIS, network administration becomes considerably easier. For instance, if *oog.org* purchases more machines for their network, it is no problem to integrate them into the network. The network manager simply edits the host file on the

---

* One such library is NISGINA, which was originally developed by Nigel Williams; this library can be found at *http://www.dcs.qmw.ac.uk/~williams/.* Be sure to check the mailing list archives found off that page for information on the latest versions of this software.

master NIS server and pushes the new version out to the slave servers. Every client in the NIS domain now "knows" about the new machine. NIS offers one-touch administration ease coupled with some redundancy (if one server goes down, a client can ask another) and load sharing (not all of the clients in a network have to rely on a single server).

With this theory in mind, let's see how Perl can help us with NIS-related tasks. We can start with the process of getting data into NIS. You may be surprised to know that we've already done the work for this task. The host files we created in the previous section can be imported into NIS by just dropping them into place in the NIS master server's source file directory, and activating the usual push mechanisms (usually by typing *make* in */var/yp*). By default, the *Makefile* in */var/yp* uses the contents of the master server's configuration files as the source for the NIS maps.

It is usually a good idea to set up a separate directory for your NIS map source files, changing the *Makefile* accordingly. This allows you to keep separate data for your NIS master server and other members of your NIS domain. For example, you might not want to have the */etc/passwd* file for your NIS master as the password map for the entire domain, and vice versa.

A more interesting task is getting data out of NIS by querying an NIS server. The easiest way to do this is via Rik Harris' **Net::NIS** module. This particular module has been in alpha release state since 1995, but it is still quite functional.[*]

Here's an example of how to grab and print the entire contents of the host map with a single function call using **Net::NIS**, similar to the NIS command *ypcat*:

```
use Net::NIS;
# get our default NIS domain name
$domain = Net::NIS::yp_get_default_domain();
# grab the map
($status, $info) = Net::NIS::yp_all($domain, "hosts.byname");
foreach my $name (sort keys %{$info}){
    print "$name => $info->{$name}\n";
}
```

First we query the local host for its default domain name. With this info, we can call **Net::NIS::yp_all()** to retrieve the entire hosts map. The function call returns a status variable (bogus, as mentioned in the footnote) and a reference to a

---

[*] There's only one true bug in the a2 version that I know of. The documentation suggests you compare the return status of this module's calls against a set of predefined constants like $Net::NIS::ERR_KEY and $Net::NIS::ERR_MAP. Unfortunately, the module never actually defines these constants. The simplest way to test for a successful query is to examine the returned data's length.

hash table containing the contents of that map. We print this information using Perl's usual dereference syntax.

If we want to look up the IP address of a single host, it is more efficient to query the server specifically for that value:

```
use Net::NIS;
$hostname = "olaf.oog.org";
$domain = Net::NIS::yp_get_default_domain();
($status,$info) = Net::NIS::yp_match($domain,"hosts.byname",$hostname);
print $info,"\n";
```

`Net::NIS::yp_match()` returns another bogus status variable and the appropriate value (as a scalar) for the info being queried.

If the `Net::NIS` module does not compile or work for you, there's always the "call an external program method." For example:

```
@hosts='<path to>/ypcat hosts'
```

or:

```
open(YPCAT,"<path to>/ypcat hosts|");
while (<YPCAT>){...}
```

Let's wind up this section with a useful example of both this technique and `Net::NIS` in action. This small but handy piece of code will query NIS for the list of NIS servers currently running and query each one of them in turn using the *yppoll* program. If any of the servers fails to respond properly, it complains loudly:

```
use Net::NIS;

$yppollex = "/usr/etc/yp/yppoll"; # full path to the yppoll executable

$domain = Net::NIS::yp_get_default_domain();

($status,$info) = Net::NIS::yp_all($domain,"ypservers");

foreach my $name (sort keys %{$info}) {
    $answer = '$yppollex -h $name hosts.byname';
    if ($answer !~ /has order number/) {
        warn "$name is not responding properly!\n";
    }
}
```

NIS+

Sun included the next version of NIS, called NIS+, with the Solaris operating system. NIS+ addresses many of the most serious problems of NIS, such as security. Unfortunately (or fortunately, since NIS+ can be a bit difficult to administer), NIS+

has not caught on in the Unix world nearly as well NIS did. Until recently, there was virtually no support for it on machines not manufactured by Sun. It is slowly making its way into standard Linux distributions thanks to the work of Thorsten Kukuk (see *http://www.suse.de/~kukuk/nisplus/index.html*), but it is far from prevalent in the Unix world and nonexistent in the NT and MacOS world.

Given its marginal status, we're not going to look any deeper into NIS+ in this book. If you need to work with NIS+ from Perl, Harris also has a `Net::NISPlus` module up to the task.

Windows Internet Name Server (WINS)

When Microsoft began to run its proprietary networking protocol NetBIOS over TCP/IP (NetBT), it also found a need to handle the name-to-IP address mapping question. The first shot was the *lmhosts* file, modeled after the standard host file. This was quickly supplemented with an NIS-like mechanism. As of NT Version 3.5, Microsoft has offered a centralized scheme called Windows Internet Name Server (WINS). WINS differs in several ways from NIS:

* WINS is specialized for the distribution of host-to-IP address mappings. It is not used like NIS to centralize distribution of other information (e.g., password, network, port mappings, and user groups).

* WINS servers receive most of the information they distribute from preconfigured client registrations (they can be pre-loaded with information). WINS clients, once they receive an IP address either manually or via Dynamic Host Configuration Protocol (DHCP), are responsible for registering and re-registering their information. This is different from NIS, in that client machines ask the server for information that has been pre-loaded, and with only one exception (passwords), do not update the information on that server.

WINS, like NIS, offers the ability to have multiple servers available for reliability and load sharing through the use of a push-pull partner model. As of Windows 2000, WINS is deprecated (read "killed off") in favor of Dynamic Domain Name Service, an extension to the basic DNS system we're just about to discuss.

Given that WINS is not long for this earth, we're not going to explore Perl code to work with it. There is currently very little support for working directly with WINS from Perl. I know of no Perl modules designed specifically to interact with WINS. Your best bet may be to call some of the command-line utilities found in the Windows NT Server Resource Kit, such as *WINSCHK* and *WINSCL*.

Domain Name Service (DNS)

As useful as they are, NIS and WINS still suffer from flaws that make them unsuit-
able for "entire-Internet" uses.

Scale

>   Even though these schemes allow for multiple servers, each server must have
>   a complete copy of the entire network topology.* This topology must be
>   duplicated to every other server, a time-consuming process if the universe
>   becomes sufficiently large. WINS also suffers because of its dynamic registra-
>   tion model. A sufficient number of WINS clients could melt down any set of
>   Internet-wide WINS servers with registration requests.

Administrative control

>   We've been talking about strictly technical issues up until now, but that's not
>   the only side of administration. NIS, in particular, requires a single point of
>   administration. Whomever controls the master server controls the entire NIS
>   domain lead by that machine. Any changes to the network namespace must
>   pass through that administrative gatekeeper. This doesn't work for a
>   namespace the size of the Internet.

A new model called Domain Name Service (DNS) was invented to deal with the
flaws inherent in maintaining host files or NIS/NIS+/WINS-like systems. Under
DNS, the network namespace is partitioned into a set of somewhat arbitrary "top-
level domains." Each top-level domain can then be subdivided into smaller
domains, each of those partitioned, and so on. At each dividing point it is possible to designate a different party to retain authoritative control over that portion of
the namespace. This handles our administrative control concern.

Network clients that reside in the individual parts of this hierarchy consult the
name server closest to them in the hierarchy. If the information the client is looking for can be found on that local server, it is returned to the client. On most networks, the majority of name-to-IP address queries are for machines on that
network, so the local servers handle most of the local traffic. This satisfies the scale
problem. Multiple DNS servers (also known as secondary or slave servers) can be
set up for redundancy and load-balancing purposes.

If a DNS server is asked about a part of the namespace that it does not control or
know about, it can either instruct the client to look elsewhere (usually higher up
in the tree) or fetch the required information on behalf of the client by contacting
other DNS servers.

---

* NIS+ offers mechanisms for a client to search for information outside of the local domain, but they are
  not as flexible as those in DNS.

In this scheme, no single server needs to know the entire network topology, most queries are handled locally, local administrators retain local control, and everybody is happy. DNS offers such an advantage compared to other systems that most other systems like NIS and WINS offer a way to integrate DNS. For instance, SunOS NIS servers can be instructed to perform a DNS query if a client asks them for a host they do not know. The results of this query are returned as a standard NIS query reply so the client has no knowledge that any magic has been performed on its behalf. Microsoft DNS servers have similar functionality: if a client asks a Microsoft DNS server for the address of a local machine that it does not know about, the server can be configured to consult a WINS server on the client's behalf.

Generating DNS Configuration Files

Production of DNS configuration files follows the same procedure that we've been using to generate host and NIS source files, namely:

- Store data in a separate database (the same database can and probably should be the source for all of the files we've been discussing).

- Convert data to the output format of our choice, checking for errors as we go.

- Use RCS (or an equivalent source control system) to store old revisions of files.

For DNS, we have to expand the second step because the conversion process is more complicated. As we launch into these complications, you may find it handy to have the *DNS and BIND* book by Paul Albitz and Cricket Liu (O'Reilly) on hand for information on the DNS configuration files we'll be creating.

Creating the administrative header

DNS configuration files begin with an administrative header that provides information about the server and the data it is serving. The most important part of this header is the Start of Authority (SOA) resource record. The SOA contains:

- The name of the administrative domain served by this DNS server

- The name of the primary DNS server for that domain

- Contact info for the DNS administrator(s)

- The serial number of the configuration file (more on this in a moment)

- Refresh and retry values for secondary servers (i.e., when they synchronize with the primary server)

- Time To Live (TTL) settings for the data being served (i.e., how long the information being provided can be safely cached)

Here's an example header:

```
@ IN SOA    dns.oog.org. hostmaster.oog.org. (
                        1998052900 ; serial
                        10800      ; refresh
                        3600       ; retry
                        604800     ; expire
                        43200)     ; TTL


@                               IN  NS  dns.oog.org.
```

Most of this information is just tacked on the front of a DNS configuration file verbatim each time it is generated. The one piece we need to worry about is the serial number. Once every *X* seconds (where *X* is determined by the refresh value from above), secondary name servers contact their primary servers looking for an update to their DNS data. Modern DNS secondary servers (like BIND v8+ or Microsoft DNS) can also be told by their master server to check for an update when the master data has changed. In both cases, the secondary servers query the primary server for its SOA record. If the SOA record contains a serial number higher than their current serial number, a zone transfer is initiated (that is, the secondary downloads a new data set). As a result, it is important to increment this number each time a new DNS configuration file is created. Many DNS problems are caused by failures to update the serial number.

There are at least two ways to make sure the serial number is always incremented:

1. Read the previous configuration file and increment the value found there.

2. Compute a new value based on an external number source "guaranteed" to increment over time (like the system clock or RCS version number of the file).

Here's some example code that uses a combination of these two methods to generate a valid header for a DNS zone file. It creates a serial number formatted as recommended in Albitz and Liu's book (YYYYMMDDXX where Y=year, M=month, D=day, and XX=a two-digit counter to allow for more than one change per day):

```perl
# get today's date in the form of YYYYMMDD
@localtime = localtime;
$today = sprintf("%04d%02d%02d",$localtime[5]+1900,
                                $localtime[4]+1,
                                $localtime[3]);

# get username on either NT/2000 or Unix
$user = ($^O eq "MSWin32")? $ENV{USERNAME} :
                        (getpwuid($<))[6]." (".(getpwuid($<))[0].")";

sub GenerateHeader{
    my($header);

    # open old file if possible and read in serial number
    # assumes the format of the old file
```

```
     if (open (OLDZONE,$target)){
         while (<OLDZONE>) {
             next unless (/(\d{8}).*serial/);
             $oldserial = $1;
             last;
         }
         close (OLDZONE);
     }
     else {
         $oldserial = "000000"; # otherwise, start with a 0 number
     }

     # if old serial number was for today, increment last 2 digits, else
     # start a new number for today
     $olddate = substr($oldserial,0,6);
     $count = (($olddate == $today) ? substr($oldserial,6,2)+1 : 0);

     $serial = sprintf("%6d%02d",$today,$count);

     # begin the header
     $header .= "; dns zone file - GENERATED BY $0\n";
     $header .= "; DO NOT EDIT BY HAND!\n;\n";
     $header .= "; Converted by $user on ".scalar((localtime))."\n;\n";

     # count the number of entries in each department and then report
     foreach my $entry (keys %entries){
         $depts{$entries{$entry}->{department}}++;
     }
     foreach my $dept (keys %depts) {
         $header .= "; number of hosts in the $dept department:
                     $depts{$dept}.\n";
     }
     $header .= "; total number of hosts: ".scalar(keys %entries)."\n;\n\n";

     $header .= <<"EOH";

@ IN SOA   dns.oog.org. hostmaster.oog.org. (
                          $serial ; serial
                          10800     ; refresh
                          3600      ; retry
                          604800    ; expire
                          43200)    ; TTL

@                         IN  NS  dns.oog.org.

EOH

     return $header;
}
```

Our code attempts to read in the previous DNS configuration file to determine the last serial number in use. This number then gets split into date and counter fields. If the date we've read is the same as the current date, we need to increment the counter. If not, we create a serial number based on the current date with a counter value of 00. Once we have our serial number, the rest of the code concerns itself with writing out a pretty header in the proper form.

Generating multiple configuration files

Now that we've covered the process of writing a correct header for our DNS configuration files, there is one more complication we need to address. A well-configured DNS server has both forward (name-to-IP address) and reverse (IP address-to-name) mapping information available for every domain, or zone, it controls. This requires two configuration files per zone. The best way to keep these synchronized is to create them both at the same time.

This is the last file generation script we'll see in this chapter, so let's put everything we've done so far together. Our script will take a simple database file and generate the necessary DNS zone configuration files.

To keep this script simple, I've made a few assumptions about the data, the most important of which has to do with the topology of the network and namespace. This script assumes that the network consists of a single class C subnet with a single DNS zone. As a result, we only create a single forward mapping file and its reverse map sibling file. Adding code to handle multiple subnets and zones (i.e., creating separate files for each) would be an easy addition.

Here's a quick walk-through:

1. Read in the database file into a hash of hashes, checking the data as we go.

2. Generate a header.

3. Write out the forward mapping (name-to-IP address) file and check it into RCS.

4. Write out the reverse mapping (IP address-to-name) file and check it into RCS.

Here is the code and its output:

```
use Rcs;

$datafile    = "./database";  # our host database
$outputfile  = "zone.$$";     # our temporary output file
$target      = "zone.db";     # our target output
$revtarget   = "rev.db";      # out target output for the reverse mapping
$defzone     = ".oog.org";    # the default zone being created
$recordsep   = "-=-\n";

# get today's date in the form of YYYYMMDD
@localtime = localtime;
$today = sprintf("%04d%02d%02d",$localtime[5]+1900,
                                $localtime[4]+1,
                                $localtime[3]);
```

```perl
# get username on either NT/2000 or Unix
$user = ($^O eq "MSWin32")? $ENV{USERNAME} :
                      (getpwuid($<))[6]." (".(getpwuid($<))[0].")";

# read in the database file
open(DATA,$datafile) or die "Unable to open datafile:$!\n";

while (<DATA>) {
    chomp; # remove record separator
    # split into key1,value1
    @record = split /:\s*|\n/m;

    $record ={};                    # create a reference to empty hash
    %{$record} = @record;           # populate that hash with @record

    # check for bad hostname
    if ($record->{name} =~ /[^-.a-zA-Z0-9]/) {
        warn "!!!! ",$record->{name} .
         " has illegal host name characters, skipping...\n";
        next;
    }

    # check for bad aliases
    if ($record->{aliases} =~ /[^-.a-zA-Z0-9\s]/) {
        warn "!!!! " . $record->{name} .
            " has illegal alias name characters, skipping...\n";
        next;
    }

    # check for missing address
    unless ($record->{address}) {
        warn "!!!! " . $record->{name} .
            " does not have an IP address, skipping...\n";
        next;
    }

    # check for duplicate address
    if (defined $addrs{$record->{address}}) {
        warn "!!!! Duplicate IP addr:" . $record->{name}.
            " & " . $addrs{$record->{address}} . ", skipping...\n";
        next;
    }
    else {
        $addrs{$record->{address}} = $record->{name};
    }

    $entries{$record->{name}} = $record; # add this to a hash of hashes

}
close(DATA);

$header = &GenerateHeader;

# create the forward mapping file
```

```perl
open(OUTPUT,"> $outputfile") or
  die "Unable to write to $outputfile:$!\n";
print OUTPUT $header;

foreach my $entry (sort byaddress keys %entries) {
    print OUTPUT
          "; Owned by ",$entries{$_}->{owner}," (",
          $entries{$entry}->{department},"): ",
          $entries{$entry}->{building},"/",
          $entries{$entry}->{room},"\n";

    # print A record
    printf OUTPUT "%-20s\tIN A     %s\n",
      $entries{$entry}->{name},$entries{$entry}->{address};

    # print any CNAMES (aliases)
    if (defined $entries{$entry}->{aliases}){
        foreach my $alias (split(' ',$entries{$entry}->{aliases})) {
            printf OUTPUT "%-20s\tIN CNAME %s\n",$alias,
                                              $entries{$entry}->{name};
        }
    }
    print OUTPUT "\n";
}

close(OUTPUT);

Rcs->bindir('/usr/local/bin');
my $rcsobj = Rcs->new;
$rcsobj->file($target);
$rcsobj->co('-l');
rename($outputfile,$target) or
  die "Unable to rename $outputfile to $target:$!\n";
$rcsobj->ci("-u","-m"."Converted by $user on ".scalar(localtime));

# now create the reverse mapping file
open(OUTPUT,"> $outputfile") or
  die "Unable to write to $outputfile:$!\n";
print OUTPUT $header;
foreach my $entry (sort byaddress keys %entries) {
    print OUTPUT
          "; Owned by ",$entries{$entry}->{owner}," (",
          $entries{$entry}->{department},"): ",
          $entries{$entry}->{building},"/",
          $entries{$entry}->{room},"\n";

    printf OUTPUT "%-3d\tIN PTR     %s$defzone.\n\n",
      (split/\./,$entries{$entry}->{address})[3],
      $entries{$entry}->{name};

}

close(OUTPUT);
$rcsobj->file($revtarget);
```

```
$rcsobj->co('-l'); # assumes target has been checked out at least once
rename($outputfile,$revtarget) or
    die "Unable to rename $outputfile to $revtarget:$!\n";
$rcsobj->ci("-u","-m"."Converted by $user on ".scalar(localtime));

sub GenerateHeader{
    my($header);
    if (open(OLDZONE,$target)){
        while (<OLDZONE>) {
            next unless (/(\d{8}).*serial/);
            $oldserial = $1;
            last;
        }
        close(OLDZONE);
    }
    else {
        $oldserial = "000000";
    }

    $olddate = substr($oldserial,0,6);
    $count = ($olddate == $today) ? substr($oldserial,6,2)+1 : 0;

    $serial = sprintf("%6d%02d",$today,$count);

    $header .= "; dns zone file - GENERATED BY $0\n";
    $header .= "; DO NOT EDIT BY HAND!\n;\n";
    $header .= "; Converted by $user on ".scalar(localtime)."\n;\n";

    # count the number of entries in each department and then report
    foreach $entry (keys %entries){
        $depts{$entries{$entry}->{department}}++;
    }
    foreach $dept (keys %depts) {
        $header .= "; number of hosts in the $dept department:
                    $depts{$dept}.\n";
    }
    $header .= "; total number of hosts: ".scalar(keys %entries)."\n#\n\n";

    $header .= <<"EOH";

@ IN SOA    dns.oog.org. hostmaster.oog.org. (
                        $serial     ; serial
                        10800       ; refresh
                        3600        ; retry
                        604800      ; expire
                        43200)      ; TTL

@                       IN  NS  dns.oog.org.

EOH

    return $header;
}
```

```
sub byaddress {
   @a = split(/\./,$entries{$a}->{address});
   @b = split(/\./,$entries{$b}->{address});
   ($a[0]<=>$b[0]) ||
   ($a[1]<=>$b[1]) ||
   ($a[2]<=>$b[2]) ||
   ($a[3]<=>$b[3]);
}
```

Here's the forward mapping file (*zone.db*) that gets created:

```
; dns zone file - GENERATED BY createdns
; DO NOT EDIT BY HAND!
;
; Converted by David N. Blank-Edelman (dnb); on Fri May 29 15:46:46 1998
;
; number of hosts in the design department: 1.
; number of hosts in the software department: 1.
; number of hosts in the IT department: 2.
; total number of hosts: 4
;

@ IN SOA   dns.oog.org. hostmaster.oog.org. (
                        1998052900 ; serial
                        10800      ; refresh
                        3600       ; retry
                        604800     ; expire
                        43200)     ; TTL


@                          IN  NS  dns.oog.org.

; Owned by Cindy Coltrane (marketing): west/143
bendir              IN A     192.168.1.3
ben                 IN CNAME bendir
bendoodles          IN CNAME bendir

; Owned by David Davis (software): main/909
shimmer             IN A     192.168.1.11
shim                IN CNAME shimmer
shimmy              IN CNAME shimmer
shimmydoodles       IN CNAME shimmer

; Owned by Ellen Monk (design): main/1116
sulawesi            IN A     192.168.1.12
sula                IN CNAME sulawesi
su-lee              IN CNAME sulawesi

; Owned by Alex Rollins (IT): main/1101
sander              IN A     192.168.1.55
sandy               IN CNAME sander
micky               IN CNAME sander
mickydoo            IN CNAME sander
```

And here's the reverse mapping file (*rev.db*):

```
; dns zone file - GENERATED BY createdns
; DO NOT EDIT BY HAND!
;
; Converted by David N. Blank-Edelman (dnb); on Fri May 29 15:46:46 1998
;
; number of hosts in the design department: 1.
; number of hosts in the software department: 1.
; number of hosts in the IT department: 2.
; total number of hosts: 4
;

@ IN SOA   dns.oog.org. hostmaster.oog.org. (
                        1998052900 ; serial
                          10800    ; refresh
                          3600     ; retry
                          604800   ; expire
                          43200)   ; TTL

@                                IN  NS  dns.oog.org.

; Owned by Cindy Coltrane (marketing): west/143
3    IN PTR    bendir.oog.org.

; Owned by David Davis (software): main/909
11   IN PTR    shimmer.oog.org.

; Owned by Ellen Monk (design): main/1116
12   IN PTR    sulawesi.oog.org.

; Owned by Alex Rollins (IT): main/1101
55   IN PTR    sander.oog.org.
```

This method of creating files opens up many more possibilities. Up to now, we've generated files using content from a single text file database. We read a record from the database and we write it out to our file, perhaps with a dash of nice formatting. Only data that appeared in the database found its way into the files we created.

Sometimes it is useful to have content added in the conversion process by the script itself. For instance, in the case of DNS configuration files generation, you may wish to embellish the conversion script so it inserts MX (Mail eXchange) records pointing to a central mail server for every host in your database. A trivial code change from:

```
# print A record
   printf OUTPUT "%-20s\tIN A     %s\n",
     $entries{$entry}->{name},$entries{$entry}->{address};
```

to:

```
# print A record
printf OUTPUT "%-20s\tIN A     %s\n",
     $entries{$entry}->{name},$entries{$entry}->{address};
```

```
# print MX record
print OUTPUT "                    IN MX 10 $mailserver\n";
```

will configure DNS so that mail destined for any host in the domain is received by the machine $mailserver instead. If that machine is configured to handle mail for its domain, we've activated a really useful infrastructure component (i.e., centralized mail handling) with just a single line of Perl code.

DNS Checking: An Iterative Approach

We've spent considerable time in this chapter on the creation of the configuration information to be served by network name services, but that's only one side of the coin for system and network administrators. Keeping a network healthy also entails checking these services once they're up and running to make sure they are behaving in a correct and consistent manner.

For instance, for a system/network administrator, a great deal rides on the question "Are all of my DNS servers up?" In a troubleshooting situation, it's equally valuable to know "Are they all serving the same information?", or, more specifically, "Are the servers responding to the same queries with the same responses? Are they in sync as intended?" We'll put these questions to good use in this section.

In Chapter 2 we saw an example of the Perl motto "There's More Than One Way To Do It." Perl's TMTOWTDI-ness makes the language an excellent prototype language in which to do "iterative development." Iterative development is one way of describing the evolutionary process that takes place when writing system administration (and other) programs to handle a particular task. With Perl it's all too possible to bang out a quick-and-dirty hack that gets a job done. Later on, you may return to this script and re-write it so it is more elegant. There's even likely to be yet a third iteration of the same code, this time taking a different approach to solving the problem.

Here are three different approaches to the same problem of DNS consistency checking. These approaches will be presented in the order someone might realistically follow while trying to solve the problem and refine the solution. This ordering reflects one view on how a solution to a problem can evolve in Perl; your take on this may differ. The third approach, using the Net::DNS module, is probably the easiest and most error-proof of the bunch. But Net::DNS may not address every situation, so we're going to walk through some "roll your own" approaches first. Be sure to note the pros and cons listed after each solution has been presented.

Here's the task: write a Perl script that takes a hostname and checks a list of DNS servers to see if they all return the same information when queried about this host. To make this task simpler, we're going to assume that the host has a single, static IP address (i.e., does not have multiple interfaces or addresses associated with it).

Before we look at each approach in turn, let me show you the "driver" code we're going to use:

```
$hostname = $ARGV[0];
@servers = qw(nameserver1 nameserver2 nameserver3); # name servers

foreach $server (@servers) {
    &lookupaddress($hostname,$server);              # populates %results
}
%inv = reverse %results;                            # invert the result hash
if (keys %inv > 1) {
    print "There is a discrepancy between DNS servers:\n";
    use Data::Dumper;
    print Data::Dumper->Dump([\%results],["results"]),"\n";
}
```

For each of the DNS servers listed in the **@servers** list, we call the **&lookupaddress()** subroutine. **&lookupaddress()** queries a specific DNS server for the IP address of a given hostname and places the results into a hash called **%results**. Each DNS server has a key in **%results** with the IP address returned by that server as its value.

There are many ways to determine if all of the values in **%results** are the same (i.e., all DNS servers returned the same thing in response to our query). Here we choose to invert **%results** into another hash table, making all of the keys into values, and vice versa. If all values in **%results** are the same, there should be exactly one key in the inverted hash. If not, we know we've got a situation on our hands, so we call **Data::Dumper->Dump()** to nicely display the contents of **%results** for the system administrator to puzzle over.

Here's a sample of what the output looks like when something goes wrong:

```
There is a discrepancy between DNS servers:
$results = {
            nameserver1 => '192.168.1.2',
            nameserver2 => '192.168.1.5',
            nameserver3 => '192.168.1.2',
          };
```

Let's take a look at the contestants for the **&lookupaddress()** subroutines.

Using nslookup

If your background is in Unix, or you've done some programming in other scripting languages besides Perl, your first attempt might look a great deal like a shell script. An external program called from the Perl script does the hard work in the following code:

```
use Data::Dumper;

$hostname = $ARGV[0];
```

```
$nslookup = "/usr/local/bin/nslookup";              # nslookup binary
@servers = qw(nameserver1 nameserver2 nameserver3); # name of the name servers
foreach $server (@servers) {
    &lookupaddress($hostname,$server);              # populates %results
}
%inv = reverse %results;                            # invert the result hash
if (scalar(keys %inv) > 1) {
    print "There is a discrepancy between DNS servers:\n";
    print Data::Dumper->Dump([\%results],["results"]),"\n";
}


# ask the server to look up the IP address for the host
# passed into this program on the command line, add info to
# the %results hash
sub lookupaddress {
    my($hostname,$server) = @_;

    open(NSLOOK,"$nslookup $hostname $server|") or
      die "Unable to start nslookup:$!\n";

    while (<NSLOOK>) {
        # ignore until we hit "Name: "
        next until (/^Name:/);
        # next line is Address: response
        chomp($results{$server} = <NSLOOK>);
        # remove the field name
        die "nslookup output error\n" unless /Address/;
        $results{$server} =~ s/Address(es)?:\s+//;
        # we're done with this nslookup
        last;
    }
    close(NSLOOK);
}
```

The benefits of this approach are:

- It's a short, quick program to write (perhaps even translated line by line from a real shell script).

- We did not have to write any messy network code.

- It takes the Unix approach of using a general purpose language to glue together other smaller, specialized programs to get a job done, rather than creating a single monolithic program.

- It may be the only approach for times when you can't code the client-server communication in Perl; for instance, you have to talk with a server that requires a special client and there's no alternative.

The drawbacks of this approach are:

- It's dependent on another program outside the script. What if this program is not available? What if this program's output format changes?

- It's slower. It has to start up another process each time it wants to make a query. We could have reduced this overhead by opening a two-way pipe to an *nslookup* process that stays running while we need it. This would take a little more coding skill, but would be the right thing to do if we were going to continue down this path and further enhance this code.

- You have less control. We are at the external program's mercy for implementation details. For instance, here *nslookup* (more specifically the resolver library *nslookup* is using) is handling server timeouts, query retries, and appending a domain search list for us.

Working with raw network sockets

If you are a "power sysadmin," you may decide calling another program is not acceptable. You might want to implement the DNS queries using nothing but Perl. This entails constructing network packets by hand, shipping them out on the wire, and then parsing the results returned from the server.

This is probably the most complicated code you'll find in this entire book, written by looking at the reference sources described below along with several examples of existing networking code (including the module by Michael Fuhr we'll see in the next section). Here is a rough overview of what is going on. Querying a DNS server consists of constructing a specific network packet header and packet contents, sending it to a DNS server, and then receiving and parsing the response from that server.*

Each and every DNS packet (of the sort we are interested in) can have up to five distinct sections:

Header
> Contains flags and counters pertaining to the query or answer (always present).

Question
> Contains the question being asked of the server (present for a query and echoed in a response).

Answer
> Contains all the data for the answer to a DNS query (present in a DNS response packet).

Authority
> Contains information on where an authoritative response may be retrieved.

Additional
> Contains any information the server wishes to return in addition to the direct answer to a query.

---

* For the nitty-gritty details, I highly recommend you open RFC1035 to the section entitled "Messages" and read along.

Our program will concern itself strictly with the first three of these. We'll be using a set of **pack()** commands to create the necessary data structure for a DNS packet header and packet contents. We pass this data structure to the IO::Socket module that handles sending this data out as a packet. The same module will also listen for a response on our behalf and return data for us to parse (using **unpack()**). Conceptually, this process is not very difficult.

There's one twist to this process that should be noted before we look at the code. RFC1035 (Section 4.1.4) defines two ways of representing domain names in DNS packets: uncompressed and compressed. The uncompressed representation places the full domain name (for example, *host.oog.org*) in the packet, and is nothing special. But, if the same domain name is found more than once in a packet, it is likely a compressed representation will be used for everything but the first mention. A compressed representation replaces the domain information or part of it with a two-byte pointer back to the first uncompressed representation. This allows a packet to mention *host1*, *host2*, and *host3* in *longsubdomain.longsubdomain.oog.org*, without having to include the bytes for *longsubdomain.longsubdomain.oog.org* each time. We have to handle both representations in our code, hence the &decompress routine below. Without further fanfare, here's the code:

```
use IO::Socket;
$hostname = $ARGV[0];
$defdomain = ".oog.org"; # default domain if not present

@servers = qw(nameserver1 nameserver2 nameserver3); # name of the name servers
foreach $server (@servers) {
    &lookupaddress($hostname,$server);              # populates %results
}
%inv = reverse %results;         # invert the result hash
if (scalar(keys %inv) > 1) {     # see how many elements it has
    print "There is a discrepancy between DNS servers:\n";
    use Data::Dumper;
    print Data::Dumper->Dump([\%results],["results"]),"\n";
}

sub lookupaddress{
    my($hostname,$server) = @_;

    my($qname,$rname,$header,$question,$lformat,@labels,$count);
    local($position,$buf);

    ###
    ### Construct the packet header
    ###
    $header = pack("n C2 n4",
            ++$id,   # query id
            1,    # qr, opcode, aa, tc, rd fields (only rd set)
            0,    # rd, ra
            1,    # one question (qdcount)
            0,    # no answers (ancount)
```

```
                    0,  # no ns records in authority section (nscount)
                    0); # no addtl rr's (arcount)


    # if we do not have any separators in the name of the host,
    # append the default domain
    if (index($hostname,'.') == -1) {
        $hostname .= $defdomain;
    }


    # construct the qname section of a packet (domain name in question)
    for (split(/\./,$hostname)) {
        $lformat .= "C a* ";
        $labels[$count++]=length;
        $labels[$count++]=$_;
    }


    ###
    ### construct the packet question section
    ###
    $question = pack($lformat."C n2",
            @labels,
                    0,  # end of labels
                    1,  # qtype of A
                    1); # qclass of IN


    ###
    ### send the packet to the server and read the response
    ###
    $sock = new IO::Socket::INET(PeerAddr => $server,
                                 PeerPort => "domain",
                                 Proto    => "udp");

    $sock->send($header.$question);
    # we're using UDP, so we know the max packet size
    $sock->recv($buf,512);
    close($sock);

    # get the size of the response, since we're going to have to keep
    # track of where we are in the packet as we parse it (via $position)
    $respsize = length($buf);


    ###
    ### unpack the header section
    ###
    ($id,
     $qr_opcode_aa_tc_rd,
     $rd_ra,
     $qdcount,
     $ancount,
     $nscount,
     $arcount) = unpack("n C2 n4",$buf);


    if (!$ancount) {
        warn "Unable to lookup data for $hostname from $server!\n";
        return;
    }
```

```
###
### unpack the question section
###
# question section starts 12 bytes in
($position,$qname) = &decompress(12);
($qtype,$qclass)=unpack('@'.$position.'n2',$buf);
# move us forward in the packet to end of question section
$position += 4;

###
### unpack all of the resource record sections
###
for ( ;$ancount;$ancount--){
    ($position,$rname) = &decompress($position);
    ($rtype,$rclass,$rttl,$rdlength)=
        unpack('@'.$position.'n2 N n',$buf);
    $position +=10;
    # this next line could be changed to use a more sophisticated
    # data structure, it currently picks the last rr returned
    $results{$server}=
        join('.',unpack('@'.$position.'C'.$rdlength,$buf));
    $position +=$rdlength;
}
}


# handle domain information that is "compressed" as per RFC1035
# we take in the starting position of our packet parse and return
# the name we found (after dealing with the compressed format pointer)
# and the place we left off in the packet at the end of the name we found
sub decompress {
    my($start) = $_[0];
    my($domain,$i,$lenoct);

    for ($i=$start;$i<=$respsize;) {
        $lenoct=unpack('@'.$i.'C', $buf); # get the length of label

        if (!$lenoct){          # 0 signals we are done with this section
            $i++;
            last;
        }

        if ($lenoct == 192) { # we've been handed a pointer, so recurse
            $domain.=(&decompress((unpack('@'.$i.'n',$buf) & 1023)))[1];
            $i+=2;
            last
        }
        else {                  # otherwise, we have a plain label
            $domain.=unpack('@'.++$i.'a'.$lenoct,$buf).'.';
            $i += $lenoct;
        }
    }
    return($i,$domain);
}
```

Note that this code is not precisely equivalent to that from the previous example because we're not trying to emulate all of the nuances of *nslookup*'s behavior (timeouts, retries, searchlists, etc.). When looking at the three approaches here, be sure to keep a critical eye out for these subtle differences.

The benefits of this approach are:

- It isn't dependent on any other programs. You don't need to know the particulars of another programmer's work.

- It may be as fast or faster than calling an external program.

- It is easier to tweak the parameters of the situation (timeouts, etc.).

The drawbacks of this approach are:

- It's likely to take longer to write and is more complex than the previous approach.

- It requires more knowledge external to the direct problem at hand (i.e., you may have to learn how to put DNS packets together by hand, something we did not need to know when we called *nslookup*).

- You may have to handle OS-specific issues yourself (hidden in the previous approach by the work already done by the external program's author).

Using Net::DNS

As mentioned in Chapter 1, *Introduction*, one of Perl's real strengths is the support of a large community of developers who churn out code for others to reuse. If there's something you need to do in Perl that seems universal, chances are good that someone else has already written a module to handle it. In our case, we can make use of Michael Fuhr's excellent **Net::DNS** module to make our job simpler. For our task, we simply have to create a new DNS resolver object, configure it with the name of the DNS server we wish to use, ask it to send a query, and then use the supplied methods to parse the response:

```
use Net::DNS;

@servers = qw(nameserver1 nameserver2 nameserver3); # name of the name servers
foreach $server (@servers) {
    &lookupaddress($hostname,$server);                # populates %results
}
%inv = reverse %results;          # invert the result hash
if (scalar(keys %inv) > 1) {    # see how many elements it has
    print "There is a discrepency between DNS servers:\n";
    use Data::Dumper;
    print Data::Dumper->Dump([\%results],["results"]),"\n";
}

# only slightly modified from example in the Net::DNS manpage
```

```
sub lookupaddress{
    my($hostname,$server) = @_;

    $res = new Net::DNS::Resolver;

    $res->nameservers($server);

    $packet = $res->query($hostname);

    if (!$packet) {
        warn "Unable to lookup data for $hostname from $server!\n";
        return;
    }
    # stores the last RR we receive
    foreach $rr ($packet->answer) {
        $results{$server}=$rr->address;
    }
}
```

The benefits of this approach are:

- The code is legible again.

- It is often faster to write.

- Depending on how the module you use is implemented (is it pure Perl or is it glue to a set of C or C++ library calls?) the code you write using this module may be just as fast as calling an external compiled program.

- It is potentially portable, depending on how much work the author of the module has done for you. Any place this module can be installed, your program can run.

- As in the first approach we looked at, writing code can be quick and easy if someone else has done the behind-the-scenes work for you. You don't have to know how the module works; you just need to know how to use it.

- Code re-use. You are not reinventing the wheel each time.

The drawbacks of this approach are:

- You are back in the dependency game. This time you need to make sure this module is available for your program to run. You need to trust that the module writer has done a decent job.

- There may not be a module to do what you need, or it may not run on the operating system of choice.

More often than not, a pre-written module is my preferred approach. However, any of these approaches will get the job done. TMTOWTDI, so go forth and do it!

Module Information for This Chapter

Module	CPAN ID	Version
Rcs	CFRETER	0.09
Net::NIS	RIK	a2
Data::Dumper (ships with Perl)	GSAR	2.101
IO::Socket (ships with Perl)	GBARR	1.20
Net::DNS	MFUHR	0.12

References for More Information

DNS and BIND, 3rd Edition, by Paul Albitz and Cricket Liu (O'Reilly, 1998).

RFC849: Suggestions For Improved Host Table Distribution, Mark Crispin, 1983.

RFC881: The Domain Names Plan and Schedule, J. Postel, 1983.

RFC882: Domain Names: Concepts And Facilities, P. Mockapetris, 1983.

RFC1035: Domain Names: Implementation And Specification, P. Mockapetris, 1987.

6

Directory Services

The larger the information system, the harder it becomes to find anything in that system or even know what's available. As networks grow and become more complex, they are well served by some sort of directory. Network users might make use of a directory service to find other users for email and other messaging services. Resources on a network, like printers and network-available disk areas, might be advertised via a directory service. Public-key and certificate infrastructures could use a directory service to distribute information. In this chapter we'll look at how to use Perl to interact with some of the more popular directory services, including Finger, WHOIS, LDAP, and ADSI.

What's a Directory?

In Chapter 7, *SQL Database Administration*, I suggest that all the system administration world is a database. Directories are a good example of this characterization. For the purpose of our discussion we'll distinguish between "database" and "directory" by observing a few salient characteristics of directories:

Networked

Directories are almost always networked. Unlike some databases that live on the same machine as their clients (like the venerable */etc/passwd* file), directory services are usually provided over a network.

Simple communication/data manipulation

Databases often have complex query languages for data queries and manipulation. We'll see the most common one, SQL, in the aforementioned Chapter 7, and in Appendix D, *The Fifteen-Minute SQL Tutorial*. Communicating with a directory is a much simpler affair. A directory client typically performs only rudimentary operations and does not use a full-fledged language as part of its communication with the server.

Hierarchical

Modern directory services encourage the building of tree-like information structures, whereas databases on the whole do not.

Read-many, write-few

Modern directory servers are optimized for a very specific data traffic pattern. Under normal use, the number of reads/queries to a directory service far outweighs the number of writes/updates.

If you encounter something that looks like a database but has the above characteristics, you're probably dealing with a directory. In the four directory services we're about to see, these characteristics will be easy to spot.

Finger: A Simple Directory Service

Finger and WHOIS are good examples of simple directory services. Finger exists primarily to provide read-only information about the users of a machine (although we'll see some more creative uses shortly). Later versions of Finger, like the GNU Finger server and its derivatives, expanded upon this basic functionality by allowing you to query one machine and receive information back from all of the machines on your network.

Finger was one of the first widely deployed directory services. Once upon a time, if you wanted to locate a user's email address at another site, or even within your own, the *finger* command was the best option. *finger harry@hogwarts.edu* would tell you whether Harry's email address was `harry`, `hpotter`, or something more obscure (along with listing all of the other Harrys at that school). Though it is still in use today, Finger's popularity has waned over time as web home pages became prevalent and the practice of freely giving out user information became problematic.

Using the Finger protocol from Perl provides another good example of TMTOWTDI. When I first looked on CPAN for something to perform Finger operations, there were no modules available for this task. If you look now, you'll find Dennis Taylor's `Net::Finger` module, which he published six months or so after my initial search. We'll see how to use it in a moment, but in the meantime, let's pretend it doesn't exist and take advantage of this opportunity to learn how to use a more generic module to talk a specific protocol when the "perfect" module doesn't exist.

The Finger protocol itself is a very simple TCP/IP-based text protocol. Defined in RFC1288, it calls for a standard TCP connect to port 79. The client passes a simple CRLF-terminated* string over the connection. This string either requests specific user information or, if empty, asks for information about all users of that machine. The server responds with the requested data and closes the connection at the end of the data stream. You can see this in action by *telnet*ing to the Finger port directly on a remote machine:

```
$ telnet kantine.diku.dk 79
Trying 192.38.109.142 ...
Connected to kantine.diku.dk.
Escape character is '^]'.
cola<CR><LF>
Login: cola                          Name: RHS Linux User
Directory: /home/cola                Shell: /bin/noshell
Never logged in.
No mail.
Plan:

Current state of the coke machine at DIKU
This file is updated every 5 seconds
At the moment, it's necessary to use correct change.
This has been the case the last 19 hours and 17 minutes

Column 1 is currently *empty*.
    It's been 14 hours and 59 minutes since it became empty.
    31 items were sold from this column before it became empty.
Column 2 contains some cokes.
    It's been 2 days, 17 hours, and 43 minutes since it was filled.
    Meanwhile, 30 items have been sold from this column.
Column 3 contains some cokes.
    It's been 2 days, 17 hours, and 41 minutes since it was filled.
    Meanwhile, 11 items have been sold from this column.
Column 4 contains some cokes.
    It's been 5 days, 15 hours, and 28 minutes since it was filled.
    Meanwhile, 26 items have been sold from this column.
Column 5 contains some cokes.
    It's been 5 days, 15 hours, and 29 minutes since it was filled.
    Meanwhile, 18 items have been sold from this column.
Column 6 contains some coke-lights.
    It's been 5 days, 15 hours, and 30 minutes since it was filled.
    Meanwhile, 16 items have been sold from this column.

Connection closed by foreign host.
$
```

In this example we've connected directly to *kantine.diku.dk*'s Finger port. We typed the user name "cola," and the server returned information about that user.

---

* Carriage return + linefeed, i.e., ASCII 13 + ASCII 10.

I chose this particular host and user just to show you some of the whimsy that accompanied the early days of the Internet. Finger servers got pressed into service for all sorts of tasks. In this case, anyone anywhere on the planet can see whether the soda machine at the Department of Computer Science at the University of Copenhagen is currently stocked. For more examples of strange devices hooked to Finger servers, you may wish to check out Bennet Yee's "Internet Accessible Coke Machines" and "Internet Accessible Machines" pages; they are available online at *http://www.cs.ucsd.edu/~bsy/fun.html.*

Let's take the network communication we just performed using a *telnet* binary back to the world of Perl. With Perl, we can also open up a network socket and communicate over it. Instead of using lower-level socket commands, we'll use Jay Roger's `Net::Telnet` module to introduce a family of modules that handle generic network discussions. Other modules in this family (some of which we use in other chapters) include Eric Arnold's *Comm.pl*, Austin Schutz's *Expect.pm,* and the venerable but outdated and nonportable *chat2.pl* by Randal L. Schwartz.

`Net::Telnet` will handle all of the connection setup work for us and provides a clean interface for sending and receiving data over this connection. Though we won't use them in this example, `Net::Telnet` also provides some handy pattern-scanning mechanisms that allow your program to watch for specific responses from the other server.

Here's a `Net::Telnet` version of a simple Finger client. This code takes an argument of the form *user@finger_server.* If the user name is omitted, a list of all users considered active by the server will be returned. If the hostname is omitted, we query the local host:

```
use Net::Telnet;

($username,$host) = split(/\@/,$ARGV[0]);
$host = $host ? $host : 'localhost';

# create a new connection
$cn = new Net::Telnet(Host => $host,
                      Port => 'finger');

# send the username down this connection
unless ($cn->print("$username")){ # could be "/W $username"
    $cn->close;
    die "Unable to send finger string: ".$cn->errmg."\n";
}

# grab all of the data we receive, stopping when the
# connection is dropped
while (defined $ret = $cn->get) {
    $data .= $ret;
}
```

```
# close the connection
$cn->close;

# display the data we collected
print $data;
```

RFC1288 specifies that a /W switch can be prepended to the username sent to the server to request it to provide "a higher level of verbosity in the user information output," hence the /W comment above.

If you need to connect to another TCP-based text protocol besides Finger, you'd use very similar code. For example, to connect to a Daytime server (which shows the local time on a machine) the code looks very similar:

```
use Net::Telnet;

$host = $ARGV[0] ? $ARGV[0] : 'localhost';

$cn = new Net::Telnet(Host => $host,
                      Port => 'daytime');

while (defined $ret = $cn->get) {
    $data .= $ret;
}
$cn->close;

print $data;
```

Now you have a sense of how easy it is to create generic TCP-based network clients. If someone has taken the time to write a module specifically designed to handle a protocol, it can be even easier. In the case of Finger, you can use Taylor's **Net::Finger** to turn the whole task into a single function call:

```
use Net::Finger;

# finger() takes a user@host string and returns the data received
print finger($ARGV[0]);
```

Just to present all of the options, there's also the fallback position of calling another executable (if it exists on the machine) like so:

```
($username,$host) = split('@',$ARGV[0]);
$host = $host ? $host : 'localhost';

# location of finger executable, MacOS users can't use this method
$fingerex = ($^O eq "MSWin32") ?
                $ENV{'SYSTEMROOT'}."\\System32\\finger" :
                "/usr/ucb/finger";   # (could also be /usr/bin/finger)

print `$fingerex ${username}\@${host}`;
```

Now you've seen three different methods for performing Finger requests. The third method is probably the least ideal because it requires spawning another process.

`Net::Finger` will handle simple Finger requests; for everything else, `Net::Telnet` or any of its kin should work well for you.

The WHOIS Directory Service

WHOIS is another useful read-only directory service. WHOIS provides a telephone directory-like service for machines, networks, and the people who run them. Some larger organizations like IBM, UC Berkeley, and MIT provide WHOIS service, but the most important WHOIS servers by far are those run by the InterNIC and other Internet registries like RIPE (European IP address allocations) and APNIC (Asia/Pacific address allocations).

If you have to contact a system administrator at another site to report suspicious network activity, you would use WHOIS to get the contact info. There are GUI and command-line based tools for making WHOIS queries available for most operating systems. Under Unix, a typical query looks like this:

```
% whois -h whois.networksolutions.com brandeis.edu
<large legal paragraph omitted>
Registrant:
Brandeis University (BRANDEIS-DOM)
    Information Technology Services
    Waltham, MA 02454-9110
    US

    Domain Name: BRANDEIS.EDU

    Administrative Contact:
        Koskovich, Bob  (BK138)  user@BRANDEIS.EDU
        +1-781-555-1212 (FAX) +1-781-555-1212
    Technical Contact, Zone Contact:
        Hostmaster, Brandeis C  (RCG51)  hostmaster@BRANDEIS.EDU
        +1-781-555-1212 (FAX) +1-781-555-1212
    Billing Contact:
        Koskovich, Bob  (BK138)  user@BRANDEIS.EDU
        +1-781-555-1212 (FAX) +1-781-555-1212

    Record last updated on 13-Oct-1999.
    Record created on 27-May-1987.
    Database last updated on 19-Dec-1999 17:42:19 EST.

    Domain servers in listed order:

    LILITH.UNET.BRANDEIS.EDU      129.64.99.12
    FRASIER.UNET.BRANDEIS.EDU     129.64.99.11
    DIAMOND.CS.BRANDEIS.EDU       129.64.2.3
    DNSAUTH1.SYS.GTEI.NET         4.2.49.2
    DNSAUTH2.SYS.GTEI.NET         4.2.49.3
```

If you needed to track down the owner of a particular IP address range, WHOIS is
also the right tool:

```
% whois -h whois.arin.net 129.64.2
Brandeis University (NET-BRANDEIS)
    415 South Street
    Waltham, MA 02254

    Netname: BRANDEIS
    Netnumber: 129.64.0.0

    Coordinator:
        Koskovich, Bob   (BK138-ARIN)   user@BRANDEIS.EDU
        617-555-1212

    Domain System inverse mapping provided by:

    BINAH.CC.BRANDEIS.EDU        129.64.1.3
    NIC.NEAR.NET                 192.52.71.4
    NOC.CERF.NET                 192.153.156.22

    Record last updated on 10-Jul-97.
    Database last updated on 9-Oct-98 16:10:44 EDT.

  The ARIN Registration Services Host contains ONLY Internet
  Network Information: Networks, ASN's, and related POC's.
  Please use the whois server at rs.internic.net for DOMAIN related
  Information and nic.mil for NIPRNET Information.
```

The previous sessions used a Unix command-line WHOIS client. Windows NT and
MacOS do not ship with clients like this, but that shouldn't stop users of those systems from accessing this information. There are many fine shareware clients available, but it is easy enough to construct a very simple client in Perl using `Net::
Whois`, originally by Chip Salzenberg and now maintained by Dana Hudes. The
following example is only slightly modified from one provided in the documentation that comes with the module:

```perl
use Net::Whois;

# query server, returning an object with results
my $w = new Net::Whois::Domain $ARGV[0] or
    die "Can't connect to Whois server\n";
die "No domain information found for $ARGV[0]\n" unless ($w->ok);

# print out parts of that object
print "Domain: ", $w->domain, "\n";
print "Name: ", $w->name, "\n";
print "Tag: ", $w->tag, "\n";
print "Address:\n", map { "    $_\n" } $w->address;
print "Country: ", $w->country, "\n";
print "Record created: ".$w->record_created."\n";
print "Record updated: ".$w->record_updated."\n";
```

```
# print out name servers ($w->servers returns a list of lists)
print "Name Servers:\n", map { "    $$_[0] ($$_[1])\n" } @{$w->servers};

# print out contact list ($w->contacts returns a hash of lists)
my($c,$t);
if ($c = $w->contacts) {
    print "Contacts:\n";
    for $t (sort keys %$c) {
        print "    $t:\n";
        print map { "\t$_\n" } @{$$c{$t}};
    }
}
```

Querying the InterNIC/Network Solutions WHOIS server is a simple process. We use `Net::Whois::Domain` to return a result object. Data is then accessed by calling the methods of that object named after the fields returned by the WHOIS query.

WHOIS will play a significant role in Chapter 8, *Electronic Mail*, but for now let's move on to more complex directory services. We've already begun that transition simply by moving from Finger to WHOIS. There's an important distinction between the Finger and WHOIS examples that you've seen so far: structure.

The output of Finger varies from one server implementation to another. Although some output conventions exist, it is freeform in nature. The InterNIC/Network Solutions WHOIS server returns data with a more consistent structure and organization. We can expect each entry to have at least **Name**, **Address**, and **Domain** fields. The `Net::Whois` module relies on this structure and parses the response into fields for us. There is another module by Vipul Ved Prakash called `Net::XWhois` which takes this a step further, providing a framework for parsing information formatted in different ways by different WHOIS servers.

Even though the WHOIS protocol itself does not have a notion of fields, the modules we are calling are starting to rely on the structure of the information. The directory services we are about to look at take this structuring more seriously.

LDAP: A Sophisticated Directory Service

LDAP and ADSI are much richer and more sophisticated directory services. LDAP stands for Lightweight Directory Access Protocol. There are two widely deployed versions of the LDAP protocol out there (Version 2 and Version 3—anything that is version specific will be clearly noted as such). This protocol is fast becoming the industry standard for directory access. System administrators have embraced LDAP because it offers them a way to centralize and make available all sorts of infrastructure information. Besides the standard "company directory," examples applications include:

- NIS-to-LDAP gateways
- Finger-to-LDAP gateways

- Authentication databases of all sorts (e.g., for use on the Web)

- Resource advertisement (i.e., which machines and peripherals are available)

LDAP is also the basis of other sophisticated directory services like Microsoft's Active Directory, which we'll see later, in the section "ADSI (Active Directory Service Interfaces)."

Even if LDAP is not used in your environment to provide anything but a fancy phone book, there are still good reasons to learn how to use the protocol. LDAP servers themselves can be administered using the same protocol they serve, similar to SQL database servers being administered via SQL. To this end, Perl offers an excellent glue environment for automating LDAP administrative tasks. Before we get there, we need to be sure we understand LDAP itself.

Appendix B, *The Ten-Minute LDAP Tutorial*, contains a quick introduction to LDAP for the uninitiated. The biggest barrier new system administrators encounter when they begin to learn about LDAP is the unwieldy nomenclature it inherited from its parent protocol, the X.500 Directory Service. LDAP is a simplified version of X.500, but unfortunately, the distillation process did not make the terminology any easier to swallow. Taking a few moments with Appendix B to get these terms under your belt will make understanding how to use LDAP from Perl easier.

LDAP Programming with Perl

Like so many other systems administration tasks in Perl, a good first step towards LDAP programming is the selection of the required Perl module. LDAP is not the most complex protocol out there, but it is not a plain text protocol. As a result, cobbling something together that speaks LDAP is not a trivial exercise. Luckily two sets of authors have already done this work for us: Graham Barr created `Net::LDAP` and Leif Hedstrom and Clayton Donley created `Mozilla::LDAP` (a.k.a. `PerLDAP`). Table 6-1 lists some of the ways that the two modules differ.

Table 6-1. Comparison of the Two Perl LDAP Modules

Feature	Net::LDAP	Mozilla::LDAP (PerLDAP)
Portability	Pure Perl	Requires the Mozilla/Netscape LDAP C-SDK (source is freely available). The SDK compiles on many Unixs, NT, and MacOS
SSL encrypted sessions	Yes	Yes
Asynchronous operations	Yes	Only with the non-object-oriented base-level API

Both of these modules have the functionality to perform the simple system administration-related tasks we'll be discussing, but they take slightly different approaches in how they offer it. This creates a rare educational opportunity because it allows us to observe how two different authors implemented substantial modules to address essentially the same niche. Careful comparison between the two modules can offer insight into the module implementation process, which we'll briefly demonstrate in Chapter 10, *Security and Network Monitoring*. To facilitate this comparison, most of the examples in this section show the syntax for both Perl LDAP modules. The `use modulename` line in each full code example will clue you in on which module we are using at the time.

For demonstration servers, we'll be using the commercial Netscape 4.0 Directory Server and the free OpenLDAP server (found at *http://www.netscape.com* and *http://www.openldap.org*) almost interchangeably. Both come with almost identical command-line utilities that you can use to prototype and crosscheck your Perl code.

The Initial LDAP Connection

Connecting with authentication is the usual first step in any LDAP client-server transaction. In LDAP-speak this is known as "binding to the server." Binding to a server before sending commands to it was required in LDAPv2 but this requirement was relaxed for LDAPv3.

When you bind to an LDAP server, you are said to be doing so in the context of a specific Distinguished name (DN), described as the *bind DN* for that session. This context is similar to logging in as a particular user on a multiuser system. On a multiuser system, your current login (for the most part) determines your level of access to data on that system. With LDAP, it is the bind DN context that determines how much data on the LDAP server you can see and modify. There is a special DN known as the *root Distinguished Name* (which is not given an acronym to avoid confusing it with Relative Distinguished Name). The root Distinguished Name is the DN context that has total control over the whole tree, just like being logged in as *root* under Unix or *Administrator* for NT/2000. Some servers also refer to this as the *manager DN*.

If a client provides no authentication information (e.g., DN and password) as part of a bind, or does not bother to bind before sending commands, this is known as *anonymous authentication*. Anonymously authenticated clients typically receive very restricted access to a server's data.

There are two flavors of binding in the LDAPv3 specification: simple and SASL. Simple binding uses plain-text passwords for authentication. SASL (Simple Authentication and Security Layer) is an extensible authentication framework defined in RFC2222 that allows client/server authors to plug in a number of different authentication schemes like Kerberos and One-Time Passwords. When a client connects to a server, it requests a particular authentication mechanism. If the server supports this mechanism, it will begin the challenge-response dialogue specific to that mechanism to authenticate the client. During this dialogue, the client and server may also negotiate a security layer (e.g., "all traffic between us will be encrypted using TLS") for use after the initial authentication has been completed.

Some LDAP servers and clients add one more authentication method to the standard simple and SASL choices. This method comes as a by-product of running LDAP over an encrypted channel via Secure Socket Layer (SSL). To set this channel up, LDAP servers and clients exchange public-key cryptography certificates just like a web server and browser do for HTTPS. The LDAP server can be told to use a trusted client's certificate as authentication information without having to bother with other authentication info. Of the Perl modules available, only PerLDAP offers LDAPS (SSL-encrypted sessions). To keep our examples from getting too complicated, we'll stick to simple authentication and unencrypted transport sessions.

Here's how you do a simple bind and unbind in Perl:

```
use Mozilla::LDAP::Conn;
# use empty $binddn and $passwd for anonymous bind
$c = new Mozilla::LDAP::Conn($server, $port, $binddn, $passwd);
die "Unable to connect to $server" unless $c;
...
$c->close();
```

or:

```
use Net::LDAP;
$c = Net::LDAP->new($server, port => $port) or
    die "Unable to connect to $server: $@\n";
# use no parameters to bind() for anonymous bind
$c->bind($binddn, password => $passwd) or
    die "Unable to bind: $@\n";
...
$c->unbind();
```

With `Mozilla::LDAP::Conn`, the creation of a new connection object also binds to the server. In `Net::LDAP` this is a two-step process. To initialize a connection without performing a bind in `Mozilla::LDAP`, you'll need to use a function (`ldap_init()`) from the non-object-oriented `Mozilla::LDAP::API` module.

Be Prepared to Carefully Quote Attribute Values

A quick tip before we do any more Perl programming: if you have an attribute in your Relative Distinguished Name with a value that contains one of the characters "+", "(space)," ",", "!", ">", "<", or ";", you must specify the value surrounded by quotation marks or with the offending character escaped by a backslash (\). If the value contains quotation marks, those marks must be escaped using backslashes. Backslashes in values are also escaped with more backslashes.

Insufficient quoting will bite you if you are not careful.

Performing LDAP Searches

The D in LDAP stands for Directory, and the one operation you perform most on a
directory is a search. Let's start our exploration of LDAP functionality by learning
how to find information. An LDAP search is specified in terms of:

Where to begin the search

> This is called the *base DN* or *search base*. A base DN is simply the DN of an
> entry in the directory tree where the search should begin.

Where to look

> This is known as the search *scope*. The scope can be: *base* (search just the
> base DN), *one* (search everything one level below the base DN, not including
> the base DN itself), or *sub* (search the base DN and all of the parts of the tree
> below it).

What to look for

> This is called the *search filter*. We'll discuss filters and how they are specified
> in just a moment.

What to return

> To speed up the search operation, you can select which attributes are returned
> for each entry found by the search filter. It is also possible to request that only
> attribute names and not their values are returned. This is useful for those times
> when you want to know which entries have a certain attribute, but you don't
> care what that attribute contains.

In Perl, a search looks like this (the bind step has been replaced with an ellipsis):

```
use Mozilla::LDAP::Conn;
...
$entry = $c->search($basedn, $scope, $filter);
die "Bad search: ". $c->getErrorString()."\n" if $c->getErrorCode();
```

or:

```
use Net::LDAP;
...
$searchobj = $c->search(base => $basedn, scope => $scope,
                        filter => $filter);
die "Bad search, errorcode #".$searchobj->code() if $searchobj->code();
```

Let's talk about the mysterious `$filter` parameter before we see a fully fleshed-
out code example. Simple search filters are of the form:

```
<attribute name> <comparison operator> <attribute value>
```

where *<comparison operator>* is specified in RFC2254 as one of the operators
listed in Table 6-2.

Table 6-2. LDAP Comparison Operators

Operator	Means
=	Exact value match. Can also be a partial value match if * is used in the `<attribute value>` specification (e.g., cn=Tim O*).
=*	Match all entries that have values for `<attribute name>`, independent of what the values are. By specifying * instead of `<attribute value>`, we test for presence of that particular attribute in an entry (e.g., cn=* would select entries that have cn attributes).
~=	Approximate value match.
>=	Greater than or equal to value.
<=	Less than or equal to value.

These look Perlish, but don't be deceived. Two misleading constructs to a Perl person are ~= and =*. The first has nothing to do with regular expression matches; it finds matches that approximate the stated value. The definition of "approximate" in this case is server dependent. Most servers use an algorithm originally invented for census-taking called **soundex** to determine the matching values, to find words that "sound like" the given value (in English) but are spelled differently.*

The other construct that may clash with your Perl knowledge is the = operator. In addition to testing for exact value matches (both string and numeric), = can also be used with prefix and suffix asterisks as wildcard characters, similar to shell globbing. For example, cn=a* will yield all of the entries that have a common name that begins with the letter "a". cn=*a* performs just as you would suspect, finding all entries whose common name attribute has a letter "a" in it.

We can take two or more of these `<attribute name>` `<comparison operator>` `<attribute value>` simple search forms and string them together with Boolean operators to make a more complex filter. This takes the form:

```
(<boolean operator> (<simple1>) (<simple2>) (<simple3>) … )
```

People with LISP experience will have no problem with this sort of syntax; everyone else will just have to remember that the operator that combines the simple search forms is written first. To filter entries that match both criteria A *and* B, you would use (&(A)(B)). For entries that match criteria A *or* B *or* C, you would use (|(A)(B)(C)). The exclamation mark negates a specific criterion: A *and not* B is (&(A)(!B)). Compound filters can be compounded themselves to make arbitrarily complex search filters. Here is an example of a compound search filter that finds all of the Finkelsteins who work in Boston:

```
(&(sn=Finkelstein)(l=Boston))
```

---

* If you want to play with the soundex algorithm, Mark Mielke's **Text::Soundex** module provides a Perl implementation.

To find anyone with the last name Finkelstein or Hinds:

```
(|(sn=Finkelstein)(sn=Hinds))
```

To find all of the Finkelsteins who do not work in Boston:

```
(&(sn=Finkelstein)(!(l=Boston)))
```

To find all the Finkelsteins or Hinds who do not work in Boston:

```
(&(|(sn=Finkelstein)(sn=Hinds))(!l=Boston))
```

Here are two code examples that take an LDAP server name and an LDAP filter and return the results of the query:

```perl
use Mozilla::LDAP::Conn;

$server = $ARGV[0];
$port   = getservbyname("ldap","tcp") || "389";
$basedn = "c=US";
$scope  = "sub";

$c = new Mozilla::LDAP::Conn($server, $port, "",""); # anonymous bind
die "Unable to bind to $server\n" unless $c;

$entry = $c->search($basedn, $scope, $ARGV[1]);
die "Error in search: ". $c->getErrorString()."\n" if $c->getErrorCode();

# process the return values from search()
while ($entry) {
    $entry->printLDIF();
    $entry = $c->nextEntry();
}
$c->close();

use Net::LDAP;
use Net::LDAP::LDIF;

$server = $ARGV[0];
$port   = getservbyname("ldap","tcp") || "389";
$basedn = "c=US";
$scope  = "sub";

$c = new Net::LDAP($server, port=>$port) or
    die "Unable to connect to $server: $@\n";
$c->bind() or die "Unable to bind: $@\n"; # anonymous bind

$searchobj = $c->search(base => $basedn, scope => $scope,
                        filter => $ARGV[1]);
die "Bad search, errorcode #".$searchobj->code() if $searchobj->code();

# process the return values from search()
if ($searchobj){
    $ldif = new Net::LDAP::LDIF("-");
    $ldif->write($searchobj->entries());
    $ldif->done();
}
```

Here's an excerpt from some sample output:

```
$ ldapsrch ldap.bigfoot.com '(sn=Pooh)'
...
dn: cn="bear pooh",mail=poohbear219@hotmail.com,c=US,o=hotmail.com
mail: poohbear219@hotmail.com
cn: bear pooh
o: hotmail.com
givenname: bear
surname: pooh
...
```

Before we develop this example any further, let's explore the code that processes the results returned by **search()**. This is one place where the two modules diverge in their programming model. Both of these code samples will output the same information in LDIF (LDAP Data Interchange Format), a format we'll explore later, but they get there in two very different ways.

The **Mozilla::LDAP** model holds true to the search parsing routines described in the RFC1823 C API specification. If a search succeeds, the first entry found is returned. To view the results, you ask for the subsequent entries one at a time. For each entry retrieved, the **printLDIF()** method is used to dump its contents.

Net::LDAP's programming model more closely resembles the protocol definition of RFC2251. LDAP search results are returned in LDAP Message objects. The code we just saw calls the **entries()** method to return a list of all of the entries in these packets. We use a method from the adjunct module **Net::LDAP::LDIF** to dump these entries out en masse. The same method, **write()**, can also be used in a manner similar to **printLDIF()** in the first example to print entries one at a time, but the call shown above is more efficient.

Let's tweak our previous example a little bit. Earlier in this chapter I mentioned that we could construct speedier searches by limiting the attributes that are returned by a search. With the **Mozilla::LDAP** module this is as simple as adding extra parameters to our **search()** method call:

```
use Mozilla::LDAP::Conn;
...
$entry = $c->search($basedn,$scope,$ARGV[1],0,@attr);
```

The first additional parameter is a Boolean flag that dictates whether attribute values are omitted from search results. The default is false (0), since most of the time we are interested in more than just the names of the attributes.

The subsequent additional parameters are a list of names of attributes to be returned. Perl-savvy readers will note that lists within lists auto-interpolate, so the last line of the above code is equivalent to (and can be written as):

```
$entry =
  $c->search($basedn,$scope,$ARGV[1],0,$attr[0],$attr[1],$attr[2],...);
```

If we change our original example code from:

```
$entry = $c->search($basedn,$scope,$ARGV[1]);
```

to:

```
@attr = qw(mail);
$entry = $c->search($basedn,$scope,$ARGV[1],0,@attr);
```

we get this output instead, which only shows the entry's DN and mail attribute:

```
...
dn: cn="bear pooh",mail=poohbear219@hotmail.com,c=US,o=hotmail.com
mail: poohbear219@hotmail.com
...
```

The change made to return specific attributes via `Net::LDAP` is similarly easy:

```
use Net::LDAP;
...
# could also add "typesonly => 1" to return just attribute types like
# optional 1st param above
$searchobj = $c->search(base => $basedn, filter => $ARGV[1],
                        attrs => \@attr);
```

Note that `Net::LDAP` takes a *reference* to an array, not values in the array like `Mozilla::LDAP`.

Entry Representation in Perl

These code samples may provoke some questions about entry representation and manipulation—that is, how are entries themselves stored and manipulated in a Perl program? Let's answer a few of those questions as a follow-up to our LDAP searching discussion, even though we will discuss them more thoroughly in the upcoming sections on addition and modification of entries.

If you've just done a search using `Mozilla::LDAP` and have an entry object instance in hand, you can access the individual attributes in that entry using the Perl hash-of-lists syntax. `$entry->{attributename}` is a *list* of the values for that attribute name. I emphasize "list" because even single-valued attributes are stored in an anonymous list referenced through this hash key. To get at the value in a single-valued attribute like this, you would use `$entry->{attributename}->[0]`. Table 6-3 lists some more methods from `Mozilla::LDAP::Entry` that come in handy when retrieving entry attributes.

Table 6-3. Mozilla::LDAP::Entry Methods

Method Call	Returns
`$entry->exists($attrname)`	*true* if that entry has an attribute with this name
`$entry->hasValue($attrname,$attrvalue)`	*true* if that entry has a named attribute with this value

Table 6-3. Mozilla::LDAP::Entry Methods (continued)

Method Call	Returns
$entry->matchValue($attrname,$attrvalue)	Same as above, except performs a regular expression match for attribute value
$entry->size($attrname)	The number of values for that attribute (usually 1 unless the attribute is multivalued)

Some of these methods have additional parameters; see the documentation on `Mozilla::LDAP::Entry` for more information.

You could probably tell from the sample search code that the method for accessing `Net::LDAP` entry attributes is a bit different. After conducting a search, all of the results are available encapsulated by a single object. To get at the individual attributes for the entries in this object, you can take one of two approaches.

First, you could ask the module to convert all of the returned entries into one large user-accessible data structure. `$searchobj->as_struct()` returns a hash-of-hash-of-lists data structure. It returns a reference to a hash whose keys are the DNs of the returned entries. The values for these keys are references to anonymous hashes keyed on the attribute names. These keys yield references to anonymous arrays that hold the actual values for those attributes. Figure 6-1 makes this clearer.

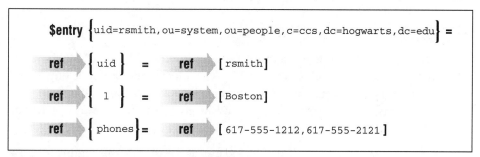

Figure 6-1. Data structure returned by as_struct()

To print the first value for the cn attributes for all of the entries in this data structure, you could use code like this:

```
$searchstruct = $searchobj->as_struct;
for (keys %$searchstruct){
    print $searchstruct->{$_}{cn}[0],"\n";
}
```

Alternatively, you can first use any one of these methods to unload an individual entry object from the object returned by a search:

```
# return a specific entry number
$entry   = $searchobj->entry($entrynum);
```

```
# acts like Perl shift() on entry list
$entry   = $searchobj->shift_entry;

# acts like Perl pop() on entry list
$entry   = $searchobj->pop_entry;

# return all of the entries as a list
@entries = $searchobj->entries;
```

Once you have an entry object, you can use one of the method calls in Table 6-4.

Table 6-4. Net::LDAP Entry Methods

Method Call	Returns
`$entry->get($attrname)`	The value of that attribute in the given entry
`$entry->attributes()`	The list of attribute names for that entry

It is possible to chain these method calls together in a fairly legible fashion. For instance, this line of code will retrieve the value of the cn attribute in the first returned entry:

```
$value = $searchobj->entry(1)->get(cn)
```

Now that you know how to access individual attributes and values returned by a search, let's look at how to get this sort of data into a directory server in the first place.

Adding Entries with LDIF

Before we look at the generic methods for adding entries to an LDAP directory, let's stay true to the title of this book and look at a technique useful mostly to system and directory administrators. This technique uses a data format that helps you to bulk load data into a directory server. We're going to look at ways of writing and reading LDIF.

LDIF, defined in a set of pre-RFC draft standards at the time of this writing, offers a simple text representation of a directory entry. Here's a simple LDIF example taken from the latest draft standard by Gordon Good:

```
version: 1
dn: cn=Barbara Jensen, ou=Product Development, dc=airius, dc=com
objectclass: top
objectclass: person
objectclass: organizationalPerson
cn: Barbara Jensen
cn: Barbara J Jensen
cn: Babs Jensen
sn: Jensen
uid: bjensen
telephonenumber: +1 408 555 1212
description: A big sailing fan.
```

```
dn: cn=Bjorn Jensen, ou=Accounting, dc=airius, dc=com
objectclass: top
objectclass: person
objectclass: organizationalPerson
cn: Bjorn Jensen
sn: Jensen
telephonenumber: +1 408 555 1212
```

The format should be almost self-explanatory to you by now. After the LDIF version number, each entry's DN, **objectClass** definitions, and attributes are listed. A line separator alone on a line (i.e., a blank line) separates individual entries.

Our first task is to learn how to write LDIF files from extant directory entries. In addition to giving us practice data for the next section (where we read LDIF files), this functionality is useful because once we have an LDIF file, we can massage it any way we like using Perl's usual text manipulation idioms.

You've already seen how to print out entries in LDIF format during our discussion of LDAP searches. Let's change the code we used in that example so it writes to a file instead:

```
use Mozilla::LDAP::Conn;
use Mozilla::LDAP::LDIF;

<perform bind & search>

open(LDIF,">$LDIFfile") or die "Unable to write to $LDIFfile:$!\n";
# create new LDIF object and pass in destination filehandle
$ldif = new Mozilla::LDAP::LDIF(\*LDIF);

while ($entry) {
    $ldif->writeOneEntry($entry);
    $entry = $c->nextEntry();
}

$c->close();
close(LDIF);
```

Mozilla::LDAP also has a **writeEntries()** method that can take an array of entries instead of just a single entry and write them out in a similar fashion.

For Net::LDAP, changing our original code is even simpler. Instead of:

```
$ldif = new Net::LDAP::LDIF("-");
```

we use:

```
$ldif = new Net::LDAP::LDIF($filename,''w'');
```

to print the output to the specified filename instead of the standard output channel.

Let's work in the opposite direction now, reading LDIF files instead of writing them. The module object methods we're about to explore will allow us to easily add entries to a directory.[*]

When you read LDIF data in via Perl, the process is exactly the reverse of what we used in the previous LDIF-writing examples. Each entry listing in the data gets read in and converted to an entry object instance that is later fed to the appropriate directory modification method. Both modules handle the data reading and parsing for you, so this is a relatively painless process. For instance, with `Mozilla::LDAP`, we can use code like the following:

```
use Mozilla::LDAP::Conn;
use Mozilla::LDAP::LDIF;

$server   = $ARGV[0];
$LDIFfile = $ARGV[1];
$port     = getservbyname("ldap","tcp") || "389";
$rootdn   = "cn=Manager, ou=Systems, dc=ccs, dc=hogwarts, dc=edu";
$pw       = "secret";

# read in an LDIF file specified as the second argument
# on the command line
open(LDIF,"$LDIFfile") or die "Unable to open $LDIFfile:$!\n";
$ldif = new Mozilla::LDAP::LDIF(\*LDIF);

# parse all of the entries, store in @entries
@entries = $ldif->readEntries();
close(LDIF);

# non-anonymous bind
$c = new Mozilla::LDAP::Conn($server,$port,$rootdn,$pw);
die "Unable to bind to $server\n" unless $c;

# iterate through our parsed entry list, attempting to add one at a time
for (@entries){
    $c->add($_); # add this entry to the directory
    warn "Error in add for ". $_->getDN().": ".$c->getErrorString()."\n"
      if $c->getErrorCode();
}
$c->close();
```

This sample also demonstrates the use of the `getErrorCode()` and `getErrorString()` methods to retrieve and report any errors that occur during the data load. Errors can manifest for any number of reasons, including DN/RDN duplication, schema violations, hierarchy problems, etc., so it is important to check for them as part of any entry modification.

---

[*] LDIF files can also contain a special `changetype:` directive that instructs the LDIF reader to delete or modify entry information rather than just add it. Of the two modules we've been working with, only `Net::LDAP` has direct support for `changetype:` via its `Net::LDAP::LDIF::read_cmd()` method.

One other quick note before we move on to the Net::LDAP equivalent: in this and the rest of the examples we're using the root or manager DN user context for demonstration purposes. In general, if you can avoid using this context for everyday work, you should. Good practice for setting up an LDAP server includes creating a powerful account or account group (which is not the root DN) for directory management. Keep this security tip in mind as you code your own applications.

With Net::LDAP, the LDIF entry addition code is similar:

```
use Net::LDAP;
use Net::LDAP::LDIF;

$server   = $ARGV[0];
$LDIFfile = $ARGV[1];
$port     = getservbyname("ldap","tcp") or "389";
$rootdn   = "cn=Manager, ou=Systems, dc=ccs, dc=hogwarts, dc=edu";
$pw       = "secret";

# read in an LDIF file specified as the second argument
# on the command line
# last parameter is "r" for open for read, "w" for write
$ldif = new Net::LDAP::LDIF($LDIFfile,"r");
@entries = $ldif->read();

$c = new Net::LDAP($server, port => $port) or
    die "Unable to connect to $server: $@\n";
$c->bind(dn => $rootdn, password => $pw) or die "Error in bind: $@\n";

for (@entries){
    $res = $c->add($_);
    warn "Error in add for ". $_->dn().": error code ".$res->code."\n"
      if $res->code();
}

$c->unbind();
```

A few notes about this code sample:

- We could chain the two LDIF **read** statements into one line if we wanted to:

  ```
  @entries = new Net::LDAP::LDIF($LDIFfile,"r")->read;
  ```

- If the **add()** fails, we request a decimal error code. For instance, we may see our code print something like this:

  ```
  Error in add for cn=Ursula Hampster, ou=Alumni Association, ou=People,
  o=University of Michigan, c=US: error code 68
  ```

  If the server returns a textual message, the **error()** method retrieves it for us, just like the error reporting code we used with Mozilla::LDAP:

  ```
  print "The error message is: ".$res->error."\n";
  ```

It is safer to test the return value of `code`, as we do in the previous example, because LDAP servers don't always populate the textual error message information in their replies. If you need to convert a decimal error code to an error message or message name, the `Net::LDAP::Util` module offers two routines for this purpose: `ldap_error_text()` and `ldap_error_name()`.

Adding Entries with Standard LDAP Operations

It's time we look under the hood of the entry addition process so we can learn how to create and populate entries manually, instead of just reading them from a file like we did in the last subsection. Our two available modules handle this process quite differently, so we'll have to deal with them separately. `Mozilla::LDAP` is closer to classic object-oriented programming style. We create a new object instance:

```
use Mozilla::LDAP::Entry;
$e = new Mozilla::LDAP::Entry()
```

and then we begin to populate it. The next step is to give the entry a DN. This accomplished with the `setDN()` method:

```
$e->setDN("uid=jay, ou=systems, ou=people, dc=ccs, dc=hogwarts, dc=edu");
```

To populate the other attributes like `objectClass` we can take one of two tacks. We can make some assumptions about the underlying data structure used to represent the entry (essentially a hash of lists) and populate the data structure directly:

```
$e->{cn} = ['Jay Sekora'];
```

Here we're using the attribute name for the hash key and a reference to an anonymous array that holds the data. The `Mozilla::LDAP` module expects an array reference as the hash value, not the data itself, so the following, as tempting as it might be, would be incorrect:

```
# evil incarnate (or at the very least, just wrong)
$e->{cn} = 'Jay Sekora';
```

Alternatively, we can play it safe and use an object method to add the data:

```
$e->addValue('cn', 'Jay Sekora');
```

To add multiple values to an attribute, you simply call `addValue()` repeatedly:

```
$e->addValue('title', 'Unix SysAdmin');
$e->addValue('title', 'Part-time Lecturer');
```

I'm partial to the second method because your code is less likely to break if future versions of the module change the underlying data representation.

Once you've populated your entry, you call the `add()` method to add this entry to the directory. Here's a small script that will add an entry to a directory. It takes a server, a user ID (to be used as part of a DN), and a common name as command-line arguments:

```
use Mozilla::LDAP::Conn;

$server   = $ARGV[0];
$port     = getservbyname("ldap","tcp") || "389";
$suffix   = "ou=People, ou=Systems, dc=ccs, dc=hogwarts, dc=edu";
$rootdn   = "cn=Manager, ou=Systems, dc=ccs, dc=hogwarts, dc=edu";
$pw       = "secret";

# non-anonymous bind
$c = new Mozilla::LDAP::Conn($server,$port,$rootdn,$pw);
die "Unable to bind to $server\n" unless $c;

$e = new Mozilla::LDAP::Entry;
# DN is uid plus a suffix detailing where to put this
# in the directory tree
$e->setDN("uid=$ARGV[1],$suffix");
$e->addValue('uid', $ARGV[1]);
$e->addValue('cn', $ARGV[2]);
$c->add($e);
die "Error in add: ". $c->getErrorString()."\n" if $c->getErrorCode();
```

Note that this code does no input error checking. If you are putting together a script that might really be used interactively, you'll need to check your input to make sure it does not include non-escaped special characters like commas. See the owl tip on attribute value quoting earlier in this section for more details.

Let's turn our attention to Net::LDAP. The entry addition process for Net::LDAP can be less object-oriented if you are so inclined. It too has an Entry module (Net::LDAP::Entry) and a constructor for an entry object instance. But it also contains an add() function that can take a naked data structure for single-step entry addition:

```
$res = $c->add(
    dn => 'uid=jay, ou=systems, ou=people, dc=ccs, dc=hogwarts, dc=edu',
    attr => [ 'cn'   => 'Jay Sekora',
              'sn'   => 'Sekora',
              'mail' => 'jayguy@ccs.hogwarts.edu',
              'title'=> ['Sysadmin','Part-time Lecturer'],
              'uid'  => 'jayguy',
            ]
    );
die "unable to add, errorcode #".$res->code() if $res->code();
```

Here we are passing two arguments to add(). The first is a DN for the entry; the second is a reference to an anonymous array of attribute-value pairs. You'll notice that multivalued attributes like title are specified using a nested anonymous array. If you are used to working with Perl data structures and have an aversion to the object-oriented programming style, this may be a more comfortable idiom.

Deleting Entries

Deleting entries from a directory is easy (and irrevocable, so be careful). Here's some code snippets, again with the bind code left out for brevity's sake:

```
use Mozilla::LDAP::Conn;
...
# if you have an entry in hand, you can use
# $c->delete($entry->getDN()) instead
$c->delete($dn) or
    die "unable to delete entry: ". $c->getErrorString()."\n";

use Net::LDAP;
...
$res = $c->delete($dn);
die "unable to delete, errorcode #".$res->code() if $res->code();
```

It is important to note that **delete()** in both modules operates on a single entry at a time. If you want to delete an entire sub-tree, you will need to first search for all of the child entries of that sub-tree using a scope of **sub** or **one** and then iterate through the return values, deleting as you go. Once the children have been deleted, then you can remove the top of that sub-tree.

Modifying Entry Names

For our final look at LDAP operations, we will focus on two kinds of modifications to LDAP entries. The first kind of modification we'll consider is a change of DN or RDN. Changing the RDN for an entry is easy and supported by both of our modules. Here's the **Mozilla::LDAP** version:

```
use Mozilla::LDAP::Conn;
...
$c->modifyRDN($newRDN,$oldDN,$delold) or
    die "unable to rename entry:". $c->getErrorString()."\n";
```

This code should be self-explanatory with the exception of the **$delold** parameter to **modifyRDN()**. When **true**, this instructs the LDAP libraries to remove the values in the entry that match the values changed in the RDN. For example, if an entry's RDN included the attribute **l** (for location), and the RDN was changed, the old **l** attribute in the entry itself would be deleted, leaving only the new value.

Here's the equivalent **Net::LDAP** code to rename an entry:

```
use Net::LDAP;
...
$res = $c->moddn($oldDN,
                 newrdn       => $newRDN,
                 deleteoldrdn => 1);
die "unable to rename, errorcode #".$res->code() if $res->code();
```

Net::LDAP's moddn() is actually more powerful than this example shows. So far we've only changed an entry's RDN, a change that does not have an effect on that entry's location in the directory tree hierarchy. Version 3 of LDAP introduces a more powerful rename operation that allows arbitrary entry relocations within the directory tree hierarchy. moddn() gives you access to this capability when called with the additional parameter **newsuperior**. If we add it like so:

```
$result = $c->moddn($oldDN,
                     newrdn       => $newRDN,
                     deleteoldrdn => 1,
                     newsuperior  => $parentDN);
     die "unable to rename, errorcode #".$res->code() if $res->code();
```

then the entry located at $oldDN will be moved to become the child of the DN specified in $parentDN. Using this method to move entries in a directory tree is more efficient than the add() or delete() sequence previously required by the protocol, but is not supported by all LDAP servers. In any case, if you've carefully designed your directory tree structure, you'll have to relocate entries less often.

Modifying Entry Attributes

Let's move on to the more common operation of modifying the attributes and attribute values in an entry. Here too we see a significant difference between Mozilla::LDAP and Net::LDAP. With Mozilla::LDAP, we use one of the method calls in Table 6-5 to change the attributes in an entry.

Table 6-5. Mozilla::LDAP Entry Modification Methods

Method Call	Effect
$entry->addValue($attrname, $attrvalue)	Adds the specified value to the named attribute in that entry.
$entry-> removeValue($attrname, $attrvalue)	Removes the specified value from the named attribute in that entry. If this value is the only value set for that attribute, the whole attribute is removed.
$entry-> setValue($attrname, $attrvalue1,...)	Changes the values for the named attribute to the specified value or values.
$entry-> remove($attrname)	Removes the named attribute (values and all) from that entry.

Once you've made all of your changes to an entry using these method calls, you must call the update() method for that LDAP connection to propagate your changes to the directory server. update() is called with a reference to the entry as an argument (i.e., $c->update($entry)).

Let's see these method calls in action as part of a global search and replace. Here's the scenario: one of the facilities at your company is being forced to move from Boston to Indiana. This code will change all of the entries with a Boston location:

```perl
use Mozilla::LDAP::Conn;

$server = $ARGV[0];
$port   = getservbyname("ldap","tcp") || "389";
$basedn = "dc=ccs,dc=hogwarts,dc=edu";
$scope  = "sub";
$rootdn = "cn=Manager, ou=Systems, dc=ccs, dc=hogwarts, dc=edu";
$pw     = "secret";

# non-anonymous bind
$c = new Mozilla::LDAP::Conn($server,$port,$rootdn,$pw);
die "Unable to bind to $server\n" unless $c;

# notice that we ask for the least amount of info
# possible for a speedy search
$entry = $c->search($basedn,$scope,"(l=Boston)",1,'');
die "Error in search:". $c->getErrorString()."\n" if $c->getErrorCode();

if ($entry){
    while($entry){
        $entry->removeValue("l","Boston");
        $entry->addValue("l","Indiana");
        $c->update($entry);
        die "Error in update:" . $c->getErrorString() . "\n"
          if $c->getErrorCode();
        $entry = $c->nextEntry();
    };
}
$c->close();
```

`Net::LDAP` takes a different approach for entry modification. It crams all of the separate `Mozilla::LDAP` method calls we just saw into one mega-method called `modify()`. The parameters passed to this method determine its functionality. Table 6-6 lists the possible choices.

Table 6-6. Net::LDAP Entry Modification Methods

Parameter	Effect
add => {$attrname => $attrvalue}	Adds a named attribute with the given value.
add => {$attrname => [$attrvalue1, $attrvalue2...]}	Adds a named attribute with the specified set of values.
delete => {$attrname => $attrvalue}	Deletes a named attribute with a specific value.
delete => {$attrname => []} delete => [$attrname1,$attrname2...]	Deletes an attribute or set of attributes independent of their value or values.

Table 6-6. Net::LDAP Entry Modification Methods (continued)

Parameter	Effect
`replace => {$attrname => $attrvalue}`	Like add, but replaces the current named attribute value. If `$attrvalue` is a reference to an empty anonymous list (`[]`), this becomes a synonym for the delete operation above.

Be sure to pay attention to the punctuation in the previous table. Some parameters call for a reference to an anonymous hash, others call for a reference to an anonymous array. Mixing the two will cause problems.

We can combine several of these parameters in the same call to `modify()`, but there's a potential problem. When you `modify()` with a set of these parameters like so:

```
$c->modify($dn,replace => {'l' => "Medford"},
               add     => {'l' => "Boston"},
               add     => {'l' => "Cambridge"});
```

there's no guarantee the additions specified will take place after the replacement. If you need your operations to take place in a specific order, you can use a similar syntax to the one we've just introduced. Instead of using a set of discrete parameters, pass in a single array containing a queue of commands. Here's how it works: `modify()` will take a **changes** parameter whose value is a list. This list is treated as a set of pairs. The first half of the pair is the operation to be performed; the second half is a reference to an anonymous array of data for that operation. For instance, if we wanted to insure that the operations in the previous code snippet happened in order, we could write:

```
$c->modify($dn, changes =>
               [ replace => ['l' => "Medford"],
                 add     => ['l' => "Boston"],
                 add     => ['l' => "Cambridge"]
               ]);
```

Take careful note of the punctuation: it is different from the other parameters we saw before.

Given this information on `modify()`, we can write the **Net::LDAP** version of our previous Boston-to-Indiana code like this:

```
use Net::LDAP;

$server   = $ARGV[0];
$port     = getservbyname("ldap","tcp") || "389";
$basedn   = "dc=ccs,dc=hogwarts,dc=edu";
$scope    = "sub";
$rootdn   = "cn=Manager, ou=Systems, dc=ccs, dc=hogwarts, dc=edu";
$pw       = "secret";
```

```
$c = new Net::LDAP($server, port => $port) or
    die "Unable to init for $server: $@\n";
$c->bind(dn => $rootdn, password => $pw) or die "Error in bind: $@\n";

$searchobj = $c->search(base  => $basedn, filter => "(l=Boston)",
                        scope => $scope,  attrs  => [''],
                        typesonly => 1);
die "Error in search: ".$searchobj->error()."\n" if ($searchobj->code());

if ($searchobj){
    @entries = $searchobj->entries;
    for (@entries){
        $res=$c->modify($_->dn(), # dn() yields the DN of that entry
                delete => {"l" => "Boston"},
                add    => {"l" => "Indiana"});
        die "unable to modify, errorcode #".$res->code() if $res->code();
    }
}

$c->unbind();
```

Putting It All Together

Now that we've toured all of the major LDAP functions, let's write some small system administration-related scripts. We'll import our machine database from Chapter 5, *TCP/IP Name Services*, into an LDAP server and then generate some useful output based on LDAP queries. Here are a couple of listings from that flat file, just to remind you of the format:

```
name: shimmer
address: 192.168.1.11
aliases: shim shimmy shimmydoodles
owner: David Davis
department: software
building: main
room: 909
manufacturer: Sun
model: Ultra60
-=-
name: bendir
address: 192.168.1.3
aliases: ben bendoodles
owner: Cindy Coltrane
department: IT
building: west
room: 143
manufacturer: Apple
model: 7500/100
-=-
```

The first thing we need to do is prepare the directory server to receive this data. We're going to use non-standard attributes, so we'll need to update the server's schema. Different servers handle this process in different ways. For instance, the

Netscape Directory server has a pleasant Directory Server Console GUI for changing details like this. Other servers require modifications to a text configuration file. With OpenLDAP, you could use something like this in a file `included` by the master configuration file to define your own object class for a machine:

```
objectclass machine
        requires
                objectClass,
                cn
        allows
                address,
                aliases,
                owner,
                department,
                building,
                room,
                manufacturer,
                model
```

Once the server is configured properly, we can think about importing the data. One approach would be to bulk load it using LDIF. If the sample from our flat-file database shown above reminded you of the LDIF format, you were right on target. This similarity makes the translation easy. Still, we'll have to watch out for a few snares:

Continuation lines

Our flat-file database does not have any entries with values spanning several lines, but if it did we'd need to make sure that output conformed to the LDIF standard. The LDIF standard dictates that all continuation lines must begin with exactly one space.

Entry separators

Our database uses the adorable character sequence -=- between each entry. Two line separators (i.e., a blank line) must separate LDIF entries, so we'll need to axe this character sequence when we see it in the input.

Attribute separators

Right now our data has only one multivalued attribute: aliases. LDIF deals with multivalued attributes by listing each value on a separate line. If we encounter multiple aliases, we'll need special code to print out a separate line for each. If it weren't for this misfeature in our data format, the code to go from our format to LDIF would be a single line of Perl.

Even with these snares, the conversion program is still pretty simple:

```
$datafile = "database";
$recordsep = "-=-\n";
$suffix  = "ou=data, ou=systems, dc=ccs, dc=hogwarts, dc=edu";
$objectclass = <<EOC;
objectclass: top
```

```
objectclass: machine
EOC

open(DATA,$datafile) or die "unable to open $datafile:$!\n";

# Perl modules break with this, even if it is in the spec
# print "version: 1\n"; #

while (<DATA>) {
    # print the header for each entry
    if (/name:\s*(.*)/){
        print "dn: cn=$1, $suffix\n";
        print $objectclass;
        print "cn: $1\n";
        next;
    }
    # handle the multi-valued aliases attribute
    if (s/^aliases:\s*//){
        @aliases = split;
        foreach $name (@aliases){
            print "aliases: $name\n";
        }
        next;
    }
    # handle the end of record separator
    if ($_ eq $recordsep){
        print "\n";
        next;
    }
    # otherwise, just print the attribute as we found it
    print;
}

close(DATA);
```

If we run this code, it prints an LDIF file that looks (in part) like this:

```
dn: cn=shimmer, ou=data, ou=systems, dc=ccs, dc=hogwarts, dc=edu
objectclass: top
objectclass: machine
cn: shimmer
address: 192.168.1.11
aliases: shim
aliases: shimmy
aliases: shimmydoodles
owner: David Davis
department: software
building: main
room: 909
manufacturer: Sun
model: Ultra60

dn: cn=bendir, ou=data, ou=systems, dc=ccs, dc=hogwarts, dc=edu
objectclass: top
objectclass: machine
cn: bendir
```

```
address: 192.168.1.3
aliases: ben
aliases: bendoodles
owner: Cindy Coltrane
department: IT
building: west
room: 143
manufacturer: Apple
model: 7500/100
...
```

With this LDIF file, we can use one of the bulk-load programs that come with our servers to load our data into the server. For instance, *ldif2ldbm*, packaged with both the OpenLDAP and the Netscape Directory Servers, reads an LDIF file and directly imports it into the directory server's native backend format without having to go through LDAP. Though you can only use this program while the server is not running, it can provide the quickest way to get lots of data into a server. If you can't take the server down, we can use the LDIF-reading Perl code we developed earlier to feed a file like this to an LDAP server.

To throw one more option into the mix, here's some code that skips the intermediary step of creating an LDIF file and imports our data directly into an LDAP server:

```perl
use Net::LDAP;
use Net::LDAP::Entry;

$datafile  = "database";
$recordsep = "-=-";
$server    = $ARGV[0];
$port      = getservbyname("ldap","tcp") || "389";
$suffix    = "ou=data, ou=systems, dc=ccs, dc=hogwarts, dc=edu";
$rootdn    = "cn=Manager, o=University of Michigan, c=US";
$pw        = "secret";

$c = new Net::LDAP($server,port => $port) or
   die "Unable to init for $server: $@\n";
$c->bind(dn => $rootdn,password => $pw) or die "Error in bind: $@\n";

open(DATA,$datafile) or die "unable to open $datafile:$!\n";

while (<DATA>) {
    chomp;
    # at the start of a new record, create a new entry object instance
    if (/^name:\s*(.*)/){
        $dn="cn=$1, $suffix";
        $entry = new Net::LDAP::Entry;
        $entry->add("cn",$1);
        next;
    }
    # special case for multivalued attribute
    if (s/^aliases:\s*//){
        $entry->add('aliases',[split()]);
```

```
        next;
    }

    # if we've hit the end of the record, add it to the server
    if ($_ eq $recordsep){
        $entry->add("objectclass",["top","machine"]);
        $entry->dn($dn);
        $res = $c->add($entry);
        warn "Error in add for " . $entry->dn() . ": error code " .
             $res->code."\n"
          if $res->code();
        undef $entry;
        next;
    }

    # add all of the other attributes
    $entry->add(split(':\s*')); # assume single valued attributes
}

close(DATA);
$c->unbind();
```

Now that we've imported the data into a server, we can start to do some interesting things. For the following examples, we'll flip-flop between the two LDAP modules. To save space, the header at the top of each sample that sets our configuration variables and the code that binds us to a server will not be repeated for each example.

So what can you do with this data when it resides in an LDAP server? You can generate a hosts file on the fly:

```
use Mozilla::LDAP;
...
$entry = $c->search($basedn,'one','(objectclass=machine)',0,
                     'cn','address','aliases');
die "Error in search:". $c->getErrorString()."\n" if $c->getErrorCode();

if ($entry){
    print "#\n\# host file - GENERATED BY $0\n
           # DO NOT EDIT BY HAND!\n#\n";
    while($entry){
        print $entry->{address}[0],"\t",
              $entry->{cn}[0]," ",
              join(' ',@{$entry->{aliases}}),"\n";
        $entry = $c->nextEntry();
    };
}
$c->close();
```

Here's the output:

```
#
# host file - GENERATED BY ldap2hosts
```

```
# DO NOT EDIT BY HAND!
#
192.168.1.11     shimmer shim shimmy shimmydoodles
192.168.1.3      bendir ben bendoodles
192.168.1.12     sulawesi sula su-lee
192.168.1.55     sander sandy mickey mickeydoo
```

You can find the names of all of our machines made by Apple:

```
use Net::LDAP;
...
$searchobj = $c->search(base  => $basedn,
                        filter => "(manufacturer=Apple)",
                        scope => 'one', attrs => ['cn']);
die "Error in search: ".$searchobj->error()."\n" if ($searchobj->code());

if ($searchobj){
    for ($searchobj->entries){
        print $_->get('cn'),"\n";
    }
}

$c->unbind();
```

Here's the output:

```
bendir
sulawesi
```

You can generate a list of machine owners:

```
use Mozilla::LDAP;
...
$entry = $c->search($basedn,'one','(objectclass=machine)',0,
                    'cn','owner');
die "Error in search:". $c->getErrorString()."\n" if $c->getErrorCode();

if ($entry){
    while($entry){
        push(@{$owners{$entry->{owner}[0]}},$entry->{cn}[0]);
        $entry = $c->nextEntry();
    };
}
$c->close();
for (sort keys %owners){
    print $_.":\t".join(' ',@{$owners{$_}})."\n";
}
```

Here's the output:

```
Alex Rollins:   sander
Cindy Coltrane: bendir
David Davis:    shimmer
Ellen Monk:     sulawesi
```

Or you can check to see if the current user ID is the owner of the current Unix machine (pseudo-authentication):

```
use Mozilla::LDAP::Conn;
use Sys::Hostname;

$user = (getpwuid($<))[6];

$hostname = hostname;
$hostname =~ s/^([^.]+)\..*/$1/; # strip domain name off of host
...
$entry = $c->search("cn=$hostname,$suffix",'base',"(owner=$user)",1,'');

if ($entry){
    print "Owner ($user) logged on to machine $hostname.\n";
}
else {
    print "$user is not the owner of this machine ($hostname)\n.";
}
$c->close();
```

These snippets should give you an idea of some of the system administration uses for LDAP access through Perl, and provide inspiration to write your own. In the next section we'll take these ideas to the next level and see a whole administration framework based on the conceptual groundwork laid by LDAP.

ADSI (Active Directory Service Interfaces)

For the final section of this chapter we'll discuss a platform-dependent directory service framework that is heavily based on the material we've just covered.

Microsoft created a sophisticated LDAP-based directory service called Active Directory for use at the heart of their Windows 2000 administration framework. Active Directory serves as the repository for all of the important configuration information (users, groups, system policies, software installation support, etc.) used in a network of Windows 2000 machines.

During the development of Active Directory, Microsoft realized a higher-level applications interface to this service was needed. ADSI, or Active Directory Service Interfaces, was invented to provide this interface. To their credit, the developers at Microsoft also realized that their new ADSI framework could be extended to cover other system administration realms like printers and NT services. This coverage makes ADSI immensely useful to people who script and automate system administration tasks. Before we show this power in action, there are a few basic concepts and terms we need to cover.

ADSI Basics

ADSI can be thought of as a wrapper around any directory service that wishes to participate in the ADSI framework. There are *providers*, as these ADSI glue implementations are called, for LDAP, WinNT 4.0, and Novell Directory Service among others. In ADSI-speak, each of these directory services and data domains (WinNT isn't a directory service) are called *namespaces*. ADSI gives you a uniform way to query and change the data found in these namespaces.

To understand ADSI, you have to know a little about the Microsoft Component Object Model (COM) upon which ADSI is built. There are many books about COM, but we can distill down to these key points:

- Everything we want to work with via COM is an *object.*[*]

- Objects have *interfaces* that provide a set of *methods* for us to use to interact with these objects. From Perl, we can use the methods provided by or inherited from the interface called *IDispatch*. Luckily most of the ADSI methods provided by the ADSI interfaces and their children (e.g., IADsUser, IADsComputer, IADsPrintQueue) are inherited from *IDispatch*.

- The values encapsulated by an object, which is queried and changed through these methods, are called *properties*. We'll refer to two kinds of properties in this chapter: *interface-defined properties* (those that are defined as part of an interface), and *schema-defined properties* (those that are defined in a schema object, more on this in just a moment). Unless we refer explicitly to "schema properties" in the following dicussion, we'll only be using interface properties.

This is standard object-oriented programming fare. It starts to get tricky when the nomenclature for ADSI/COM and other object-oriented worlds like LDAP collide.

For instance, in ADSI we speak of two different kinds of objects: *leaf* and *container*. Leaf objects encapsulate real data; container objects hold, or *parent*, other objects. In LDAP-speak a close translation for these terms might be "entry" and "branching point." On one hand we talk about objects with properties and on the other, entries with attributes. So how do you deal with this discrepancy, since both names refer to the exact same data?

Here's one way to think about it: an LDAP server does indeed provide access to a tree full of entries and their associated attributes. When you use ADSI instead of native LDAP to get at an entry in that tree, ADSI sucks the entry out of the LDAP server, wraps it up in a few layers of shiny wrapping paper, and hands it to you as a COM object. You use the necessary methods to get the contents of that parcel,

---

[*] COM is in fact the protocol used to communicate with these objects as part of the larger framework called OLE, for Object Linking and Embedding. In this section, I've tried to keep us out of the Microsoft morass of acronyms, but if you want to dig deeper, there are some good resources that are available at *http://www.microsoft.com/com*.

which are now called "properties." If you make any changes to the properties of this object, you can hand the object back to ADSI, which will take care of unwrapping the information and putting it back in the LDAP tree for you.

A reasonable question at this point is "Why not go directly to the LDAP server?" Two good answers: once we know how to use ADSI to communicate with one kind of directory service, we know how to communicate with them all (or at least the ones that have ADSI providers). The second answer will be demonstrated in a few moments when we see how ADSI's encapsulation can make directory service programming a little easier.

To head in the direction of ADSI programming from Perl, we need to introduce *ADsPaths*. ADsPaths give us a unique way to refer to objects in any of our namespaces. They look like this:

```
<progID>:<path to object>
```

`<progID>` is the programmatic identifier for a provider (e.g., WinNT or LDAP), and `<path to object>` is a provider-specific way of finding the object in its namespace. The `<progID>` portion is *case-sensitive*. Using `winnt`, `ldap`, or `WINNT` instead of `WinNT` and `LDAP` will cause your programs to fail.

Here are some ADsPath examples taken from the ADSI SDK documentation:

```
WinNT://MyDomain/MyServer/User
WinNT://MyDomain/JohnSmith,user
LDAP://ldapsvr/CN=TopHat,DC=DEV,DC=MSFT,DC=COM,O=Internet
LDAP://MyDomain.microsoft.com/CN=TopH,DC=DEV,DC=MSFT,DC=COM,O=Internet
```

It's no coincidence that these look like URLs, since both URLs and ADsPaths serve roughly the same purpose. They both try to provide an unambiguous way to reference a piece of data made available by different data services. In the case of LDAP ADsPaths, we are using the LDAP URL syntax from the RFC we mention in Appendix B (RFC2255).

We'll look more closely at ADsPaths when we discuss the two namespaces, *WinNT* and *LDAP*, referenced earlier. Before we get there, let's see how ADSI in general is used from Perl.

Using ADSI from Perl

The `Win32::OLE` family of modules maintained by Jan Dubois and Gurusamy Sarathy give us the Perl bridge to ADSI (which is built on COM as part of OLE). After loading the main module, we use it to request an ADSI object:

```
use Win32::OLE;

$adsobj = Win32::OLE->GetObject($ADsPath) or
    die "Unable to retrieve the object for $ADsPath\n";
```

The Tools of the ADSI Trade

To use the material in this chapter you will need ADSI installed on at least one machine on your network. This machine can act (via DCOM) as an ADSI gateway for the other machines. See Toby Everett's site, given below, for more information on how to set ADSI up to work with DCOM.

Any machine running Windows 2000 has ADSI built into the OS. For all other Win32 machines, you will need to download and install the free ADSI 2.5 distribution found at *http://www.microsoft.com/adsi*. At this link you will also find crucial ADSI documentation including *adsi25.chm*, a compressed HTML help file that contains some of the best ADSI documentation available.

Even if you are using Windows 2000, I recommend downloading the ADSI SDK found at the Microsoft URL because it provides this documentation and a handy ADSI object browser called *ADsVW*. The SDK comes with ADSI programming examples in a number of languages including Perl. Unfortunately, the examples in the current ADSI distribution rely on the deprecated *OLE.pm* module, so at best you might be able to pick up a few tips, but you should not use these examples as your starting point.

Before you begin to code, you will also want to pick up Toby Everett's ADSI object browser (written in Perl) from *http://opensource.activestate.com/authors/tobyeverett*. It will help you navigate around the ADSI namespaces. Be sure to visit this site early in your ADSI programming career because it is one of the best available on using ADSI from Perl.

`Win32::OLE->GetObject()` takes an OLE *moniker* (a unique identifier to an object, which in this case is an ADsPath) and returns an ADSI object for us. This call also handles the process of *binding* to the object, a process you should be familiar with from our LDAP discussion. By default we bind to the object using the credentials of the user running the script.

Here's a tip that may save you some consternation. If you run these two lines of code in the Perl debugger and examine the contents of the returned object reference, you might see something like this:

```
DB<3> x $adsobj
0  Win32::OLE=HASH(0x10fe0d4)
      empty hash
```

Don't panic. `Win32::OLE` uses the power of tied variables. The seemingly empty data structure you see here will magically yield information from our object when we access it properly.

Perl's hash reference syntax is used to access the interface property values of an ADSI object:

```
$value = $adsobj->{key}
```

For instance, if that object had a **Name** property defined as part of its interface (and they all do), you could:

```
print $adsobj->{Name}."\n";
```

Interface property values can be assigned using the same notation:

```
$adsobj->{FullName}= "Oog";  # set the property in the cache
```

An ADSI object's properties are stored in an in-memory cache (called the *property cache*). The first request for an object's properties populates this cache. Subsequent queries for the same property will retrieve the information from this cache, *not the directory service*. If you want to populate the cache by hand, you can call that object instance's **GetInfo()** or **GetInfoEx()** (an extended version of **GetInfo()**) method using the syntax we'll see in a moment.

Because the initial fetch is automatic, **GetInfo()** and **GetInfoEx()** are often overlooked. Though we won't see any in this book, there are cases where you will need them. Two example cases:

1. Some object properties are only fetched by an explicit **GetInfoEx()** call. Microsoft Exchange 5.5's LDAP provider offers a particularly egregious example because many of its properties are not available without calling **GetInfoEx()** first. *See http://opensource.activestate.com/authors/tobyeverett* for more details on this inconsistency.

2. If you have a directory that multiple people can change, an object you may have just retrieved could be changed while you are still working with it. If this happens, the data in your property cache for that object will be stale. **GetInfo()** and **GetInfoEx()** will refresh this cache for you.

To actually update the backend directory service and data source provided through ADSI, you *must* call the special method **SetInfo()** after changing an object. **SetInfo()** flushes the changes from the property cache to the actual directory service and data source. (This should remind you of our need in **Mozilla::LDAP** to call the **update()** method. It's the same concept.)

Calling methods from an ADSI object instance is easy:

```
$adsobj->Method($arguments...)
```

So, if we changed an object's properties as mentioned in the previous warning, we might use this line right after the code that made the change:

```
$adsobj->SetInfo();
```

This would flush the data from the property cache back into the underlying directory service or data source.

One `Win32::OLE` call you'll want to use often is `Win32::OLE->LastError()`. This will return the error, if any, generated by the last OLE operation. Using the *-w* switch with Perl (e.g., *perl -w script*) also causes any OLE failures to complain in a verbose manner. Often these error messages are all the debugging help you have, so be sure to make good use of them.

The ADSI code we've shown so far should look like fairly standard Perl to you, because on the surface, it is. Now let's introduce a few of the plot complications.

Dealing with Container/Collection Objects

Early in this section we mentioned there are two kinds of ADSI objects: leaf and container. Leaf objects represent pure data, whereas container objects (also called collection objects in OLE/COM terms) contain other objects. Another way to distinguish between the two in the ADSI context is by noting that leaf objects have no children in a hierarchy, but container objects do.

Container objects require special handling, since most of the time we're interested in the data encapsulated by their child objects. There are two ways to access these objects from Perl. `Win32::OLE` offers a special function called `in()`, which is not available by default when the module is loaded in the standard fashion. We have to use the following at the beginning of our code to make use of it:

```
use Win32::OLE 'in';
```

`in()` will return a list of references to the child objects held by that container. This allows us to write easy-to-read Perl code like:

```
foreach $child (in $adsobj){
    print $child->{Name}
}
```

Alternatively, we can load one of `Win32::OLE`'s helpful progeny, which is called `Win32::OLE::Enum`. `Win32::OLE::Enum->new()` will create an enumerator object from one of our container objects:

```
use Win32::OLE::Enum;

$enobj = Win32::OLE::Enum->new($adsobj);
```

We can then call a few methods on this enumerator object to get at `$adsobj`'s children. These methods should remind you of the methods we used with `Mozilla::LDAP`'s search operations; it is the same process.

`$enobj->Next()` will return a reference to the next child object instance (or the next X objects if given an optional parameter). `$enobj->All` returns a list of object instance references. `Win32::OLE::Enum` offers a few more methods (see the documentation for details), but these are the ones you'll use most often.

Identifying a Container Object

You can't know if an object is a container object *a priori*. There is no way to ask an object itself about its "containerness" from Perl. The closest you can come is to try to create an enumerator object and fail gracefully if this does not succeed. Here's some code that does just that:

```
use Win32::OLE;
use Win32::OLE::Enum;

eval {$enobj = Win32::OLE::Enum->new($adsobj)};
print "object is " . ($@ ? "not " : "") . "a container\n";
```

Alternatively, you can look to other sources that describe the object. This segues nicely into our third plot complication.

So How Do You Know Anything About an Object?

We've avoided the biggest and perhaps the most important question until now. In a moment we'll be dealing with objects in two of our namespaces. We understand how to retrieve and set object properties and how to call object methods for these objects, but only if we already know the names of these properties and methods. Where did these names come from? How did we find them in the first place?

There's no single place to find an answer to these questions, but there are a few sources we can draw upon to get most of the picture. The first place is the ADSI documentation, especially the help file mentioned in the earlier sidebar, "The Tools of the ADSI Trade." This file has an huge amount of material. For the answer to our question about property and methods names, the place to start in the file is *Active Directory Service Interfaces 2.5→ADSI Reference→ADSI System Providers*.

The documentation is sometimes the only place to find method names, but there's a second, more interesting approach we can take when looking for property names. We can use metadata provided by ADSI itself. This is where the schema properties concept we mentioned earlier comes into the picture.

Every ADSI object has a property called **Schema** that yields an ADsPath to its schema object. For instance, the following code:

```
use Win32::OLE;

$ADsPath = "WinNT://BEESKNEES,computer";
$adsobj  = Win32::OLE->GetObject($ADsPath) or
    die "Unable to retrieve the object for $ADsPath\n";
print "This is a ".$adsobj->{Class}."object, schema is at:\n".
      $adsobj->{Schema},"\n";
```

will print:

```
This is a Computer object, schema is at: WinNT://DomainName/Schema/Computer
```

The value of $adsobj→{Schema} is an ADsPath to an object that describes the schema for the objects of class Computer in that domain. Here we're using the term "schema" in the same way we used it when talking about LDAP schemas. In LDAP, schemas define which attributes can and must be present in entries of specific object classes. In ADSI, a schema object holds the same information about objects of a certain class and their schema properties.

If we want to see the possible attribute names for an object, we can look at the values of two properties in its schema object: MandatoryProperties and OptionalProperties. Let's change the print statement above to the following:

```
$schmobj = Win32::OLE->GetObject($adsobj->{Schema}) or
                die "Unable to retrieve the object for $ADsPath\n";
print join("\n",@{$schmobj->{MandatoryProperties}},
                @{$schmobj->{OptionalProperties}}),"\n";
```

This prints:

```
Owner
Division
OperatingSystem
OperatingSystemVersion
Processor
ProcessorCount
```

Now we know the possible schema interface property names in the WinNT namespace for our Computer objects. Pretty nifty.

Schema properties are retrieved and set in a slightly different manner than interface properties. You recall that interface properties are retrieved and set like this:

```
# retrieving and setting INTERFACE properties
$value = $obj->{property};
$obj->{property} = $value;
```

Schema properties are retrieved and set using special methods:

```
# retrieving and setting SCHEMA properties
$value = $obj->Get("property");
$obj->Put("property","value");
```

Everything we've talked about so far regarding interface properties holds true for schema properties as well (i.e., property cache, SetInfo( ), etc). Besides the need to use special methods to retrieve and set values, the only other place where you'll need to distinguish between the two is in their names. Sometimes the same object may have two different names for essentially the same property, one for the interface property and one for the schema property. For example, these two retrieve the same basic setting for a user:

```
$len = $userobj->{PasswordMinimumLength};  # the interface property
$len = $userobj->Get("MinPasswordLength"); # the same schema property
```

There are two kinds of properties because interface properties exist as part of the underlying COM model. When developers define an interface as part of developing a program, they also define the interface properties. Later on, if they want to extend the property set, they have to modify both the COM interface and any code that uses that interface. In ADSI, developers can change the schema properties in a provider without having to modify the underlying COM interface for that provider. It is important to become comfortable with dealing with both kinds of properties because sometimes a piece of data in an object is only made available from within one kind of property and not in the other.

On a practical note, if you are just looking for interface or schema property names and don't want to bother writing a program to find them, I recommend using the Toby Everett ADSI browser mentioned earlier. Figure 6-2 is a sample screen shot of this browser in action.

Alternatively, there is a program called *ADSIDump* in the *General* folder of the SDK samples that can dump the contents of an entire ADSI tree for you.

Searching

This is the last complication we'll discuss before moving on. In "LDAP: A Sophisticated Directory Service," we spent considerable time talking about LDAP searches. But here in ADSI-land, we've breathed hardly a word about the subject. This is because from Perl (and any other language that uses the same OLE automation interface), searching with ADSI is a pain—that is, sub-tree searches, or searches that entail anything but the simplest of search filters are excruciatingly painful. (Others are not so bad.) Complex searches are troublesome because they require you to step out of the ADSI framework and use a whole different methodology to get at your data (not to mention learn more Microsoft acronyms).

But people who do system administration are trained to laugh at pain, so let's start with simple searches before tackling the hard stuff. Simple searches that encompass one object (scope of **base**) or an object's immediate children (scope of **one**) can be handled manually with Perl. Here's how:

- For a single object, retrieve the properties of interest and use the normal Perl comparison operators to determine if this object is a match:

  ```
  if ($adsobj->{cn} eq "Mark Sausville" and $adsobj->{State} eq "CA"){...}
  ```

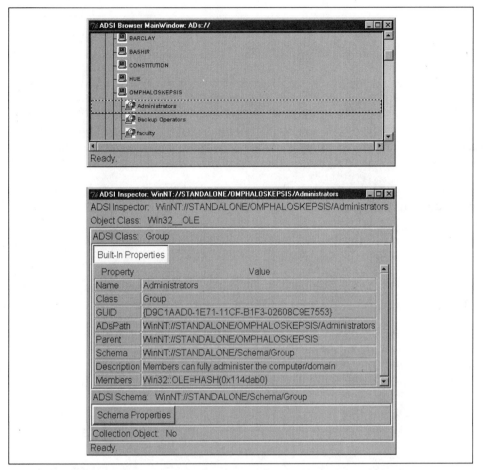

Figure 6-2. Everett's ADSI browser displaying an Administrators group object

- To search the children of an object, use the container object access techniques we discussed previously and then examine each child object in turn. We'll see some examples of this type of search in a moment.

If you want to do more complex searches like those that entail searching a whole directory tree or sub-tree, you need to switch to using a different "middleware" technology called ADO (ActiveX Data Objects). ADO offers scripting languages an interface to Microsoft's OLE DB layer. OLE DB provides a common database-oriented interface to data sources like relational databases and directory services. In our case we'll be using ADO to talk to ADSI (which then talks to the actual directory service). Because ADO is a database-oriented methodology, the code you are about to see foreshadows the ODBC material we cover in Chapter 7.

ADO only works when talking to the LDAP ADSI provider. It will not work for the WinNT namespace.

ADO is a whole subject in itself that is only peripherally related to the subject of directory services, so we're only going to look at one example and provide a little bit of explanation before moving on to some more relevant ADSI examples. For more information on ADO itself, please see *http://www.microsoft.com/ado*.

Here's some code that displays the name of all of the groups to be found in a given domain. We'll go through this code piece by piece in a moment.

```
use Win32::OLE 'in';

# get ADO object, set the provider, open the connection
$c = Win32::OLE->new("ADODB.Connection");
$c->{Provider} = "ADsDSOObject";
$c->Open("ADSI Provider");
die Win32::OLE->LastError() if Win32::OLE->LastError();

# prepare and then execute the query
$ADsPath = "LDAP://ldapserver/dc=example,dc=com";
$rs = $c->Execute("<$ADsPath>;(objectClass=Group);Name;SubTree");
die Win32::OLE->LastError() if Win32::OLE->LastError();

until ($rs->EOF){
    print $rs->Fields(0)->{Value},"\n";
    $rs->MoveNext;
}

$rs->Close;
$c->Close;
```

The block of code after the module load gets an ADO Connection object instance sets that object instance's provider name, and then instructs it to open the connection. This connection is opened on behalf of the user running the script, though we could have set some other object properties to change this.

We then perform the actual search using **Execute()**. This search can be specified using one of two "dialects," SQL or ADSI.* The ADSI dialect, as shown, uses a

---

* If you know SQL, you may find the SQL dialect a little easier. The SQL dialect offers some interesting possibilities. For instance, MS SQL Server 7 can be configured to know about ADSI providers in addition to normal databases. This means that you can execute SQL queries which simultaneously access Active-Directory objects via ADSI.

command string consisting as four arguments, each separated by semicolons.* The arguments are:

- An ADsPath (in angle brackets) that sets the server and base DN for the search
- A search filter (using the same LDAP filter syntax we saw before)
- The name or names (separated by commas) of the properties to return
- A search scope of either Base, OneLevel, or SubTree (as per the LDAP standard)

`Execute()` returns a reference to the first of the ADO `RecordSet` objects returned by our query. We ask for each `RecordSet` object in turn, unpacking the objects it holds and printing the `Value` property returned by the `Fields()` method for each of these objects. The `Value` property contains the value we requested in our command string (the name of the `Group` object). Here's some sample output from a Windows 2000 machine:

```
Administrators
Users
Guests
Backup Operators
Replicator
Server Operators
Account Operators
Print Operators
DHCP Users
DHCP Administrators
Domain Computers
Domain Controllers
Schema Admins
Enterprise Admins
Cert Publishers
Domain Admins
Domain Users
Domain Guests
Group Policy Admins
RAS and IAS Servers
DnsAdmins
DnsUpdateProxy
```

Performing Common Tasks Using the WinNT and LDAP Namespaces

Now that we've safely emerged from our list of complications, we can turn to performing some common administrative tasks using ADSI from Perl. The goal is to

---

* Be careful of this ADSI ADO provider quirk: there cannot be any whitespace around the semicolons or the query will fail.

give you a taste of the things you can do with the ADSI information we've presented. Then you can use the code we're going to see as starter recipes for your own programming.

For these tasks, we'll use one of two namespaces. The first namespace is *WinNT*, which gives us access to Windows 4.0 objects like users, groups, printers, services, etc.

The second is our friend *LDAP*. *LDAP* becomes the provider of choice when we move on to Windows 2000 and its LDAP-based Active Directory. Most of the *WinNT* objects can be accessed via *LDAP* as well. But even with Windows 2000, there are still tasks that can only be performed using the WinNT namespace (like the creation of local machine accounts).

The code that works with these different namespaces looks similar (after all, that's part of the point of using ADSI), but you should note two important differences. First, the ADsPath format is slightly different. The WinNT ADsPath takes one of these forms according to the ADSI SDK:

```
WinNT:[//DomainName[/ComputerName[/ObjectName[,className]]]]
WinNT:[//DomainName[/ObjectName[,className]]]
WinNT:[//ComputerName,computer]
WinNT:
```

The LDAP ADsPath looks like this:

```
LDAP://HostName[:PortNumber][/DistinguishedName]
```

Note that the LDAP ADsPath requires a server hostname under NT4 (this changes in Windows 2000). This means that the LDAP namespace isn't browsable from its top-level like the WinNT namespace, since you have to point it at a starting server. With the WinNT namespace, one can begin with an ADsPath of just `WinNT:` to start drilling down into the domain hierarchy.

Also note that the properties of the objects in the two namespaces are similar, but they are not the same. For instance, you can access the same user objects from both the WinNT and LDAP namespaces, but you can only get to some Active Directory properties for a particular user object through the LDAP namespace.

It's especially important to pay attention to the differences between the schema found in the two namespaces. For example, the `User` class for WinNT has no mandatory properties while the LDAP `User` class requires `cn` and `samAccountName` to be present in every user object.

With these differences in mind, let's look at some actual code. To save space, we're going to omit most of the error checking, but you'll want to run your scripts with the *-w* switch and liberally sprinkle lines like this throughout your code:

```
die "OLE error :".Win32::OLE->LastError() if Win32::OLE->LastError();
```

Working with Users via ADSI

To dump the list of users in a domain:

```
use Win32::OLE 'in';

$AdsPath = "WinNT://DomainName/PDCName,computer";
$c = Win32::OLE->GetObject($ADsPath) or die "Unable to get $ADsPath\n";
foreach $adsobj (in $c){
    print $adsobj->{Name},"\n" if ($adsobj->{Class} eq "User");
}
```

To create a user and set her or his Full Name:

```
use Win32::OLE;

$ADsPath="WinNT://DomainName/ComputerName,computer";
$c = Win32::OLE->GetObject($ADsPath) or die "Unable to get $ADsPath\n";

# create and return a User object
$u = $c->Create("user",$username);
$u->SetInfo();  # we have to create the user before we modify it

# no space between "Full" and "Name" allowed with WinNT: namespace
$u->{FullName} = $fullname;
$su->SetInfo();
```

If ComputerName is a Primary Domain Controller, then a domain user is created. If not, that user is local to the specified machine.

The equivalent code to create a global user (you can't create local users using LDAP) in an Active Directory looks like this:

```
use Win32::OLE;

$AdsPath = "LDAP://ldapserver,CN=Users,dc=example,dc=com";

$c = Win32::OLE->GetObject($ADsPath) or die "Unable to get $ADsPath\n";

# create and return a User object
$u=$c->Create("user","cn=".$commonname);
$u->{samAccountName} = $username;
# we have to create the user in the dir before we modify it
$u->SetInfo();

# space between "Full" and "Name" required with LDAP: namespace, sigh
$u->{'Full Name'} = $fullname;
$u->SetInfo();
```

Deleting a user requires just a small change:

```
use Win32::OLE;

$AdsPath = "WinNT://DomainName/ComputerName,computer";
$c = Win32::OLE->GetObject($ADsPath) or die "Unable to get $ADsPath\n";
```

```
# delete the User object, note that we are bound to the container object
$c->Delete("user",$username);
$u->SetInfo();
```

Changing a user's password is a single method's work:

```
use Win32::OLE;

$AdsPath = "WinNT://DomainName/ComputerName/".$username;
$u = Win32::OLE->GetObject($ADsPath) or die "Unable to get $ADsPath\n";

$u->ChangePasssword($oldpassword,$newpassword);
$u->SetInfo();
```

Working with Groups via ADSI

You can enumerate the available groups with just a minor tweak of our user enumeration code above. The one changed line is:

```
print $adsobj->{Name},"\n" if ($adsobj->{Class} eq "Group");
```

Creation and deletion of groups is performed using the same **Create()** and **Delete()** methods we just saw for user account and creation. The only difference is the first argument needs to be "group." For example:

```
$g = $c->Create("group",$groupname);
```

To add a user to a group (specified as a **GroupName**) once you've created it:

```
use Win32::OLE;

$AdsPath = "WinNT://DomainName/GroupName,group";

$g = Win32::OLE->GetObject($ADsPath) or die "Unable to get $ADsPath\n";

# this uses the ADsPath to a specific user object
$g->Add($userADsPath);
```

The same rules we saw before about local versus domain (global) users apply here as well. If we want to add a domain user to our group, our **$userADsPath** should reference the user at the PDC for that domain.

To remove a user from a group, use:

```
$c->Remove($userADsPath);
```

Working with File Shares via ADSI

Now we start to get into some of the more interesting ADSI esoterica. It is possible to use ADSI to instruct a machine to start sharing a part of its local storage to other computers:

```
use Win32::OLE;

$AdsPath = "WinNT://ComputerName/lanmanserver";

$c = Win32::OLE->GetObject($ADsPath) or die "Unable to get $ADsPath\n";

$s = $c->Create("fileshare",$sharename);
$s->{path}        = 'C:\directory';
$s->{description} = "This is a Perl created share";
$s->SetInfo();
```

File shares are deleted using the `Delete()` method.

Before we move on to other tasks, let me take this opportunity to remind you to closely consult the SDK documentation before using any of these ADSI objects. Sometimes, you'll find useful surprises. If you look at this section in the ADSI 2.5 help file: *Active Directory Service Interfaces 2.5→ADSI Reference→ADSI Interfaces→Persistent Object Interfaces→IADsFileShare*, you'll see that a `fileshare` object has a `CurrentUserCount` property that shows how many users are currently connected to this file share. This could be a very handy detail.

Working with Print Queues and Print Jobs via ADSI

Here's how to determine the names of the queues on a particular server and the models of the printers being used to serve those queues:

```
use Win32::OLE 'in';

$ADsPath="WinNT://DomainName/PrintServerName,computer";

$c = Win32::OLE->GetObject($ADsPath) or die "Unable to get $ADsPath\n";

foreach $adsobj (in $c){
    print $adsobj->{Name}.":".$adsobj->{Model}."\n"
        if ($adsobj->{Class} eq "PrintQueue");
}
```

Once you have the name of a print queue, you can bind to it directly to query and control it:

```
use Win32::OLE 'in';

# this table comes from this section in the ADSI 2.5 SDK:
# 'Active Directory Service Interfaces 2.5->ADSI Reference->
# ADSI Interfaces->Dynamic Object Interfaces->IADsPrintQueueOperations->
# IADsPrintQueueOperations Property Methods' (phew)

%status =
  (0x00000001 => 'PAUSED',            0x00000002 => 'PENDING_DELETION',
```

```
        0x00000003 => 'ERROR' ,           0x00000004 => 'PAPER_JAM',
        0x00000005 => 'PAPER_OUT',        0x00000006 => 'MANUAL_FEED',
        0x00000007 => 'PAPER_PROBLEM',    0x00000008 => 'OFFLINE',
        0x00000100 => 'IO_ACTIVE',        0x00000200 => 'BUSY',
        0x00000400 => 'PRINTING',         0x00000800 => 'OUTPUT_BIN_FULL',
        0x00001000 => 'NOT_AVAILABLE',    0x00002000 => 'WAITING',
        0x00004000 => 'PROCESSING',       0x00008000 => 'INITIALIZING',
        0x00010000 => 'WARMING_UP',       0x00020000 => 'TONER_LOW',
        0x00040000 => 'NO_TONER',         0x00080000 => 'PAGE_PUNT',
        0x00100000 => 'USER_INTERVENTION', 0x00200000 => 'OUT_OF_MEMORY',
        0x00400000 => 'DOOR_OPEN',        0x00800000 => 'SERVER_UNKNOWN',
        0x01000000 => 'POWER_SAVE');

    $ADsPath = "WinNT://PrintServerName/PrintQueueName";

    $p = Win32::OLE->GetObject($ADsPath) or die "Unable to get $ADsPath\n";

    print "The printer status for " . $c->{Name} . " is " .
        ((exists $p->{status}) ? $status{$c->{status}} : "NOT ACTIVE") . "\n";
```

The `PrintQueue` object offers the set of print queue control methods you'd hope for: `Pause()`, `Resume()`, and `Purge()`. These allow us to control the actions of the queue itself. But what if we want to examine or manipulate the actual jobs in this queue?

To get at the actual jobs, you call a `PrintQueue` object method called `PrintJobs()`. `PrintJobs()` returns a collection of `PrintJob` objects, each of which has a set of properties and methods. For instance, here's how to show the jobs in a particular queue:

```
    use Win32::OLE 'in';

    # this table comes from this section in the ADSI 2.5 SDK:
    # 'Active Directory Service Interfaces 2.5->ADSI Reference->
    # ADSI Interfaces->Dynamic Object Interfaces->IADsPrintJobOperations->
    # IADsPrintJobOperations Property Methods' (double phew)

    %status = (0x00000001 => 'PAUSED',  0x00000002 => 'ERROR',
               0x00000004 => 'DELETING',0x00000010 => 'PRINTING',
               0x00000020 => 'OFFLINE', 0x00000040 => 'PAPEROUT',
               0x00000080 => 'PRINTED', 0x00000100 => 'DELETED');

    $ADsPath = "WinNT://PrintServerName/PrintQueueName";

    $p = Win32::OLE->GetObject($ADsPath) or die "Unable to get $ADsPath\n";

    $jobs = $p->PrintJobs();
    foreach $job (in $jobs){
      print $job->{User} . "\t" . $job->{Description} . "\t" .
            $status{$job->{status}} . "\n";
    }
```

Each job can be `Pause()`d and `Resume()`d as well.

Working with NT/2000 Services via ADSI

For our last set of examples, we're going to look at how to locate, start, and stop the services on an NT/2000 machine. Like the other examples in this chapter, these code snippets must be run from an account with sufficient privileges on the target computer to effect changes.

To list the services on a computer and their status, we could use this code:

```
use Win32::OLE 'in';

# this table comes from this section in the ADSI 2.5 SDK:
# 'Active Directory Service Interfaces 2.5->ADSI Reference->
# ADSI Interfaces->Dynamic Object Interfaces->IADsServiceOperations->
# IADsServiceOperations Property Methods'

%status =
  (0x00000001 => 'STOPPED',         0x00000002 => 'START_PENDING',
   0x00000003 => 'STOP_PENDING',    0x00000004 => 'RUNNING',
   0x00000005 => 'CONTINUE_PENDING',0x00000006 => 'PAUSE_PENDING',
   0x00000007 => 'PAUSED',          0x00000008 => 'ERROR');

$ADsPath = "WinNT://DomainName/ComputerName,computer";

$c = Win32::OLE->GetObject($ADsPath) or die "Unable to get $ADsPath\n";

foreach $adsobj (in $c){
  print $adsobj->{DisplayName} . ":" . $status{$adsobj->{status}} . "\n"
      if ($adsobj->{Class} eq "Service");
}
```

To start, stop, pause, or continue a service, we call the obvious method (**Start()**, **Stop()**, etc.). Here's how we might start the Network Time service on a Windows 2000 machine if it were stopped:

```
use Win32::OLE;

$ADsPath = "WinNT://DomainName/ComputerName/W32Time,service";

$s = Win32::OLE->GetObject($ADsPath) or die "Unable to get $ADsPath\n";

$s->Start();
# may wish to check status at this point, looping until it is started
```

To avoid potential user- and computer name conflicts, the previous code can also be written as:

```
use Win32::OLE;

$d = Win32::OLE->GetObject("WinNT://Domain");
$c = $d->GetObject("Computer", $computername);
$s = $c->GetObject("Service", "W32Time");

$s->Start();
```

Stopping it is just a matter of changing the last line to:

```
$s->Stop();
# may wish to check status at this point, looping until it is stopped
```

These examples should give you some idea of the amount of control ADSI from Perl can give you over your system administration work. Directory services and their interfaces can be a very powerful part of your computing infrastructure.

Module Information for This Chapter

Name	CPAN ID	Version
Net::Telnet	JROGERS	3.01
Net::Finger	FIMM	1.05
Net::Whois	DHUDES	1.9
Net::LDAP	GBARR	0.20
Mozilla::LDAP	LEIFHED	1.4
Sys::Hostname (ships with Perl)		
Win32::OLE (ships with ActiveState Perl)	JDB	1.11

References for More Information

Finger

RFC1288:The Finger User Information Protocol, D. Zimmerman, 1991.

WHOIS

ftp://sipb.mit.edu/pub/whois/whois-servers.list is a list of most major WHOIS servers.

RFC954:NICNAME/WHOIS, K. Harrenstien, M. Stahl, and E. Feinler, 1985.

LDAP

An Internet Approach to Directories, Netscape, 1997 (found at *http://developer. netscape.com/docs/manuals/ldap/ldap.html*) is an excellent white paper introduction to LDAP.

An LDAP Roadmap & FAQ, Jeff Hodges, 1999 (found at *http://www.kingsmountain. com/ldapRoadmap.shtml*).

http://www.ogre.com/ldap/ and *http://www.linc-dev.com/* are the home pages for the co-developers of PerLDAP.

http://www.openldap.org/ is a free LDAP server under active development.

http://www.umich.edu/~dirsvcs/ldap/index.html is home of the parent of both the OpenLDAP and Netscape directory servers. Some of the introduction documentation is still quite useful.

Implementing LDAP, by Mark Wilcox (Wrox Press, 1999).

LDAP-HOWTO, Mark Grennan, 1999 (found at *http://www.grennan.com/ldap-HOWTO.html*).

LDAP Overview Presentation, Bruce Greenblatt, 1999 (found at *http://www.directory-applications.com/presentation/*).

LDAP:Programming Directory-Enabled Applications With Lightweight Directory Access Protocol, by Tim Howes and Mark Smith (Macmillan Technical Publishing, 1997).

Netscape Directory Server Administrator's/Installation/Deployment Guides and SDK documentation (found at *http://developer.netscape.com/docs/manuals/directory.html*).

RFC1823:The LDAP Application Program Interface, T. Howes and M. Smith, 1995.

RFC2222:Simple Authentication and Security Layer (SASL), J. Myers, 1997.

RFC2251:Lightweight Directory Access Protocol (v3), M. Wahl, T. Howes, and S.Kille, 1997.

RFC2252:Lightweight Directory Access Protocol (v3):Attribute Syntax Definitions, M.Wahl, A. Coulbeck, T. Howes, and S. Kille, 1997.

RFC2254:The String Representation of LDAP Search Filters, T. Howes, 1997.

RFC2255:The LDAP URL Format, T. Howes and M. Smith, 1997.

RFC2256:A Summary of the X.500(96) User Schema for use with LDAPv3, M. Wahl, 1997.

The LDAP Data Interchange Format (LDIF)—Technical Specification (work in progress), Gordon Good, 1999 (found at *http://search.ietf.org/internet-drafts/draft-good-ldap-ldif-0X.txt* where X is the current version number).

Understanding and Deploying Ldap Directory Services, by Tim Howes, Mark Smith, and Gordon Good (Macmillan Technical Publishing, 1998).

Understanding LDAP, Heinz Jonner, Larry Brown, Franz-Stefan Hinner, Wolfgang Reis, and Johan Westman, 1998 (found at *http://www.redbooks.ibm.com/abstracts/sg244986.html*). A superb "Redbook" introduction to LDAP.

ADSI

http://cwashington.netreach.net/ is another good (non-Perl specific) site on scripting ADSI and other Microsoft technologies.

http://www.microsoft.com/adsi is the canonical source for ADSI information; be sure to download the ADSI SDK from here.

http://opensource.activestate.com/authors/tobyeverett contains Toby Everett's collection of documentation on using ADSI from Perl.

http://www.15seconds.com is another good (non–Perl specific) site on scripting ADSI and other Microsoft technologies.

Windows 2000 Active Directory, by Alistair G. Lowe-Norris (O'Reilly, 1999).

7

SQL Database Administration

What's a chapter on database administration doing in a system administration book? There are three strong reasons for people with interests in Perl and system administration to become database-savvy:

1. A not-so-subtle thread running through several chapters of this book is the increasing importance of databases to modern-day system administration. We've used (albeit simple) databases to keep track of user and machine information; that's just the tip of the iceberg. Mailing lists, password files, and even the Windows NT/2000 registry are all examples of databases you probably see every day. All large-scale system administration packages (e.g., offerings from CA, Tivoli, HP, and Microsoft) are dependent on database backends. If you are planning to do any serious system administration, you are bound to bump into a database eventually.

2. Database administration is a play-within-a-play for system administrators. Database Administrators (DBAs) have to contend with, among other things:

    Logins/users
    Log files
    Storage management (disk space, etc.)
    Process management
    Connectivity issues
    Backup
    Security

Sound familiar? We can and should learn from both knowledge domains.

3. Perl is a glue language, arguably one of the best. Much work has gone into Perl/database integration, thanks mostly to the tremendous energy surrounding Web development. We can put this effort to work for us. Though Perl can integrate with several different database formats like Unix DBM, Berkeley DB, etc., we're going to pay attention in this chapter to the Perl's interface with large-scale database products. Other formats are addressed elsewhere in this book.

In order to be a database-literate system administrator, you have to speak a little Structured Query Language (SQL), the *lingua franca* of most commercial and several noncommercial databases. Writing scripts in Perl for database administration requires some SQL knowledge because these scripts will contain simple embedded SQL statements. See Appendix D, *The Fifteen-Minute SQL Tutorial*, for enough SQL to get you started. The examples in this chapter use the same databases in previous chapters to keep us from straying from the system administration realm.

Interacting with an SQL Server from Perl

There are two standard frameworks for communication with an SQL server: DBI (DataBase Interface) and ODBC (Open DataBase Connectivity). Once upon a time, DBI was the Unix standard and ODBC the Win32 standard, but this distinction has started to blur now that ODBC has become available in the Unix world and DBI has been ported to Win32. Further blurring the lines is the DBD::ODBC package, a DBD module that speaks ODBC from within the DBI framework.*

DBI and ODBC are very similar in intent and execution, so we'll show you how to use both simultaneously. Both DBI and ODBC can be thought of as "middleware." They form a layer of abstraction that allows the programmer to write code using generic DBI/ODBC calls, without having to know the specific API of any particular database. It is then up to the DBI/ODBC software to hand these calls off to a database-specific layer. The DBI module calls a DBD driver for this; the ODBC Manager calls the data source-specific ODBC driver. This database-specific driver takes care of the nitty-gritty details necessary for communicating with the server in question. Figure 7-1 shows the DBI and ODBC architectures. In both cases, there is a (at least) three-tiered model:

1. An underlying database (Oracle, MySQL, Sybase, Microsoft SQL Server, etc.).
2. A database-specific layer that makes the actual server-specific requests to the server on behalf of the programmer. Programmers don't directly communicate with this layer; they use the third tier. In DBI, a specific DBD module handles

---

* In addition to the standards we are going to discuss, there are some excellent server and OS-specific Perl mechanisms. *Sybperl* by Michael Peppler for Perl-Sybase communication is one example. Many of these nonstandard mechanisms are also available as DBI-ified modules. For instance, most *Sybperl* functionality is now available in DBD::Sybase. On Win32 platforms the ActiveX Data Objects (ADO) framework mentioned in the previous chapter is starting to see wider use.

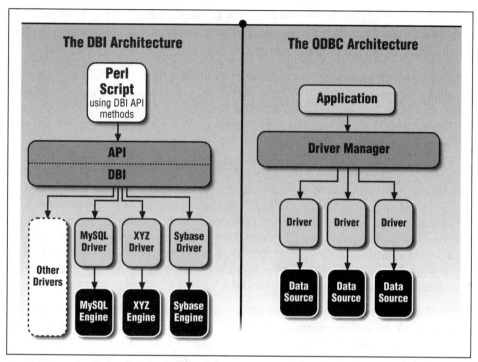

Figure 7-1. DBI and ODBC architectures

this layer. When talking with an Oracle database, the `DBD::Oracle` module would be invoked. DBD modules are usually linked during the building process to a server-specific client library provided by the server vendor. With ODBC, a data-source-specific ODBC driver provided by the vendor handles this layer.

3. A database-independent Application Programming Interface (API) layer. Soon, we'll be writing Perl scripts that will communicate with this layer. In DBI, this is known as the DBI layer (i.e., we'll be making DBI calls). In ODBC, one typically communicates with the ODBC Driver Manager via ODBC API calls.

The beauty of this system is that code written for DBI or ODBC is extremely portable between different servers from different vendors. The API calls made are the same, independent of the underlying database. That's the idea at least, and it holds true for most database programming. Unfortunately, the sort of code we're most likely to write (i.e., database administration) is bound to be server-specific, since virtually no two servers are administered in even a remotely similar fashion.* Experienced system administrators love portable solutions, but they don't expect them.

---

* MS-SQL was initially derived from Sybase source code, so it's one of the rare counter-examples.

That somber thought aside, let's look at how to use DBI and ODBC. Both technologies follow the same basic steps, so you may notice a little redundancy in the explanations, or at least in the headings.

The next sections assume you've installed a database server and the necessary Perl modules. For some of our DBI example code, we're going to use the MySQL server; for ODBC, we'll use Microsoft's SQL Server.

Bridging the Unix-NT/2000 Database Divide

A common question asked by multiplatform system administrators is "How can I talk to my Microsoft SQL Server from my Unix machine?" If an environment's central administration or monitoring system is Unix-based, then a new MS-SQL server installation presents a challenge. I know of three ways to deal with this situation. Choices 2 and 3 below are not SQL-server–specific, so even if you are not using Microsoft SQL Server in your environment, you may find these techniques will come in handy some day.

1. Build and use DBD::Sybase. DBD::Sybase will require some underlying database communication libraries. There are two sets of libraries available that will fit the bill. The first one, Sybase OpenClient libraries, may be available for your platform (e.g., they ship for free with some Linux distributions as part of the Sybase Adaptive Server Enterprise). If your MS-SQL server is Version 6.5 or lower, DBD::Sybase built with these libraries will work. If it is 7.0 or higher, you may need to get a compatibility patch from Microsoft. For information on this patch, see *http://support.microsoft.com/support/kb/articles/q239/8/83.asp* (KB article Q239883). Your second option is to install the FreeTDS libraries found at *http://www.freetds.org*. See the instructions on this site for building the correct protocol version for the server you will be using.

2. Use DBD::Proxy. There is a DBD module that ships with DBI called DBD::Proxy. It allows you to run a small network server on your MS-SQL server machine to transparently proxy requests from your Unix clients to the server.

3. Acquire and use Unix ODBC software via DBD::ODBC. Several vendors, including MERANT (*http://www.merant.com*) and OpenLink Software (*http://www.openlinksw.com*), will sell this to you or you can attempt to use the work of the various Open Source developers. For more information, see Brian Jepson's *freeODBC* page at *http://users.ids.net/~bjepson/ freeODBC*. You will need both an ODBC driver for your Unix platform (provided by the database vendor) and an ODBC manager (such as unixODBC or iODBC).

Using the DBI Framework

Here are the basic steps for using DBI. For more information on DBI, see *Programming the Perl DBI* by Alligator Descartes and Tim Bunce (O'Reilly).

Step 1: Load the necessary Perl module

Nothing special here, you need to just:

```
use DBI;
```

Step 2: Connect to the database and receive a connection handle

The Perl code to establish a DBI connection to a MySQL database and return a database handle looks like this:

```
# connect using to the database named $database using given
# username and password, return a database handle
$database = "sysadm";
$dbh = DBI->connect("DBI:mysql:$database",$username,$pw);
die "Unable to connect: $DBI::errstr\n" unless (defined $dbh);
```

DBI will load the low-level DBD driver for us (**DBD::mysql**) prior to actually connecting to the server. We then test if the **connect()** succeeded before continuing. DBI provides **RaiseError** and **PrintError** options for **connect()**, should we want DBI to perform this test or automatically complain about errors when they happen. For example, if we used:

```
$dbh = DBI->connect("DBI:mysql:$database",
                    $username,$pw,{RaiseError => 1});
```

then DBI would call **die** for us if the **connect()** failed.

Step 3: Send SQL commands to the server

With our Perl module loaded and a connection to the database server in place, it's showtime! Let's send some SQL commands to the server. We'll use some of the SQL tutorial queries from Appendix D for examples. These queries will use the Perl q convention for quoting (i.e., **something** is written as q{something}), just so we don't have to worry about single or double quotes in the actual queries themselves. Here's the first of the two DBI methods for sending commands:

```
$results=$dbh->do(q{UPDATE hosts
                    SET bldg = 'Main'
                    WHERE name = 'bendir'});
die "Unable to perform update:$DBI::errstr\n" unless (defined $results);
```

$results will receive either the number of rows updated or **undef** if an error occurs. Though it is useful to know how many rows were affected, that's not going to cut it for statements like **SELECT** where we need to see the actual data. This is where the second method comes in.

To use the second method you first **prepare** a SQL statement for use and
then you ask the server to **execute** it. Here's an example:

```
$sth = $dbh->prepare(q{SELECT * from hosts}) or
   die "Unable to prep our query:".$dbh->errstr."\n";
$rc = $sth->execute or
   die "Unable to execute our query:".$dbh->errstr."\n";
```

prepare() returns a new creature we haven't seen before: the statement handle. Just like a database handle refers to an open database connection, a statement handle refers to a particular SQL statement we've **prepare()**d. Once we
have this statement handle, we use **execute** to actually send the query to our
server. Later on, we'll be using the same statement handle to retrieve the
results of our query.

You might wonder why we bother to **prepare()** a statement instead of just
executing it directly. **prepare()**ing a statement gives the DBD driver (or more
likely the database client library it calls) a chance to parse the SQL query.
Once a statement has **prepare()**d, we can execute it repeatedly via our
statement handle without parsing it over and over. Often this is a major efficiency win. In fact, the default **do()** DBI method does a **prepare()** and then
execute() behind the scenes for each statement it is asked to execute.

Like the **do** call we saw earlier, **execute()** returns the number of rows
affected. If the query affects zero rows, the string **0E0** is returned to allow a
Boolean test to succeed. **−1** is returned if the number of rows affected is
unknown by the driver.

Before we move on to ODBC, it is worth mentioning one more twist supported by most DBD modules on the **prepare()** theme: placeholders. Placeholders, also called positional markers, allow you to **prepare()** an SQL
statement that has holes in it to be filled at **execute()** time. This allows you
to construct queries on the fly without paying most of the parse time penalty.
The question mark character is used as the placeholder for a single scalar
value. Here's some Perl code to demonstrate the use of placeholders:

```
@machines = qw(bendir shimmer sander);
$sth = $dbh->prepare(q{SELECT name, ipaddr FROM hosts WHERE name = ?});
foreach $name (@machines){
   $sth->execute($name);
   do-something-with-the-results
}
```

Each time we go through the **foreach** loop, the **SELECT** query is executed
with a different **WHERE** clause. Multiple placeholders are straightforward:

```
$sth->prepare(
   q{SELECT name, ipaddr FROM hosts
      WHERE (name = ? AND bldg = ? AND dept = ?)});
$sth->execute($name,$bldg,$dept);
```

Now that we know how to retrieve the number of rows affected by non-**SELECT** SQL queries, let's look into retrieving the results of our **SELECT** requests.

Step 4: Retrieve SELECT results

The mechanism here is similar to our brief discussion of cursors during the SQL tutorial in Appendix D. When we send a **SELECT** statement to the server using `execute()`, we're using a mechanism that allows us to retrieve the results one line at a time.

In DBI, we call one of the methods in Table 7-1 to return data from the result set.

Table 7-1. DBI Methods for Returning Data

Name	Returns	Returns If No More Rows
`fetchrow_arrayref()`	An array reference to an anonymous array with values that are the columns of the next row in a result set	`undef`
`fetchrow_array()`	An array with values that are the columns of the next row in a result set	An empty list
`fetchrow_hashref()`	A hash reference to an anonymous hash with keys that are the column names and values that are the values of the columns of the next row in a result set	`undef`
`fetchall_arrayref()`	A reference to an array of arrays data structure	A reference to an empty array

Let's see these methods in context. For each of these examples, assume the following was executed just prior:

```
$sth = $dbh->prepare(q{SELECT name,ipaddr,dept from hosts}) or
   die "Unable to prepare our query: ".$dbh->errstr."\n";
$sth->execute or die "Unable to execute our query: ".$dbh->errstr."\n";
```

Here's `fetchrow_arrayref()` in action:

```
while ($aref = $sth->fetchrow_arrayref){
  print "name: "   . $aref->[0] . "\n";
  print "ipaddr: " . $aref->[1] . "\n";
  print "dept: "   . $aref->[2] . "\n";
}
```

The DBI documentation mentions that `fetchrow_hashref()` is less efficient than `fetchrow_arrayref()` because of the extra processing it entails, but it can yield more readable code. Here's an example:

```
while ($href = $sth->fetchrow_hashref){
  print "name: "   . $href->{name}  . "\n";
  print "ipaddr: " . $href->{ipaddr}. "\n";
  print "dept: "   . $href->{dept}  . "\n";
}
```

Finally, let's take a look at the "convenience" method, `fetchall_arrayref()`. This method sucks the entire result set into one data structure, returning a reference to an array of references. Be careful to limit the size of your queries when using this method because it does pull the entire result set into memory. If you have a 100GB result set, this may prove to be a bit problematic.

Each reference returned looks exactly like something we would receive from `fetchrow_arrayref()`. See Figure 7-2.

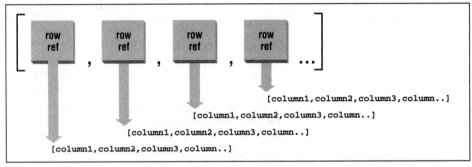

Figure 7-2. The data structure returned by fetchrow_arrayref

Here's some code that will print out the entire query result set:

```
$aref_aref = $sth->fetchall_arrayref;
foreach $rowref (@$aref_aref){
  print "name: "    . $rowref->[0] . "\n";
  print "ipaddr: " . $rowref->[1] . "\n";
  print "dept: "    . $rowref->[2] . "\n";
  print '-'x30,"\n";
}
```

This code sample is specific to our particular data set because it assumes a certain number of columns in a certain order. For instance, we assume the machine name is returned as the first column in the query (`$rowref->[0]`).

We can use some magic attributes (often called metadata) of statement handles to rewrite our result retrieval code to make it more generic. Specifically, if we look at `$sth->{NUM_OF_FIELDS}` after a query, it will tell us the number of fields (columns) in our result set. `$sth->{NAME}` contains a reference to an array with the names of each column. Here's a more generic way to write the last example:

```
$aref_aref = $sth->fetchall_arrayref;
foreach $rowref (@$aref_aref){
  for ($i=0; $i < $sth->{NUM_OF_FIELDS};i++;){
    print $sth->{NAME}->[$i].": ".$rowref->[$i]."\n";
  }
  print '-'x30,"\n";
}
```

Be sure to see the DBI documentation for more metadata attributes.

Step 5: Close the connection to the server

In DBI this is simply:

```
# tells server you will not need more data from statement handle
# (optional, since we're just about to disconnect)
$sth->finish;
# disconnects handle from database
$dbh->disconnect;
```

DBI Leftovers

There are two remaining DBI topics worth mentioning before we move on to ODBC. The first is a set of methods I call "shortcut" methods. The methods in Table 7-2 combine steps 3 and 4 from above.

Table 7-2. DBI Shortcut Methods

Name	Combines These Methods into a Single Method
selectrow_arrayref($stmnt)	prepare($stmnt), execute(), fetchrow_arrayref()
selectcol_arrayref($stmnt)	prepare($stmnt), execute(), (@{fetchrow_arrayref()})[0] (i.e., returns first column for each row)
selectrow_array($stmnt)	prepare($stmnt), execute(), fetchrow_array()

The second topic worth mentioning is DBI's ability to bind variables to query results. The methods bind_col() and bind_columns() are used to tell DBI to automatically place the results of a query into a specific variable or list of variables. This usually saves a step or two when coding. Here's an example using bind_columns() that makes its use clear:

```
$sth = $dbh->prepare(q{SELECT name,ipaddr,dept from hosts}) or
  die "Unable to prep our query:".$dbh->errstr."\n";
$rc = $sth->execute or
  die "Unable to execute our query:".$dbh->errstr."\n";

# these variables will receive the 1st, 2nd, and 3rd columns
# from our SELECT
$rc = $sth->bind_columns(\$name,\$ipaddr,\$dept);

while ($sth->fetchrow_arrayref){
    # $name, $ipaddr, and $dept are automagically filled in from
    # the fetched query results row
    do-something-with-the-results
}
```

Using the ODBC Framework

The basic steps for using ODBC are similar to the DBI steps we just discussed.

Step 1: Load the necessary Perl module

```
use Win32::ODBC;
```

Step 2: Connect to the database and receive a connection handle

ODBC requires one preliminary step before making a connection. We need to create a *Data Source Name*. A DSN is a named reference that stores the configuration information (e.g., server and database name) needed to reach an information source like an SQL server. DSNs come in two flavors, *user* and *system*, distinguishing between connections available to a single user on a machine and connections available to any user or service.[*]

DSNs can be created either through the ODBC control panel under Windows NT/2000, or programmatically via Perl. We'll take the latter route, if just to keep the snickering down among the Unix folks. Here's some code to create a user DSN to our database on an MS-SQL server:

```
# creates a user DSN to a Microsoft SQL Server
# note: to create a system DSN, substitute ODBC_ADD_SYS_DSN
# for ODBC_ADD_DSN
if (Win32::ODBC::ConfigDSN(
                ODBC_ADD_DSN,
                "SQL Server",
                ("DSN=PerlSysAdm",
                 "DESCRIPTION=DSN for PerlSysAdm",
                 "SERVER=mssql.happy.edu",   # server name
                 "ADDRESS=192.168.1.4",      # server IP addr
                 "DATABASE=sysadm",          # our database
                 "NETWORK=DBMSSOCN",         # TCP/IP Socket Lib
                ))){
                        print "DSN created\n";
                }
else {
    die "Unable to create DSN:" . Win32::ODBC::Error() . "\n";
}
```

Once we have a DSN in place, we can use it to open a connection to our database:

```
# connect to the named DSN, returns a database handle
$dbh=new Win32::ODBC("DSN=PerlSysAdm;UID=$username;PWD=$pw;");
die "Unable to connect to DSN PerlSysAdm:" . Win32::ODBC::Error() . "\n"
  unless (defined $dbh);
```

---

[*] There's a third flavor, *file*, which writes the DSN configuration information out to a file so it can be shared among several computers, but it isn't created by the Win32::ODBC method call we're about to use.

Step 3: Send SQL commands to the server

The ODBC equivalent of DBI's do(), prepare(), and execute() is a little bit simpler because the Win32::ODBC module has a single method, Sql(), for sending commands to a server. Though ODBC theoretically has a notion of prepared statements and placeholders, they are not implemented in the current Win32::ODBC module.* Win32::ODBC also does not use statement handles; all communication takes place through the initial database handle opened by the new method above. We're left with the simplest of command structures:

```
$rc = $dbh->Sql(q{SELECT * from hosts});
```

 An important distinction between the ODBC and DBI methods: unlike DBI's do(), the ODBC Sql() call returns undef if it *succeeds*, and some non-zero number if it fails.

If you need to know how many rows were affected by an INSERT, DELETE, or UPDATE query, you would use the RowCount() method. Win32::ODBC's documentation notes that not all ODBC drivers implement this call (or implement it for all SQL operations), so be sure to test your driver before relying on it. Like the return code for DBI's execute(), RowCount() will return −1 if the number of rows returned is not available to the driver.

Here's the equivalent ODBC code for the DBI do() example in the previous section:

```
if (defined $dbh->Sql(q{UPDATE hosts
                        SET bldg = 'Main'
                        WHERE name = 'bendir'})){
  die "Unable to perform update: ".Win32::ODBC::Error()."\n";
}
else {
  $results = $dbh->RowCount();
}
```

Step 4: Retrieve SELECT results

Retrieving the results of a SELECT query under ODBC is performed in a fashion similar to DBI's method, with one twist. First, *fetching* the data from the server and *accessing* it are two separate steps under Win32::ODBC. FetchRow() gets the next row, returning 1 if it succeeds, undef if it does not. Once we've got the row we can choose one of two methods to access it.

---

* At the time of this writing, Dave Roth was beta testing a new version of Win32::ODBC that allows for parameter binding. It uses a similar syntax to DBI (i.e., Prepare() and then Sql()) with a few ODBC twists thrown in. See *http://www.roth.net* for more information.

`Data()` returns a list of the returned columns when called in a list context. It returns all of the columns concatenated together if called in a scalar context. `Data()` can take an optional list argument to specify which columns are returned and in what order (otherwise they are returned in an "unspecified" order according to the documentation).

`DataHash()` returns a hash with the column names as keys for the column values. This is similar to DBI's `fetchrow_hashref()` except it returns a hash instead of a *hash reference*. Like `Data()`, `DataHash()` can also take an optional list argument to specify which columns are returned.

In context, they look like this:

```
if ($dbh->FetchRow()){
  @ar = $dbh->Data();
  do-stuff-with-@ar-values
}
```

and:

```
if ($dbh->FetchRow()){
  $ha = $dbh->DataHash('name','ipaddr');
  do-stuff-with-$ha{name}-and-$ha{ipaddr}
}
```

Just for parity's sake in this discussion, the information we found through DBI's statement handle attribute `{NAME}` can be found in `Win32::ODBC`-land via the `FieldNames()` call. If you need to know the number of fields (like in `{NUM_OF_FIELDS}`), you'll have to count the number of elements in the list returned by `FieldNames()`.

Step 5: Close the connection to the server

```
$dbh->close();
```

If you created a DSN and want to delete it to clean up after yourself, use a statement similar to the one used to create it:

```
# replace ODBC_REMOVE_DSN with ODBC_REMOVE_SYS_DSN if you created a system DSN
if (Win32::ODBC::ConfigDSN(ODBC_REMOVE_DSN,
                           "SQL Server","DSN=PerlSysAdm")){
  print "DSN deleted\n";
}
else {
  die "Unable to delete DSN:".Win32::ODBC::Error()."\n";
}
```

You now know how to work with a database from Perl using both DBI and ODBC. Let's put your knowledge to work with some more extended examples from the database administration realm.

Server Documentation

A great deal of time and energy goes into the configuration of an SQL server and the objects that reside on it. Having a way to document this sort of information can come in handy in a number of situations. If a database gets corrupted and there's no backup, you may be called upon to recreate all of its tables. You may have to migrate data from one server to another; knowing the source and destination configuration can be important. Even for your own database programming, being able to see a table map can be very helpful.

To give you a flavor of the nonportable nature of database administration, let me show you an example of the same simple task as written for three different SQL servers using both DBI and ODBC. Each of these programs does the exact same thing: print out a listing of all of the databases on a server, their tables, and the basic structure of each table. These scripts could easily be expanded to show more information about each object. For instance, it might be useful to show which columns in a table had NULL or NOT NULL set. The output of all three programs looks roughly like this:

```
---sysadm---
        hosts
                    name [char(30)]
                    ipaddr [char(15)]
                    aliases [char(50)]
                    owner [char(40)]
                    dept [char(15)]
                    bldg [char(10)]
                    room [char(4)]
                    manuf [char(10)]
                    model [char(10)]
---hpotter---
        customers
                    cid [char(4)]
                    cname [varchar(13)]
                    city [varchar(20)]
                    discnt [real(7)]
        agents
                    aid [char(3)]
                    aname [varchar(13)]
                    city [varchar(20)]
                    percent [int(10)]
        products
                    pid [char(3)]
                    pname [varchar(13)]
                    city [varchar(20)]
                    quantity [int(10)]
                    price [real(7)]
        orders
                    ordno [int(10)]
                    month [char(3)]
```

```
                           cid [char(4)]
                           aid [char(3)]
                           pid [char(3)]
                           qty [int(10)]
                           dollars [real(7)]
   ...
```

MySQL Server via DBI

Here's a DBI way of pulling this information from a MySQL server. MySQL's addition of the *SHOW* command makes this task pretty easy:

```perl
use DBI;

print "Enter user for connect: ";
chomp($user = <STDIN>);
print "Enter passwd for $user: ";
chomp($pw = <STDIN>);

$start= "mysql"; # connect initially to this database

# connect to the start MySQL database
$dbh = DBI->connect("DBI:mysql:$start",$user,$pw);
die "Unable to connect: ".$DBI::errstr."\n" unless (defined $dbh);

# find the databases on the server
$sth=$dbh->prepare(q{SHOW DATABASES}) or
   die "Unable to prepare show databases: ". $dbh->errstr."\n";
$sth->execute or
   die "Unable to exec show databases: ". $dbh->errstr."\n";
while ($aref = $sth->fetchrow_arrayref) {
    push(@dbs,$aref->[0]);
}
$sth->finish;

# find the tables in each database
foreach $db (@dbs) {
    print "---$db---\n";

    $sth=$dbh->prepare(qq{SHOW TABLES FROM $db}) or
     die "Unable to prepare show tables: ". $dbh->errstr."\n";
    $sth->execute or
      die "Unable to exec show tables: ". $dbh->errstr."\n";

    @tables=();
    while ($aref = $sth->fetchrow_arrayref) {
        push(@tables,$aref->[0]);
    }

    $sth->finish;

   # find the column info for each table
   foreach $table (@tables) {
```

```
            print "\t$table\n";

            $sth=$dbh->prepare(qq{SHOW COLUMNS FROM $table FROM $db}) or
              die "Unable to prepare show columns: ". $dbh->errstr."\n";
            $sth->execute or
              die "Unable to exec show columns: ". $dbh->errstr."\n";

            while ($aref = $sth->fetchrow_arrayref) {
                print "\t\t",$aref->[0]," [",$aref->[1],"]\n";
            }

            $sth->finish;
    }
}
$dbh->disconnect;
```

A few quick comments about this code:

- We connect to a start database only to satisfy the DBI connect semantics, but this context is not necessary thanks to the SHOW commands. This won't be the case in our next two examples.

- If you thought the SHOW TABLES and SHOW COLUMNS prepare and execute statements looked like excellent candidates for placeholders, you're absolutely right. Unfortunately, this particular DBD driver/server combination doesn't support placeholders in this context (at least not when this book was being written). We'll see a similar situation in our next example.

- We prompt for a database user and password interactively because the alternatives (hard coding them into the script or passing them on the command line where they can be found by anyone running a process table dump) are even worse evils. This prompt will echo the password characters as typed. To be really careful, we should use something like Term::Readkey to turn off character echo.

Sybase Server via DBI

Here's the Sybase equivalent. Peruse the code and then we'll talk about a few salient points:

```
use DBI;

print "Enter user for connect: ";
chomp($user = <STDIN>);
print "Enter passwd for $user: ";
chomp($pw = <STDIN>);

$dbh = DBI->connect('dbi:Sybase:',$user,$pw);
die "Unable to connect: $DBI::errstr\n"
  unless (defined $dbh);
```

```
# find the databases on the server
$sth = $dbh->prepare(q{SELECT name from master.dbo.sysdatabases}) or
  die "Unable to prepare sysdatabases query: ".$dbh->errstr."\n";
$sth->execute or
  die "Unable to execute sysdatabases query: ".$dbh->errstr."\n";

while ($aref = $sth->fetchrow_arrayref) {
    push(@dbs, $aref->[0]);
}
$sth->finish;

foreach $db (@dbs) {
    $dbh->do("USE $db") or
      die "Unable to use $db: ".$dbh->errstr."\n";
    print "---$db---\n";

    # find the tables in each database
    $sth=$dbh->prepare(q{SELECT name FROM sysobjects WHERE type="U"}) or
      die "Unable to prepare sysobjects query: ".$dbh->errstr."\n";
    $sth->execute or
      die "Unable to exec sysobjects query: ".$dbh->errstr."\n";

    @tables=();
    while ($aref = $sth->fetchrow_arrayref) {
        push(@tables,$aref->[0]);
    }
    $sth->finish;

    # we need to be "in" the database for the next step
    $dbh->do("use $db") or
          die "Unable to change to $db: ".$dbh->errstr."\n";

    # find the column info for each table
    foreach $table (@tables) {
        print "\t$table\n";

      $sth=$dbh->prepare(qq{EXEC sp_columns $table}) or
            die "Unable to prepare sp_columns query: ".$dbh->errstr."\n";
        $sth->execute or
            die "Unable to execute sp_columns query: ".$dbh->errstr."\n";

        while ($aref = $sth->fetchrow_arrayref) {
            print "\t\t",$aref->[3]," [",$aref->[5],"(",
                $aref->[6],")]\n";
        }
        $sth->finish;
    }
}
$dbh->disconnect or
  warn "Unable to disconnect: ".$dbh->errstr."\n";
```

Here are the promised salient points:

- Sybase keeps information on its databases and tables in the special system tables *sysdatabases* and *sysobjects*. Each database has a *sysobjects* table, but the server keeps track of the databases in a single *sysdatabases* table located in the master database. We use the more explicit `databases.owner.table` syntax in the first **SELECT** to unambiguously reference this table. To get at the per-database *sysobjects*, we could just use this syntax instead of explicitly switching database context with **USE**. But like *cd*ing to a directory, this context makes the other queries a little simpler to write.

- The **SELECT** from *sysobjects* uses a **WHERE** clause to only return user-defined tables. This was done to limit the size of the output. If we wanted to include all of the system tables too, we would change this to:

  ```
  WHERE type="U" AND type="S"
  ```

- Placeholders in `DBD::Sybase` are implemented in such a way as to prohibit their use with stored procedures. If this weren't the case, we'd surely use them for the **EXEC** `sp_columns`.

MS-SQL Server via ODBC

Finally, here's the code for pulling the same information from a MS-SQL server via ODBC. You'll notice that the actual SQL needed is almost identical to the previous example thanks to the Sybase/MS-SQL connection. The interesting changes between this example and the last are:

- The use of a DSN, which also gives us a default database context, so we don't have to be explicit about where to look for the *sysdatabases* table.

- The use of `$dbh->DropCursor()` as the rough analogue to `$sth->finish`.

- The annoying syntax you need to use to execute a stored procedure. See the `Win32::ODBC` web pages for more detail on dealing with stored procedures and other anomalies like this.

Here's the code:

```perl
use Win32::ODBC;

print "Enter user for connect: ";
chomp($user = <STDIN>);
print "Enter passwd for $user: ";
chomp($pw = <STDIN>);

$dsn="sysadm"; # name of the DSN we will be using

# find the available DSNs, creating $dsn if it doesn't exist already
die "Unable to query available DSN's".Win32::ODBC::Error()."\n"
```

```perl
    unless (%dsnavail = Win32::ODBC::DataSources());
if (!defined $dsnavail{$dsn}) {
    die "unable to create DSN:".Win32::ODBC::Error()."\n"
       unless (Win32::ODBC::ConfigDSN(ODBC_ADD_DSN,
                     "SQL Server",
                     ("DSN=$dsn",
                      "DESCRIPTION=DSN for PerlSysAdm",
                      "SERVER=mssql.happy.edu",
                      "DATABASE=master",
                      "NETWORK=DBMSSOCN", # TCP/IP Socket Lib
                     )));
}

# connect to the master database
$dbh = new Win32::ODBC("DSN=$dsn;UID=$user;PWD=$pw;");
die "Unable to connect to DSN $dsn:".Win32::ODBC::Error()."\n"
    unless (defined $dbh);

# find the databases on the server
if (defined $dbh->Sql(q{SELECT name from sysdatabases})){
    die "Unable to query databases:".Win32::ODBC::Error()."\n";
}

while ($dbh->FetchRow()){
    push(@dbs, $dbh->Data("name"));
}
$dbh->DropCursor();

# find the user tables in each database
foreach $db (@dbs) {
    if (defined $dbh->Sql("use $db")){
        die "Unable to change to database $db:" .
            Win32::ODBC::Error() . "\n";
    }
    print "---$db---\n";
    @tables=();
    if (defined $dbh->Sql(q{SELECT name from sysobjects
                            WHERE type="U"})){
        die "Unable to query tables in $db:" .
            Win32::ODBC::Error() . "\n";
    }
    while ($dbh->FetchRow()) {
        push(@tables,$dbh->Data("name"));
    }
    $dbh->DropCursor();

    # find the column info for each table
    foreach $table (@tables) {
        print "\t$table\n";
        if (defined $dbh->Sql(" {call sp_columns (\'$table\')} ")){
            die "Unable to query columns in
                $table:".Win32::ODBC::Error() . "\n";
        }
        while ($dbh->FetchRow()) {
```

```
                @cols=();
                @cols=$dbh->Data("COLUMN_NAME","TYPE_NAME","PRECISION");
                print "\t\t",$cols[0]," [",$cols[1],"(",$cols[2],")]\n";
            }
            $dbh->DropCursor();
        }
    }
    $dbh->Close();

    die "Unable to delete DSN:".Win32::ODBC::Error()."\n"
        unless (Win32::ODBC::ConfigDSN(ODBC_REMOVE_DSN,
                                "SQL Server","DSN=$dsn"));
```

Database Logins

As mentioned before, database administrators have to deal with some of the same issues system administrators contend with, like maintaining logins and accounts. For instance, at my day job we teach database programming classes. Each student who takes a class gets a login on our Sybase server and her or his very own (albeit small) database on that server to play with. Here's a simplified version of the code we use to create these databases and logins:

```
use DBI;

# USAGE: syaccreate <username>

$admin = 'sa';
print "Enter passwd for $admin: ";
chomp($pw = <STDIN>);
$user=$ARGV[0];

# generate a *bogus* password based on user name reversed
# and padded to at least 6 chars with dashes
$genpass = reverse join('',reverse split(//,$user));
$genpass .= "-" x (6-length($genpass));

# here's a list of the SQL commands we will execute in order
# we: 1) create the database on the USER_DISK device,
#        with the log on USER_LOG
#     2) add a login to the server for the user,
#        making the new database the default
#     3) switch to the newly created database
#     4) change its owner to be this user
@commands = ("create database $user on USER_DISK=5 log on USER_LOG=5",
             "sp_addlogin $user,\"$genpass\",$user",
             "use $user",
             "sp_changedbowner $user");

# connect to the server
$dbh = DBI->connect('dbi:Sybase:',$admin,$pw);
die "Unable to connect: $DBI::errstr\n"
  unless (defined $dbh);
```

```
# loop over the command array, execute each command in turn
for (@commands) {
    $dbh->do($_) or die "Unable to $_: " . $dbh->errstr . "\n";
}

$dbh->disconnect;
```

Because this task consists of running a set of commands that don't return data sets, we can write this as a very compact loop that just calls $dbh->do() repeatedly. We could use an almost identical script to delete these accounts and their databases when the class has concluded:

```
use DBI;

# USAGE: syacdelete <username>

$admin = 'sa';
print "Enter passwd for $admin: ";
chomp($pw = <STDIN>);
$user=$ARGV[0];

# here's a list of the SQL commands we will execute in order
# we: drop the user's database
#      drop the user's server login
@commands = ("drop database $user",
             "sp_droplogin $user");

# connect to the server
$dbh = DBI->connect('dbi:Sybase:',$admin,$pw);
die "Unable to connect: $DBI::errstr\n"
  unless(defined $dbh);

# loop over the command array, execute each command in turn
for (@commands) {
    $dbh->do($_) or die "Unable to $_: " . $dbh->errstr . "\n";
}

$dbh->disconnect or
  warn "Unable to disconnect: " . $dbh->errstr . "\n";
```

There are many login-related functions that can be coded up. Here are a few ideas:

Password checker

> Connect to the server and get a listing of databases and logins. Attempt to connect using weak passwords (login names, blank passwords, default passwords).

User mapping

> Generate a listing of which logins can access which databases.

Password control

> Write a pseudo-password expiration system.

Monitoring Server Health

For our final set of examples, we'll take a look at several ways to monitor the health of an SQL server. This sort of routine monitoring is similar in nature to the network service monitoring we saw in Chapter 5, *TCP/IP Name Services*.

Space Monitoring

To get technical for a moment, database servers are places to hold stuff. If you run out of space to hold stuff, this is known as either "a bad thing" or "a very bad thing." As a result, programs that help us monitor the amount of space allocated and used on a server are very useful indeed. Let's look at a DBI program designed to look at the space situation on a Sybase server.

Here's a snippet of output from a program that shows graphically how space is used in each database on the server. Each section shows a bar chart of the percentage of allocated data and log space in use in a database. In the following chart, d stands for data space and 1 stands for log space. For each bar the percentage of space used and the total available space is indicated:

```
                   |ddddddd                                  |15.23%/5MB
    hpotter--------|                                         |
                   |                                         |0.90%/5MB

                   |ddddddd                                  |15.23%/5MB
    dumbledore-----|                                         |
                   |                                         |1.52%/5MB


                   |dddddddd                                 |16.48%/5MB
    hgranger-------|                                         |
                   |                                         |1.52%/5MB

                   |ddddddd                                  |15.23%/5MB
    rweasley-------|                                         |
                   |1                                        |3.40%/5MB

                   |ddddddddddddddddddddddddddddd            |54.39%/2MB
    hagrid---------|                                         |
                   |- no log                                 |
```

Here's how we generated this output:

```
use DBI;

$admin = 'sa';
print "Enter passwd for $admin: ";
chomp($pw = <STDIN>);
$pages = 2; # data is stored in 2k pages
```

```
# connect to the server
$dbh = DBI->connect('dbi:Sybase:',$admin,$pw);
die "Unable to connect: $DBI::errstr\n"
  unless (defined $dbh);

# get the name of the databases on the server
$sth = $dbh->prepare(q{SELECT name from sysdatabases}) or
  die "Unable to prepare sysdatabases query: ".$dbh->errstr."\n";
$sth->execute or
  die "Unable to execute sysdatabases query: ".$dbh->errstr."\n";

while ($aref = $sth->fetchrow_arrayref) {
    push(@dbs, $aref->[0]);
}
$sth->finish;

# retrieve stats for each of the databases
foreach $db (@dbs) {

    # get and total the size column from all non-log segments
    $size    = &querysum(qq{SELECT size FROM master.dbo.sysusages
                       WHERE  dbid = db_id(\'$db\')
                       AND    segmap != 4});
    # get and total the size column for the log segment
    $logsize = &querysum(qq{SELECT size FROM master.dbo.sysusages
                       WHERE  dbid = db_id(\'$db\')
                       AND    segmap = 4});

    # change to the database and retrieve usage stats
    $dbh->do(q{use $db}) or
      die "Unable to change to $db: ".$dbh->errstr."\n";

    # we used the reserved_pgs function to return the number of pages
    # used by both the data (doampg) and index (ioampg) part
    # of the database
    $used=&querysum(q{SELECT reserved_pgs(id,doampg)+reserved_pgs(id,ioampg)
                    FROM sysindexes
                    WHERE id != 8});

    # same, except this time we look at the log usage
    $logused=&querysum(q{SELECT reserved_pgs(id, doampg)
                       FROM sysindexes
                       WHERE id=8});

    # show this information graphically
    &graph($db,$size,$logsize,$used,$logused);
}
$dbh->disconnect;

# prepare/exec a given single-column SELECT query, return
# the sum of the results
sub querysum {
    my($query) = shift;
    my($sth,$aref,$sum);
```

```
        $sth = $dbh->prepare($query) or
            die "Unable to prepare $query: ".$dbh->errstr."\n";
        $sth->execute or
            die "Unable to exec $query: ".$dbh->errstr."\n";

        while ($aref=$sth->fetchrow_arrayref) {
            $sum += $aref->[0];
        }
        $sth->finish;

        $sum;

    }

# print out nice chart given database name, size, log size,
# and usage info
sub graph {
    my($dbname,$size,$logsize,$used,$logused) = @_;

    # line for data space usage
    print ' 'x15 . '|'.'d'x (50 *($used/$size)) .
          ' 'x (50-(50*($used/$size))) . '|';

    # percentage used and total M for data space
    printf("%.2f",($used/$size*100));
    print "%/". (($size * $pages)/1024)."MB\n";
    print $dbname.'-'x(14-length($dbname)).'-|'.(' 'x 49)."|\n";

    if (defined $logsize) { # line for log space usage
        print ' 'x15 . '|' . 'l'x (50 *($logused/$logsize)) .
              ' 'x (50-(50*($logused/$logsize))) . '|';
        # percentage used and total M for log space
        printf("%.2f",($logused/$logsize*100));
        print "%/". (($logsize * $pages)/1024)."MB\n";
    }
    else { # some databases do not have separate log space
        print ' 'x15 . "|- no log".(' 'x 41)."|\n";
    }
    print "\n";
}
```

SQL-savvy folks will probably wonder why a special subroutine (querysum) is being invoked to total the contents of a single column instead of using the perfectly good SUM calculation operator in SQL. querysum() is just meant to be an example of the sort of manipulation on the fly one can do from Perl. A Perl subroutine is probably more appropriate for more complex jobs. For instance, if we need to keep separate running totals based on a regular expression, that's probably best done from Perl rather than asking the server to perform the tabulation (even if it could).

Where Does the Work Get Done?

One question that may come up when writing SQL programs from within Perl is "Should I manipulate my data on the server using SQL, or on my client using Perl?" Often there is an overlap between the SQL functions offered by a server (e.g., SUM()) and Perl's operators.

For example, it is probably more efficient to use the DISTINCT keyword to eliminate duplicates from a returned data set before they get to your Perl program, even though this is an operation you could easily do in Perl.

Unfortunately, there are too many variables to be able to provide a hard and fast rule for deciding which method to use. Here are some factors you may wish to consider:

- How efficiently does the server handle a particular query?

- How much data is in play?

- How much do you have to manipulate the data and how complex is that manipulation?

- What are the speeds of the server, client, and intervening network (if there is one)?

- Do you want your code to be portable between database servers?

Often you just have to try it both ways before deciding.

Monitoring the CPU Health of a SQL Server

For the final example of this chapter, we'll use DBI to show us a minute-by-minute status line display of the CPU health of a SQL server. Just to make it more interesting, we'll monitor two separate servers simultaneously from the same script. We'll comment on this code in a moment:

```
use DBI;

$syadmin = "sa";
print "Sybase admin passwd: ";
chomp($sypw = <STDIN>);

$msadmin = "sa";
print "MS-SQL admin passwd: ";
chomp($mspw = <STDIN>);

# connect to Sybase server
$sydbh = DBI->connect("dbi:Sybase:server=SYBASE",$syadmin,$sypw);
die "Unable to connect to sybase server: $DBI::errstr\n"
  unless (defined $sydbh);
```

```
# turn on the ChopBlanks option to remove trailing whitespace in columns
$sydbh->{ChopBlanks} = 1;

# connect to MS-SQL server (handy that we can use DBD::Sybase for this!)
$msdbh = DBI->connect("dbi:Sybase:server=MSSQL",$msadmin,$mspw);
die "Unable to connect to mssql server: $DBI::errstr\n"
  unless (defined $msdbh);
# turn on the ChopBlanks option to remove trailing whitespace in columns
$msdbh->{ChopBlanks} = 1;

$|=1; # turn off STDOUT IO buffering

# initialize the signal handler so we can cleanup nicely
$SIG{INT} = sub {$byebye = 1;};

# infinitely loop unless our interrupt flag has been set
while (1) {
    last if ($byebye);

    # run the stored procedure sp_monitor
    $systh = $sydbh->prepare(q{sp_monitor}) or
        die "Unable to prepare sy sp_monitor:".$sydbh->errstr."\n";
    $systh->execute or
        die "Unable to execute sy sp_monitor:".$sydbh->errstr."\n";
    # loop to retrieve the lines from the output we need.
    # We know we have all of it when we see the cpu_busy information
    while($href = $systh->fetchrow_hashref or
          $systh->{syb_more_results}) {
            # got what we needed, stop asking
            last if (defined $href->{cpu_busy});
    }
    $systh->finish;

    # substitute out everything but the % number from
    # the values we receive
    for (keys %{$href}) {
        $href->{$_} =~ s/.*-(\d+%)/\1/;
    }

    # collect all the data we need into a single line
    $info = "Sybase: (".$href->{cpu_busy}." CPU), ".
                "(".$href->{io_busy}." IO), ".
                "(".$href->{idle}." idle)    ";

    # ok, now let's do it all over again for the second server (MS-SQL)
    $mssth = $msdbh->prepare(q{sp_monitor}) or
        die "Unable to prepare ms sp_monitor:".$msdbh->errstr."\n";
    $mssth->execute or
        die "Unable to execute ms sp_monitor:".$msdbh->errstr."\n";
    while($href = $mssth->fetchrow_hashref or
          $mssth->{syb_more_results}) {
            # got what we needed, stop asking
            last if (defined $href->{cpu_busy});
    }
```

```
$mssth->finish;

# substitute out everything but the % number from
# the values we receive
for (keys %{$href}) {
    $href->{$_} =~ s/.*-(\d+%)/\1/;
}

$info .= "MSSQL: (" . $href->{'cpu_busy'}." CPU), ".
                "(".$href->{'io_busy'}." IO), ".
                "(".$href->{'idle'}." idle)";
print " "x78,"\r";
print $info,"\r";

sleep(5) unless ($byebye);
}

# only end up here if we've broken out of the loop thanks to an interrupt
$sydbh->disconnect;
$msdbh->disconnect;
```

This script keeps this line on your screen, which is refreshed every five seconds:

```
Sybase: (33% CPU), (33% IO), (0% idle)   MSSQL: (0% CPU), (0% IO), (100% idle)
```

The heart of this program is the stored procedure **sp_monitor** that exists both on Sybase and MS-SQL. **sp_monitor**'s output looks like this:

last_run	current_run	seconds
Aug 3 1998 12:05AM	Aug 3 1998 12:05AM	1

cpu_busy	io_busy	idle
0(0)-0%	0(0)-0%	40335(0)-0%

packets_received	packets_sent	packet_errors
1648(0)	1635(0)	0(0)

total_read	total_write	total_errors	connections
391(0)	180(0)	0(0)	11(0)

Unfortunately, **sp_monitor** exposes a nonportable Sybase-ism that was carried over to MS-SQL: multiple result sets. Each of the lines returned comes back as a separate result set. DBD::Sybase handles this by setting a special statement attribute. That's why you see this test:

```
while($href = $systh->fetchrow_hashref or
        $systh->{syb_more_results}) {
```

and why we exit this loop early once we've seen the columns we're looking for:

```
# got what we needed, stop asking
last if (defined $href->{cpu_busy});
```

The program itself loops forever until it receives an interrupt signal (most likely from the user pressing Ctrl-C). When we receive this signal, we do the safest thing possible in a signal handler and set an exit flag. This is the technique recommended by the *perlipc* manpage for safe signal handling. Receiving the INT signal will set a flag that punts us out of the loop on the next iteration. Catching this signal allows the program to nicely close its database handles before shuffling off this mortal coil.

This small program just scratches the surface of the sort of server monitoring we can do. It would be easy to take the results we get from `sp_monitor` and graph them over time to get a better notion of how our server is being used. Let creeping featurism be your muse.

Module Information for This Chapter

Module	CPAN ID	Version
DBI	TIMB	1.13
Msql-Mysql modules (`DBD::mysql`)	JWIED	1.2210
`DBD::Sybase`	MEWP	0.21
`Win32::ODBC` (from *http://www.roth.net*)	GBARR	970208

References for More Information

SQL

http://w3.one.net/~jhoffman/sqltut.htm contains James Hoffman's excellent SQL tutorial; try the links at the end of the tutorial for more good SQL sites.

DBI

Advanced Perl Programming, by Sriram Srinivasan (O'Reilly, 1997).

http://www.symbolstone.org/technology/perl/DBI/index.html is the official DBI home page; this should be your first stop.

Programming the Perl DBI, by Alligator Descartes and Tim Bunce (O'Reilly, 2000).

ODBC

http://www.microsoft.com/odbc contains Microsoft's ODBC information. You may also want to search for ODBC on the *http://msdn.microsoft.com* site, looking carefully at the library material on ODBC in the MDAC SDK.

http://www.roth.net/perl/odbc/ is the official `Win32::ODBC` home page.

Win32 Perl Programming: The Standard Extensions, by Dave Roth (Macmillan Technical Publishing, 1999). By the author of `Win32::ODBC`, currently the best reference for Win32 Perl module programming.

Other Topics

http://sybooks.sybase.com is where Sybase puts its entire documentation set online with an easy to navigate and easy to search interface. This sometimes comes in handy not just for Sybase/MS-SQL related questions, but for general SQL questions as well.

http://www.mbay.net/~mpeppler/ is the home page of Michael Peppler (author of *SybPerl* and `DBD::Sybase`). Contains some useful information not just on Sybase, but also on SQL and database programming in general.

In this chapter:
- *Sending Mail*
- *Common Mistakes in Sending Email*
- *Receiving Mail*
- *Module Information for This Chapter*
- *References for More Information*

8

Electronic Mail

Unlike the other chapters in this book, this chapter does not discuss how to administer a particular service, technology, or knowledge domain. Instead, we're going to look at how to use email from Perl as a tool for system administration.

Perl can help us in an administrative context with both sending and receiving email. Email is a great notification mechanism: often we want a program to tell us when something goes wrong, provide the results of an automatic process (like a late night *cron* or scheduler service job), or let us know when something we care about changes. We'll explore how to send mail from Perl for these purposes and then look at some of the pitfalls associated with the practice of sending ourselves mail.

Similarly, we'll look at how Perl can be used to post-process mail we receive to make it more useful to us. Perl can be useful for dealing with spam and managing user questions.

This chapter will assume that you already have a solid and reliable mail infrastructure. We're also going to assume that your mail system, or one that you have access to, uses protocols that follow the IETF specifications for sending and receiving mail. The examples in this chapter will use protocols like SMTP (Simple Mail Transfer Protocol, RFC821) and expect messages to be RFC822-compliant. We'll go over these terms in due course.

Sending Mail

Let's talk about the mechanics of sending email first and then tackle the more sophisticated issues. The traditional (Unix) Perl mail sending code often looks something like this example from the Perl Frequently Asked Questions list:

```
# assumes we have sendmail installed
open(SENDMAIL, "|/usr/lib/sendmail -oi -t -odq") or
  die "Can't fork for sendmail: $!\n";
print SENDMAIL <<"EOF";
From: User Originating Mail <me\@host>
```

```
To: Final Destination <you\@otherhost>
Subject: A relevant subject line

Body of the message goes here after the blank line
in as many lines as you like.
EOF
close(SENDMAIL) or warn "sendmail didn't close nicely";
```

 When the array interpolation rules were changed between Perl Version 4 and Perl Version 5, it broke many scripts that sent mail. Even now, be on the lookout for code like this:

```
$address = "fred@example.com";
```

This needs to be changed to one of these lines to work properly:

```
$address="fred\@example.com";
$address='fred@example.com';
$address= join('@', 'fred', 'example.com');
```

Code that calls *sendmail* like our example above works fine under many circumstances, but it doesn't work on any operating system that lacks a mail transport agent called "sendmail" installed (e.g., NT or MacOS). On those operating systems, this leaves you with a few choices.

Getting sendmail (or Similar Mail Transport Agent)

On Win32, you're in luck because I know of at least three Win32 ports of *sendmail* itself:

- Cygwin *sendmail* port (*http://dome/weeg.uiowa.edu/pub/domestic/sos/ports*)

- Mercury Systems' commercial *sendmail* port (*http://www.demobuilder.com/sendmail.htm*)

- Sendmail, Inc.'s commercial *Sendmail for NT* (*http://www.sendmail.com*)

If you'd like something more lightweight, and are willing to make small modifications to your Perl code to support different command-line arguments, other Win32 programs like these will do the trick:

- *blat* (*http://www.interlog.com/~tcharron/blat.html*)

- *netmail95* (*http://www.geocities.com/SiliconValley/Lakes/2382/netmail.html*)

- *wmailto* (*http://www.impaqcomp.com/jgaa/wmailto.html*)

The advantage of this approach is it offloads much of the mail-sending complexity from your script. A good Mail Transport Agent (MTA) handles the process of retrying a destination mail server if it's unreachable, selecting the right destination server (finding and choosing between Mail eXchanger DNS records), rewriting the headers if necessary, dealing with bounces, and so on. If you can avoid having to take care of all of that in Perl, that's often a good thing.

Using the OS-Specific IPC Framework.

On MacOS or Windows NT, you can drive a mail client using the native interprocess communication (IPC) framework.

I haven't seen any MacOS ports of *sendmail*, but under MacOS, we can ask Perl to use AppleScript to drive an email client:

```
$to="someone\@example.com";
$from="me\@example.com";
$subject="Hi there";
$body="message body\n";

MacPerl::DoAppleScript(<<EOC);
tell application "Eudora"

    make message at end of mailbox "out"

    -- 0 is the current message
    set field \"from\" of message 0 to \"$from\"
    set field \"to\" of message 0 to \"$to\"
    set field \"subject\" of message 0 to \"$subject\"
    set body of message 0 to \"$body\"
    queue message 0
    connect with sending without checking
    quit
end tell
EOC
```

This code executes a very simple AppleScript that communicates with the email client *Eudora* by Qualcomm. The script creates a new message, populates and queues the message for sending, and then instructs Eudora to send its queued messages before quitting.

Another slightly more efficient way to write this same code would be to use the `Mac::Glue` module we saw in Chapter 2, *Filesystems*:

```
use Mac::Glue ':glue';

$e=new Mac::Glue 'Eudora';
$to="someone\@example.com";
$from="me\@example.com";
$subject="Hi there";
$body="message body";

$e->make(
    new => 'message',
    at => location(end => $e->obj(mailbox => 'Out'))
);
```

```
$e->set($e->obj(field => from     => message => 0), to => $from);
$e->set($e->obj(field => to       => message => 0), to => $to);
$e->set($e->obj(field => subject => message => 0), to => $subject);
$e->set($e->prop(body => message => 0), to => $body);

$e->queue($e->obj(message => 0));
$e->connect(sending => 1, checking => 0);
$e->quit;
```

Under NT, we can use Microsoft's Collaborative Data Objects Library (previously called Active Messaging), an ease-of-use layer built on top of their MAPI (Messaging Application Programming Interface) architecture. To call this library to drive a mail client like Outlook, we could use the `Win32::OLE` module like so:

```
$to="me\@example.com";
$subject="Hi there";
$body="message body\n";

use Win32::OLE;

# init OLE, COINIT_OLEINITIALIZE required when using MAPI.Session objects
Win32::OLE->Initialize(Win32::OLE::COINIT_OLEINITIALIZE);
die Win32::OLE->LastError(),"\n" if Win32::OLE->LastError();

# create a session object that will call Logoff when it is destroyed
my $session = Win32::OLE->new('MAPI.Session','Logoff');
die Win32::OLE->LastError(),"\n" if Win32::OLE->LastError();

# log into that session using the default OL98 Internet Profile
$session->Logon('Microsoft Outlook Internet Settings');
die Win32::OLE->LastError(),"\n" if Win32::OLE->LastError();

# create a message object
my $message = $session->Outbox->Messages->Add;
die Win32::OLE->LastError(),"\n" if Win32::OLE->LastError();

# create a recipient object for that message object
my $recipient = $message->Recipients->Add;
die Win32::OLE->LastError(),"\n" if Win32::OLE->LastError();

# populate the recipient object
$recipient->{Name} = $to;
$recipient->{Type} = 1; # 1 = "To:", 2 = "Cc:", 3 = "Bcc:"

# all addresses have to be resolved against a directory
# (in this case probably your Address book). Full addresses
# usually resolve to themselves, so this line in most cases will
# not modify the recipient object.
$recipient->Resolve();
die Win32::OLE->LastError(),"\n" if Win32::OLE->LastError();

# populate the Subject: line and message body
$message->{Subject} = $subject;
$message->{Text} = $body;
```

```
# queue the message to be sent
# 1st argument = save copy of message
# 2nd argument = allows user to change message w/dialog box before sent
# 3rd argument = parent window of dialog if 2nd argument is True
$message->Send(0, 0, 0);
die Win32::OLE->LastError(),"\n" if Win32::OLE->LastError();

# explicitly destroy the $session object, calling $session->Logoff
# in the process
undef $session;
```

Unlike the previous example, this code just queues the message to be sent. It is up to the mail client (like Outlook) or transport infrastructure (like Exchange) to periodically initiate message delivery. There is a CDO/AM 1.1 method for the `Session` object called `DeliverNow()` that is supposed to instruct MAPI to flush all incoming and outgoing mail queues. Unfortunately, it is not available and does not work under some circumstances, so it is not included in the previous code example.

The previous code drives MAPI "by hand" using OLE calls. If you'd like to use MAPI without getting your hands that dirty, Amine Moulay Ramdane has put together a `Win32::MAPI` module (found at *http://www.generation.net/~aminer/ Perl/)* that can take some of the work out of the process.

Programs that rely on AppleScript/Apple Events or MAPI are equally as non-portable as calling a *sendmail* binary. They offload some of the work, but are relatively inefficient. They should probably be your methods of last resort.

Speaking to the Mail Protocols Directly

Our final choice is to write code that speaks to the mail server in its native language. Most of this language is documented in RFC821. Here's a basic SMTP (Simple Mail Transport Protocol) conversation. The data we send is in bold:

```
% telnet example.com 25          -- connect to the SMTP port on example.com
Trying 192.168.1.10 ...
Connected to example.com.
Escape character is '^]'.
220 mailhub.example.com ESMTP Sendmail 8.9.1a/8.9.1; Sun, 11 Apr 1999 15:32:16 -
0400 (EDT)
HELO client.example.com          -- identify the machine we are connecting from
                                    (can also use EHLO)
250 mailhub.example.com Hello dnb@client.example.com [192.168.1.11], pleased to
meet you
MAIL FROM: <dnb@example.com>     -- specify the sender
250 <dnb@example.com>... Sender ok
RCPT TO: <dnb@example.com>       -- specify the recipient
250 <dnb@example.com>... Recipient ok
DATA                             -- begin to send message, note we send several key header lines
354 Enter mail, end with "." on a line by itself
From: David N. Blank-Edelman (David N. Blank-Edelman)
```

```
To: dnb@example.com
Subject: SMTP is a fine protocol

Just wanted to drop myself a note to remind myself how much I love SMTP.
    Peace,
        dNb
.                                    -- finish sending the message
250 PAA26624 Message accepted for delivery
QUIT                                 -- end the session
221 mailhub.example.com closing connection
Connection closed by foreign host.
```

It is not difficult to script a network conversation like this. We could use the
`Socket` module or even something like `Net::Telnet` as seen in Chapter 6, *Directory Services*. But there are good mail modules out there that make our job easier,
like Jenda Krynicky's `Mail::Sender`, Milivoj Ivkovic's `Mail::Sendmail`, and
`Mail::Mailer` in Graham Barr's *MailTools* package. All three of these packages
are operating-system–independent and will work almost anywhere a modern Perl
distribution is available. We'll look at `Mail::Mailer` because it offers a single
interface to two of the mail-sending methods we've discussed so far. Like most
Perl modules written in an object-oriented style, the first step is to construct an
instance of new object:

```
use Mail::Mailer;

$from="me\@example.com";
$to="you\@example.com";
$subject="Hi there";
$body="message body\n";

$type="smtp";
$server="mail.example.com";

my $mailer = Mail::Mailer->new($type, Server => $server) or
    die "Unable to create new mailer object:$!\n";
```

The `$type` variable allows you to choose one of the following behaviors:

smtp

> Send the mail using the `Net::SMTP` module (part of Barr's *libnet* package),
> available for most non-Unix ports of Perl as well. If you are using *MailTools*
> Version 1.13 and above, you can specify the SMTP server name using the `=>`
> notation as demonstrated above. If not, you will have to configure the server
> name as part of the *libnet* install procedure.

mail

> Send the mail using the Unix mail user agent *mail* (or whatever binary you
> specify as an optional second argument). This is similar to our use of Apple-
> Script and MAPI above.

sendmail

> Send the mail using the *sendmail* binary, like our first method of this section.

You can also set the environment variable `PERL_MAILERS` to change the default locations used to find the binaries like *sendmail* on your system.

Calling the `open()` method of our `Mail::Mailer` object causes our object to behave like a filehandle to an outgoing message. In this call, we pass in the headers of the message as a reference to an anonymous hash:

```
$mailer->open({From => $from,
               To => $to,
               Subject => $subject}) or
   die "Unable to populate mailer object:$!\n";
```

We `print` our message body to this pseudo-filehandle and then close it to send the message:

```
print $mailer $body;
$mailer->close;
```

That's all it takes to send mail portably via Perl.

Depending on which `$type` behavior we choose when using this module, we may or may not be covered regarding the harder MTA issues mentioned earlier. The previous code uses the `smtp` behavior, which means our code needs to be smart enough to handle error conditions like unreachable servers. As written, it's not that smart. Be sure any production code you write is prepared to deal with these issues.

Common Mistakes in Sending Email

Now we can begin using email as a notification method. However, when we start to write code that performs this function, we quickly find that the *how* to send mail is not nearly as interesting as the *when* and *what* to send.

This section explores those questions by taking a contrary approach. If we look at what and how *not* to send mail we'll get a deeper insight into these issues. Let's talk about some of the most common mistakes made when writing system administration programs that send mail.

Overzealous Message Sending

By far, the most common mistake is sending too much mail. It is a great idea to have scripts send mail. If there's a service disruption, normal email or email sent to a pager are good ways to bring this problem to the attention of a human. But under most circumstances it is a very *bad* idea to have your program send mail about the problem every five minutes or so. Overzealous mail generators are quickly added to the mail filters of the very humans who should be reading the mail. The end result is that important mail is routinely ignored.

Controlling the frequency of mail

The easiest way to avoid what I call "mail beaconing" is to build safeguards into the programs to gate the delay between messages. If your script runs constantly, it is easy to stash the time of the last mail message sent in a variable like this:

```
$last_sent = time;
```

If your program is started up every N minutes or hours via Unix's *cron* or NT scheduler service mechanisms, this information can be written to a one-line file and read again the next time the program is run. Be sure in this case to pay attention to some of the security precautions listed in Chapter 1, *Introduction.*

Depending on the situation, you can get fancy about your delay times. This code shows an exponential backoff:

```
$max  = 24*60*60; # maximum amount of delay in seconds (1 day)
$unit = 60;       # increase delay by measures of this unit (1 min)

# provide a closure with the time we last sent a message and
# the last power of 2 we used to compute the delay interval.
# The subroutine we create will return a reference to an
# anonymous array with this information
sub time_closure {
    my($stored_sent,$stored_power)=(0,-1);
    return sub {
        (($stored_sent,$stored_power) = @_) if @_;
        [$stored_sent,$stored_power];
    }
};

$last_data=&time_closure; # create our closure

# return true first time called and then once after an
# exponential delay
sub expbackoff {
    my($last_sent,$last_power) = @{&$last_data};

    # reply true if this is the first time we've been asked, or if the
    # current delay has elapsed since we last asked. If we return true,
    # we stash away the time of our last affirmative reply and increase
    # the power of 2 used to compute the delay.
    if (!$last_sent or
        ($last_sent +
          (($unit * 2**$last_power >= $max) ?
              $max : $unit * 2**$last_power) <= time())){
                &$last_data(time(),++$last_power);
                return 1;
    }
    else {
        return 0;
    }
}
```

The subroutine `expbackoff()` returns `true` (1) if email should be sent and `false` (0) if not. It begins by returning `true` the first time it is called, then rapidly increases the delay time until eventually `true` is only returned once a day.

To make this code more interesting, I've used a peculiar programming construct called a *closure* to stash away the last message-sent time and the last power of two used to compute the delay. We're using the closure as a way of hiding our important variables from the rest of the program. In this small program it is just a curiosity, but the usefulness of this technique becomes readily apparent in a larger program where it is more likely that other code might inadvertently stomp on our variables. In brief, here's how closures work.

The subroutine `&time_closure()` returns a reference to an anonymous subroutine, essentially a little piece of code without a name. Later on we'll use that reference to run this code using the standard symbolic reference syntax: `&$last_data`. The code in our anonymous subroutine returns a reference to an array, hence the punctuation parking lot in this line used to access the returned data:

```
my($last_sent,$last_power) = @{&$last_data};
```

Here's the magic that makes a closure: because the reference is created in the same enclosing block as the `my()`ed variables `$stored_sent` and `$stored_power`, it traps those variables in a unique context. `$stored_sent` and `$stored_power` can be read and changed only while the code in this reference is executing. They also retain their values between invocations of the code reference. For instance:

```
# create our closure
$last_data=&time_closure;

# call the subroutine that sets our variables
&$last_data(1,1);

# attempt to change them outside of the sub
$stored_sent = $stored_power = 2;

# show their current value using the subroutine
print "@{&$last_data}\n";
```

will print "1 1" even though it appears we changed the values of `$stored_sent` and `$stored_power` in the third line of code. We certainly changed the value of the global variables with those names, but we couldn't touch the copies protected by the closure.

It may help you to think of a variable in a closure as a satellite in orbit around a wandering planet. The satellite is trapped by the gravity of the planet; where the planet goes, so too goes the satellite. The satellite's position can be described only in reference to the planet: to find the satellite, you first locate the planet. Each time you find this particular planet, the satellite should be there, just where you left it.

Think of the variables in a closure as being in orbit around their anonymous sub-routine code reference, separate from the rest of your program's galaxy.

Setting astrophysics aside, let's return to our discussion of mail sending. Sometimes it is more appropriate to have your program act like a two-year-old, complaining more often as time goes by. Here's some code similar to the previous example. This time we increase the number of messages sent over time. It starts off giving the go-ahead to send mail once a day and then rapidly decreases the delay time until it hits a minimum delay of five minutes:

```perl
$max  = 60*60*24; # maximum amount of delay in seconds (1 day)
$min  = 60*5;     # minimum amount of delay in seconds (5 minutes)
$unit = 60;       # decrease delay by measures of this unit (1 min)

$start_power = int log($max/$unit)/log(2); # find the closest power of 2

sub time_closure {
    my($last_sent,$last_power)=(0,$start_power+1);
    return sub {
      (($last_sent,$last_power) = @_) if @_;
      # keep exponent positive
      $last_power = ($last_power > 0) ? $last_power : 0;
      [$last_sent,$last_power];
    }
};

$last_data=&time_closure; # create our closure

# return true first time called and then once after an
# exponential ramp up
sub exprampup {
    my($last_sent,$last_power) = @{&$last_data};

    # reply true if this is the first time we've been asked, or if the
    # current delay has elapsed since we last asked. If we send, we
    # stash away the time of our last affirmative reply and increased
    # power of 2 used to compute the delay.
    if (!$last_sent or
        ($last_sent +
        (($unit * 2**$last_power <= $min) ?
            $min : $unit * 2**$last_power) <= time())){
            &$last_data(time(),--$last_power);
            return 1;
    }
    else {
      return 0;
    }
}
```

In both examples we called an additional subroutine (`&$last_data`) to find when the last message was sent and how the delay was computed. Later, if we decide to change how the program is run, this compartmentalization will allow us to change how we store that state. For example, if we change our program to run periodically rather than running all the time, we could easily replace the closure with a normal subroutine that saves and retrieves the data to and from a plain text file.

Controlling the amount of mail

Another subclass of the "overzealous message sending" syndrome is the "everybody on the network for themselves" problem. If all of the machines on your network decide to send you a piece of mail, you may miss something important in the subsequent message blizzard. A better approach is to have them all report to a central repository of some sort. The information can then be collated and mailed out later in a single mail message.

Let's consider a moderately contrived example. For this scenario, assume each machine in your network drops a one-line file into a shared directory.* Named for each machine, that file will contain each machine's summary of the results of last night's scientific computation. It would have a single line of this form:

```
hostname success-or-failure number-of-computations-completed
```

A program that collates the information and mails the results might look like this:

```perl
use Mail::Mailer;
use Text::Wrap;

# the list of machines reporting in
$repolist = "/project/machinelist";
# the directory where they write files
$repodir  = "/project/reportddir";
# filesystem separator for portability,
# could use File::Spec module instead
$separator= "/";
# send mail "from" this address
$reportfromaddr = "project\@example.com";
# send mail to this address
$reporttoaddr    = "project\@example.com";
# read the list of machine reporting in into a hash.
# Later we de-populate this hash as each machine reports in,
# leaving behind only the machine which are missing in action
open(LIST,$repolist) or die "Unable to open list $repolist:$!\n";
while(<LIST>){
    chomp;
    $missing{$_}=1;
    $machines++;
}

# read all of the files in the central report directory
```

---

* Another good rendezvous spot for status information like this would be in a database.

```perl
# note: this directory should be cleaned out automatically
# by another script
opendir(REPO,$repodir) or die "Unable to open dir $repodir:$!\n";

while(defined($statfile=readdir(REPO))){
    next unless -f $repodir.$separator.$statfile;

    # open each status file and read in the one-line status report
    open(STAT,$repodir.$separator.$statfile)
      or die "Unable to open $statfile:$!\n";

    chomp($report = <STAT>);

    ($hostname,$result,$details)=split(' ',$report,3);

    warn "$statfile said it was generated by $hostname!\n"
      if($hostname ne $statfile);

    # hostname is no longer considered missing
    delete $missing{$hostname};
    # populate these hashes based on success or failure reported
    if ($result eq "success"){
        $success{$hostname}=$details;
        $succeeded++;
    }
    else {
        $fail{$hostname}=$details;
        $failed++;
    }
    close(STAT);
}
closedir(REPO);

# construct a useful subject for our mail message
if ($successes == $machines){
    $subject = "[report] Success: $machines";
}
elsif ($failed == $machines or scalar keys %missing >= $machines) {
    $subject = "[report] Fail: $machines";
}
else {
    $subject = "[report] Partial: $succeeded ACK, $failed NACK".
      ((%missing) ? ", ".scalar keys %missing." MIA" : "");
}

# create the mailer object and populate the headers
$type="sendmail";
my $mailer = Mail::Mailer->new($type) or
  die "Unable to create new mailer object:$!\n";

$mailer->open({From=>$reportfromaddr, To=>$reporttoaddr, Subject=>$subject}) or
  die "Unable to populate mailer object:$!\n";
```

```
# create the body of the message
print $mailer "Run report from $0 on " . scalar localtime(time) . "\n";

if (keys %success){
    print $mailer "\n==Succeeded==\n";
    foreach $hostname (sort keys %success){
      print $mailer "$hostname: $success{$hostname}\n";
    }
}

if (keys %fail){
    print $mailer "\n==Failed==\n";
    foreach $hostname (sort keys %fail){
      print $mailer "$hostname: $fail{$hostname}\n";
    }
}

if (keys %missing){
    print $mailer "\n==Missing==\n";
    print $mailer wrap("","",join(" ",sort keys %missing)),"\n";
}

# send the message
$mailer->close;
```

The code first reads a list of the machine names that will be participating in this scheme. Later on it will use a hash based on this list to check if there are any machines that have not placed a file in the central reporting directory. We open each file in this directory and extract the status information. Once we've collated the results, we construct a mail message and send it out.

Here's an example of the resulting mail:

```
Date: Wed, 14 Apr 1999 13:06:09 -0400 (EDT)
Message-Id: <199904141706.NAA08780@example.com>
Subject: [report] Partial: 3 ACK, 4 NACK, 1 MIA
To: project@example.com
From: project@example.com

Run report from reportscript on Wed Apr 14 13:06:08 1999

==Succeeded==
barney: computed 23123 oogatrons
betty: computed 6745634 oogatrons
fred: computed 56344 oogatrons

==Failed==
bambam: computed 0 oogatrons
dino: computed 0 oogatrons
pebbles: computed 0 oogatrons
wilma: computed 0 oogatrons

==Missing==
mrslate
```

Another way to collate results like this is to create a custom logging daemon and have each machine report in over a network socket. Let's look at code for the server first. This example reuses code from the previous example. We'll talk about the important new code right after you see the listing:

```perl
use IO::Socket;
use Text::Wrap; # used to make the output prettier

# the list of machine reporting in
$repolist = "/project/machinelist";
# the port number clients should connect to
$serverport = "9967";

&loadmachines; # load the machine list

# set up our side of the socket
$reserver = IO::Socket::INET->new(LocalPort => $serverport,
                                  Proto     => "tcp",
                                  Type      => SOCK_STREAM,
                                  Listen    => 5,
                                  Reuse     => 1)
  or die "Unable to build our socket half: $!\n";

# start listening on it for connects
while(($connectsock,$connectaddr) = $reserver->accept()){

    # the name of the client that has connected to us
    $connectname = gethostbyaddr((sockaddr_in($connectaddr))[1],AF_INET);

    chomp($report=$connectsock->getline);

    ($hostname,$result,$details)=split(' ',$report,3);

    # if we've been told to dump our info, print out a ready-to-go mail
    # message and reinitialize all of our hashes/counters
    if ($hostname eq "DUMPNOW"){
      &printmail($connectsock);
      close($connectsock);
      undef %success;
      undef %fail;
      $succeeded = $failed = 0;
      &loadmachines;
      next;
    }

    warn "$connectname said it was generated by $hostname!\n"
      if($hostname ne $connectname);
    delete $missing{$hostname};
    if ($result eq "success"){
      $success{$hostname}=$details;
      $succeeded++;
    }
```

```
      else {
        $fail{$hostname}=$details;
        $failed++;
      }
      close($connectsock);
  }
  close($reserver);

# loads the list of machines from the given file
sub loadmachines {
    undef %missing;
    undef $machines;
    open(LIST,$repolist) or die "Unable to open list $repolist:$!\n";
    while(<LIST>){
      chomp;
      $missing{$_}=1;
      $machines++;
    }
}

# prints a ready to go mail message. The first line is the subject,
# subsequent lines are all the body of the message
sub printmail{
    ($socket) = $_[0];

    if ($successes == $machines){
      $subject = "[report] Success: $machines";
    }
    elsif ($failed == $machines or scalar keys %missing >= $machines) {
      $subject = "[report] Fail: $machines";
    }
    else {
      $subject = "[report] Partial: $succeeded ACK, $failed NACK".
        ((%missing) ? ", ".scalar keys %missing." MIA" : "");
    }

    print $socket "$subject\n";

    print $socket "Run report from $0 on ".scalar localtime(time)."\n";

    if (keys %success){
      print $socket "\n==Succeeded==\n";
      foreach $hostname (sort keys %success){
        print $socket "$hostname: $success{$hostname}\n";
        }
    }

    if (keys %fail){
      print $socket "\n==Failed==\n";
      foreach $hostname (sort keys %fail){
        print $socket "$hostname: $fail{$hostname}\n";
        }
    }

    if (keys %missing){
      print $socket "\n==Missing==\n";
```

```
        print $socket wrap("","",join(" ",sort keys %missing)),"\n";
    }
}
```

Besides moving some of the code sections to their own subroutines, the key
change is the addition of the networking code. The `IO::Socket` module makes
the process of opening and using sockets pretty painless. Sockets are usually
described using a telephone metaphor. We start by setting up our side of the
socket (`IO::Socket->new()`), essentially turning on our phone, and then wait
for a call from a network client (`IO::Socket->accept()`). Our program will
pause (or "block") until a connection comes in. As soon as it arrives, we note the
name of the connecting client. We then read a line of input from the socket.

This line of input is expected to look just like those we read from individual files
in our previous example. The one difference is the magic hostname *DUMPNOW.* If
we see this hostname, we print the subject and body of a ready-to-mail message to
the connecting client and reset all of our counters and hash tables. The client is
then responsible for actually sending the mail it receives from the server. Let's look
at our sample client and what it can do with this message:

```
use IO::Socket;

# the port number clients should connect to
$serverport = "9967";
# and the name of the server
$servername = "reportserver";
# name to IP address
$serveraddr = inet_ntoa(scalar gethostbyname($servername));
$reporttoaddr   = "project\@example.com";
$reportfromaddr  = "project\@example.com";


$reserver = IO::Socket::INET->new(PeerAddr => $serveraddr,
                                  PeerPort => $serverport,
                                  Proto    => "tcp",
                                  Type     => SOCK_STREAM)
    or die "Unable to build our socket half: $!\n";


if ($ARGV[0] ne "-m"){
    print $reserver $ARGV[0];
}
else {
    use Mail::Mailer;

    print $reserver "DUMPNOW\n";
    chomp($subject = <$reserver>);
    $body = join("",<$reserver>);

    $type="sendmail";
    my $mailer = Mail::Mailer->new($type) or
        die "Unable to create new mailer object:$!\n";
```

```
        $mailer->open({
              From => $reportfromaddr,
              To => $reporttoaddr,
              Subject => $subject
          }) or
              die "Unable to populate mailer object:$!\n";

        print $mailer $body;
        $mailer->close;
    }

    close($reserver);
```

This code is simpler. First, we open up a socket to the server. In most cases, we pass it our status information (received on the command line as $ARGV[0]) and drop the connection. If we were really going to set up a logging client-server like this, we would probably encapsulate this client code in a subroutine and call it from within a much larger program after its processing had been completed.

If this script is passed an *−m* flag, it instead sends "DUMPNOW" to the server and reads the subject line and body returned by the server. Then this output is fed to `Mail::Mailer` and sent out via mail using the same code we've seen earlier.

To limit the example code size and keep the discussion on track, the server and client code presented here is as bare bones as possible. There's no error or input checking, access control or authentication (anyone on the Net who can get to our server can feed and receive data from it), persistent storage (what if the machine goes down?), or any of a number of routine precautions in place. On top of this, we can only handle a single request at a time. If a client should stall in the middle of a transaction, we're sunk. For more sophisticated server examples, I recommend the client-server treatments in Sriram Srinivasan's *Advanced Perl Programming,* and Tom Christiansen and Nathan Torkington's *Perl Cookbook,* both published by O'Reilly. Jochen Wiedmann's `Net::Daemon` module will also help you write more sophisticated daemon programs.

Let's move on to the other common mistakes made when writing system administration programs that send mail.

Subject Line Waste

A *Subject:* line is a terrible thing to waste. When sending mail automatically, it is possible to generate a useful *Subject:* line on the fly for each message. This means there is very little excuse to leave someone with a mailbox that looks like this:

```
Super-User     File history database merge report
Super-User     File history database merge report
Super-User     File history database merge report
Super-User     File history database merge report
```

```
Super-User        File history database merge report
Super-User        File history database merge report
Super-User        File history database merge report
```

when it could look like this:

```
Super-User        Backup OK, 1 tape, 1.400 GB written.
Super-User        Backup OK, 1 tape, 1.768 GB written.
Super-User        Backup OK, 1 tape, 2.294 GB written.
Super-User        Backup OK, 1 tape, 2.817 GB written.
Super-User        Backup OK, 1 tape, 3.438 GB written.
Super-User        Backup OK, 3 tapes, 75.40 GB written.
```

Your *Subject:* line should be a concise and explicit summary of the situation. It should be very clear from the subject line whether the program generating the message is reporting success, failure, or something in between. A little more programming effort will pay off handsomely in reduced time reading mail.

Insufficient Information in the Message Body

This falls into the same "a little verbosity goes a long way" category as the previous mistake. If your script is going to complain about problems or error conditions in email, there are certain pieces of information it should provide in that mail. They boil down to the canonical questions of journalism:

Who?

Which script is complaining? Include the contents of $0 (if you haven't set it explicitly) to show the full path to the current script. Mention the version of your script if it has one.

Where?

Give some indication of the place in your script where trouble occurred. The Perl function `caller()` returns all sorts of useful information for this:

```
# note: what caller() returns can be specific to a
# particular Perl version, be sure to see the perlfunc docs
($package, $filename, $line, $subroutine, $hasargs, $wantarray,
 $evaltext, $is_require) = caller($frames);
```

$frames above is the number of stack frames (if you've called subroutines from within subroutines) desired. Most often you'll want $frames set to 1. Here's a sample list returned by the `caller()` function when called in the middle of the server code from our last full code example:

```
('main','repserver',32,'main::printmail',1,undef)
```

This shows the script was in the main package while running from the filename *repserver* at line 32 in the script. At that point it was executing code in the `main::printmail` subroutine (which has arguments and has not been called in a list context).

If you want to use `caller()` without doing it by hand, the **Carp** module also provides an excellent problem report.

When?

Describe the program state at the time of the error. For instance, what was the last line of input read?

Why?

If you can, answer the reader's unspoken question: "Why are you bothering me with a mail message?" The answer may be as simple as "the accounting data has not been fully collated," "DNS service is not available now," or "the machine room is on fire." This provides context to the reader (and perhaps some motivation to investigate).

What?

Finally, don't forget to mention what went wrong in the first place.

Here's some simple Perl code that covers all of these bases:

```
use Text::Wrap;

sub problemreport {
# $shortcontext should be a one-line description of the problem
# $usercontext should be a detailed description of the problem
# $nextstep should be the best suggestion for how to remedy the problem
    my($shortcontext,$usercontext,$nextstep) = @_;
    my($filename, $line, $subroutine) = (caller(1))[1,2,3];

    push(@return,"Problem with $filename: $shortcontext\n");

    push(@return,"*** Problem report for $filename ***\n\n");
    push(@return,fill("","","- Problem: $usercontext")."\n\n");
    push(@return,"- Location: line $line of file $filename in
                $subroutine\n\n");
    push(@return,"- Occurred: ".scalar localtime(time)."\n\n");

    push(@return,"- Next step: $nextstep\n");

    \@return;
}

sub fireperson {
    $report = &problemreport("the computer is on fire",<<EOR,<<EON);
While running the accounting report, smoke started pouring out of the
back of the machine. This occurred right after we processed the ORA
pension plan.
EOR
Please put fire out before continuing.
EON

  print @{$report};

}

&fireperson;
```

&problemreport will output a problem report, subject line first, suitable for feeding to Mail::Mailer as per our previous examples. &fireperson is an example test of this subroutine.

Now that we've explored sending mail, let's see the other edge of the sword.

Receiving Mail

When we discuss receiving mail in this section, we're not going to be speaking of *fetching* mail. Transferring mail from one machine to another is not particularly interesting. Mail::POP3Client by Sean Dowd and Mail::Cclient by Malcolm Beattie can easily perform the necessary POP (Post Office Protocol) or IMAP (Internet Message Access Protocol) mail transfers for you. It is more instructive to look at what to do with this mail once it has arrived, and that's where we'll focus our attention.

Let's start with the basics and look at the tools available for the dissection of both a single mail message and an entire mailbox. For the first topic, we will again turn to Graham Barr's *MailTools* package, this time to use the Mail::Internet and Mail::Header modules.

Dissecting a Single Message

The Mail::Internet and Mail::Header modules offer a convenient way to slice and dice the headers of an RFC822-compliant mail message. RFC822 dictates the format of a mail message, including the names of the acceptable header lines and their formats.

To use Mail::Internet, you first feed it an open filehandle to a message file or a reference to an array that already holds the lines of a message:

```
use Mail::Internet;

$messagefile = "mail";

open(MESSAGE,"$messagefile") or die "Unable to open $messagefile:$!\n";
$message = new Mail::Internet \*MESSAGE;
close(MESSAGE);
```

If we want to parse a message arriving in a stream of input (i.e., piped to us on our standard input), we could do this:

```
use Mail::Internet;

$message = new Mail::Internet \*STDIN;
```

Mail::Internet hands us back a message object instance. We'll commonly use two methods with this instance: body() and head(). body() return a reference to an anonymous array that contains the lines of the body of the message. `head()` is more interesting and offers a nice segue to the `Mail::Header` module.

`Mail::Header` is implicitly loaded whenever we load `Mail::Internet`. If we call `Mail::Internet`'s `head()` method, it returns a `Mail::Header` header object instance. This is the same object instance we would get if we changed our first `Mail::Internet` example code to use `Mail::Header` explicitly:

```
use Mail::Header;

$messagefile = "mail";

open(MESSAGE,"$messagefile") or die "Unable to open $messagefile:$!\n";
$header = new Mail::Header \*MESSAGE;
close(MESSAGE);
```

The `$header` object holds the headers of that message and offers us several handy methods to get at this data. For instance, to print a sorted list of the header names (which the module calls "tags") appearing in the message, we could add this to the end of the previous code:

```
print join("\n",sort $header->tags);
```

Depending on the message, we'd see something like this:

```
Cc
Date
From
Message-Id
Organization
Received
Reply-To
Sender
Subject
To
```

We need to retrieve all of the *Received:* headers from a message. Here's how:

```
@received = $header->get("Received");
```

Often we use the `Mail::Header` methods in conjunction with a `Mail::Internet` object. If we were using `Mail::Internet` to return an object that contained both the body and the headers of a message, we might chain some of the methods from both modules together like this:

```
@received = $message->head->get("Received");
```

Note that we're calling `get()` in a list context. In a scalar context, it will return the first occurrence of that tag unless you provide it with an occurrence number as an optional second argument. For instance, `get("Received",2)` will return the second `Received:` line in the message. There are other methods provided by

`Mail::Header` to add and delete tags in a header; see the documentation for more information.

Dissecting a Whole Mailbox

Taking this subject to the next level where we slice and dice entire mailboxes, is straightforward. If our mail is stored in "classical Unix mbox" format or *qmail* (another Message Transfer Agent (MTA) à la *sendmail*) format, we can use `Mail::Folder` by Kevin Johnson. Many common non-Unix mail agents like Eudora store their mail in classical Unix mbox format as well, so this module can be useful on multiple platforms.

The drill is very similar to the examples we've seen before:

```
use Mail::Folder::Mbox; # for classic Unix mbox format

$folder = new Mail::Folder('mbox',"filename");
```

The `new()` constructor takes the mailbox format type and the filename to parse. It returns a `folder` object instance through which we can query, add, remove, and modify messages. To retrieve the sixth message in this folder:

```
$message = $folder->get_message(6);
```

`$message` now contains a `Mail::Internet` object instance. With this object instance you can use all of the methods we just discussed. If you need just the header of the same message:

```
$header = $folder->get_header(6);
```

No surprises here; a reference to a `Mail::Header` object instance is returned. See the `Mail::Folder` documentation for the other available methods.

Tracking Down Spam

Now we know how to take a message apart; let's look at two places where this skill comes in handy. The first such domain we'll consider is UCE—Unsolicited Commercial Email (pronounced "spam"). On the whole, users dislike receiving unsolicited commercial email. System administrators detest UCE because it fills mail spool directories and log files unnecessarily. Plus, each UCE mailing generates complaints from users, so the amount of annoying mail in a system administrator's mailbox often increases in a 1:10 ratio for each UCE message received.

The best way to fight back against this annoyance is to create a climate where spam is not tolerated and becomes too much trouble to send. Complaining to the spammer's Internet Service Provider (most of which have strict acceptable use policies) frequently causes the spammer to be booted off that service. If this happens at every ISP the spammer works from, eventually it becomes harder and harder to find a host ISP. The harder a spammer has to work to continue his or her business, the less likely he or she will stay in that business.

Complaining to the right ISP or is made difficult by the following factors:

- Spammers frequently forge parts of their email in an attempt to cover their tracks. This fact in itself is another reason to dislike spammers. At the very least, it speaks volumes about their intent.

- Spammers frequently pass their trash through innocent (misconfigured) mail servers. This process is known as "relaying" because in most cases the mail neither originates from, nor is intended for, anyone at that mail server. The mail server is just acting as a relay. System administrators at open relay sites often find themselves in a world of pain. Their hijacked mail server starts to suffer under unintended load (perhaps disrupting real service), their site gets blacklisted, and a sizable portion of the legitimate mail that does get through consists of hate mail from the spammed sites.

Perl can help us with the process of dissecting a spam message to find its source. We'll start small and then get progressively fancier by exercising some of the skills we learned in Chapter 5, *TCP/IP Name Services*, and Chapter 6. If you'd like to see a related and very sophisticated Perl spam-fighting script, I recommend you take a look at *adcomplain* by Bill McFadden, found at *http://www.rdrop.com/users/billmc/adcomplain.html*.

Here's a copy of a real piece of spam with the message body changed to avoid giving the spammer any satisfaction:

```
Received: from isiteinc.com (www.isiteinc.com [206.136.243.2])
    by mailhost.example.com (8.8.6/8.8.6) with ESMTP id NAA14955
    for <webadmin@example.com>; Fri, 7 Aug 1998 13:55:41 -0400 (EDT)
From: responses@example.com
Received: from extreme (host-209-214-9-150.mia.bellsouth.net
    [209.214.9.150])
    by isiteinc.com (8.8.3/8.8.3) with SMTP id KAA19050 for
    webadmin@example.com; Fri, 7 Aug 1998 10:48:09 -0700 (EDT)
Date: Fri, 7 Aug 1998 10:48:09 -0700 (EDT)
Received: from login_0246.whynot.net mx.whynot.net[206.212.231.88])
    by whynot.net (8.8.5/8.7.3) with SMTP id XAA06927 for
    <webadmin@example.com>; Fri, 7 August 1998 13:48:11 -0700 (EDT)
To: <webadmin@example.com>
Subject: ***ADVERTISE VACATION RENTALS - $25/year*** - http://www.example.com
Reply-To: sample@whynot.net
X-PMFLAGS: 10322341.10
X-UIDL: 10293287_192832.222
Comments: Authenticated Sender is <user122@whynot.net>
Message-Id: <77126959_36550609>
```

> We are proud to announce the all new http://www.example.com website brought to you
> by Extreme Technologies, Inc.
>
> Our exciting new travel resource contains some of the most visually appealing
> vacation listings available on the WWW. Within our site you will find information
> on properties for rent, properties for sale, international properties, bed &
> breakfast and Inns presented in a highly efficient, and easily navigable fashion.
> Our listings come complete with color photos, animated graphics, concise
> descriptions, and information on how to contact the renter/seller directly. Plus,
> we change our site graphics every month!

Let's look at this message with a critical eye. First, most of the message headers are suspect. As you saw in the previous section of this chapter, most of the headers (*To:*, *From:*, etc.) are fed to our mailer during the DATA portion of the message transfer. The one set of headers that are hard to forge are those added by the mail transfer agent (e.g., *sendmail*) as it passes through each mail system.

In particular, we need to look closely at the *Received:* headers. A spammer can add forged *Received:* lines, but he or she can't take away the ones added by subsequent mail systems. It is possible to fake even those out, but it requires a certain level of sophistication (such as forging TCP/IP packets or spoofing DNS entries) that hit-and-run spammers vary rarely possess.

Let's begin by extracting the *Received:* headers from the message and displaying them in a more readable form. We'll print them in the order a message was transmitted, starting from the first mail server that received the message and ending at its final destination (our site):

```perl
use Mail::Header;

$header = new Mail::Header \*STDIN;

$header->unfold('Received');
@received = $header->get('Received');

for (reverse @received){
    chomp;
    parseline($_);
    if (!defined $ehelo and !defined $validname and !defined $validip){
      print "$_\n";
    }
    else {
      write;
    }
}

format STDOUT =
@<<<<<<<<<<<<<<<<<<<<<<<  @<<<<<<<<<<<<<<<<<<<<<  @<<<<<<<<<<<<<<<
$ehelo,$validname,$validip
.

sub parseline {
```

```
my $line = $_;

# "normal" -- from HELO (REAL [IP])
if (/from\s+(\w\S+)\s*\((\S+)\s*\[(\d+\.\d+\.\d+\.\d+)/){
  ($ehelo,$validname,$validip) = ($1,$2, $3);
}
# can't reverse resolve -- from HELO ([IP])
elsif (/from\s+(\w\S+)\s+\(\[(\d+\.\d+\.\d+\.\d+)\]/){
  ($ehelo,$validname,$validip) = ($1,undef, $2);
}
# exim -- from [IP] (helo=[HELO IP])
elsif (/from\s+\[(\d+\.\d+\.\d+\.\d+)\]\s+\(helo=\[(\d+\.\d+\.\d+\.\d+)\]/){
  ($validip,$ehelo,$validname) = ($1,$2, undef);
}
# Sun Internet Mail Server -- from [IP] by HELO
elsif (/from\s+\[(\d+\.\d+\.\d+\.\d+)\]\s+by\s+(\S+)/){
  ($validip,$ehelo,$validname) = ($1,$2, undef);
}
# Microsoft SMTPSVC -- from HELO - (IP)
elsif (/from\s+(\S+)\s+-\s+(\d+\.\d+\.\d+\.\d+)\s+/){
  ($ehelo,$validname,$validip) = ($1,$2, $3);
}
else { # punt!
  $ehelo = $validname = $validip = undef;
}

return [$ehelo,$validname,$validip];
}
```

This code first **unfold()**s and extracts the *Received:* headers from the message. **unfold()** simply removes the new lines and continuation characters from the given set of header lines. We do this to make parsing easier.

We iterate through these lines in the reverse order they are found in the message. We are essentially operating from the core of the message out, since each system that handles the message envelops it in another layer of *Received:* headers. And the bulk of the work is done by the **&parseline** subroutine. This subroutine attempts to use a set of regular expressions to extract the following from a *Received:* header:

A HELO/EHLO hostname

The name presented at the HELO or EHLO stage of the SMTP conversation.

A "valid" IP address

The IP address of the connecting client as noted by the mail transport agent at time of connect. It is more likely to be "valid" because it uses information that is independent from the information provided by the client during its SMTP conversation. This is important because a spammer's client is likely to be a compulsive liar. The word *valid* is quoted because there are ways to spoof this information.

A "valid" name

 The name of the client found when the mail transfer agent performs a reverse-DNS lookup of the client's IP address. Like the previous item, this information does not come from the client (though it too can be faked).

The format of a proper *Received:* line is suggested by RFC821 and RFC822. However, if you look at a collection of the mail you have received (as I did when generating the regular expressions used earlier), you'll see that not all mail transfer agents agree on this format. We deal with the most common formats in our program, but there are other variations loose in the wild that you'll have to handle if you plan to extend this code. See the *adcomplain* script for an idea of the variety of formats in use.

Here's the output of our program, run on the message cited earlier:

```
login_0246.whynot.net   mx.whynot.net             206.212.231.88
extreme                 host-209-214-9-150.mia    209.214.9.150
isiteinc.com            www.isiteinc.com          206.136.243.2
```

The first column lists the name the machine used when identifying itself, the second column shows the name of the machine according to the server connection, and the last coluimn is the IP address of that connection's originator. As we mentioned previously, this list is ordered so the last line of output corresponds to the machine that handed the message to our mail server for delivery to us.

Though spammers can't remove *Received:* lines, they can influence the contents of these lines by providing a fake name in their HELO or EHLO greeting. You can see it has happened in the second line of this example because the hostname in the first column looks nothing like the hostname in the second, more "valid" column.

But supposing they do match, how do you know if a *Received:* line is forged? One method is to check the "valid" IP address on each *Received:* line against the "valid" hostname and flag anomalies. The subroutine below will return **true** (1) if our lookup of the hostname does not match our reverse lookup of the IP address, and vice versa. We'll plug this code into a larger program shortly:

```perl
use Socket;

sub checkrev{
    my($ip,$name) = @_;

    return 0 unless ($ip and $name);

    my $namelook = gethostbyaddr(inet_aton($ip),AF_INET);
    my $iplook   = gethostbyname($name);

    $iplook = inet_ntoa($iplook) if $iplook;

    # may be recorded with different capitalization
```

```
    if ($iplook eq $ip and lc $namelook eq lc $name){
        return 0;
    }
    else {
        return 1;
    }
}
```

This check is not truly reliable because, although not desired, it is certainly possible to have legitimate hosts with different or missing reverse IP address pointers. Additionally, name servers can be told to respond with bogus information (i.e., gethostbyaddr() can't really be trusted).

There's more we can divine from these *Received:* headers before we track down the owners of each mail hop. For instance, do we or anyone else consider any of the mail hops to be a known source of spam?

Checking against a local blacklist

Some sites keep a local blacklist of hosts spammers are known to use for distributing their messages. This practice was adopted in the early days of the spam industry when it was found that certain ISPs refused to take action against even their most notorious spam-producing customers. In response, mechanisms were added to the major MTAs to deny connections from a list of antisocial hosts and domains.

We can use this list to help us identify if a message has passed through any of the sites listed as known spammers in our local blacklist. We know the site that delivered the mail to us isn't in this list (otherwise we would not have allowed the connect in the first place), but all of the other mail servers listed in a mail's *Received:* headers are suspect.

There's no one way to write generic code that checks a site against all possible MTA blacklists because different MTAs store this information in different formats. The majority of sites on the Internet currently use *sendmail* as their mail transport agent, so we'll use its blacklist format for this part of our example. Recent versions of *sendmail* store their blacklist database using the Berkeley DB 2.X libraries available from *http://www.sleepycat.com*.

Paul Marquess has released a module called BerkeleyDB specifically to use the Berkeley 2.x/3.x libraries. This may be a bit confusing because the documentation for DB_File, Marquess' other famous module found in the core Perl distribution, also recommends using the 2.x/3.x libraries. DB_File uses the Berkeley DB 2.x/3.x libraries in "compatible mode" (for example, the library is built using the --enable-compat185 flag so the version 1.x API is available). The BerkeleyDB module lets a Perl programmer use the expanded functionality provided by the native 2.x/3.x API.

sendmail uses the native Berkeley DB 2.x/3.x format, so we need to press the `BerkeleyDB` module into service. Here's some code that will display the contents of a local blacklist:

```perl
$blacklist = "/etc/mail/blacklist.db";

use BerkeleyDB;

# tie the hash %blist to the blacklist file, using Berkeley DB
# to retrieve values
tie %blist, 'BerkeleyDB::Hash', -Filename => $blacklist
   or die "Cannot open file $filename: $! $BerkeleyDB::Error\n" ;

# iterate over each key and value in this file, printing only
# the REJECT entries
while(($key,$value) = each %blist){
    # the entry in the list can also be marked "OK", "RELAY", etc.
    next if ($value ne "REJECT");

    print "$key\n";
}
```

Building on this code, we can create a subroutine that checks to see if a given host, or the domain it is in, can be found in our local blacklist. If we are asked about the host *mailserver.spammer.com*, we need to cycle through all of the entries in our blacklist (which could contain *mailserver.spammer.com*, *spammer.com*, or even just *spammer*) to see if any of entries can be found in that hostname.

There are many ways in Perl to write code that compares a list of values against some input, but to keep the code both efficient and interesting, we'll use two moderately advanced Perl techniques. These techniques are designed to reduce the amount of regular expression compilation that takes place during a program's execution. Every time our program uses a "new" regular expression in an interpolated matching situation, the Perl regular expression engine needs to compile the expression. For example, in this code snippet we force the Perl regular expression engine to chew on a new interpolated value each time we go through the loop:

```perl
# imagine another loop around this one that calls this code a
# kerjillion times
foreach $match (qw(alewife davis porter harvard central kendall park)){
    $station =~ /$match/ and print "found our station stop!";
}
```

This process is computationally expensive, so if we can cut down on the amount of compilation needed, our program will run more efficiently. Regular expression compilation time becomes an issue mostly in code that iterates over a list of different regular expressions.

Here's an example of the first technique designed to deal with this issue:

```
use BerkeleyDB;

$blacklist = "/etc/mail/blacklist.db";

&loadblist;

# take a host name as a command-line argument and complain
# if it is in the blacklist
if (defined &checkblist($ARGV[0])){
       print "*** found $found in our blacklist\n";
    }

# load the blacklist into an array of anonymous subroutines
sub loadblist{
    tie %blist, 'BerkeleyDB::Hash', -Filename  => $blacklist
      or die "Cannot open file $filename: $! $BerkeleyDB::Error\n" ;

    while(my($key,$value) = each %blist){
        # the blacklist can also say "OK", "RELAY", and etc.
        next if ($value ne "REJECT");
        push(@blisttests, eval 'sub {$_[0] =~ /\Q$key/o and $key}');
    }
}

sub checkblist{
    my($line) = shift;

    foreach $subref (@blisttests){
        return $found if ($found = &$subref($line));
    }
    return undef;
}
```

This example uses the anonymous subroutine technique demonstrated in Joseph Hall's book *Effective Perl Programming* (Addison Wesley). For each blacklist entry, we create an anonymous subroutine. Each subroutine checks its input against one of the entries in the blacklist. If it matches, we return the entry. References to these subroutines are stored in a list as we create them. Here's the line of code that creates a subroutine and pushes a reference to that code on to a list:

```
push(@blisttests, eval 'sub {$_[0] =~ /\Q$key/o and $key}');
```

So if our blacklist had an entry *spammer*, then the code reference pushed on the array would essentially point to:

```
sub {
   $_[0] =~ /\Qspammer/o and "spammer";
}
```

The \Q at the beginning of the regular expression is there to prevent periods (as in
.com) or other reserved punctuation from being treated as regular expression
metacharacters.

Later in the program we iterate over the list of code references and run each little
anonymous subroutine against our input. If any of them return true, we hand
back the return value of the subroutine:

```
return $found if ($found = &$subref($line));
```

The regular expression compilation we're concerned about takes place only once,
when the code reference is being created. We can call each subroutine as often as
we want without paying the time penalty for regular expression compilation.

There's another, slightly less advanced technique for writing this code if you are
using Perl Version 5.005 or later. Perl Version 5.005 introduced a new syntactic
construct called "precompiled regular expressions," which makes this task a little
more straightforward. If we wanted to rewrite this code using this new construct,
we might do something like this:

```
sub loadblist{
    tie %blist, 'BerkeleyDB::Hash', -Filename => $blacklist
        or die "Cannot open file $filename: $! $BerkeleyDB::Error\n" ;

    while(my($key,$value) = each %blist){
        # the blacklist can also say "OK", "RELAY", and etc.
        next if ($value ne "REJECT");
        push(@blisttests,[qr/\Q$key/,$key]);
    }
}

sub checkblist{
    my($line) = shift;

    foreach my $test (@blisttests){
        my($re,$key) = @{$test};
        return $key if ($line =~ /$re/);
    }
    return undef;
}
```

This time we drop a reference to an anonymous array in @blisttest. The first
element of that anonymous array is a compiled regular expression, created using
the new "quote regular expression" syntax, qr//. This allows us to store a regular
expression after it has been compiled. This precompiled regular expression will
provide a significant speed increase when we later perform the match. The second element of our anonymous array is the blacklist entry itself, to be returned if
the compiled regular expression is successfully matched.

Checking against Internet-wide blacklists

Our last code example provided our site's opinion on the "Is this a spammer?" question for a particular host or domain, but it didn't draw upon the experiences of the rest of the Internet community. There are somewhat controversial* services that offer easy access to Internet-wide blacklists of spammers or known open relay hosts. Two well-known services of this type are the Mail Abuse Prevention System's Realtime Blackhole List (RBL) and the Open Relay Behaviour-modification System (ORBS). To access these lists:

1. Reverse the order of the elements of the IP address you are checking. For instance, 192.168.1.34 becomes 34.1.168.192.

2. Append a special domain name to the resulting dotted-quad. To check against the RBL, you would use 34.1.168.192.rbl.maps.vix.com.

3. Fire off a DNS query for this address.

If you receive a positive response (i.e., it returns an A resource record), then the IP address in question is on the list and has been blacklisted.

A little less controversial is the Dial-up User List, also maintained by the Mail Abuse Prevention System folks. This is a voluntary list of IP address ranges for dynamically-assigned modem pools. The theory is that SMTP connections should not originate from any of these hosts. Those hosts should be sending their mail through their ISP's mail server (which is not on this list).

Here's one way you might check to see if an IP address is on any of these lists:

```
sub checkaddr{
    my($ip,$domain) = @_;

    return undef unless (defined $ip);

    my $lookupip = join('.',reverse split(/\./,$ip));

    if (gethostbyname($lookupip.$domain)){
        return $ip;
    }
    else {
        return undef;
    }
}
```

We'll roll this subroutine into this section's penultimate example in a moment. First, now that we've got significantly more detail about each of our *Received:*

---

* The controversy stems over whether such blacklists should be kept, who should maintain them, how they should be applied, under what circumstances sites should be added and removed, and any other political issue you can imagine. For more information on these services, see *http://www.maps.vix.com* and *http://www.orbs.org*.

headers, let's make an attempt to locate the human or humans responsible for administering each of the machines listed. The `Net::Whois` module we saw in Chapter 6 would probably be your first guess for the right tool for this task.

Unfortunately, that module is specialized to receive name-to-domain information only. It also expects the information be in the form used by the InterNIC, not any of the other registries. We may need to receive IP address-to-domain mappings from the WHOIS servers at *http://whois.arin.net* (American Registry for Internet Numbers), *http://whois.ripe.net* (European IP Address Allocations), and *http://whois.apnic.net* (Asia Pacific Address Allocations). The lack of an appropriate module is the first hurdle we're going to have to conquer.

But even if we know how to connect to all of the registries and process their different output formats, it's not clear, given any random IP address, which registry we need to ask. Determining which server to ask is our second hurdle. Luckily, if we ask ARIN for an address in a range not in its database, it will refer us to the proper registry. So if we asked ARIN about a Japanese network address, it will point us at APNIC.

To get over the first hurdle, we could use a general-purpose network communications module like the `Net::Telnet` module we used in Chapter 6. Another option is the `IO::Socket` module we saw earlier in this chapter. Choosing between them is mostly a matter of personal choice and their availability for the platform you'll be using.

The WHOIS service runs on TCP port 43, though we'll use the service name to force a lookup just for caution sake. Talking to a WHOIS server is easy. You connect, provide a query string (in this case an IP address), and receive the answer back. Code to query a random WHOIS server is as simple as this:

```perl
sub getwhois{
    my($ip) = shift;
    my($info);

    $cn = new Net::Telnet(Host => $whoishost,
                          Port => 'whois',
                          Errmode => "return",
                          Timeout => 30)
        or die "Unable to set up $whoishost connection:$!\n";

    unless ($cn->print($ip."\n")){
        $cn->close;
        die "Unable to send $ip to $whoishost: ".$cn->errmsg."\n";
    }

    while ($ret = $cn->get){
        $info .=$ret;
    };
```

```
        $cn->close;

        return $info;
    }
```

To deal with the second hurdle of choosing the right registry, we have at least two choices. We can query *http://whois.arin.net* and parse the output. For instance, here's a transcript of the example I gave earlier of querying ARIN for the IP address of a Japanese machine. Bold type is used to indicate our input in the conversation:

```
% telnet whois.arin.net 43
Trying 192.149.252.22 ...
Connected to whois.arin.net.
Escape character is '^]'.
210.161.92.226
Asia Pacific Network Information Center (NETBLK-APNIC-CIDR-BLK)
    Level 1 - 33 Park Road
    Milton, 4064
    AU

    Netname: APNIC-CIDR-BLK2
    Netblock: 210.0.0.0 - 211.255.255.0

    Coordinator:
        Administrator, System  (SA90-ARIN)  sysadm@APNIC.NET
        +61-7-3367-0490

    Domain System inverse mapping provided by:

    SVC01.APNIC.NET            202.12.28.131
    NS.TELSTRA.NET             203.50.0.137
    NS.KRNIC.NET               202.30.64.21
    NS.RIPE.NET                193.0.0.193

    *** please refer to whois.apnic.net for more information ***
    *** before contacting APNIC                             ***
    *** use whois -h whois.apnic.net <object>               ***

    Record last updated on 04-Mar-99.
    Database last updated on 19-Apr-99 16:14:16 EDT.
```

Once we get output like this, we know we need to ask the question again at *http://whois.apnic.net*.

Alternatively, we can query a "smart" WHOIS server to do the work for us. My favorite site for this is *http://whois.geektools.com*.[*] This server will analyze your query, send the request off to the correct WHOIS server on your behalf, and return

---

[*] As an interesting aside, the GeekTools WHOIS proxy server is written in Perl. For more information about this service or for a copy of the code, see *http://www.geektools.com*.

the result. A user of this service does not have to know or care about which site actually holds the information.

To keep our example code from getting too large and keep this discussion on target, we'll take the second (and easier) option.

Let's wrap all of these little queries into one big package and run it. If we run this code to call all of the above subroutines on our example spam message:

```perl
use Mail::Header;
use Socket;
use BerkeleyDB;
use Net::Telnet;

$header = new Mail::Header \*STDIN;

$header ->unfold('Received');
@received = $header->get('Received');

$rbldomain  = ".rbl.maps.vix.com";
$orbsdomain = ".relays.orbs.org";
$duldomain  = ".dul.maps.vix.com";
$blacklist  = "/etc/mail/blacklist.db";
$whoishost  = "whois.geektools.com";

&loadblist;

for (reverse @received){
    chomp;


    parseline($_);
    if (!defined $ehelo and !defined $validname and !defined $validip){
       print "$_\n";
    }
    else {
     $flags  = (&checkaddr($validip,$rbldomain)   ? "R" : "");  # in RBL?
     $flags .= (&checkaddr($validip,$orbsdomain)  ? "O" : "");  # in ORBS?
     $flags .= (&checkaddr($validip,$duldomain)   ? "D" : "");  # in DUL?
     $flags .= (&checkblist($_)                   ? "B" : "");  # in our list?
     $flags .= (&checkrev($validip,$validname)    ? "L" : "");  # rev-lookup?
      push(@iplist,$validip);

      write;
    }
}

for (@iplist){
    print "\nWHOIS info for $_:\n";
    print &getwhois($_);
}

format STDOUT =
```

```
@<<<<<<<<<<<<<<<<<<<<<<  @<<<<<<<<<<<<<<<<<<<<<<<  @<<<<<<<<<<<<<<<< @<<<<
$ehelo,$validname,$validip,$flags
.
```

we get output that looks like this (slightly abridged):

```
login_0246.whynot.net  mx.whynot.net              206.212.231.88   L
extreme                host-209-214-9-150.mia     209.214.9.150    DB
isiteinc.com           www.isiteinc.com           206.136.243.2    OB

WHOIS info for 206.212.231.88:

WHOIS info for 209.214.9.150:
BellSouth.net Inc. (NETBLK-BELLSNET-BLK4)
   1100 Ashwood Parkway
   Atlanta, GA 30338

   Netname: BELLSNET-BLK4
   Netblock: 209.214.0.0 - 209.215.255.255
   Maintainer: BELL

   Coordinator:...

WHOIS info for 206.136.243.2:
Brainsell Incorporated (NET-ISITEINC)
   4105-R Laguna St.
   Coral Gables, FL 33146
   US

   Netname: ISITEINC
   Netnumber: 206.136.243.0

   Coordinator:...
```

Much nicer! Now we know:

- The spammer gave misleading HELO/EHLO responses.
- The first site is probably bogus (it had a lookup failure and there was no WHOIS information).
- The spam message was probably injected into the Net via a dial-up machine.
- Two of these addresses are already on our blacklist.
- ORBS doesn't like them either.
- Contact information for the ISP and site we might want to contact.

Perl has helped us get well on our way towards dealing with this particular piece of unsolicited commercial email.

But spam is such an unpleasant subject. Let's move on to a cheerier topic, like interacting with users via email.

Support Mail Augmentation

Even if you do not have a "help desk" at your site, you probably have some sort of support email address for user questions and problems. Email as a support communications medium has certain advantages:

- It can be stored and tracked, unlike hallway conversations.

- It is asynchronous; the system administrator can read and answer mail during the more rational nighttime hours.

- It can be a unicast, multicast, or broadcast medium by choice. If 14 people write in (let's say, about a spam message), it is possible to respond to all of them simultaneously when the problem is resolved.

- It can be easily forwarded to someone else who might know the answer or have authority over that service domain.

These are all strong reasons to make email an integral part of any support relationship. However, email does have certain disadvantages:

- If there is a problem with your email system itself, or if the user is having email-related problems, another medium must be used.

- Users can and will type anything they want into an email message. There's no guarantee that this message will contain the information you need to fix the problem or assist the user. You may not gain even a superficial understanding of the purpose of the email. This leads us to the conundrum we'll attempt to address in this section.

My favorite support email of all time is reproduced in its entirety with only the name of the sender changed to protect the guilty:

```
Date: Sat, 28 Sep 1996 12:27:35 -0400 (EDT)
From: Special User <user@example.com>
To: systems@example.com
Subject: [Req. #9531] printer help


something is wrong and I have know idea what
```

If the user hadn't mentioned "printer" in the subject of her mail, we would have no clue where to begin and would probably have chalked the situation up to existential angst. Granted, this was perhaps the most extreme example. More often you receive mail like this:

```
From: Another user <user2@example.com>
Subject: [Req #14563] broken macine
To: systems@example.com
Date: Wed, 11 Mar 1998 10:59:42 -0500 (EST)


There is something wrong with the following machine:

krakatoa.example.com
```

A user does not send mail devoid of contextual content like this out of malice. I believe the root cause of these problems is an impedance mismatch between the user's and the system administrator's mental model of the computing environment.

In the case of most users, the visible structure of the computing environment is limited to the client machine they are logged into, the nearby printer, and their storage (i.e., home directory). For a system administrator the structure of the computing environment is considerably different. She sees a set of servers providing services to clients, all of which may have a myriad of different peripheral devices. Each machine may have a different set of software that is installed and a different state (system load, configuration, etc.).

To a user, the question "Which machine is having a problem?" seems strange. They are talking about *the* computer, the one they are using *now*. Isn't that obvious? To a system administrator, a request for "help with *the* printer" is equally odd; after all, there are many printers in her charge.

So too it goes with the specifics of a problem. System administrators around the world grit their teeth every day when they receive mail that says, "My machine isn't working, can you help me?" They know "not working" could mean a whole panoply of symptoms, each with its own array of causes. To a user that has experienced three screen freezes in the last week, "not working" is unambiguous.

One way to address this disconnect is to constrain the material sent in email. Some sites force the user to send in trouble reports using a custom support application or web form. The problem with this approach is that very few users enjoy engaging in a click-and-scroll fest just to report a problem or ask a question. The more pain involved in the process, the less likely someone will go to the trouble of using these mechanisms. It doesn't matter how carefully constructed or beautifully designed your web form is if no one is willing to use it. Hallway requests will become the norm again. Back to square one?

Well, with the help of Perl, maybe not. Perl can help us augment normal mail receiving to assist us in the support process. One of the first steps in this process for a system administrator is the identification of locus: "Where is the problem? Which printer? Which machine?" And so on.

Here is a program I call *suss*, which provides a bare-bones example of this augmentation. It looks at an email message and attempts to guess the name of a machine associated with that message. The upshot of this is that we often can determine the hostname for the "My machine has a problem" category of email without having to engage in a second round of email with the vague user. This hostname is more than likely going to be a good starting point in the troubleshooting process.

suss uses an extremely simple algorithm to guess the name the machine in question (basically just a hash lookup for every word in the message). First, it examines the message subject, then the body of the message, and finally looks at the *Received:* headers on the message. Here's a simplified version of the code that expects to be able to read an */etc/hosts* file to determine the names of our hosts:

```perl
use Mail::Internet;
$localdomain = ".example.com";

# read in our host file
open(HOSTS,"/etc/hosts") or die "Can't open host file\n";
while(defined($_ = <HOSTS>)){
    next if /^#/;         # skip comments
    next if /^$/;         # skip blank lines
    next if /monitor/i;   # an example of a misleading host

    $machine = lc((split)[1]);  # extract the first host name & downcase
    $machine =~ s/\Q$localdomain\E$//oi; # remove our domain name
    $machines{$machine}++ unless $machines{$machine};
}

# parse the message
$message = new Mail::Internet \*STDIN;
$message->head->unfold();

# check in the subject line
my $subject = $message->head->get('Subject');
$subject  =~ s/[.,;?]//g;
for (split(/\s+/,$subject)) {
    if (exists $machines{lc $_}) {
      print "subject: $_\n";
       $found++;
      }
}
exit if $found;

# check in the body of the message
chomp(my @body = @{$message->body()});
my $body = join(" ",@body);
$body =~ s/[^\w\s]/ /g;               # remove punctuation
@body{split(' ', lc $body)} = ();     # uniq'ify the body
for (keys %body) {
    if (exists $machines{lc $_}) {
      print "body: $_\n";
       $found++;
      }
}
exit if $found;

# last resort: check the last Received: line
$received = (reverse $message->head->get('Received'))[0];
$received =~ s/\Q$localdomain\E//g;
for (split(/\s+/,$received)) {
```

```
    if (exists $machines{lc $_}) {
      print "received: $_\n";
    }
}
```

Two comments on this code:

- The simplicity of our word check becomes painfully apparent when we encounter perfectly reasonable hostnames like *monitor*. If you have host-names that are likely to appear in support messages, you will either have to special-case them as we do with `next if /monitor/i`, or preferably create a more complicated parsing scheme.

- We're using a hash slice construct (`@body{...}`) to help speed up our search of the body of the message. In one step, we've extracted all of the unique words from the text. To understand this construct, you can read it from the inside out. First, the `split()` returns a list of all of the "words" (lowercased) in the message. These words are used as keys to populate the hash `%body`. Because a hash can only contain one instance of any given key, the hash will contain keys consisting of all of the unique words found in the body of the message. It is magic like this that can make programming Perl fun.

Let's take this code out for a spin. Here are two real support messages:

```
Received: from strontium.example.com (strontium.example.com [192.168.1.114])
        by mailhub.example.com (8.8.4/8.7.3) with ESMTP id RAA27043
        for <systems>; Thu, 27 Mar 1997 17:07:44 -0500 (EST)
From: User Person <user@example.com>
Received: (user@localhost)
        by strontium.example.com (8.8.4/8.6.4) id RAA10500
        for systems; Thu, 27 Mar 1997 17:07:41 -0500 (EST)
Message-Id: <199703272207.RAA10500@strontium.example.com>
Subject: [Req #11509] Monitor
To: systems@example.com
Date: Thu, 27 Mar 1997 17:07:40 -0500 (EST)

Hi,
My monitor is flickering a little bit and it is tiresome
whe working with it to much.
Is it possible to fix it or changing the monitor?

Thanks.

User.
-------------------------------------
Received: from example.com (user2@example.com [192.168.1.7])
        by mailhost.example.com (8.8.4/8.7.3) with SMTP id SAA00732
        for <systems@example.com>; Thu, 27 Mar 1997 18:34:54 -0500 (EST)
Date: Thu, 27 Mar 1997 18:34:54 -0500 (EST)
From: Another User <user2@example.com>
To: systems@example.com
Subject: [Req #11510] problems with two computers
```

```
Message-Id: <Pine.SUN.3.95.970327183117.23440A-100000@example.com>

In Jenolen (in room 292), there is a piece of a disk stuck in it. In intrepid,
there is a disk with no cover (or whatever you call that silver thing) stuck in
it. We tried to turn off intrepid, but it wouldn't work. We (the proctor on duty
and I) tried to get the disk piece out, but it didn't work. The proctor in charge
decided to put signs on them saying 'out of order'

AnotherUser
```

Aiming our code at these two messages yields:

```
received: strontium
```

and:

```
body: jenolen
body: intrepid
```

Both hostname guesses were right on the money, and that's with just a little bit of
simple code. To take things one step further, let's assume you get this email:

```
Received: from [192.168.1.118] (buggypeak.example.com [192.168.1.118])
        by mailhost.example.com (8.8.6/8.8.6) with SMTP id JAA16638
        for <systems>; Tue, 4 Aug 1998 09:07:15 -0400 (EDT)
Message-Id: <v02130502b1ecb78576a9@[192.168.1.118]>
Date: Tue, 4 Aug 1998 09:07:16 -0400
To: systems@example.com
From: user@example.com (Nice User)
Subject: [Req #15746] printer

Could someone please persuade my printer to behave and print like a nice printer
should?  Thanks much :)

-Nice User.
```

The user may not realize that you are responsible for a herd of 30 printers. But we
can use Perl and a basic observation to help make an educated guess. Users tend
to print to printers that are geographically close to the machine they are using at
the time. If we can determine which machine they sent mail from, we can probably can pick the printer. There are many ways to retrieve a machine-to-printer
mapping, e.g., from a separate file, from a field in the host database we mentioned in Chapter 5, or even a directory service from LDAP. Here's some code that
uses a simple hostname-to-associated-printer database:

```
use Mail::Internet;
use DB_File;

$localdomain = ".example.com";

# printdb is a Berkeley DB file with a host for a key and a
# printer for a value
$printdb    = "printdb";
```

```
# parse the message
$message = new Mail::Internet \*STDIN;
$message->head->unfold();

# check in the subject line
my $subject = $message->head->get('Subject');
if ($subject =~ /print(er|ing)?/i){
    # find sending machine (assumes Sendmail's header format)
    $received = (reverse $message->head->get('Received'))[0];
    ($host) =
        $received =~ /^from \S+ \((?:\S+@)?(\S+)\Q$localdomain\E \[/;
}

tie %printdb, "DB_File",$printdb  or die "Can't tie $printdb database:$!\n";

print "Problem on $host may be with the printer called " .
        $printdb{$host} . ".\n";

untie %printdb;
```

If the message mentions "print," "printer," or "printing" in its subject line, we pull out the hostname from the *Received:* header. Unlike our UCE examples, we know the format our mail hub uses for *Received:* headers, so we can use a single regular expression to extract this information. With hostname in hand, we can look up the associated printer in a Berkeley DB database. The end result:

```
Problem on buggypeak may be with the printer called hiroshige.
```

If you take a moment to examine the fabric of your environment, you will see other ways to augment the receiving of your support email. The examples in this section are small and designed to get you thinking about the possibilities. What other help could programs that read mail (perhaps mail sent by other programs) provide you? Perl gives you many ways to analyze your email, place it in a larger context, and then act upon that information.

Module Information for This Chapter

Module	CPAN ID	Version
Mac::Glue	CNANDOR	0.58
Win32::OLE (ships with ActiveState Perl)	JDB	1.11
Mail::Mailer (found in *MailTools*)	GBARR	1.13
Text::Wrap (found in *Text-Tabs+Wrap* and also ships with Perl)	MUIR	98.112902
IO::Socket (found in IO and also ships with Perl)	GBARR	1.20
Mail::Internet (found in *MailTools*)	GBARR	1.13
Mail::Header (found in *MailTools*)	GBARR	1.13
Mail::Folder::Mbox (found in Mail::Folder)	KJOHNSON	0.07

Module	CPAN ID	Version
Socket (ships with Perl)		
BerkeleyDB	PMQS	0.10
Net::Telnet	JROGERS	3.01
DB_File (ships with Perl)	PMQS	1.72

References for More Information

Advanced Perl Programming, by Sriram Srinivasan (O'Reilly, 1997) has a good section on programming network servers.

Effective Perl Programming, by Joseph Hall with Randal Schwartz (Addison Wesley, 1998) is a useful book for picking up Perl idioms.

http://www.cauce.org/ is a site from Coalition Against Unsolicited Email. There are many sites devoted to fighting Unsolicited Commercial Email; this site is a good place to start. It has pointers to many other sites, including those that go into greater detail about the analysis of mail headers for this process.

http://www.eudora.com/developers/scripting.html contains information for scripting Eudora with pointers to other AppleScript references.

http://www.microsoft.com and *http://msdn.microsoft.com* have information on "MAPI," "active messaging," and "CDO." The name of this technology has changed twice so far, so I'm hesitant to give you a specific pointer. There is plenty of good information at the Microsoft sites (especially in the MSDN library section) on these topics, but it tends to move around a bit.

Perl Cookbook, by Tom Christiansen and Nathan Torkington (O'Reilly, 1998), also addresses the programming of network servers.

RFC821:Simple Mail Transfer Protocol, J. Postel, 1982.

RFC822:Standard for the format of ARPA Internet text messages, D. Crocker, 1982.

RFC954:NICNAME/WHOIS, K. Harrenstien, M. Stahl, and E. Feinler, 1985.

9

Log Files

If this weren't a book on system administration, an entire chapter on log files would seem peculiar. But system administrators have a very special relationship with log files. Like Doctor Doolittle, who could talk to the animals, system administrators are expected to be able to communicate with a large menagerie of software and hardware. Much of this communication takes place through log files, so we become log file linguists. Perl can be a big help in this process.

It is impossible to touch on all of the different kinds of processing and analysis you can do with logs. Entire books have been devoted to just statistical analysis of this sort of data. However, this chapter should give you some general approaches to the topic and Perl tools to whet your appetite for more.

Text Logs

Logs come in different flavors, so we need several approaches for dealing with them. The most common type of log file is one composed entirely of lines of text. Popular server packages like Apache (web), INN (Usenet news), and Sendmail (email) spew log text in voluminous quantities. Most logs on Unix machines look similar because they are created by a centralized logging facility known as *syslog*. For our purposes, we can treat files created by *syslog* like any other text file.

Here's a simple Perl program to scan for the word "error" in a text-based log file:

```
open(LOG,"logfile") or die "Unable to open logfile:$!\n";
while(<LOG>){
    print if /\berror\b/i;
}
close(LOG);
```

Perl-savvy readers are probably itching to turn it into a one-liner. For those folks:

```
perl -ne 'print if /\berror\b/i' logfile
```

Binary Log Files

Sometimes it's not that easy writing programs to deal with log files. Instead of nice, easily parseable text lines, some logging mechanisms produce nasty, gnarly binary files with proprietary formats that can't be parsed with a single line of Perl. Luckily, Perl isn't afraid of these miscreants. Let's look at a few approaches we can take when dealing with these files. We're going to look at two different examples of binary logs: Unix's *wtmp* file and NT/2000's event logs.

Back in Chapter 3, *User Accounts*, we touched briefly on the notion of logging in and logging out of a Unix host. Login and logout activity is tracked in a file called *wtmp* on most Unix variants. It is common to check this file whenever there is a question about a user's connection habits (e.g., from what hosts does this person usually log in?).

On NT/2000, the event logs play a more generalized role. They are used as a central clearinghouse for logging practically all activity that takes place on these machines including login and logout activity, OS messages, security events, etc. Their role is analogous to the Unix *syslog* service we mentioned earlier.

Using unpack()

Perl has a function called **unpack()** especially designed to parse binary and structured data. Let's take a look at how we might use it to deal with the *wtmp* files. The format of *wtmp* differs from Unix variant to Unix variant. For this specific example we'll look at the *wtmp* files found on SunOS 4.1.4 and Digital Unix 4.0 because they are pretty simple. Here's a plain text translation of the first three records in a SunOS 4.1.4 *wtmp* file:

```
0000000    ~   \0  \0  \0  \0  \0  \0  \0   r   e   b   o   o   t  \0  \0
0000020   \0  \0  \0  \0  \0  \0  \0  \0  \0  \0  \0  \0  \0  \0  \0  \0
0000040    ,   /   ;   4   c   o   n   s   o   l   e  \0   r   o   o   t
0000060   \0  \0  \0  \0  \0  \0  \0  \0  \0  \0  \0  \0  \0  \0  \0  \0
0000100   \0  \0  \0  \0   ,   /   ; 203   c   o   n   s   o   l   e  \0
0000120   \0  \0  \0  \0  \0  \0  \0  \0  \0  \0  \0  \0  \0  \0  \0  \0
0000140   \0  \0  \0  \0  \0  \0  \0  \0   ,   /   < 230
```

Unless you are already familiar with the structure of this file, that "ASCII dump" (as it is called) of the data looks like line noise or some other kind of semi-random garbage. So how do we become acquainted with this file's structure?

The easiest way to understand the format of this file is to look at the source code for programs that read and write to it. If you are not literate in the C language, this may seem like a daunting task. Luckily, we don't actually have to understand or even look at most of the source code; we can just examine the portion that defines the file format.

All of the operating system programs that read and write to the *wtmp* file get their file definition from a single, short C include file, which is very likely to be found at */usr/include/utmp.h*. The part of the file we need to look at begins with a definition of the C data structure that will be used to hold the information. If you search for **struct utmp {** you'll find the portion we need. The next lines after **struct utmp {** define each of the fields in this structure. These lines should be each be commented using the **/* text */** C comment convention.

Just to give you an idea of how different two versions of *wtmp* can be, compare the relevant excerpts from *utmp.h* on these two operating systems.

SunOS 4.1.4:

```
struct utmp {
        char    ut_line[8];     /* tty name */
        char    ut_name[8];     /* user id */
        char    ut_host[16];    /* host name, if remote */
        long    ut_time;        /* time on */
};
```

Digital Unix 4.0:

```
struct utmp {
        char    ut_user[32];    /* User login name */
        char    ut_id[14];      /* /etc/inittab id- IDENT_LEN in init */
        char    ut_line[32];    /* device name (console, lnxx) */
        short   ut_type;        /* type of entry */
        pid_t   ut_pid;         /* process id */
        struct exit_status {
            short e_termination; /* Process termination status */
            short e_exit;        /* Process exit status */
        } ut_exit;               /* The exit status of a process
                                 * marked as DEAD_PROCESS.
                                 */
        time_t  ut_time;        /* time entry was made */
        char    ut_host[64];    /* host name same as MAXHOSTNAMELEN */
};
```

These files provide all of the clues we need to compose the necessary **unpack()** statement. **unpack()** takes a data format template as its first argument. It uses this template to determine how to disassemble the (usually) binary data it receives in its second argument. **unpack()** will take apart the data as instructed, returning a list where each element of the list corresponds to an element of your template.

Let's construct our template piece by piece based on the C structure from the SunOS *utmp.h* include file above. There are many possible template letters we can use. I've translated the ones we'll use below, but you should check the **pack()** section of the *perlfunc* manual page for more information. Constructing these templates is not always straightforward; C compilers occasionally pad values out to satisfy alignment constraints. The command *pstruct* that ships with Perl can often help with quirks likes these.

We do not have any of these complications with our data format. Table 9-1 gives the *utmp.h* breakdown.

Table 9-1. Translating the utmp.h C Code to an unpack() Template

C Code	unpack() Template	Template Letter/Repeat # Translation
char ut_line[8];	A8	ASCII string (space padded), 8 bytes long
char ut_name[8];	A8	ASCII string (space padded), 8 bytes long
char ut_host[16];	A16	ASCII string (space padded), 16 bytes long
long ut_time;	l	A signed "long" value (may not be the same as the size of a "long" value on a particular machine)

Having constructed our template, let's use it in a real piece of code:

```
# this is the template we're going to feed to unpack()
$template = "A8 A8 A16 l";
# this uses pack() to help us determine the size (in bytes)
# of a single record
$recordsize = length(pack($template,()));

# open the file
open(WTMP,"/var/adm/wtmp") or die "Unable to open wtmp:$!\n";

# read it in one record at a time
while (read(WTMP,$record,$recordsize)) {
    # unpack it, using our template
    ($tty,$name,$host,$time)=unpack($template,$record);
    # handle the records with a null character specially
    # (see below)
    if ($name and substr($name,0,1) ne "\0"){
        print "$tty:$name:$host:" ,
                scalar localtime($time),"\n";
    }
    else {
        print "$tty:(logout):(logout):",
                scalar localtime($time),"\n";
    }
}

# close the file
close(WTMP);
```

Here's the output of this little program:

```
~:reboot::Mon Nov 17 15:24:30 1997
:0:dnb::0:Mon Nov 17 15:35:08 1997
ttyp8:user:host.mcs.anl.go:Mon Nov 17 18:09:49 1997
```

```
ttyp6:dnb:limbo-114.ccs.ne:Mon Nov 17 19:03:44 1997
ttyp6:(logout):(logout):Mon Nov 17 19:26:26 1997
ttyp1:dnb:traal-22.ccs.neu:Mon Nov 17 23:47:18 1997
ttyp1:(logout):(logout):Tue Nov 18 00:39:51 1997
```

Here are two small comments on the code:

- Under SunOS, logouts from a particular tty are marked with a null character in the first position, hence:

  ```
  if ($name and substr($name,1,1) ne "\0"){
  ```

- **read()** takes a number of bytes to read as its third argument. Rather than hardcode in a record size like "32", we use a handy property of the **pack()** function. When handed an empty list, **pack()** returns a null or space-padded string the size of a record. This allows us to feed **pack()** an arbitrary record template and have it tell us how big a record is:

  ```
  $recordsize = length(pack($template,()));
  ```

Calling an OS (or Someone Else's) Binary

Groveling through *wtmp* files on systems is such a common task that Unix systems ship a command for printing a human readable dump of the binary file called *last.* Here's some sample output showing approximately the same data as the output of our previous example:

```
dnb        ttyp6     traal-22.ccs.neu Mon Nov 17 23:47 - 00:39   (00:52)
dnb        ttyp1     traal-22.ccs.neu Mon Nov 17 23:47 - 00:39   (00:52)
dnb        ttyp6     limbo-114.ccs.ne Mon Nov 17 19:03 - 19:26   (00:22)
user       ttyp8     host.mcs.anl.go Mon Nov 17 18:09 - crash (27+11:50)
dnb        :0        :0              Mon Nov 17 15:35 - 17:35 (4+02:00)
reboot     ~                         Mon Nov 17 15:24
```

We can easily call binaries like *last* from Perl. This code will show all of the unique user names found in our current *wtmp* file:

```
# location of the last command binary
$lastexec = "/usr/ucb/last";

open(LAST,"$lastexec|") or die "Unable to run $lastexec:$!\n";
while(<LAST>){
    $user = (split)[0];
    print "$user","\n" unless exists $seen{$user};
    $seen{$user}='';
}
close(LAST) or die "Unable to properly close pipe:$!\n";
```

So why use this method when **unpack()** looks like it can serve all of your needs? Portability. As we've shown, the format of the *wtmp* file differs from Unix variant to Unix variant. On top of this, a vendor can change the format of *wtmp* between OS releases, rendering your perfectly good **unpack()** template invalid.

However, one thing you *can* reasonably depend on is the continued presence of a *last* command that will read this format, independent of any underlying format changes. If you use the unpack() method, you have to create and maintain separate template strings for each different *wtmp* format you plan to parse.*

The biggest disadvantage of using this method over unpack() is the increased sophistication of the field parsing you need to do in the program. With unpack(), all of the fields are automatically extracted from the data for you. Using our *last* example, you may find yourself with split() or regular-expression–resistant output like this, all in the same output:

```
user    console                      Wed Oct 14 20:35 - 20:37  (00:01)
user    pts/12         208.243.191.21  Wed Oct 14 09:19 - 18:12  (08:53)
user    pts/17         208.243.191.21  Tue Oct 13 13:36 - 17:09  (03:33)
reboot  system boot                   Tue Oct  6 14:13
```

Your eye has little trouble picking out the columns, but any program that parses this output will have to deal with the missing information in lines one and four. unpack() can still be used to tease apart this output because it has fixed field widths, but that's not always possible.

Using the OS's Logging API

For this approach, let's switch our focus to Windows NT/2000's Event Log Service. As we mentioned before, it unfortunately does not log to plain text files. The best, and only, supported way to get to the data is through a set of special API calls. Most users rely on the *Event Viewer* program, shown in Figure 9-1, to retrieve this data for them.

Luckily, there is a Perl module written by Jesse Dougherty (updated by Martin Pauley and Bret Giddings) that allows easy access to the Event Log API calls.† Here's a simple program that just dumps a listing of events in the *System* event log in a *syslog*-like format. We'll walk through a more complex version of this program later in this chapter.

```
use Win32::EventLog;
# each event has a type, this is a translation of the common types
%type = (1   => "ERROR",
         2   => "WARNING",
         4   => "INFORMATION",
         8   => "AUDIT_SUCCESS",
         16  => "AUDIT_FAILURE");
```

---

* There's a bit of handwaving here, since you still have to track where the *last* executable is found in each Unix environment and compensate for any differences in the format of each program's output.

† Log information in Windows 2000 can also be retrieved using the Window Management Instrumentation (WMI) framework we touched on in Chapter 4, *User Activity*. Win32::EventLog is easier to use and understand.

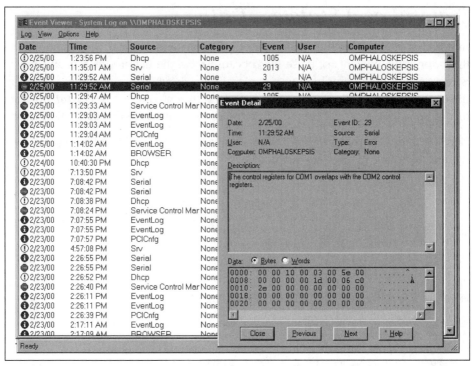

Figure 9-1. The NT4 Event Viewer

```
# if this is set, we also retrieve the full text of every
# message on each Read()
$Win32::EventLog::GetMessageText = 1;

# open the System event log
$log = new Win32::EventLog("System")
  or die "Unable to open system log:$^E\n";

# read through it one record at a time, starting with the first entry
while ($log->Read((EVENTLOG_SEQUENTIAL_READ|EVENTLOG_FORWARDS_READ),
          1,$entry)){
    print scalar localtime($entry->{TimeGenerated})." ";
    print $entry->{Computer}."[".($entry->{EventID} &
        0xffff)."] ";
    print $entry->{Source}.":".$type{$entry->{EventType}};
    print $entry->{Message};
}
```

Command-line utilities like *last* that dump event logs into plain ASCII format also
exist for NT/2000. We'll see one of these utilities in action later in this chapter.

Stateful and Stateless Data

In addition to the format in which the log file presents its data, it is important to think about the contents of these files because *what* the data represents and *how* it is represented both contribute to our plan of attack when programming. With log file contents, often a distinction can be made between data that is *stateful* and data that is *stateless*. Let's see a couple of examples that will make this distinction clear.

Here's a three-line snippet from an Apache web server log. Each line represents a request answered by the web server:

```
esnet-118.dynamic.rpi.edu - - [13/Dec/1998:00:04:20 -0500] "GET home/u1/tux/
tuxedo05.gif

HTTP/1.0" 200 18666 ppp-206-170-3-49.okld03.pacbell.net - - [13/Dec/1998:00:04:21
-0500] "GET home/u2/news.htm

HTTP/1.0" 200 6748 ts007d39.ftl-fl.concentric.net - - [13/Dec/1998:00:04:22 -0500]
"GET home/u1/bgc.jpg HTTP/1.1" 304 -
```

Here are a few lines from a printer daemon log file:

```
Aug 14 12:58:46 warhol  printer: cover/door open
Aug 14 12:58:58 warhol  printer: error cleared
Aug 14 17:16:26 warhol  printer: offline or intervention needed
Aug 14 17:16:43 warhol  printer: error cleared
Aug 15 20:40:45 warhol  printer: paper out
Aug 15 20:40:48 warhol  printer: error cleared
```

In both cases, each line of the log file is independent of every other line in the file. We can find patterns or aggregate lines together gathering statistics, but there's nothing inherent in the data that connects the log file entries to each other.

Now consider some slightly doctored entries from a *sendmail* mail log:

```
Dec 13 05:28:27 mailhub sendmail[26690]: FAA26690: from=<user@has.a.godcomplex.
com>, size=643, class=0, pri=30643, nrcpts=1, msgid=<199812131032.CAA22824@has.a.
godcomplex.com>, proto=ESMTP, relay=user@has.a.godcomplex.com [216.32.32.176]

Dec 13 05:29:13 mailhub sendmail[26695]: FAA26695: from=<root@host.ccs.neu.edu>,
size=9600, class=0, pri=39600, nrcpts=1, msgid=<199812131029.FAA15005@host.ccs.
neu.edu>, proto=ESMTP, relay=root@host.ccs.neu.edu [129.10.116.69]

Dec 13 05:29:15 mailhub sendmail[26691]: FAA26690: to=<user@ccs.neu.edu>,
delay=00:00:02, xdelay=00:00:01, mailer=local, stat=Sent

Dec 13 05:29:19 mailhub sendmail[26696]: FAA26695: to="|IFS=' '&&exec /usr/bin/
procmail -f-||exit 75 #user", ctladdr=user (6603/104), delay=00:00:06, xdelay=00:
00:06, mailer=prog, stat=Sent
```

Unlike the previous examples, there is a definite connection between the lines in the file. Figure 9-2 makes that connection explicit.

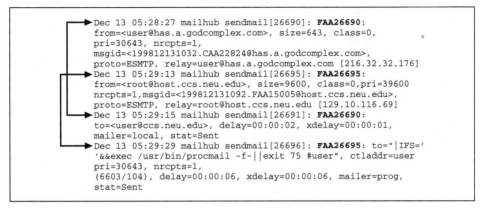

```
Dec 13 05:28:27 mailhub sendmail[26690]: FAA26690:
from=<user@has.a.godcomplex.com>, size=643, class=0,
pri=30643, nrcpts=1,
msgid=<199812131032.CAA22824@has.a.godcomplex.com>,
proto=ESMTP, relay=user@has.a.godcomplex.com [216.32.32.176]
Dec 13 05:29:13 mailhub sendmail[26695]: FAA26695:
from=<root@host.ccs.neu.edu>, size=9600, class=0,pri=39600
nrcpts=1,msgid=<199812131092.FAA15005@host.ccs.neu.edu>,
proto=ESMTP, relay=root@host.ccs.neu.edu [129.10.116.69]
Dec 13 05:29:15 mailhub sendmail[26691]: FAA26690:
to=<user@ccs.neu.edu>, delay=00:00:02, xdelay=00:00:01,
mailer=local, stat=Sent
Dec 13 05:29:29 mailhub sendmail[26696]: FAA26695: to="|IFS='
'&&exec /usr/bin/procmail -f-||exit 75 #user", ctladdr=user
pri=30643, nrcpts=1,
(6603/104), delay=00:00:06, xdelay=00:00:06, mailer=prog,
stat=Sent
```

Figure 9-2. Related entries in the sendmail log

Each line has at least one partner entry that shows the source and destinations of each message. When a message enters the system it is assigned a unique "Message-ID," highlighted above, which identifies that message while it is in play. This Message-ID allows us to associate related lines in an interleaved log file, essentially giving a message an existence or "state" in between entries of a log file.

Sometimes we care about the "distance" between state transitions. Take, for instance, the *wtmp* file we saw earlier in this chapter. Not only are we interested in when someone logs in and when they log out (the two state transitions in the log), but in the time between these two events, i.e., how long they were logged in.

The most sophisticated log files can add another twist. Here are some excerpts from a POP (Post Office Protocol) server's log file while the server is in debug mode. The names and IP addresses have been changed to protect the innocent:

```
Jan 14 15:53:45 mailhub popper[20243]: Debugging turned on
Jan 14 15:53:45 mailhub popper[20243]: (v2.53) Servicing request from "client" at
129.X.X.X
Jan 14 15:53:45 mailhub popper[20243]: +OK QPOP (version 2.53) at mailhub
starting.
Jan 14 15:53:45 mailhub popper[20243]: Received: "USER username"
Jan 14 15:53:45 mailhub popper[20243]: +OK Password required for username.
Jan 14 15:53:45 mailhub popper[20243]: Received: "pass xxxxxxxxx"
Jan 14 15:53:45 mailhub popper[20243]: +OK username has 1 message (26627 octets).
Jan 14 15:53:46 mailhub popper[20243]: Received: "LIST"
Jan 14 15:53:46 mailhub popper[20243]: +OK 1 messages (26627 octets)
Jan 14 15:53:46 mailhub popper[20243]: Received: "RETR 1"
Jan 14 15:53:46 mailhub popper[20243]: +OK 26627 octets
<message text appears here>
Jan 14 15:53:56 mailhub popper[20243]: Received: "DELE 1"
Jan 14 15:53:56 mailhub popper[20243]: Deleting message 1 at offset 0 of length
26627
Jan 14 15:53:56 mailhub popper[20243]: +OK Message 1 has been deleted.
Jan 14 15:53:56 mailhub popper[20243]: Received: "QUIT"
```

```
Jan 14 15:53:56 mailhub popper[20243]: +OK Pop server at mailhub signing off.
Jan 14 15:53:56 mailhub popper[20243]: (v2.53) Ending request from "user" at
(client) 129.X.X.X
```

Not only do we encounter connections ("Servicing request from…") and disconnections ("Ending request from…"), but we have information detailing what took
place in between these state transitions.

Each of these middle events also provides potentially useful "distance" information. If there was a problem with our POP server, we might look to see how long
each step in the above output took.

In the case of an FTP server, you may be able to draw some conclusions from this
data about how people interact with your site. On average, how long do people
stay connected before they transfer files? Do they pause between commands for a
long time? Do they always travel from one part of your site to another before
downloading the same file? The interstitial data can be a rich source of information.

Disk Space Problems

The downside to having programs that can provide useful or verbose logging output is the amount of disk space this output can consume. This is a concern for all
three operating systems covered in this book: Unix, MacOS, and Windows NT/
2000. Of the three, NT/2000 is probably the least troublesome of the lot because
its central logging facility has built-in autotrimming support. MacOS does not have
a central logging facility, but it too can run servers that will happily produce
enough logging output to fill your disks if given the chance.

Usually, the task of keeping the log files down to a reasonable size is handed off
to the system administrator. Most Unix vendors provide some sort of automated
log size management mechanism with the OS, but it often only handles the select
set of log files shipped with the machine. As soon as you add another service to a
machine that creates a separate log file, it becomes necessary to tweak (or even
toss) the vendor-supplied solution.

Log Rotation

The usual solution to the space problem is to rotate your log files. (We'll see an
unusual solution later in this section.) After a specific duration has passed or a file
size has been reached, the current log file is moved to another name, e.g., *logfile.0*.
The logging process is then continued into an empty file. At the next interval or
limit, we repeat the process, first moving the backup file (*logfile.0*) to another
name (like *logfile.1*). This process is repeated until a set number backup files have
been created. The oldest backup file at that point is deleted. Figure 9-3 shows a
picture of this process.

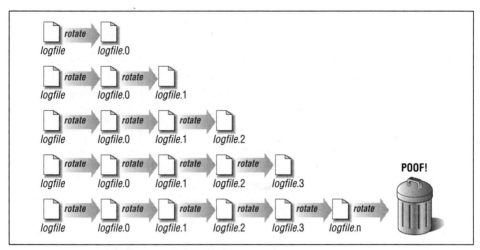

Figure 9-3. A pictorial representation of log rotation

This method allows us to keep a reasonable, finite amount of log data around. Table 9-2 provides one recipe for log rotation and the Perl functions needed to perform each step.

Table 9-2. A Recipe for Log Rotation in Perl

Process	Perl
Move the older backup logs out of the way (i.e., move each one to a new name in the sequence).	`rename()` or `&File::Copy::move()` if moving files cross-filesystem.
If necessary, signal the process creating this particular log file to close the current file and cease logging to disk until told otherwise.	`kill()` for programs that take signals, `system()` or ` `` ` (backticks) if another administrative program has to be called for this purpose.
Copy or move the log file that was just in use to another file.	`&File::Copy` to copy, `rename()` to rename (or `&File::Copy::move()` if moving files cross-filesystem).
If necessary, truncate the current log file.	`truncate()` or `open(FILE,"> filename")`.
If necessary, signal the logging process to resume logging.	See step 2 of this table.
If desired, compress or post-process the copied file.	`system()` or backticks to run a compression program or other code for post-processing.
Delete other, older log file copies.	`stat()` to examine file sizes and dates, `unlink()` to delete files.

There are many variations on this theme. Everyone and their aunt's vendor have written their own script to do log rotation. It should come as no surprise that there

is a Perl module to handle log rotation. Let's take a quick look at `Logfile::`
`Rotate` by Paul Gampe.

`Logfile::Rotate` uses the object-oriented programming convention of first creating a new log file object instance and then running a method of that instance.
First, we create a new instance with the parameters found in Table 9-3.

Table 9-3. Logfile::Rotate Parameters

Parameter	Purpose
`File`	Name of log file to rotate
`Count` (optional, default: 7)	Number of backup files to keep around
`Gzip` (optional, default: Perl's default as found during the Perl build)	Full path to *gzip* compression program executable
`Signal`	Code to be executed after the rotation has been completed, as in step 5 of Table 9-2

Here's some example code that uses these parameters:

```
use Logfile::Rotate;
$logfile = new Logfile::Rotate(
                File   => "/var/adm/log/syslog",
                Count  => 5,
                Gzip   => "/usr/local/bin/gzip",
                Signal =>
                   sub {
                       open PID, "/etc/syslog.pid" or
                           die "Unable to open pid file:$!\n";
                       chomp($pid = <PID>);
                       close PID;
                       # should check validity first
                       kill 'HUP', $pid;
                       }
                );
```

This locks the log file you've specified and prepares the module for rotating it.
Once you've created this object, actually rotating the log is trivial:

```
$logfile->rotate();
undef $logfile;
```

The **undef** line is there to be sure that the log file is unlocked after rotation (it
stays locked while the logfile object is still in existence).

As mentioned in the documentation, if this module is run by a privileged user (like
root) there are a few concerns. First, `Logfile::Rotate` makes a system call to
run the *gzip* program, potentially a security hole. Second, the **Signal** subroutine
must be coded in a defensive manner. In the previous example, we don't check to
see that the process ID retrieved from */etc/syslog.pid* is actually the correct PID for

syslog. It would be better to use one of the process table listing strategies we discussed in Chapter 4, *User Activity*, before sending the signal via `kill()`. See Chapter 1, *Introduction*, for more tips on coding defensively.

Circular Buffering

We've just discussed the traditional log rotation method for dealing with storage of ever-growing logs. Let me show you a more unusual approach that you can add to your toolkit.

Here's a common scenario: you're trying to debug a server daemon that provides a torrent of log output. You're only interested in a small part of the total output, perhaps just the lines the server produces after you run some sort of test with a special client. Saving all of the log output to disk as per usual would fill your disk quickly. Rotating the logs as often as needed with this volume of output would slow down the server. What do you do?

I wrote a program called *bigbuffy* to deal with this conundrum. The approach is pretty straightforward. *bigbuffy* reads from its usual "standard" or "console" input one line at a time. These lines are stored in a circular buffer of a set size. When the buffer is full, it starts filling from the top again. This read-store process continues forever until *bigbuffy* receives a signal from the user. Upon receiving this signal, it dumps the current contents of the buffer to a file and returns to its normal cycle. What's left behind on disk is essentially a window into the log stream, showing just the data you need.

bigbuffy can be paired with a service-monitoring program like those found in Chapter 5, *TCP/IP Name Services*. As soon as the monitor detects a problem, it can signal *bigbuffy* to dump its log buffer. Now you've got a snapshot of the log localized to the failure instance (assuming your buffer is large enough and your monitor noticed the problem in time).

Here's a simplified version of *bigbuffy*. The code is longer than the examples we've seen so far in this chapter, but it is not very complex. We'll use it in a moment as a springboard for addressing some important issues like input blocking and security:

```
$buffsize = 200; # default circular buffer size (in lines)

use Getopt::Long;

# parse the options
GetOptions("buffsize=i" => \$buffsize,
           "dumpfile=s" => \$dumpfile);

# set up the signal handler and initialize a counter
&setup;
```

```perl
# and away we go! (with just a simple
# read line-store line loop)
while (<>){
    # insert line into data structure
    # note, we do this first, even if we've caught a signal.
    # Better to dump an extra line than lose a line of data if
    # something goes wrong in the dumping process

    $buffer[$whatline] = $_;

    # where should the next line go?
     ($what_line %= $buff_size)++;

    # if we receive a signal, dump the current buffer
    if ($dumpnow) {
        &dodump();
    }
}


sub setup {
    die "USAGE: $0 [--buffsize=<lines>] --dumpfile=<filename>"
      unless (length($dumpfile));

    $SIG{'USR1'} = \&dumpnow; # set a signal handler for dump

    $whatline = 1; # start line in circular buffer
}

# simple signal handler that just sets an exception flag,
# see perlipc(1)
sub dumpnow {
    $dumpnow = 1;
}

# dump the circular buffer out to a file, appending to file if
# it exists
sub dodump{
    my($line);      # counter for line dump
    my($exists);    # flag, does the output file exist already?
    my(@firststat,@secondstat); # to hold output of lstats

    $dumpnow = 0;  # reset the flag and signal handler
    $SIG{'USR1'} = \&dumpnow;

    if (-e $dumpfile and (! -f $dumpfile or -l $dumpfile)) {
      warn "ALERT: dumpfile exists and is not a plain file,
            skipping dump.\n";
      return undef;
    }

    # we have to take special precautions when we're doing an
    # append. The next set of "if" statements perform a set of
    # security checks while opening the file for append
    if (-e $dumpfile) {
        $exists = 1;
        unless(@firststat = lstat $dumpfile){
```

```
                warn "Unable to lstat $dumpfile,
                     skipping dump.\n";
                return undef;
        }
        if ($firststat[3] != 1) {
            warn "$dumpfile is a hard link, skipping dump.\n";
            return undef;
        }
    }

    unless (open(DUMPFILE,">>$dumpfile")){
        warn "Unable to open $dumpfile for append,
             skipping dump.\n";
        return undef;
    }
    if ($exists) {
        unless (@secondstat = lstat DUMPFILE){
            warn "Unable to lstat opened $dumpfile,
                 skipping dump.\n";
            return undef;
        }

        if ($firststat[0] != $secondstat[0] or # check dev num
            $firststat[1] != $secondstat[1] or # check inode
            $firststat[7] != $secondstat[7])   # check sizes
          {
            warn "SECURITY PROBLEM: lstats don't match,
                 skipping dump.\n";
            return undef;
          }
    }

    $line = $whatline;
    print DUMPFILE "-".scalar(localtime).("-"x50)."\n";
    do {
        # in case buffer was not full
        last unless (defined $buffer[$line]);
        print DUMPFILE $buffer[$line];
        $line = ($line == $buffsize) ? 1 : $line+1;
    } while ($line != $whatline);

    close(DUMPFILE);

    # zorch the active buffer to avoid leftovers
    # in future dumps
    $whatline = 1;
    $buffer = ();

    return 1;
}
```

A program like this can stir up a few interesting implementation issues.

Input blocking in log processing programs

I mentioned earlier that this is a simplified version of *bigbuffy*. For ease of implementation, especially cross-platform, this version has an unsavory characteristic: while dumping data to disk, it can't continue reading input. During a buffer dump, the program sending output to *bigbuffy* may be told by the OS to pause operation pending the drain of its output buffer. Luckily, the dump is fast, so the window where this could happen is very small, but this is still less passive than we'd like.

Two possible solutions to this problem include:

- Rewriting *bigbuffy* to use a double-buffered, multitasking approach. Instead of using a single storage buffer, two would be employed. Upon receiving the signal, the program would begin to log to a second buffer while a child process or another thread handled the dumping of the first buffer. At the next signal, buffers are swapped again.

- Rewriting *bigbuffy* to interleave reading and writing while it is dumping. The simplest version of this approach would involve writing some number of lines to the output file each time a new line is read. This gets a bit tricky if the log output being read is "bursty" instead of arriving as constant flow. You wouldn't want to wait for a new line of output before you could receive the requested log buffer dump. You'd have to use some sort of timeout or internal clock mechanism to get around this problem.

Both approaches are hard to pull off portably in a cross-platform environment, hence the simplified version shown in this book.

Security in log processing programs

You may have noticed that *bigbuffy* troubles itself more than usual with the opening and writing of its output file. This is an example of the defensive coding style mentioned earlier in "Log Rotation." If this program is to be used to debug server daemons, it is likely to be run by privileged users on a system. It is important to think about unpleasant situations that might allow this program to be abused.

For example, take the case where the output file we've specified is maliciously swapped with a link to another file. If we naively opened and wrote to the file, we might find ourselves inadvertently stomping on an important file like */etc/passwd* instead. Even if we checked the output file before opening it, a nasty person may have switched it on us before we began to write to it. To avoid this scenario:

- We check if the output file exists already. If it does, we `lstat()` it to get file-system information.

- We open the file in append mode.

- Before we actually write to this file, we `lstat()` the open filehandle and check that it is still the same file we expect it to be and it hasn't been switched since we initially checked it. If it is not the same file (e.g., someone swapped the file with a link right before the **open**), we do *not* write to the file and complain loudly. This last step avoids a race condition as mentioned in Chapter 1.

If we didn't have to append, we could have opened a temporary file with a randomized name (so it couldn't be guessed ahead of time) and renamed the temporary file into place.

These sorts of gyrations are necessary on most Unix systems because Unix was not originally designed with security as a high priority. Symbolic-link security breaches are not a problem under NT4 since they are a little-used part of the POSIX subsystem, and MacOS, which doesn't have the notion of "privileged user."[*]

Log Analysis

Some system administrators never get past the rotation phase in their relationship with their log files. As long as the necessary information exists on disk when it is needed for debugging, they never put any thought into using their log file information for any other purpose. I'd like to suggest that this is a shortsighted view, and that a little log file analysis can go a long way. We're going to look at a few approaches you can use for performing log file analysis in Perl, starting with the most simple and getting more complex as we go along.

Most of the examples in this section use Unix log files for demonstration purposes, since the average Unix system has more log files than sample systems from either of the other two operating systems put together, but the approaches offered here are not OS-specific.

Stream Read-Count

The easiest approach is the simple "read-and-count." We read through a stream of log data, looking for interesting data, and increment a counter when we find it. Here's a simple example, which counts the number of times a machine has rebooted based on the contents of a Solaris 2.6 *wtmpx* file:[†]

```
# template for Solaris 2.6 wtmpx, see the pack() doc
# for more information
$template = "A32 A4 A32 l s s2 x2 l2 l x20 s A257 x";

# determine the size of a record
$recordsize = length(pack($template,()));
```

---

[*] In fairness, both NT and MacOS have their own unique security weaknesses. Also, there is considerable time and effort these days being spent to "harden" various Unix distributions (e.g., OpenBSD).

[†] *wtmpx* is a file that uses an extended form of the *u/wtmp* format. It was designed to record events without some of the field length constraints of the classic format (e.g., 16-character remote hostnames). Under Solaris, each login/logout is logged to both *wtmp* and *wtpmx.*

```
# open the file
open(WTMP,"/var/adm/wtmpx") or die "Unable to open wtmpx:$!\n";

# read through it one record at a time
while (read(WTMP,$record,$recordsize)) {
    ($ut_user,$ut_id,$ut_line,$ut_pid,$ut_type,$ut_e_termination,
     $ut_e_exit,$tv_sec,$tv_usec,$ut_session,$ut_syslen,$ut_host)=
       unpack($template,$record);

    if ($ut_line eq "system boot"){
        print "rebooted ".scalar localtime($tv_sec)."\n";
        $reboots++;
    }
}

close(WTMP);
print "Total reboots: $reboots\n";
```

Let's extend this methodology and see an example of statistics gathering using the Windows NT Event Log facility. As mentioned before, NT has a well-developed and fairly sophisticated system-logging mechanism. This sophistication makes it a bit trickier for the beginning Perl programmer. We'll have to use some Win32-specific Perl module routines to get at the basic log information.

NT programs and operating system components log their activities by posting "events" to one of several different event logs. These events are recorded by the OS with basic information like when the event was posted, which program or OS function is posting the event, what kind of event (informational or something more serious) is being posted, etc.

Unlike Unix, the actual description of the event, or log message, is not actually stored with the event entry. Instead, an EventID is posted to the log. This EventID contains a reference to a specific message compiled into a program library (*.dll*). Retrieving a log message given an EventID is tricky. The process involves looking up the proper library in the Registry and loading the library by hand. Luckily, the current version of `Win32::EventLog` performs this process for us automatically (see `$Win32::EventLog::GetMessageText` in our first `Win32::Eventlog` example earlier, "Using the OS's Logging API."

For our next example, we're going to generate some simple statistics on the number of entries currently in the *System* log, where they have come from, and their level of severity. We'll write this program in a slightly different manner than the first NT logging example in this chapter.

Our first step is to load the `Win32::EventLog` module that contains the glue between Perl and the Win32 event log routines. We then initialize a hash table that will be used to contain the results of our calls to the log-reading routines. Perl would normally take care of this for us, but sometimes it is good to add code like this for the benefit of others who will be reading the program. Finally, we set up a small list of event types that we will use later for printing statistics:

```
use Win32::EventLog;

my %event=('Length',NULL,
           'RecordNumber',NULL,
           'TimeGenerated',NULL,
           'TimeWritten',NULL,
           'EventID',NULL,
           'EventType',NULL,
           'Category',NULL,
           'ClosingRecordNumber',NULL,
           'Source',NULL,
           'Computer',NULL,
           'Strings',NULL,
           'Data',NULL,);

# partial list of event types, i.e., Type 1 is "Error",
# 2 is "Warning", etc.
@types = ("","Error","Warning","","Information");
```

Our next step is to open up the *System* event log. The `Open()` places an *EventLog* handle into `$EventLog` that we can use as our connection to this particular log:

```
Win32::EventLog::Open($EventLog,'System','')
   or die "Could not open System log:$^E\n";
```

Once we have this handle, we can use it to retrieve the number of events in the log and the number of the oldest record:

```
$EventLog->Win32::EventLog::GetNumber($numevents);
$EventLog->Win32::EventLog::GetOldest($oldestevent);
```

We use this information as part of our first `Read()` statement, which positions us to the place in the log right before the first record. This is the equivalent of `seek()`ing to the beginning of a file:

```
$EventLog->Win32::EventLog::Read((EVENTLOG_SEEK_READ |
                                  EVENTLOG_FORWARDS_READ),
                                 $numevents + $oldestevent, $event);
```

And then from here on in, it is a simple loop to read each log entry in turn. The `EVENTLOG_SEQUENTIAL_READ` flag says "continue reading from the position of the last record read." The `EVENTLOG_FORWARDS_READ` flag moves us forward in chronological order.* The third argument to `Read()` is the record offset, in this case 0, because we want to pick up right where we left off. As we read each record, we record its `Source` and `EventType` in a hash table of counters.

---

* Here's another place where the Win32 event log routines are more flexible than usual. Our code could have moved to the to the end of the log and read backwards in time if we wanted to do that for some reason.

```
# loop through all of the events, recording the number of
# Source and EventTypes
for ($i=0;$i<$numevents;$i++) {
    $EventLog->Read((EVENTLOG_SEQUENTIAL_READ |
                    EVENTLOG_FORWARDS_READ),
                    0, $event);
    $source{$event->{Source}}++;
    $types{$event->{EventType}}++;
}

# now print out the totals
print "-->Event Log Source Totals:\n";
for (sort keys %source) {
    print "$_: $source{$_}\n";
}
print "-"x30,"\n";
print "-->Event Log Type Totals:\n";
for (sort keys %types) {
    print "$types[$_]: $types{$_}\n";
}
print "-"x30,"\n";
print "Total number of events: $numevents\n";
```

My results look like this:

```
--> Event Log Source Totals:
Application Popup: 4
BROWSER: 228
DCOM: 12
Dhcp: 12
EventLog: 351
Mouclass: 6
NWCWorkstation: 2
Print: 27
Rdr: 12
RemoteAccess: 108
SNMP: 350
Serial: 175
Service Control Manager: 248
Sparrow: 5
Srv: 201
msbusmou: 162
msi8042: 3
msinport: 162
mssermou: 151
qic117: 2
------------------------------
--> Event Log Type Totals:
Error: 493
Warning: 714
Information: 1014
------------------------------
Total number of events: 2220
```

As promised, here's some sample code that relies on a *last*-like program to dump the contents of the event log. It uses a program called *ElDump* by Jesper Lauritsen, downloaded from *http://www.ibt.ku.dk/jesper/JespersNTtools.htm*. *ElDump* is similar to *DumpEl* found in the NT Resource Kit:

```perl
$eldump = 'c:\bin\eldump';       # path to ElDump
# output data field separated by ~ and without full message
# text (faster)
$dumpflags = '-l system -c ~ -M';

open(ELDUMP,"$eldump $dumpflags|") or die "Unable to run $eldump:$!\n";

print STDERR "Reading system log.";

while(<ELDUMP>){
    ($date,$time,$source,$type,$category,$event,$user,$computer) =
    split('~');
    $$type{$source}++;
    print STDERR ".";
}
print STDERR "done.\n";

close(ELDUMP);

# for each type of event, print out the sources and number of
# events per source
foreach $type (qw(Error Warning Information
                  AuditSuccess AuditFailure)){
    print "-" x 65,"\n";
    print uc($type)."s by source:\n";
    for (sort keys %$type){
        print "$_ ($$type{$_})\n";
    }
}
print "-" x 65,"\n";
```

Here's a snippet from the output:

```
ERRORs by source:
BROWSER (8)
Cdrom (2)
DCOM (15)
Dhcp (2524)
Disk (1)
EventLog (5)
RemoteAccess (30)
Serial (24)
Service Control Manager (100)
Sparrow (2)
atapi (2)
i8042prt (4)
-------------------------------------------------------------
```

```
WARNINGs by source:
BROWSER (80)
Cdrom (22)
Dhcp (76)
Print (8)
Srv (82)
```

A simple stream read-count variation

A simple variation of the stream read-count approach involves taking multiple passes through the data. This is sometimes necessary for large data sets and cases where it takes an initial scan through the data before you can determine the difference between interesting and non-interesting data. Programmatically, this means after the first pass through the input, either:

*   Moving back to the beginning of the data stream (which could just be a file) using seek() or an API-specific call, or

*   Closing and re-opening the filehandle. This is often the only choice when you are reading the output of a program like *last*.

Here's an example where a multiple-pass read-count approach might be useful. Imagine you have to deal with a security breach where an account on your system has been compromised. One of the first questions you might want to ask is "Has any other account been compromised from the same source machine?" Finding a comprehensive answer to this seemingly simple question turns out to be trickier than you might expect. Let's take a first shot at the problem. This SunOS-specific code (see the initial template) takes the name of a user as its first argument and an optional regular expression as a second argument for filtering out hosts we wish to ignore:

```
$template      = "A8 A8 A16 l"; # for SunOS 4.1.x
$recordsize    = length(pack($template,()));
($user,$ignore) = @ARGV;

print "-- scanning for first host contacts from $user --\n";
open(WTMP,"/var/adm/wtmp") or die "Unable to open wtmp:$!\n";
while (read(WTMP,$record,$recordsize)) {
    ($tty,$name,$host,$time)=unpack($template,$record);

    if ($user eq $name){
        next if (defined $ignore and $host =~ /$ignore/o);
        if (length($host) > 2 and !exists $contacts{$host}){
            $connect = localtime($time);
            $contacts{$host}=$time;
            write;
        }
    }
}

print "-- scanning for other contacts from those hosts --\n";
```

```
    die "Unable to seek to beginning of wtmp:$!\n"
      unless (seek(WTMP,0,0));

  while (read(WTMP,$record,$recordsize)) {
      ($tty,$name,$host,$time)=unpack($template,$record);

      # if it is not a logout, and we're looking for this host,
      # and this is a connection from a user *other* than the
      # compromised account, then record
      if (substr($name,1,1) ne "\0" and
            exists $contacts{$host} and
            $name ne $user){
                $connect = localtime($time);
                write;
      }
  }
}
close(WTMP);

# here's the output format, may need to be adjusted based on template
format STDOUT =
@<<<<<<<<    @<<<<<<<<<<<<<<   @<<<<<<<<<<<<<<<<<<<<
$name,$host,$connect
.
```

First the program scans through a *wtmp* file looking for all logins from the compromised user. As it finds them, it compiles a hash of all of the hosts from which these logins took place. It then rolls back to the beginning of the file and scans for connections from that host list, printing matches as it finds them. It would be easy to modify this program to scan all of the files in a directory of rotated *wtmp* log files.

One problem with this program is that it is too specific. It will only match exact hostnames. If an intruder is coming in from a dialup modem bank of an ISP (which they often are), chances are the hostnames will change with each dial-up connection. Still, partial solutions like this often help a great deal.

Besides its simplicity, the stream read-count approach we've been discussing has the advantage of being faster and less memory-intensive than other method. It works best with the stateless type of log files we discussed early on in the chapter. But sometimes, especially when dealing with stateful data, we need to use a different plan of attack.

Read-Remember-Process

The opposite extreme of our previous approach, where we passed by the data as fast as possible, is to read it into memory and deal with it after reading. Let's look at a few versions of this strategy.

First, an easy example: let's say you have an FTP transfer log and you want to know which files have been transferred the most often. Here are some sample lines from a *wu-ftpd* FTP server transfer log:

```
Sun Dec 27 05:18:57 1998 1 nic.funet.fi 11868 /net/ftp.funet.fi/CPAN/MIRRORING.
FROM a _ o a cpan@perl.org ftp 0 *
Sun Dec 27 05:52:28 1998 25 kju.hc.congress.ccc.de 269273 /CPAN/doc/FAQs/FAQ/
PerlFAQ.html a _ o a mozilla@ ftp 0 *
Sun Dec 27 06:15:04 1998 1 rising-sun.media.mit.edu 11868 /CPAN/MIRRORING.FROM b _
o a root@rising-sun.media.mit.edu ftp 0 *
Sun Dec 27 06:15:05 1998 1 rising-sun.media.mit.edu 35993 /CPAN/RECENT.html b _ o
a
root@rising-sun.media.mit.edu ftp 0 *
```

Here's the list of fields for each line of the previous output (please see the *wu-ftpd* server manpage *xferlog(5)* for details on each field).

Field #	Field Name
0	current-time
1	transfer-time (in seconds)
2	remote-host
3	filesize
4	filename
5	transfer-type
6	special-action-flag
7	direction
8	access-mode
9	username
10	service-name
11	authentication-method
12	authenticated-user-id

Here's some code to show which files have been transferred most often:

```
$xferlog = "/var/adm/log/xferlog";

open(XFERLOG,$xferlog) or die "Unable to open $xferlog:$!\n";

while (<XFERLOG>){
    $files{(split)[8]}++;
}

close(XFERLOG);

for (sort {$files{$b} <=> $files{$a}||$a cmp $b} keys %files){
    print "$_:$files{$_}\n";
}
```

We read each line of the file, using the name of the file as a hash key and incrementing the value for that key. The name of the file is extracted from each log line using an array index that references a specific element of the list returned by the `split()` function:

```
$files{(split)[8]}++;
```

You may notice that the specific element we reference (8) is different from the 8th field in the *xferlog* field listing above. This is an unfortunate result of the lack of field delimiters in the original file. We are splitting on whitespace (the default for `split()`), so the date field becomes five separate list items.

One subtle trick in this code sample is in the anonymous **sort** function we use to sort the values:

```
for (sort {$files{$b} <=> $files{$a}||$a cmp $b} keys %files){
```

Note that the places of `$a` and `$b` have been switched from their alphabetical order in the first portion. This causes **sort** to return the items in descending order, thus showing us the more frequently transferred files first. The second portion of the anonymous **sort** function (`||$a cmp $b`) assures that we list files with the same number of transfers in a sorted order.

If we want to limit this script to counting only certain files or directories, we could let the user specify a regular expression as the first argument to this script. For example, adding:

```
next unless /$ARGV[0]/o;
```

to the `while()` loop allows you to specify a regular expression to limit which files will be counted.

Regular Expressions

Regular expression crafting is often one of the most important parts of log parsing. Regexps are used like programmatic sieves to extract the interesting data from the non-interesting data in your logs. The regular expressions used in this chapter are very basic, but you'll probably be creating more sophisticated regexps for your own use. You may wish to use the subroutine or compiled regular expression techniques introduced in the previous chapter to use them even more efficiently.

Any time you spend learning how to wield regexp power will benefit you in many ways. One of the best for learning about regular expressions is Jeffrey Friedl's book, *Mastering Regular Expressions* (O'Reilly).

Let's take a look at another example of the read-remember-process approach using our "breach-finder" program from the previous section. Our earlier code only showed us *successful* logins from the intruder sites. We have no way of knowing about unsuccessful attempts. For that information, we're going to have to bring in another log file.

This problem exposes one of Unix's flaws: Unix systems tend to store log information in a number of different places and formats. Few tools are provided for dealing with these disparities (luckily we have Perl). It is not uncommon to need more than one data source to solve problems like these.

The log file that will be the most help to us in this endeavor is the one generated through *syslog* by Wietse Venema's Unix security tool *tcpwrappers*. *tcpwrappers* provides gatekeeper programs and libraries that can be used to control access to network services. An individual network service like *telnet* can be configured so that a *tcpwrappers* program first handles all network connections to this service. After a connection is made, the *tcpwrappers* program will *syslog* the connection attempt and then either pass the connection off to the real service or take some action (like dropping the connection). The choice of whether to let the connection through is based on some simple user-provided rules (e.g., allow only certain originating hosts). *tcpwrappers* can also take preliminary precautions to make sure the connection is coming from the place it purports to come from using a DNS reverse-lookup. It can also be configured to log the name of the user who made the connection (via the RFC931 ident protocol) if possible. For a more detailed description of *tcpwrappers*, see Simson Garfinkel and Gene Spafford's book *Practical Unix & Internet Security* (O'Reilly).

For our purposes, we can just add some code to our previous breach-finder program that scans the *tcpwrappers* log (*tcpdlog* in this case) for connections from the suspect hosts we found in our scan of *wtmp*. If we add the following code to the end of our previous code sample:

```
# tcpd log file location
$tcpdlog        = "/var/log/tcpd/tcpdlog";
$hostlen        = 16;  # max length of hostname in wtmp file

print "-- scanning tcpdlog --\n";
open(TCPDLOG,$tcpdlog) or die "Unable to read $tcpdlog:$!\n";
while(<TCPDLOG>){
    next if !/connect from /; # we only care about connections
    ($connecto,$connectfrom) = /(.+):\s+connect from\s+(.+)/;
    $connectfrom =~ s/^.+@//;
```

```
           # tcpwrappers can log the entire hostname, not just the first N
           # characters like some wtmp logs. As a result, we need to truncate
           # the hostname at the same place as the wtmp file if we want to
           # perform a hash lookup below
           $connectfrom = substr($connectfrom,0,$hostlen);
           print if (exists $contacts{$connectfrom} and
                     $connectfrom !~ /$ignore/o);
     }
```

we get output that looks like this:

```
-- scanning for first host contacts from user --
user        host.ccs.neu  Fri Apr  3 13:41:47
-- scanning for other contacts from those hosts --
user2       host.ccs.neu  Thu Oct  9 17:06:49
user2       host.ccs.neu  Thu Oct  9 17:44:31
user2       host.ccs.neu  Fri Oct 10 22:00:41
user2       host.ccs.neu  Wed Oct 15 07:32:50
user2       host.ccs.neu  Wed Oct 22 16:24:12
-- scanning tcpdlog --
Jan 12 13:16:29 host2 in.rshd[866]: connect from user4@host.ccs.neu.edu
Jan 13 14:38:54 host3 in.rlogind[4761]: connect from user5@host.ccs.neu.edu
Jan 15 14:30:17 host4 in.ftpd[18799]: connect from user6@host.ccs.neu.edu
Jan 16 19:48:19 host5 in.ftpd[5131]: connect from user7@host.ccs.neu.edu
```

You may have noticed that the output above found connections from two different time ranges. We found connections in *wtmp* from April 3 to October 22, while the *tcpwrappers* data appeared to show only January connections. The difference in dates is an indication that our *wtmp* files and our *tcpwrappers* files are rotated at different speeds. You need to be aware of these details when writing code that tacitly assumes the two log files being correlated refer to the same time period.

For a final and more sophisticated example of the read-remember-process approach, let's look at a task that requires combining stateful and stateless data. If you wanted a more comprehensive picture of the activity on a *wu-ftpd* server, you might want to use code to correlate the login and logout activity logged in a machine's *wtmp* file with the file transfer information recorded by *wu-ftpd* in its *xferlog* file. It might be nice if you could see output that showed when an FTP session started and finished, and what transfers took place during that session.

Here's a snippet of sample output from the code we're about to assemble. It shows four FTP sessions in March. The first session shows one file being transferred to the machine. The next two show files being transferred from that machine, and the last shows a connection without any transfers:

```
Thu Mar 12 18:14:30 1998-Thu Mar 12 18:14:38 1998 pitpc.ccs.neu.ed
        -> /home/dnb/makemod

Sat Mar 14 23:28:08 1998-Sat Mar 14 23:28:56 1998 traal-22.ccs.neu
        <- /home/dnb/.emacs19
```

```
Sat Mar 14 23:14:05 1998-Sat Mar 14 23:34:28 1998 traal-22.ccs.neu
        <- /home/dnb/lib/emacs19/cperl-mode.el
        <- /home/dnb/lib/emacs19/filladapt.el

Wed Mar 25 21:21:15 1998-Wed Mar 25 21:36:15 1998 traal-22.ccs.neu
        (no transfers in xferlog)
```

Producing this output turns out to be non-trivial, since we need to pigeonhole stateless data into a stateful log. The *xferlog* transfer log shows only the time and the host that initiated the transfer. The *wtmp* log shows the connection and disconnections from other hosts to the server. Let's walk through how to combine the two types of data using a read-remember-process approach. We'll define some variables for the program, and then call the subroutines to perform each task:

```perl
# for date->Unix time (secs from Epoch) conversion
use Time::Local;

$xferlog = "/var/log/xferlog"; # location of transfer log
$wtmp = "/var/adm/wtmp";       # location of wtmp
$template = "A8 A8 A16 l";     # SunOS 4.1.4 template for wtmp
$recordsize = length(pack($template,())); # size of each wtmp entry
$hostlen = 16;    # max length of the hostname in wtmp
# month name to number mapping
%month = qw{Jan 0 Feb 1 Mar 2 Apr 3 May 4 Jun 5 Jul 6
            Aug 7 Sep 8 Oct 9 Nov 10 Dec 11};

&ScanXferlog;    # scan the transfer log
&ScanWtmp;       # scan the wtmp log
&ShowTransfers;  # correlate and print transfers
```

Now let's look at the procedure that reads the *wu-ftpd xferlog* logfile:

```perl
# scans a wu-ftpd transfer log and populates the %transfers
# data structure
sub ScanXferlog {
    local($sec,$min,$hours,$mday,$mon,$year);
    my($time,$rhost,$fname,$direction);

    print STDERR "Scanning $xferlog...";
    open(XFERLOG,$xferlog) or
        die "Unable to open $xferlog:$!\n";

    while (<XFERLOG>){
        # use an array slice to select the fields we want
        ($mon,$mday,$time,$year,$rhost,$fname,$direction) =
            (split)[1,2,3,4,6,8,11];

        # add the direction of transfer to the filename,
        # i is "transferred in"
        $fname = ($direction eq 'i' ? "-> " : "<- ") . $fname;

        # convert the transfer time to Unix epoch format
        ($hours,$min,$sec) = split(':',$time);
        $unixdate =
```

```
            timelocal($sec,$min,$hours,$mday,$month{$mon},$year);

        # put the data into a hash of lists of lists:
        push(@{$transfers{substr($rhost,0,$hostlen)}},
             [$unixdate,$fname]);
    }
    close(XFERLOG);
    print STDERR "done.\n";
}
```

The **push()** line of Perl in the previous code probably deserves a little explanation. This line creates a hash of lists of lists that looks something like this:

```
$transfers{hostname} =
    ([time1, filename1], [time2, filename2],[time3, filename3]...)
```

The **%transfers** hash is keyed on the name of the host that initiated the transfer. We truncate that name to the largest string size our *wtmp* can hold as we create each hash entry.

For each host, we store a list of transfer pairs, each pair recording when a file was transferred and the name of that file. We're choosing to store the time in "seconds since the epoch" for ease of comparison later.* The subroutine **timelocal()** from the module **Time::Local** helps us convert to that standard. Because we're scanning a file transfer log written in chronological order, these lists of pairs are built in chronological order as well, a property that will come in handy later.

Let's move on to scanning *wtmp*:

```
# scans the wtmp file and populates the @sessions structure
# with ftp sessions
sub ScanWtmp {
    my($record,$tty,$name,$host,$time,%connections);

    print STDERR "Scanning $wtmp...\n";
    open(WTMP,$wtmp) or die "Unable to open $wtmp:$!\n";

    while (read(WTMP,$record,$recordsize)) {

        # don't even bother to unpack if record does not begin
        # with ftp. NOTE: this creates a wtmp format dependency
        # as a trade-off for speed
        next if (substr($record,0,3) ne "ftp");

        ($tty,$name,$host,$time)=unpack($template,$record);

        # if we find an open connection record, then
        # create a hash of list of lists. The LoL will be used
        # as a stack below.
```

---

* This is seconds since some arbitrary starting point. For example, the epoch on most Unix machines is 00:00:00 GMT on January 1, 1970.

```
         if ($name and substr($name,0,1) ne "\0"){
             push(@{$connections{$tty}},[$host,$time]);
         }
     # if we find a close connection record, we try to pair
     # it with a previous open connection record we recorded
     # before
         else {
                 unless (exists $connections{$tty}){
                 warn "found lone logout on $tty:" .
                     scalar localtime($time)."\n";
                 next;
             }
         # we'll use the previous open connect and this
         # close connect to record this as a single session.
         # To do that we create a list of lists where each
         # list is (hostname, login, logout)
         push(@sessions,
             [@{shift @{$connections{$tty}}},$time]);

             # if no more connections on the stack for that
             # tty, remove from hash
             delete $connections{$tty}
                 unless (@{$connections{$tty}});
         }
     }
     close(WTMP);
     print STDERR "done.\n";
 }
```

Let's look at what's going in this code. We read through *wtmp* one record at a
time. If that record begins with `ftp`, we know that this is an FTP session. As the
comment says, the line of code that makes that decision has an implicit assumption about the format of a *wtmp* record. If `tty` was not the first field in the record,
this test would not work. However, being able to test whether a line is of interest
without having to `unpack()` is worth it.

Once we've found a line that begins with `ftp`, we take it apart to determine if it
describes opening or closing of an FTP session. If it is an opening of a connection, we record that in `%connections`, a data structure that keeps tabs on all the
open sessions. Like `%transfers` in our previous subroutine, it is a hash of list of
lists, this time keyed on the tty (i.e., terminal) of each connection. Each of the values in this hash is a set of pairs detailing the connection hostname and time.

Why use such a complicated data structure to keep track of the open connections? Unfortunately, there isn't a simple "open-close open-close open-close" pair-
ing of lines in *wtmp*. For instance, take a look at these lines from *wtmp* (as printed
by our first *wtmp* program earlier in this chapter):

```
ftpd1833:dnb:ganges.ccs.neu.e:Fri Mar 27 14:04:47 1998
ttyp7:(logout):(logout):Fri Mar 27 14:05:11 1998
ftpd1833:dnb:hotdiggitydog-he:Fri Mar 27 14:05:20 1998
```

```
ftpd1833:(logout):(logout):Fri Mar 27 14:06:20 1998
ftpd1833:(logout):(logout):Fri Mar 27 14:06:43 1998
```

Notice the two open FTP connection records on the same tty (lines 1 and 3). If we just stored a single connection per tty in a plain hash, we'd lose the first connection record when we found the second one.

Instead, we use the list of lists keyed off every tty in %connections as a stack. When we see a connection opening, we add a *(host, login-time)* pair for the connection to the stack kept for that tty. Each time we see a close connection line for this tty, we "pop" one of the open connection records off the stack and store our complete information about the session as a whole in another data structure. That's the purpose of this line of code:

```
push(@sessions,[@{shift @{$connections{$tty}}},$time]);
```

Let's untangle this line from the inside out to make sure everything is clear. The part in bold type returns a reference to the stack/list of open connection pairs for a specific tty:

```
push(@sessions,[@{shift @{$connections{$tty}}},$time]);
```

This pops the reference to the first connection pair off that stack:

```
push(@sessions,[@{shift @{$connections{$tty}}},$time]);
```

We dereference it to get at the actual *(host, login-time)* connection pair list. If we place this pair at the beginning of another list that ends with the connection time, Perl will interpolate the connection pair and we'll have a single, three-element list. This gives us a triad of *(host, login-time, logout-time)*:

```
push(@sessions,[@{shift @{$connections{$tty}}},$time]);
```

Now that we have all of the parts (initiating host, connection start, and end) of an FTP session in a single list, we can push a reference to that list on to the @sessions lists of lists for future use:

```
push(@sessions,[@{shift @{$connections{$tty}}},$time]);
```

We have a list of sessions thanks to this one, very busy line of code.

To finish the job in our &ScanWtmp subroutine we check if the stack is empty for a tty, i.e., there are no more open connection requests pending. If this is the case we can delete that tty's entry from the hash; we know the connection has ended:

```
delete $connections{$tty} unless (@{$connections{$tty}});
```

Time to do the actual correlation between our two different data sets. This task falls to our &ShowTransfers subroutine. For each session, it prints out the connection triad, and then the files transferred during this session.

```
# iterate over the session log, pairing sessions
# with transfers
sub ShowTransfers {
    local($session);

    foreach $session (@sessions){

        # print session times
        print scalar localtime($$session[1]) . "-" .
            scalar localtime($$session[2]) .
            " $$session[0]\n";

        # find all files transferred in this connection triad
        # and print them
        print &FindFiles(@{$session}),"\n";
    }
}
```

Here's the hard part, deciding whether a particular login session had any transfers:

```
# returns all of the files transferred for a given connect
# session triad
sub FindFiles{
    my($rhost,$login,$logout) = @_;
    my($transfer,@found);

    # easy case, no transfers in this login
    unless (exists $transfers{$rhost}){
        return "\t(no transfers in xferlog)\n";
    }

    # easy case, first transfer we have on record is
    # after this login
    if ($transfers{$rhost}->[0]->[0] > $logout){
        return "\t(no transfers in xferlog)\n";
    }

    # find any files transferred in this session
    foreach $transfer (@{$transfers{$rhost}}){

        # if transfer happened before login
        next if ($$transfer[0] < $login);

        # if transfer happened after logout
        last if ($$transfer[0] > $logout);

        # if we've already used this entry
        next unless (defined $$transfer[1]);

        push(@found,"\t".$$transfer[1]."\n");
        undef $$transfer[1];
    }
    ($#found > -1 ? @found : "\t(no transfers in xferlog)\n")
}
```

We can eliminate the easy cases first. If we've never seen transfers initiated by this host, or the first transfer associated with this host occurs after the session triad we are checking has ended, we know no files have been transferred during that session.

If we can't eliminate the easy cases, we need to look through our lists of transfers. We check if each transfer made from the host in question occurred after the session started, but before the session ended. We skip to the next transfer if either of these conditions isn't true. We also avoid testing the other transfers for the host as soon as we've found a transfer that takes place after the session has ended. Remember we mentioned that all of the transfers are added to the data structure in chronological order? Here's where it pays off.

The last test we make before considering a transfer entry to be valid may look a little peculiar:

```
# if we've already used this entry
next unless (defined $$transfer[1]);
```

If two anonymous FTP sessions from the same host overlap in time, we have no way of knowing which session is responsible for initiating a transfer of that file. There is simply no information from either of our logs that can help us make that determination. The best we can do in this case is make up a standard and keep to it. The standard here is "attribute the transfer to the first session possible." This test line above, and the subsequent **undef**ing of the filename value as a flag, enforces that standard.

If this final test passes, we declare victory and add the filename to the list of files transferred in that session. The session and its accompanying file transfers are printed.

Read-remember-process programs that have to do this sort of correlation can get fairly sophisticated, especially when they are bringing together data sources where the correlation is a bit fuzzy. So in good Perl spirit, let's see if we can take an easier approach.

Black Boxes

In the Perl world, if you are trying to write something generally useful, another person may have beat you to it and published their code for the task. This gives you an opportunity to simply feed your data into their module in a prescribed way and receive results without having to know how the task was performed. This is often known as a "black box approach."

One example is the **SyslogScan** package by Rolf Harold Nelson. Earlier in this chapter we noted that parsing a mail log file from *sendmail* can be tricky because the lines are stateful. Each line often has one or more sibling lines interspersed with other lines later in the log. The `SyslogScan` package offers an easy way to refer to each mail delivery without having to manually scan the file and pair up all of the relevant lines. It can filter for certain addresses and keep track of some rudimentary statistics for the messages it has seen.

`SyslogScan` is object-oriented, so the first step is to load the module and create a new object instance:

```
use SyslogScan::DeliveryIterator;

# a list of mail syslog files
$maillogs = ["/var/log/mail/maillog"];

$iterator = new SyslogScan::DeliveryIterator(syslogList => $maillogs);
```

The **new** method of `SyslogScan::DeliveryIterator` returns an *iterator*, essentially a pointer into the file that shuttles forward message delivery by message delivery. By using an iterator, we are spared from the actual work of scanning ahead in the file looking for all of the lines related to a particular message. If we call the **next()** method of that iterator, it will hand us back a delivery object. This object encapsulates the information about that delivery previously spread over several lines in the log. For example, this code:

```
while ($delivery = $iterator -> next()){
    print $delivery->{Sender}." -> ".
            join(",",@{$delivery->{ReceiverList}}),"\n";
}
```

prints out information like:

```
root@host.ccs.neu.edu -> user1@cse.scu.edu
owner-freebsd-java-digest@freebsd.org -> user2@ccs.neu.edu
root@host.ccs.neu.edu -> user3@ccs.neu.edu
```

It gets even snazzier. If we feed a `SyslogScan` iterator object to the **new** method of the `SyslogScan::Summary` module, **new** will take all of the output from that iterator's **next** method and return a summary object. This summary object contains usage summaries for all of the delivery objects that iterator could possible return.

But the `SyslogScan` package takes this functionality to still another level. If we now feed a summary object to the **new** method of `SyslogScan::ByGroup`, we get a bygroup object that has grouped all of the summaries into domains and compiled stats for those groups. Here's the magic we just described in action:

```
use SyslogScan::DeliveryIterator;
use SyslogScan::Summary;
use SyslogScan::ByGroup;
use SyslogScan::Usage;
```

```
# the location of our maillog
$maillogs = ["/var/log/mail/maillog"];

# get an iterator for this file
$iterator = new SyslogScan::DeliveryIterator(syslogList => $maillogs);

# feed this iterator to ::Summary, receive a summary object
$summary = new SyslogScan::Summary($iterator);

# feed this summary object to ::ByGroup and receive a
# stats-by-group object
$bygroup = new SyslogScan::ByGroup($summary);

# print the contents of this object
foreach $group (sort keys %$bygroup){
    ($bmesg,$bbytes)=@{$bygroup->{$group}->
                        {groupUsage}->getBroadcastVolume()};
    ($smesg,$sbytes)=@{$bygroup->{$group}->
                        {groupUsage}->getSendVolume()};
    ($rmesg,$rbytes)=@{$bygroup->{$group}->
                        {groupUsage}->getReceiveVolume()};
    ($rmesg,$rbytes)=@{$bygroup->{$group}->
                        {groupUsage}->getReceiveVolume()};
    write;
}

format STDOUT_TOP =
Name                               Bmesg  BByytes  Smesg  SBytes   Rmesg  Rbytes
--+------------------------        -----  -------- ------ -------- ------ -------
.

format STDOUT =
@<<<<<<<<<<<<<<<<<   @>>>>> @>>>>>>> @>>>>> @>>>>>>> @>>>>> @>>>>>>>
$group,$bmesg,$bbytes,$smesg,$sbytes,$rmesg,$rbytes
.
```

The result is a report detailing the number and bytes of broadcast, sent, and received messages. Here's an excerpt from some sample output:

Name	Bmesg	BByytes	Smesg	SBytes	Rmesg	Rbytes
getreminded.com	1	3420	1	3420	0	0
gillette.com	1	984	1	984	4	7812
gis.net	3	10830	3	10830	1	787
globalserve.net	1	1245	1	1245	0	0
globe.com	0	0	0	0	1	2040

The plus side of the black box approach is that you can often get a great deal done, thanks to the hard work of the module or script author, with very little code of your own. The minus side to using the black box approach is the trust you have to place in another author's code. It may have subtle bugs or use an approach that does not scale for your needs. It is best to look over the code before you drop it into production in your site.

Using Databases

The last approach we'll discuss requires the most knowledge outside of the Perl domain to implement. As a result, we'll only take a very simple look at a technique that over time will probably become more prevalent.

The previous examples we've seen work fine on reasonably-sized data sets when run on machines with a reasonable amount of memory, but they don't scale. For situations where you have lots of data, especially if the data comes from different sources, databases are the natural tool.

There are at least two ways to make use of databases from Perl. The first is one I'll call a "Perl-only" method. With this method, all of the database activity takes place in Perl, or libraries tightly coupled to Perl. The second way uses Perl modules like the DBI family to make Perl a client of another database like MySQL, Oracle, or MS-SQL. Let's use both of these approaches for log processing and analysis.

Using Perl-only databases

As long as the data set is not too large, we can probably stick to a Perl-only solution. We'll extend our ubiquitous breach-finder for an example. So far our code just dealt with connections on a single machine. If we wanted to find out about logins from intruders on any of our machines, how would we do it?

Our first step is to drop all of the *wtmp* data for our machines into a database of some sort. For the purpose of this example, assume that all of the machines in question have direct access to some shared directory via some network file system like NFS. Before we proceed, we need to choose a database format.

My "Perl database format" of choice is the Berkeley DB format. I use quotes around "Perl database format" because, while the support for DB is shipped with the Perl sources, the actually DB libraries must be procured from another source (*http:// www.sleepycat.com*) and installed before the Perl support can be built. Table 9-4 provides a comparison between the different supported database formats.

Table 9-4. Comparison of the Supported Perl Database Formats

Name	Unix Support	NT/2000 Support	Mac Support	Key or Value Size Limits	Byte-Order Independent
"old" dbm	Yes	No	No	1K	No
"new" dbm	Yes	No	Yes	4K	No
Sdbm	Yes	Yes	No	1K (default)	No
Gdbm	Yes [a]	Yes [b]	No	None	No
DB	Yes [a]	Yes [a]	Yes	None	Yes

[a] Actual database libraries may have to be downloaded separately.
[b] Database library and Perl module must be downloaded from the net (*http://www.roth.net*).

I like the Berkeley-DB format because it can handle larger data sets and is byte-order independent. The byte-order independence is particularly important for the Perl code we're about to see, since we'll want to read and write to the same file from different machines which may have different architectures.

We'll start off by populating the database. For the sake of simplicity and portability, we're calling the *last* program to avoid having to **unpack()** several different *wtmp* files ourselves. Here's the code, with an explanation to follow:

```perl
use DB_File;
use FreezeThaw qw(freeze thaw);
use Sys::Hostname; # to get the current hostname
use Fcntl;         # for the definition of O_CREAT and O_RDWR

# find the executable for the last program
(-x "/bin/last" and $lastex = "/bin/last") or
  (-x "/usr/ucb/last" and $lastex = "/usr/ucb/last");

$userdb    = "userdata";    # user database file
$connectdb = "connectdata"; # connection database file
$thishost  = &hostname;

open(LAST,"$lastex|") or
    die "Can't run the program $lastex:$!\n";

# read each line of the output from "last"
while (<LAST>){
    next if /^reboot\s/ or /^shutdown\s/ or
            /^ftp\s/    or /^wtmp\s/;
    ($user,$tty,$host,$day,$mon,$date,$time) = split;
    next if $tty =~ /^:0/ or $tty =~ /^console$/;
    next if (length($host) < 4);
    $when = $mon." ".$date." ".$time;

    # save each record in a hash of list of lists
    push(@{$users{$user}},[$thishost,$host,$when]);
    push(@{$connects{$host}},[$thishost,$user,$when]);
}

close(LAST);

# tie to a database file, creating it (for Read & Write); if
# it does not exist see the footnote in the text re: $DB_BTREE
tie %userdb, "DB_File",$userdb,O_CREAT|O_RDWR, 0600, $DB_BTREE
  or die "Unable to open $userdb database for r/w:$!\n";

# iterate through the users and store the info in our
# database using freeze
foreach $user (keys %users){
    if (exists $userdb{$user}){
        ($userinfo) = thaw($userdb{$user});
        push(@{$userinfo},@{$users{$user}});
        $userdb{$user}=freeze $userinfo;
    }
```

```
        else {
            $userdb{$user}=freeze $users{$user};
        }
    }
    untie %userdb;

    # do the same for the connections
    tie %connectdb, "DB_File",$connectdb,O_CREAT|O_RDWR,
                    0600, $DB_BTREE
      or die "Unable to open $connectdb database for r/w:$!\n";
    foreach $connect (keys %connects){
        if (exists $connectdb{$connect}){
            ($connectinfo) = thaw($connectdb{$connect});
            push(@{$connectinfo},@{$connects{$connect}});
            $connectdb{$connect}=freeze($connectinfo);
        }
        else {
            $connectdb{$connect}=freeze($connects{$connect});
        }
    }
    untie %connectdb;
```

Our code takes the output from the *last* program and does the following:

1. Filters out the lines that are not useful.

2. Squirrels away the output in two hash of list of lists data structures that look
   like this:

   ```
   $users{username} =
       [[current host, connecting host, connect time],
        [current host, connecting host, connect time]
        ...
       ];
   $connects{host} =
       [[current host, username1, connect time],
        [current host, username2, connect time],
        ...
       ];
   ```

3. Takes this data structure in memory and attempts to merge it into a database.

This last step is the most interesting, so let's explore it more carefully. We tie the
hashes **%userdb** and **%connectdb** to database files.* This magic allows us to
access those hashes transparently, while Perl handles storing and retrieving data to
the database files behind the scenes. But hashes only store simple strings. How do
we get our "hashes of list of lists" into a single hash value for storage?

---

* You don't usually have to use the BTREE form of storage when using DB_File, but this program can
  store some very long values. Those values caused the Version 1.85 DB_HASH storage method to croak
  in testing (causing corrupted data), while the BTREE storage method seemed to handle the pounding.
  Later versions of the DB libraries may not have this bug.

Ilya Zakharevich's `FreezeThaw` module is used to store our complex data structure in a single scalar that can be used as a hash value. `FreezeThaw` can take an arbitrary Perl data structure and encode it as a string. There are other modules like this, `Data::Dumper` by Gurusamy Sarathy (shipped with Perl) and `Storable` by Raphael Manfredi being the most prevalent. `FreezeThaw` offers the most compact representation of a complex data structure, hence its use here. Each of these modules has its strong points, so be sure to investigate all three if you have a task like ours.

In our program we check if an entry for this user or host exists. If it doesn't, we simply "freeze" the data structure into a string and store that string in the database using our tied hash. If it does exist, we "thaw" the existing data structure found in the database back into memory, add our data, then re-freeze and re-store it.

If we run this code on several machines, we'll have a database with some potentially useful information to feed to the next version of our breach-finder program.

An excellent time to populate a database like this is just after a log rotation of a *wtmp* file has taken place.

The database population code presented here is too bare-bones for production use. One glaring deficiency is the lack of a mechanism to prevent multiple instances of the program from updating the database at the same time. Given that file locking over NFS is known to be dicey at best, it might be easier to call code like this from a larger program that serializes the process of collecting information from each machine in turn.

Now that we have a database full of data, let's walk through our new improved breach-finder program that uses this information:

```perl
use DB_File;
use FreezeThaw qw(freeze thaw);
use Fcntl;

# accept the username and hosts to ignore as command-line arguments
($user,$ignore) = @ARGV;

# database files we'll be using
$userdb    ="userdata";
$connectdb ="connectdata";

tie %userdb, "DB_File",$userdb,O_RDONLY,666,$DB_BTREE
   or die "Unable to open $userdb database for reading:$!\n";
tie %connectdb, "DB_File",$connectdb,O_RDONLY,666,$DB_BTREE
   or die "Unable to open $connectdb database
          for reading:$!\n";
```

We've loaded the modules we need, taken our input, set a few variables, and tied them to our database files. Now it's time to do some work:

```
# we can exit if we've never seen a connect from this user
unless (exists $userdb{$user}){
    print "No logins from that user.\n";
    untie %userdb;
    untie %connectdb;
    exit;
}

($userinfo) = thaw($userdb{$user});

print "-- first host contacts from $user --\n";
foreach $contact (@{$userinfo}){
    next if (defined $ignore and $contact->[1] =~ /$ignore/o);
    print $contact->[1] . " -> " . $contact->[0] .
          " on ".$contact->[2]."\n";
    $otherhosts{$contact->[1]}='';
}
```

This code says: if we've seen this user at all, we reconstitute that user's contact records in memory using **thaw()**. For each contact, we test to see if we've been asked to ignore the host it came from. If not, we print a line for that contact and record the originating host in the **%otherhosts** hash.

We use a hash here as a simple way of collecting the unique list of hosts from all of the contact records. Now that we have the list of hosts the intruder may have connected from, we need to find out all of the other users who have connected from these potentially compromising hosts.

Finding this information will be easy because when we recorded which users logged in to which machines, we also recorded the inverse (i.e., which machines were logged into by which users) in another database file. We now look at all of the records from the hosts we identified in the previous step. If we are not told to ignore a host, and we have connection records for it, we capture a unique list of users who have logged into that host using the **%userseen** hash:

```
print "-- other connects from source machines  --\n";
foreach $host (keys %otherhosts){
    next if (defined $ignore and $host =~ /$ignore/o);
    next unless (exists $connectdb{$host});

    ($connectinfo) = thaw($connectdb{$host});

    foreach $connect (@{$connectinfo}){
        next if (defined $ignore and $connect->[0] =~ /$ignore/o);
        $userseen{$connect->[1]}='';
    }
}
```

The final act of this three-step drama has a nice circular flair. We return to our original user database to find all of the connections made by suspect users from suspect machines:

```perl
foreach $user (sort keys %userseen){
    next unless (exists $userdb{$user});

    ($userinfo) = thaw($userdb{$user});

    foreach $contact (@{$userinfo}){
        next if (defined $ignore and $contact->[1] =~ /$ignore/o);
        write if (exists $otherhosts{$contact->[1]});
    }
}
```

All that's left is to sweep up the theater and go home:

```perl
untie %userdb;
untie %connectdb;

format STDOUT =
@<<<<<<<< @<<<<<<<<<<<<<<< -> @<<<<<<<<<<<<<<< on @<<<<<<<<<<<
$user.":",$contact->[1],$contact->[0],$contact->[2]
.
```

Here's some example output from the program (again, with the user and host-names changed to protect the innocent):

```
-- first host contacts from baduser --
badhost1.exampl -> machine1.ccs.neu.edu on Jan 18 09:55
badhost2.exampl -> machine2.ccs.neu.edu on Jan 19 11:53
-- other connects from source machines  --
baduser2:   badhost1.exampl -> machine2.ccs.neu.e on Dec 15 13:26
baduser2:   badhost2.exampl -> machine2.ccs.neu.e on Dec 11 12:45
baduser3:   badhost1.exampl -> machine1.ccs.neu.ed on Jul 13 16:20
baduser4:   badhost1.exampl -> machine1.ccs.neu.ed on Jun 9 11:53
baduser:    badhost1.exampl -> machine1.ccs.neu.ed on Jan 18 09:55
baduser:    badhost2.exampl -> machine2.ccs.neu.e on Jan 19 11:53
```

This is a lovely example program, but it doesn't really scale past a small cluster of machines. For every subsequent run of the program, it may have to read a record from the database, `thaw()` it back into memory, add some new data to the record, `freeze()` it again, and store it back in the database. This can be CPU-time-and memory-intensive. The whole process potentially happens once per user and machine connection, so things slow down very quickly.

Using Perl-cliented SQL databases

Let's look at one way you might deal with very large datasets. You may need to load your data into a more sophisticated SQL database (commercial or otherwise) and query the information you need from it using SQL. If you're not familiar with

SQL, I recommend you take a quick peek at Appendix D, *The Fifteen-Minute SQL Tutorial*, before looking at this section.

Populating the database could look like this:

```
use DBI;
use Sys::Hostname;

$db = "dnb"; # the name of the database we're using

# locate the last executable
(-x "/bin/last" and $lastex = "/bin/last") or
  (-x "/usr/ucb/last" and $lastex = "/usr/ucb/last");

# connect to a Sybase database using user "dnb" and a password
# provided on the command line
$dbh = DBI->connect('dbi:Sybase:','dnb',$ARGV[0]);
die "Unable to connect: $DBI::errstr\n"
  unless (defined $dbh);

# change to the database we'll be using
$dbh->do("use $db") or
  die "Unable to change to $db: ".$dbh->errstr."\n";

# create the lastinfo table if it doesn't exist
unless ($dbh->selectrow_array(
          q{SELECT name from sysobjects WHERE name="lastinfo"})){
          $dbh->do(q{create table lastinfo (username char(8),
                                            localhost char(40),
                                            otherhost varchar(75),
                                            when char(18))}) or
      die "Unable to create lastinfo: ".$dbh->errstr."\n";
}

$thishost = &hostname;

$sth = $dbh->prepare(
   qq{INSERT INTO lastinfo(username,localhost,otherhost,when)
    VALUES (?,'$thishost', ?, ?)}) or
    die "Unable to prepare insert: ".$dbh->errstr."\n";

open(LAST,"$lastex|") or die "Can't run the program $lastex:$!\n";

while (<LAST>){
    next if /^reboot\s/ or /^shutdown\s/ or
            /^ftp\s/    or /^wtmp\s/;
    ($user,$tty,$host,$day,$mon,$date,$time) = split;
    next if $tty =~ /^:0/ or $tty =~ /^console$/;
    next if (length($host) < 4);
    $when = $mon." ".$date." ".$time;

    $sth->execute($user,$host,$when);
}
```

```
close(LAST);
$dbh->disconnect;
```

This creates a table called *lastinfo* with *username*, `localhost`, `otherhost`, and *when* columns. We iterate over the output of *last*, inserting non-bogus entries into this table.

Now we can use databases to do what they do so well. Here is a set of sample SQL queries that could easily be wrapped in Perl using the DBI or ODBC interfaces we explored in Chapter 7, *SQL Database Administration*:

```
-- how many entries in the database?
select count (*) from lastinfo;


-----------
      10068
-- how many users have logged in?
select count (distinct username) from lastinfo;


-----------
        237


-- how many separate hosts have connected to our machines?
select count (distinct otherhost) from lastinfo;


-----------
       1000


-- which local hosts has the user "dnb" logged into?
select distinct localhost from lastinfo where username = "dnb";
 localhost
---------------------------------------
 host1
 host2
```

These examples should give you a taste of the sort of "data mining" you can do once all of the data is in a real database. Each of those queries took only a second or so to run. Databases can be fast, powerful tools for system administration.

The subject of log analysis is a vast one. Hopefully this chapter has given you a few tools and a little inspiration.

Module Information for This Chapter

Modules	CPAN ID	Version
Win32::EventLog (ships with ActivePerl)		0.062
Logfile::Rotate	PAULG	1.03
Getopt::Long (ships with Perl)		2.20
Time::Local (ships with Perl)		1.01

Modules	CPAN ID	Version
SyslogScan	RHNELSON	0.32
DB_File (ships with Perl)	PMQS	1.72
FreezeThaw	ILYAZ	0.3
Sys::Hostname (ships with Perl)		
Fcntl (ships with Perl)		1.03
DBI	TIMB	1.13

References for More Information

Essential System Administration, (2nd Edition), by Æleen Frisch (O'Reilly, 1995) has a good, short intro to *syslog*.

http://www.heysoft.de/index.htm is the home of Frank Heyne software, a provider of Win32 Event Log-parsing software. Also has a good Event Log FAQ list.

http://www.le-berre.com/ is Philippe Le Berre's home page, and contains an excellent write-up on the use of Win32::EventLog and other Win32 packages.

"Managing NT Event Logs with Perl for Win32," Bob Wells, *Windows NT Magazine*, February/March 1998.

Practical Unix & Internet Security, (2nd Edition), by Simson Garfinkel and Gene Spafford (O'Reilly, 1996). Another good (and slightly more detailed) intro to *syslog*, also includes *tcpwrappers* information.

Windows NT Event Logging, by James D. Murray (O'Reilly, 1998).

10

Security and Network Monitoring

Any discussion of *security* is fraught with peril. There are at least three snares that can doom a discussion on security:

1. Security means different things to different people. If you walked into a conference of Greco-Roman scholars and asked about Rome, the first scholar would rise dramatically to her feet and begin to lecture about aqueducts (infrastructure and delivery), the second *Pax Romana* (ideology and policies), a third would expound on the Roman legions (enforcement), a fourth on the Roman Senate (administration), and so on. The need to deal with every facet of security at once is security's first trap.

2. People think that something can be secure, be it a program, a computer, a network, etc. This chapter will never claim to show you how to make anything secure; it will try to help you make something *more* secure, or at least recognize when something is *less* secure. Security is a continuum.

3. Finally, one of the most deadly traps in this business is specificity. It is true that the deity of security is often in the details, but it is an ever-shifting set of details. Patching security holes A, B, and C on your system only guarantees (and perhaps not even) that those particular holes will not be a source of trouble. It does nothing to help when hole D is found. That's why this chapter will focus on principles and tools for improving security. It will not tell you how to fix any particular buffer overflow, vulnerable registry key, or world-writable system file.

One good way to get into a discussion of these principles is to examine how security manifests itself in the physical world. In both the real and virtual worlds, it all comes down to *fear*. Will something I care about be damaged, lost, or revealed? Is there something I can do to prevent this from happening? Is it happening *right now?*

If we look at how this fear is faced in the physical world, we can learn ways to deal with it in our domain as well. One way we deal with this fear is to invent stronger ways of partitioning space. With physical space we use constructs like bank vaults; with intellectual space we use data-hiding methods like "top secret clearance" or encryption. But this is a never-ending pursuit. For every hour spent designing a security system, there is at least an hour spent looking for a way to evade it. In our case, there are also hordes of bored teenagers with computers and disgruntled former employees looking for something to do with excess energy.

A slightly better approach to improving security that has persisted over the ages is the use of a designated person to allay these fears. Once upon a time, there was nothing so comforting as the sound of the night watchman's footsteps as he or she walked through the town, jiggling doors handles to make sure everything was locked and secure. We'll use this quaint image as the jump point for our exploration into security and network monitoring with Perl.

Noticing Unexpected or Unauthorized Changes

A good watchman notices change. He or she knows when things are in the wrong place in your environment. If your precious Maltese falcon gets replaced with a forgery, the watchman is the first person that should notice. Similarly, if someone modifies or replaces key files on your system, you want sirens to blare and klaxons to sound. More often than not, the change will be harmless. But the first time someone breaches your security and mucks with */bin/login, msgina.dll,* or *Finder,* you'll be so glad you noticed that you will excuse any prior false alarms.

Local Filesystem Changes

Filesystems are an excellent place to begin our exploration into change-checking programs. We're going to explore ways to check if important files like operating system binaries and security-related files (e.g., */etc/passwd* or *msgina.dll*) have changed. Changes to these files made without the knowledge of the administrator are often signs of an intruder. There are some relatively sophisticated cracker toolkits available on the Net that do a very good job of installing Trojan versions of important files and covering up their tracks. That's the most malevolent kind of change we can detect. On the other end of the spectrum, sometimes it is just nice to know when important files have been changed (especially in environments where multiple people administer the same systems). The techniques we're about to explore will work equally well in both cases.

The easiest way to tell if a file has changed is to use the Perl functions `stat()` and `lstat()`. These functions take a filename or a filehandle and return an array with information about that file. The only difference between the two functions manifests itself on operating systems like Unix that support symbolic links. In these cases `lstat()` is used to return information about the target of a symbolic link instead of the link itself. On all other operating systems the information returned by `lstat()` should be the same as that returned by `stat()`.

Using `stat()` or `lstat()` is easy:

```
@information = stat("filename");
```

As demonstrated in Chapter 3, *User Accounts*, we can also use Tom Christiansen's `File::Stat` module to provide this information using an object-oriented syntax.

The information returned by `stat()` or `lstat()` is operating-system–dependent. `stat()` and `lstat()` began as Unix system calls, so the Perl documentation for these calls is skewed towards the return values for Unix systems. Table 10-1 shows how these values compare to those returned by `stat()` on Windows NT/2000 and MacOS. The first two columns show the Unix field number and description.

Table 10-1. stat() Return Value Comparison

#	Unix Field Description	Valid for NT/2000	Valid for MacOS
0	Device number of filesystem	Yes (drive #)	Yes (but is vRefNum)
1	Inode number	No (always 0)	Yes (but is fileID/dirID)
2	File mode (type and permissions)	Yes	Yes (but is 777 for dirs and applications, 666 for unlocked documents, 444 for locked documents)
3	Number of (hard) links to the file	Yes (for NTFS)	No (always 1)
4	Numeric user ID of file's owner	No (always 0)	No (always 0)
5	Numeric group ID of file's owner	No (always 0)	No (always 0)
6	The device identifier (special files only)	Yes (drive #)	No (always null)
7	Total size of file, in bytes	Yes (but does not include the size of any alternate data streams)	Yes (but returns size of data fork only)

Table 10-1. stat( ) Return Value Comparison (continued)

#	Unix Field Description	Valid for NT/2000	Valid for MacOS
8	Last access time since the epoch	Yes	Yes (but epoch is 66 years earlier than Unix, at 1/1/1904, and value is same as field #9)[a]
9	Last modify time since the epoch	Yes	Yes (but epoch is 1/1/1904 and value is same as field #8)
10	Inode change time since the epoch	Yes (but is file *creation* time)	Yes (but epoch is 1/1/1904 and is file *creation* time)
11	Preferred block size for filesystem I/O	No (always null)	Yes
12	Actual number of blocks allocated	No (always null)	Yes

[a] Also, MacOS epoch is counted from *local* time, not Universal Time Coordinated (UTC). So if the clocks in two MacOS computers are synchronized, but one has a time zone setting (TZ) of -0800 and the other has a TZ of -0500, the values for time() on these computers will be three hours apart.

In addition to `stat()` and `lstat()`, other non-Unix versions of Perl have special functions to return attributes of a file that are peculiar to that OS. See Chapter 2, *Filesystems*, for discussions of functions like `MacPerl::GetFileInfo()` and `Win32::FileSecurity::Get()`.

Once you have queried the `stat()`ish values for a file, the next step is to compare the "interesting" values against a known set of values for that file. If the values changed, something about the file must have changed. Here's a program that both generates a string of `lstat()` values and checks files against a known set of those values. We intentionally exclude field #8 from the above table (last access time) because it changes every time a file is read.

This program takes either a *−p filename* argument to print `lstat()` values for a given file or a *−c filename* argument to check the `lstat()` values all of the files listed in *filename*.

```
use Getopt::Std;

# we use this for prettier output later in &printchanged()
@statnames = qw(dev ino mode nlink uid gid rdev
                size mtime ctime blksize blocks);

getopt('p:c:');

die "Usage: $0 [-p <filename>|-c <filename>]\n"
  unless ($opt_p or $opt_c);

if ($opt_p){
    die "Unable to stat file $opt_p:$!\n"
      unless (-e $opt_p);
```

```
        print $opt_p,"|",join('|',(lstat($opt_p))[0..7,9..12]),"\n";
        exit;
}


if ($opt_c){
    open(CFILE,$opt_c) or
        die "Unable to open check file $opt_c:$!\n";
    while(<CFILE>){
        chomp;
        @savedstats = split('\|');
        die "Wrong number of fields in line beginning with
            $savedstats[0]\n"
          unless ($#savedstats == 12);
        @currentstats = (lstat($savedstats[0]))[0..7,9..12];

        # print the changed fields only if something has changed
        &printchanged(\@savedstats,\@currentstats)
          if ("@savedstats[1..13]" ne "@currentstats");
    }
    close(CFILE);
}


# iterates through attributes lists and prints any changes between
# the two
sub printchanged{
    my($saved,$current)= @_;

    # print the name of the file after popping it off of the array read
    # from the check file
    print shift @{$saved},":\n";

    for (my $i=0; $i < $#{$saved};$i++){
        if ($saved->[$i] ne $current->[$i]){
            print "\t".$statnames[$i]." is now ".$current->[$i];
            print " (should be ".$saved->[$i].")\n";
        }
    }
}
```

To use this program, we might type *checkfile –p /etc/passwd >> checksumfile*. *checksumfile* should then contain a line that looks like this:

```
/etc/passwd|1792|11427|33060|1|0|0|24959|607|921016509|921016509|8192|2
```

We would then repeat this step for each file we want to monitor. Then, running the script with *checkfile –c checksumfile* will show any changes. For instance, if I remove a character from */etc/passwd*, this script will complain like this:

```
/etc/passwd:
        size is now 606 (should be 607)
        mtime is now 921020731 (should be 921016509)
        ctime is now 921020731 (should be 921016509)
```

There's one quick Perl trick in this code to mention before we move on. The following line demonstrates a quick-and-dirty way of comparing two lists for equality (or lack thereof):

```
if ("@savedstats[1..12]" ne "@currentstats");
```

The contents of the two lists are automatically "stringified" by Perl by concatenating the list elements with a space between them:

```
join(" ",@savedstats[1..12]))
```

and then the resulting strings are compared. For short lists where the order and number of the list elements is important, this technique works well. In most other cases, you'll need an iterative or hash solution like the ones documented in the Perl FAQs.

Now that you have file attributes under your belt, I've got bad news for you. Checking to see that a file's attributes have not changed is a good first step, but it doesn't go far enough. It is not difficult to alter a file while keeping attributes like the access and modification times the same. Perl even has a function, `utime()`, for changing the access or modification times of a file. Time to pull out the power tools.

Detecting change in data is one of the fortes of a particular set of algorithms known as "message-digest algorithms." Here's how Ron Rivest describes a particular message-digest algorithm called the "RSA Data Security, Inc. MD5 Message-Digest Algorithm" in RFC1321:

> The algorithm takes as input a message of arbitrary length and produces as output a 128-bit "fingerprint" or "message digest" of the input. It is conjectured that it is computationally infeasible to produce two messages having the same message digest, or to produce any message having a given prespecified target message digest.

For our purposes this means that if we run MD5 on a file, we'll get a unique fingerprint. If the data in this file were to change in any way, no matter how small, the fingerprint for that file will change. The easiest way to harness this magic from Perl is through the `Digest` module family and its `Digest::MD5` module.

The `Digest::MD5` module is easy to use. You create a `Digest::MD5` object, add the data to it using the `add()` or `addfile()` methods, and then ask the module to create a digest (fingerprint) for you.

To compute the MD5 fingerprint for a password file on Unix, we could use something like this:

```
use Digest::MD5 qw(md5);

$md5 = new Digest::MD5;

open(PASSWD,"/etc/passwd") or die "Unable to open passwd:$!\n";
```

```
$md5->addfile(PASSWD);
close(PASSWD);

print $md5->hexdigest."\n";
```

The `Digest::MD5` documentation demonstrates that we can string methods together to make the above program more compact:

```
use Digest::MD5 qw(md5);

open(PASSWD,"/etc/passwd") or die "Unable to open passwd:$!\n";
print Digest::MD5->new->addfile(PASSWD)->hexdigest,"\n";
close(PASSWD);
```

Both of these code snippets print out:

```
a6f905e6b45a65a7e03d0809448b501c
```

If we make even the slightest change to that file, the output changes. Here's the output after I transpose just *two characters* in the password file:

```
335679c4c97a3815230a4331a06df3e7
```

Any change in the data now becomes obvious. Let's extend our previous attribute-checking program to include MD5:

```
use Getopt::Std;
use Digest::MD5 qw(md5);

@statnames =
 qw(dev ino mode nlink uid gid rdev size mtime ctime blksize blocks md5);

getopt('p:c:');

die "Usage: $0 [-p <filename>|-c <filename>]\n"
  unless ($opt_p or $opt_c);

if ($opt_p){
    die "Unable to stat file $opt_p:$!\n"
      unless (-e $opt_p);

    open(F,$opt_p) or die "Unable to open $opt_p:$!\n";
    $digest = Digest::MD5->new->addfile(F)->hexdigest;
    close(F);

    print $opt_p,"|";join('|',(lstat($opt_p))[0..7,9..12]),
        "|$digest","\n";
    exit;
}

if ($opt_c){
    open(CFILE,$opt_c) or
      die "Unable to open check file $opt_c:$!\n";

    while (<CFILE>){
```

```
        chomp;
        @savedstats = split('\|');
        die "Wrong number of fields in \'$savedstats[0]\' line.\n"
          unless ($#savedstats == 13);

        @currentstats = (lstat($savedstats[0]))[0..7,9..12];

        open(F,$savedstats[0]) or die "Unable to open $opt_c:$!\n";
        push(@currentstats,Digest::MD5->new->addfile(F)->hexdigest);
        close(F);

        &printchanged(\@savedstats,\@currentstats)
          if ("@savedstats[1..13]" ne "@currentstats");
    }
    close(CFILE);
}

sub printchanged {
    my($saved,$current)= @_;

    print shift @{$saved},":\n";

    for (my $i=0; $i <= $#{$saved};$i++){
        if ($saved->[$i] ne $current->[$i]){
            print " ".$statnames[$i]." is now ".$current->[$i];
            print " (".$saved->[$i].")\n";
        }
    }
}
```

Network Service Changes

We've looked at ways to detect change on our local filesystem. How about notic-ing changes on other machines or in the services they provide? In Chapter 5, *TCP/IP Name Services*, we saw ways to query NIS and DNS. It would be easy to check repeated queries to these services for changes. For instance, if our DNS servers are configured to allow this, we can pretend to be a secondary server and request a dump (i.e., a "zone transfer") of that server's data for a particular domain:

```
use Net::DNS;

# takes two command-line arguments: the first is the name server
# to query, the # second is the domain to query from that name server
$server = new Net::DNS::Resolver;
$server->nameservers($ARGV[0]);

print STDERR "Transfer in progress...";
@zone = $server->axfr($ARGV[1]);
die $server->errorstring unless (defined @zone);
print STDERR "done.\n";

for $record (@zone){
  $record->print;
}
```

Combine this idea with MD5. Instead of printing the zone information, let's take a digest of it:

```
use Net::DNS;
use FreezeThaw qw{freeze};
use Digest::MD5 qw(md5);

$server = new Net::DNS::Resolver;
$server->nameservers($ARGV[0]);

print STDERR "Transfer in progress...";
@zone = $server->axfr($ARGV[1]);
die $server->errorstring unless (defined @zone);
print STDERR "done.\n";

$zone = join('',sort map(freeze($_),@zone));

print "MD5 fingerprint for this zone transfer is: ";
print Digest::MD5->new->add($zone)->hexdigest,"\n";
```

MD5 works on a scalar chunk of data (a message), not a Perl list-of-hashes data structure like **@zone**. That's where this line of code comes into play:

```
$zone = join('',sort map(freeze($_),@zone));
```

We're using the **FreezeThaw** module we saw in Chapter 9, *Log Files*, to flatten each **@zone** record data structure into a plain text string. Once flattened, the records are sorted before being concatenated into one large scalar value. The sort step allows us to ignore the order in which the records are returned in the zone transfer.

Dumping the contents of an entire server's zone file is a bit extreme, especially for large zones, so it may make more sense to monitor only an important subset of addresses. See Chapter 5 for an example of this. Also, it is a good idea to restrict the ability to do zone transfers to as few machines as possible for security reasons.

The material we've seen so far doesn't get you completely out of the woods. Here are a few questions you might want to ponder:

- What if someone tampers with your database of MD5 digests and substitutes valid fingerprints for their Trojan file replacements or service changes?

- What if someone tampers with your script so it only *appears* to check the digests against your database?

- What if someone tampers with the MD5 module on your system?

- For the ultimate in paranoia, what if someone manages to tamper with the Perl executable, one of its shared libraries, or the operating system core itself?

The usual answers to these questions (poor as they may be) involve keeping known good copies of everything related to the process (digest databases, modules, statically-linked Perl, etc.) on read-only medium.

This conundrum is another illustration of the continuum of security. It is always possible to find more to fear.

Noticing Suspicious Activities

A good night watchman needs more than just the ability to monitor for change. She or he also needs to be able to spot suspicious activities and circumstances. A hole in the perimeter fence or unexplained bumps in the night need to be brought to someone's attention. We can write programs to play this role.

Local Signs of Peril

It's unfortunate, but learning to be good at spotting signs of suspicious activity often comes as a result of pain and the desire to avoid it in the future. After the first few security breaches, you'll start to notice that intruders often follow certain patterns and leave behind telltale clues. Spotting these signs, once you know what they are, is often easy in Perl.

After each security breach, it is vitally important that you take a few moments to perform a postmortem of the incident. Document (to the best of your knowledge) where the intruders came in, what tools or holes they used, what they did, who else they attacked, what you did in response, and so on.

It is tempting to return to normal daily life and forget the break-in. If you can resist this temptation, you'll find later that you've gained something from the incident, rather than just losing time and effort. The Nietzchean principle of "that which does not kill you makes you stronger" is often applicable in the system administration realm as well.

For instance, intruders, especially the less-sophisticated kind, often try to hide their activities by creating "hidden" directories to store their data. On Unix and Linux systems they will put exploit code and sniffer output in directories with names like "…" (dot dot dot), ". " (dot space), or " Mail" (space Mail). These names are likely to be passed over in a cursory inspection of *ls* output.

We can easily write a program to search for these names using the tools we learned about in Chapter 2. Here's a program based on the **File::Find** module (as called by *find.pl*) which looks for anomalous directory names.

```
require "find.pl";

# Traverse desired filesystems

&find('.');
```

```
sub wanted {

    (-d $_) and                          # is a directory
      $_ ne "." and $_ ne ".." and       # is not . or ..

        (/[^-.a-zA-Z0-9+,:;_~$#()]/ or   # contains a "bad" character
         /^\.{3,}/ or                    # or starts with at least 3 dots
         /^-/) and                       # or begins with a dash

        print "'".&nice($name)."'\n";
}

# print a "nice" version of the directory name, i.e., with control chars
# explicated. This subroutine barely modified from &unctrl() in Perl's
# stock dumpvar.pl
sub nice {
    my($name) = $_[0];
    $name =~ s/([\001-\037\177])/'^'.pack('c',ord($1)^64)/eg;

    $name;
}
```

Remember the sidebar "Regular Expressions" in Chapter 9? Filesystem sifting programs like these are another example where this holds true. The effectiveness of these programs often hinges on the quality and quantity of their regular expressions. Too few regexps and you miss things you might want to catch. Too many regexps or regexps that are inefficient gives your program an exorbitant runtime and resource usage. If you use regexps that are too loose, the program will generate many false positives. It is a delicate balance.

Finding Problematic Patterns

Let's use some of the things we learned in Chapter 9 to move us along in our discussion. We've just talked about looking for suspicious objects; now let's move on to looking for *patterns* that may indicate suspicious activity. We can demonstrate this with a program that does some primitive logfile analysis to determine potential break-ins.

This example is based on the following premise: most users logging in remotely do so consistently from the same place or a small list of places. They usually log in remotely from a single machine, or from the same ISP modem bank each time. If you find an account that has logged in from more than a handful of domains, it's a good indicator that this account has been compromised and the password has been widely distributed. Obviously this premise does not hold for populations of highly mobile users, but if you find an account that has been logged into from Brazil and Finland in the same two-hour period, that's a pretty good indicator that something is fishy.

Let's walk through some code that looks for this indicator. This code is Unix-centric, but the techniques demonstrated in it are platform independent. First, here's our built-in documentation. It's not a bad idea to put something like this near the top of your program for the sake of other people who will read your code. Before we move on, be sure to take a quick look at the arguments the rest of the program will support:

```
sub usage {
    print <<"EOU"
lastcheck - check the output of the last command on a machine
            to determine if any user has logged in from > N domains
            (inspired by an idea from Daniel Rinehart)

   USAGE:  lastcheck [args], where args can be any of:
    -i:          for IP #'s, treat class C subnets as the same "domain"
    -h:          this help message
    -f <domain>  count only foreign domains, specify home domain
    -l <command>: use <command> instead of default /usr/ucb/last
                 note: no output format checking is done!
    -m <#>:      max number of unique domains allowed, default 3
    -u <user>:   perform check for only this username
EOU
    exit;
}
```

First we parse the user's command-line arguments. The **getopts** line below will look at the arguments to the program and set $opt_*<flag letter>* appropriately. The colon after the letter means that option takes an argument:

```
use Getopt::Std;        # standard option processor
getopts('ihf:l:m:u:'); # parse user input

&usage if (defined $opt_h);

# number of unique domains before we complain
$maxdomains = (defined $opt_m) ? $opt_m : 3;
```

The following lines reflect the portability versus efficiency decision we discussed in the Chapter 9. Here we're opting to call an external program. If you wanted to make the program less portable and a little more efficient, you could use **unpack()** as discussed in that chapter:

```
$lastex = (defined $opt_l) ? $opt_l : "/usr/ucb/last";

open(LAST,"$lastex|") || die "Can't run the program $lastex:$!\n";
```

Before we get any further into the program, let's take a quick look at the hash of lists data structure this program uses as it processes the data from *last*. This hash will have a username as its key and a reference to a list of the unique domains that user has logged in from as its value.

For instance, a sample entry might be:

```
$userinfo { laf } = [ 'ccs.neu.edu', 'xerox.com', 'foobar.edu' ]
```

This entry shows the account *laf* has logged in from the *ccs.neu.edu*, *xerox.com*, and *foobar.edu* domains.

We begin by iterating over the input we get from *last*; the output on our system looks like this:

```
cindy     pts/10   sinai.ccs.neu.ed  Fri Mar 27 13:51   still logged in
michael   pts/3    regulus.ccs.neu.  Fri Mar 27 13:51   still logged in
david     pts/5    fruity-pebbles.c  Fri Mar 27 13:48   still logged in
deborah   pts/5    grape-nuts.ccs.n  Fri Mar 27 11:43 - 11:53  (00:09)
barbara   pts/3    152.148.23.66     Fri Mar 27 10:48 - 13:20  (02:31)
jerry     pts/3    nat16.aspentec.c  Fri Mar 27 09:24 - 09:26  (00:01)
```

You'll notice that the hostnames (column 3) in our *last* output have truncated names. We've seen this hostname length restriction before in Chapter 9, but up until now we've sidestepped the challenge it represents. We'll stare danger right in the face in a moment when we start populating our data structure.

Early on in the `while` loop, we try to skip lines that contain cases we don't care about. In general it is a good idea to check for special cases like this at the beginning of your loops before any actual processing of the data (e.g., a `split()`) takes place. This lets the program quickly identify when it can skip a particular line and continue reading input:

```perl
while (<LAST>){

    # ignore special users
    next if /^reboot\s|^shutdown\s|^ftp\s/;

    # if we've used -u to specify a specific user, skip all entries
    # that don't pertain to this user (whose name is stored in $opt_u
    # by getopts for us).
    next if (defined $opt_u && !/^$opt_u\s/);

    # ignore X console logins
    next if /:0\s+:0/;

    # find the user's name, tty, and remote hostname
    ($user, $tty,$host) = split;

    # ignore if the log had a bad username after parsing
    next if (length($user) < 2);

    # ignore if no domain name info in name
    next if $host !~ /\./;

    # find the domain name of this host (see explanation below)
    $dn = &domain($host);
```

```
    # ignore if you get a bogus domain name
    next if (length ($dn) < 2);

    # ignore this input line if it is in the home domain as specified
    # by the -f switch
    next if (defined $opt_f && ($dn =~ /^$opt_f/));

    # if we've never seen this user before, simply create a list with
    # the user's domain and store this in the hash of lists.
    unless (exists $userinfo{$user}){
        $userinfo{$user} = [$dn];
    }
    # otherwise, this can be a bit hairy; see the explanation below
    else {
        &AddToInfo($user,$dn);
    }
}
}
close(LAST);
```

Now let's take a look at the individual subroutines that handle the tricky parts of this program. Our first subroutine, &domain(), takes a Fully Qualified Domain Name (FQDN), i.e., a hostname with the full domain name attached, and returns its best guess at the domain name of that host. It has to be a little smart for two reasons:

1. Not all hostnames in the logs will be actual names. They may be simple IP addresses. In this case, if the user has set the *–i* switch, we assume any IP address we get is a class C network subnetted on the standard byte boundary. In practical terms this means that we treat the first three octets as the "domain name" of the host. This allows us to treat logins from 192.168.1.10 as coming from the same logical source as logins from 192.168.1.12. This may not be the best of assumptions, but it is the best we can do without consulting another source of information (and it works most of the time). If the user does not use the *–i* switch, we treat the entire IP address as the domain of record.

2. As mentioned before, the hostnames may be truncated. This leaves us to deal with partial entries like **grape-nuts.ccs.n** and **nat16.aspentec.c**. This is not as bad as it might sound, since each host will have its FQDN truncated at the same point every time it is stored in the log. We attempt to work around this restriction as best we can in the **&AddToInfo()** subroutine we'll discuss in a moment.

Back to the code:

```
    # take a FQDN and attempt to return FQD
    sub domain{
        # look for IP addresses
        if ($_[0] =~ /^\d+\.\d+\.\d+\.\d+$/) {
```

```
            # if the user did not use -i, simply return the IP address as is
            unless (defined $opt_i){
                return $_[0];
            }

            # otherwise, return everything but the last octet
            else {
                $_[0] =~ /(.*)\.\d+$/;
                return $1;
            }
        }

    # if we are not dealing with an IP address
    else {
        # downcase the info to make later processing simpler and quicker
        $_[0] = lc($_[0]);

        # then return everything after first dot
        $_[0] =~ /^[^.]+\.(.*)/;
        return $1;
    }
}
```

This next subroutine, short as it is, encapsulates the hardest part of this program. Our &AddToInfo() subroutine has to deal with truncated hostnames and the storing of information into our hash table. We're going to use a substring matching technique that you may find useful in other contexts.

In this case, we'd really like all of the following domain names to be treated and stored as the same domain name in our array of unique domains for a user:

```
ccs.neu.edu
ccs.neu.ed
ccs.n
```

When the uniqueness of a domain name is in question, we check three things:

1. Is this domain name an *exact match* of anything we have stored for this user?

2. Is this domain name a *substring* of already stored data?

3. Is the *stored* domain data a substring of the domain name we are checking?

If any of these are the case, we don't need to add a new entry to our data structure because we already have a substring equivalent stored in the user's domain list. If case #3 is true, we'll want to replace the stored data entry with our current entry, assuring we've stored the largest string possible. Astute readers will also note that cases #1 and #2 can be checked simultaneously since an exact match is equivalent to a substring match where all the characters match.

If all of these cases are false, we do need to store the new entry. Let's take a look at the code first and then talk about how it works:

```
sub AddToInfo{
    my($user, $dn) = @_;

    for (@{$userinfo{$user}}){

        # case #1 & #2 from above: is this either exact or substring match?
        return if (index($_,$dn) > -1);

        # check case #3 from above, i.e. is the stored domain data
        # a substring of the domain name we are checking?
        if (index($dn,$_) > -1){
          $_ = $dn; # swap current & stored values
          return;
        }
    }

    # otherwise, this is a new domain, add it to the list
    push @{$userinfo{$user}}, $dn;
}
```

@{$userinfo{$user}} returns the list of domains we've stored for the specified user. We iterate over each item in this list to see if $dn can be found in any item. If it can, we have a substring equivalent already stored, so we exit the subroutine.

If we pass this test, we look for case #3 above. Each entry in the list is checked to see if it can be found in our current domain. If it is a match, we overwrite the list entry with the current domain data, thus storing the larger of the two strings. This happens even when there is an exact match, since it does no harm. We overwrite the entry using a special property of the **for** and **foreach** Perl operators. Assigning to $_ in the middle of a **for** loop like this actually assigns to the current element of the list at that point in the loop. The loop variable becomes an alias for the list variable. If we've made this swap, we can leave the subroutine. If we pass all three tests, then the final line adds the domain name in question to the user's domain list.

That's it for the gory details of iterating over the file and building our data structure. To wrap this program up, let's run through all of the users we found and check how many unique domains each has logged into (i.e., the size of the list we've stored for each). For those entries that have more domains than our comfort level, we print the contents of their entry:

```
for (sort keys %userinfo){
    if ($#{$userinfo{$_}} > $maxdomains){
        print "\n\n$_ has logged in from:\n";
        print join("\n",sort @{$userinfo{$_}});
    }
}
print "\n";
```

Now that you've seen the code, you might wonder if this approach really works. Here's some real sample output of our program for a user who had her password sniffed at another site:

```
username has logged in from:
38.254.131
bu.edu
ccs.neu.ed
dac.neu.ed
hials.no
ipt.a
tnt1.bos1
tnt1.bost
tnt1.dia
tnt2.bos
tnt3.bos
tnt4.bo
toronto4.di
```

Some of these entries look normal for a user in the Boston area. However, the *toronto4.di* entry is a bit suspect and the *hials.no* site is in Norway. Busted!

This program could be further refined to include the element of time or correlations with another log file like that from *tcpwrappers*. But as you can see, pattern detection is often very useful by itself.

SNMP

Let's move away from security and towards more general monitoring topics. In the previous section we looked at a method for monitoring a specific network service. The Simple Network Management Protocol (SNMP) takes a quantum leap forward by offering a general way to remotely monitor and configure network devices and networked computers. Once you master the basics of SNMP, you can use it to keep tabs on (and often configure) practically every device on your network.

Truth be told, the *Simple* Network Management Protocol isn't particularly simple. There's a respectable learning curve associated with this subject. If you aren't already familiar with SNMP, see Appendix E, *The Twenty-Minute SNMP Tutorial*, for a tutorial on it.

Using SNMP from Perl

One way we could use SNMP from Perl is to call command-line programs like the UCD-SNMP ones used for demonstration purposes in Appendix E. It would be a straightforward process, no different any of the examples of calling external programs we've seen earlier in this book. Since there's nothing new to learn there, we won't spend any time with this technique. I will offer one caveat: if you are using

SNMPv1 or SNMPv2C, chances are you'll have to put the community name on the command line. If this program runs on a multiuser box, anyone who can list the process table may be able to see this community name and steal the keys to the kingdom. This threat is present in our command-line examples in Appendix E, but it becomes more acute with automated programs that repeatedly make external program calls like this. For demonstration purposes only, the following examples also take the target hostname and community name string on the command line. You should change that for production code.

If we don't call an external program to perform SNMP operations from Perl, our other choice is to use a Perl SNMP module. There are at least three separate but similar modules available: **Net::SNMP** by David M. Town, *SNMP_Session.pm* written by Simon Leinen, and the "SNMP Extension Module v3.1.0 for the UCD SNMPv3 Library" (which we'll call just call **SNMP** because of the way it is loaded) by G.S. Marzot. All of these modules implement SNMPv1. **Net::SNMP** and **SNMP** offer some SNMPv2 support. Only **SNMP** offers any SNMPv3 support.

The most significant difference between these three modules besides their level of SNMP support is their reliance on libraries external to the core Perl distribution. The first two (**Net::SNMP** and *SNMP_Session.pm*) are implemented in Perl alone, while **SNMP** needs to be linked against a separate pre-built UCD-SNMP library. The main drawback to using **SNMP** is this added dependency and build step (presuming you can build the UCD-SNMP library on your platform).

The plus side of depending on the UCD-SNMP library is the extra power it provides to the module. For instance, **SNMP** can parse Management Information Base (MIB) description files and print raw SNMP packet dumps for debugging, two functions the other modules do not provide. There are other modules that can help reduce this disparity in functionality (for instance, **SNMP::MIB::Compiler** by Fabien Tassin can handle MIB parsing tasks), but if you are looking for one module to do the whole job, **SNMP** is your best bet.

Let's start with a small Perl example. If we need to know the number of interfaces a particular device has, we could query the `interfaces.ifNumber` variable. Using **Net::SNMP**, it is this easy:

```
use Net::SNMP;

# requires a hostname and a community string as its arguments
($session,$error) = Net::SNMP->session(Hostname => $ARGV[0],
                                       Community => $ARGV[1]);

die "session error: $error" unless ($session);

# iso.org.dod.internet.mgmt.mib-2.interfaces.ifNumber.0 =
#   1.3.6.1.2.1.2.1.0
$result = $session->get_request("1.3.6.1.2.1.2.1.0");
```

```
die "request error: ".$session->error unless (defined $result);

$session->close;

print "Number of interfaces: ".$result->{"1.3.6.1.2.1.2.1.0"}."\n";
```

When pointed at a workstation with an Ethernet and a loopback interface, it will print **Number of interfaces: 2**; a laptop with Ethernet, loopback, and PPP interfaces returns **Number of interfaces: 3**; and a small router returns **Number of interfaces: 7**.

One key thing to notice is the use of Object Identifiers (OIDs) instead of variable names. Both **Net::SNMP** and *SNMP_Session.pm* handle SNMP protocol interactions only. They make no pretense of handling the peripheral SNMP-related tasks like parsing SNMP MIB descriptions. For this functionality you will have to look to other modules such as **SNMP::MIB::Compiler** or *SNMP_util.pm* by Mike Mitchell for use with **SNMP_Session.pm** (not to be confused with **SNMP::Util** by Wayne Marquette, for use with the **SNMP** module).

If you want to use textual identifiers instead of numeric OIDs without coding in the mapping yourself or using an additional module, your only choice is to use the **SNMP** module, which has a built-in MIB parser. Let's do a table walk of the Address Resolution Protocol (ARP) table of a machine using this module:

```
use SNMP;

# requires a hostname and a community string as its arguments
$session = new SNMP::Session(DestHost => $ARGV[0], Community => $ARGV[1],
                             UseSprintValue => 1);

die "session creation error: $SNMP::Session::ErrorStr" unless
  (defined $session);

# set up the data structure for the getnext command
$vars = new SNMP::VarList(['ipNetToMediaNetAddress'],
                          ['ipNetToMediaPhysAddress']);

# get first row
($ip,$mac) = $session->getnext($vars);
die $session->{ErrorStr} if ($session->{ErrorStr});

# and all subsequent rows
while (!$session->{ErrorStr} and
       $$vars[0]->tag eq "ipNetToMediaNetAddress"){
   print "$ip -> $mac\n";
   ($ip,$mac) = $session->getnext($vars);
};
```

Here's an example of the output this produces:

```
192.168.1.70 -> 8:0:20:21:40:51
192.168.1.74 -> 8:0:20:76:7c:85
192.168.1.98 -> 0:c0:95:e0:5c:1c
```

This code looks similar to the previous `Net::SNMP` example. We'll walk through it to highlight the differences:

```
use SNMP;

$session = new SNMP::Session(DestHost => $ARGV[0], Community => $ARGV[1],
                             UseSprintValue => 1);
```

After loading the `SNMP` module, we create a session object just like we did in the `Net::SNMP` example. The additional `UseSprintValue => 1` argument just tells the `SNMP` module to pretty-print the return values. If we didn't do this, the Ethernet addresses listed above would be printed in an encoded form.

```
# set up the data structure for the getnext command
$vars = new SNMP::VarList(['ipNetToMediaNetAddress'],
                          ['ipNetToMediaPhysAddress']);
```

`SNMP` is willing to use simple strings like `sysDescr.0` with its commands, but it prefers to use a special object it calls a "Varbind." It uses these objects to store return values from queries. For example, the code we're looking at calls the `getnext()` method to send a `get-next-request`, just like in the IP route table example in Appendix E. Except this time, `SNMP` will store the returned indices in a Varbind for us so we don't have to keep track of them by hand. With this module, you can just hand the Varbind back to the `getnext` method each time you want the next value.

Varbinds are simply anonymous Perl arrays with four elements: `obj`, `iid`, `val`, and `type`. For our purposes, we only need to worry about `obj` and `iid`. The first element, `obj`, is the object you are querying. `obj` can be specified in one of several formats. In this case, we are using a *leaf identifier* format, i.e., specifying the leaf of the tree we are concerned with. `IpNetToMediaNetAddress` is the leaf of the tree:

```
.iso.org.dod.internet.mgmt.mib-2.ip.ipNetToMediaTable.ipNetToMediaEntry.
ipNetToMediaNetAddress
```

The second element in a Varbind is the `iid`, or instance identifier. In our previous discussions, we've always used a 0 here (e.g., `system.sysDescr.0`), because we've only seen objects that have a single instance. Shortly we'll see examples where the `iid` can be something other than 0. For instance, later on we'll want to refer to a particular network interface on a multi-interface Ethernet switch. `obj` and `iid` are the only two parts of a Varbind you need to specify for a `get`. `getnext` does not need an `iid` since it will return the next instance by default.

The line of code above uses `VarList()`, which creates a list of two Varbinds, each with just the `obj` element filled in. We feed this list to the `getnext()` method:

```
# get first row
($ip,$mac) = $session->getnext($vars);
die $session->{ErrorStr} if ($session->{ErrorStr});
```

`getnext()` returns the values it received back from our request and updates the Varbind data structures accordingly. Now it is just a matter of calling `getnext()` until we fall off the end of the table:

```
while (!$session->{ErrorStr} and
       $$vars[0]->tag eq "ipNetToMediaNetAddress"){
        print "$ip -> $mac\n";
        ($ip,$mac) = $session->getnext($vars);
};
```

For our final SNMP example, let's return to the world of security. We'll pick a task that would be tricky, or at least annoying, to do well with the command-line SNMP utilities.

Here's the scenario: you've been asked to track down a misbehaving user on your switched Ethernet network. The only info you have is the Ethernet address of the machine that user is on. It's not an Ethernet address you have on file (which could be kept in our host database from Chapter 5 if we extended it), and you can't sniff your switched net, so you are going to have to be a little bit clever about tracking this machine down. Your best bet in this case may be to ask one or all of your Ethernet switches if they've seen that address on one of their ports.

Just to make this example more concrete so we can point at specific MIB variables, we'll say that your network consists of several Cisco Catalyst 5500 switches. The basic methodology we're going to use to solve this problem will apply to other products and other vendors as well. Any switch or vendor-specific information will be noted as we go along. Let's walk through this problem step by step.

As before, first we have to go search through the correct MIB module files. With a little jumpstart from Cisco's tech support, we realize we'll need to access four separate objects:

- The `vlanTable`, found at `enterprises.cisco.workgroup.ciscoStack-MIB.vlanGrp` in the *CISCO-STACK-MIB* description.

- The `dot1dTpFdbTable` (transparent port forwarding table), found at `dot1dBridge.dot1dTp` in the RFC1493 *BRIDGE-MIB* description.

- The `dot1dBasePortTable`, found at `dot1dBridge.dot1dBase` in the same RFC.

- The `ifXTable`, found in the RFC1573 *IF-MIB* (Interfaces) description.

Why four different tables? Each table has a piece to contribute to the answer, but no one table has the specific information we seek. The first table provides us with a list of the VLANS (Virtual Local Area Networks), or virtual "network segments," on the switch. Cisco has chosen to keep separate tables for each VLAN on a switch, so we will need to query for information one VLAN at a time. More on this in a moment.

The second table provides us with a list of Ethernet addresses and the number of the switch's *bridge port* on which each address was last seen. Unfortunately, a bridge port number is an internal reckoning for the switch; it does not correspond to the name of a physical port on that switch. We need to know the physical port name, i.e., from which card and port the machine with that Ethernet address last spoke, so we have to dig further.

There is no table that maps bridge port to physical port name (that would be too easy), but the `dot1dBasePortTable` can provide a bridge port to interface number mapping. Once we have the interface number, we can look it up in `ifXTable` and retrieve the port name.

Figure 10-1 shows a picture of the four-layer deference necessary to perform our desired task.

Here's the code to put these four tables together to dump the information we need:

```
use SNMP;

# These are the extra MIB module files we need, found in the same
# directory as this script
$ENV{'MIBFILES'}=
   "CISCO-SMI.my:FDDI-SMT73-MIB.my:CISCO-STACK-MIB.my:BRIDGE-MIB.my";

# Connect and get the list of VLANs on this switch
$session = new SNMP::Session(DestHost => $ARGV[0],
                             Community => $ARGV[1]);
die "session creation error: $SNMP::Session::ErrorStr" unless
   (defined $session);

# enterprises.cisco.workgroup.ciscoStackMIB.vlanGrp.vlanTable.vlanEntry
# in CISCO-STACK-MIB
$vars = new SNMP::VarList(['vlanIndex']);

$vlan = $session->getnext($vars);
die $session->{ErrorStr} if ($session->{ErrorStr});

while (!$session->{ErrorStr} and $$vars[0]->tag eq "vlanIndex"){

    # VLANS 1000 and over are not "real" ON A CISCO CATALYST 5XXX
    # (this limit is likely to be different on different switches)
    push(@vlans,$vlan) if $vlan < 1000;
```

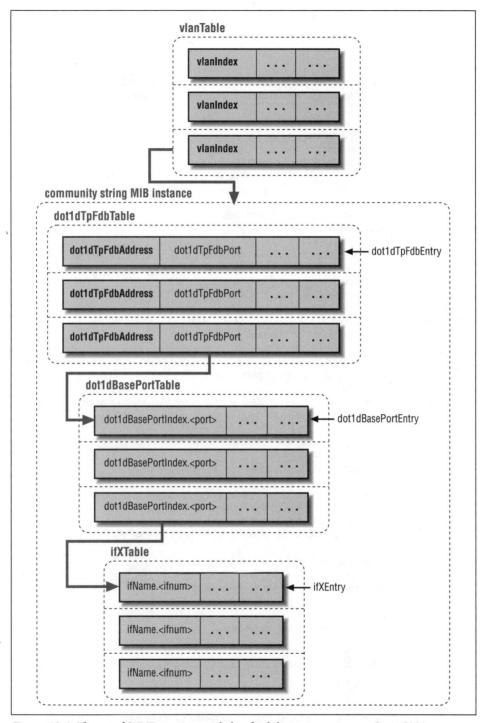

Figure 10-1. The set of SNMP queries needed to find the port name on a Cisco 5000

```
        $vlan = $session->getnext($vars);
};

undef $session,$vars;

# for each VLAN, query for the bridge port, the interface number
# associated with that port, and then the interface name for that
# port number
foreach $vlan (@vlans){
    # note our use of "community string indexing" as part
    # of the session setup
    $session = new SNMP::Session(DestHost => $ARGV[0],
                                 Community => $ARGV[1]."@".$vlan,
                                 UseSprintValue => 1);

    die "session creation error: $SNMP::Session::ErrorStr"
      unless (defined $session);

    # from transparent forwarding port table at
    # dot1dBridge.dot1dTp.dot1dTpFdbTable.dot1dTpFdbEntry
    # in RFC1493 BRIDGE-MIB
    $vars = new SNMP::VarList(['dot1dTpFdbAddress'],['dot1dTpFdbPort']);

    ($macaddr,$portnum) = $session->getnext($vars);
    die $session->{ErrorStr} if ($session->{ErrorStr});

    while (!$session->{ErrorStr} and
           $$vars[0]->tag eq "dot1dTpFdbAddress"){

        # dot1dBridge.dot1dBase.dot1dBasePortTable.dot1dBasePortEntry
        # in RFC1493 BRIDGE-MIB
        $ifnum =
          (exists $ifnum{$portnum}) ? $ifnum{$portnum} :
            ($ifnum{$portnum} =
               $session->get("dot1dBasePortIfIndex\.$portnum"));

        # from ifMIB.ifMIBObjects.ifXTable.ifXEntry in RFC1573 IF-MIB
        $portname =
          (exists $portname{$ifnum}) ? $portname{$ifnum} :
            ($portname{$ifnum}=$session->get("ifName\.$ifnum"));

        print "$macaddr on VLAN $vlan at $portname\n";

        ($macaddr,$portnum) = $session->getnext($vars);
    };

    undef $session, $vars, %ifnum, %portname;
}
```

If you've read Appendix E, most of this code will look familiar. Here are some comments on the new stuff:

```
$ENV{'MIBFILES'}=
  "CISCO-SMI.my:FDDI-SMT73-MIB.my:CISCO-STACK-MIB.my:BRIDGE-MIB.my";
```

This code sets the `MIBFILES` environment variable for the UCD-SNMP package library. When set, this variable instructs the library to parse the listed set of additional files for MIB object definitions. The only strange MIB module file in that list is *FDDI-SMT73-MIB.my*. This is included because *CISCO-STACK-MIB.my* has the following statement at the top to include certain definitions from other MIB entries:

```
IMPORTS
        MODULE-IDENTITY, OBJECT-TYPE, Integer32, IpAddress, TimeTicks,
        Counter32, Counter64, NOTIFICATION-TYPE
                FROM SNMPv2-SMI
        DisplayString, RowStatus
                FROM SNMPv2-TC
        fddimibPORTSMTIndex, fddimibPORTIndex
                FROM FDDI-SMT73-MIB
        OwnerString
                FROM IF-MIB
        MODULE-COMPLIANCE, OBJECT-GROUP
                FROM SNMPv2-CONF
        workgroup
                FROM CISCO-SMI;
```

Even though we don't reference any objects that use `fddimibPORTSMTIndex` or `fddimibPORTIndex`, we still (by choice) include that file in the file list to keep the MIB parser from complaining. All of the other MIB definitions in this `IMPORTS` statement are included either in our parse list or the library's default list. You often need to look for the `IMPORTS` section of a MIB module to see that module's dependencies when going MIB groveling.

Moving on in our code, here's another strange statement:

```
$session = new SNMP::Session(DestHost => $ARGV[0],
                             Community => $ARGV[1]."@".$vlan,
                             UseSprintValue => 1);
```

Instead of just passing on the community name as provided by the user, we're appending something of the form *@VLAN-NUMBER*. In Cisco parlance, this is "community string indexing." When dealing with VLANs and bridging, Cisco devices keep track of several "instances" of the MIB, one for each VLAN. Our code makes the same queries once per each VLAN found on the switch:

```
$ifnum =
        (exists $ifnum{$portnum}) ? $ifnum{$portnum} :
          ($ifnum{$portnum} =
            $session->get("dot1dBasePortIfIndex\.$portnum"));
```

Two comments on this piece of code. First, for variety's sake, we're using a simple string argument to `get()`. We could easily have used something more Varbind-ish:

```
($ifnum{$portnum}=$session->get(['dot1dBasePortIfIndex',$portnum]));
```

Second, note that we're doing some very simple caching here. Before we actually perform a `get()`, we look in a simple hash table (`%ifnum`) to see if we've already made this query. If we haven't, we make the query and populate the hash table with the result. At the end of each VLAN pass, we delete the cache hash (`undef %ifnum`) to prevent previous VLAN information from providing false information.

This is a good technique to remember when programming SNMP code. It is important to query as little and as seldom as possible if you want to be kind to your network and network devices. A device may have to take horsepower away from its usual tasks to respond to your slew of queries if you are not prudent.

Here's an excerpt from our code in action:

```
"00 10 1F 2D F8 FB " on VLAN 1 at 1/1
"00 10 1F 2D F8 FD " on VLAN 1 at 1/1
"08 00 36 8B A9 03 " on VLAN 115 at 2/18
"08 00 36 BA 16 03 " on VLAN 115 at 2/3
"08 00 36 D1 CB 03 " on VLAN 115 at 2/15
```

It's not hard to see how this program could be enhanced. Besides prettier or more orderly output, it could save state between runs. Each time it ran, the program could let you know how things have changed: new addresses appearing, ports being changed, etc. One quick caveat: most switches are of the "learning" variety, so they will age out entries for addresses that they haven't heard from in a while. This just means that your program will need to run at least as often as the standard port aging time.

Danger on the Wire

SNMP is good for proactive monitoring (and some reactive monitoring situations when using SNMP traps), but it doesn't always help with unplanned situations like network emergencies. In these situations, you may need to monitor the network in ways that are not covered by the available SNMP variables.

Perl Saves the Day

Here's a true story that shows how Perl can help in these times. One Saturday evening I casually logged into a machine on my network to read my email. Much to my surprise, I found our mail and web servers near death and fading fast. Attempts to read and send mail or look at web content yielded slow responses, hung connections, and outright connection failures. Our mail queue was starting to reach critical mass.

I looked first at the state of the servers. Interactive response was fine, and the CPU load was high, but not deadly. One sign of trouble was the number of mail processes running. According to the mail logs, there were more processes running than expected because many transactions were not completing. Processes that had started up to handle incoming connections from the outside were hanging, driving up the load. This load was then capping any new outgoing connections from initiating. This strange network behavior led me to examine the current connection table of the server using *netstat.*

The last column of the *netstat* output told me that there were indeed many connections in progress on that machine from many different hosts. The big shocker was the state of those connections. Instead of looking like this:

```
tcp   0   0  mailhub.3322   mail.mel.aone.ne.smtp   ESTABLISHED
tcp   0   0  mailhub.3320   edunet.edunet.dk.smtp   CLOSE_WAIT
tcp   0   0  mailhub.1723   kraken.mvnet.wne.smtp   ESTABLISHED
tcp   0   0  mailhub.1709   plover.net.bridg.smtp   CLOSE_WAIT
```

they looked more like this:

```
tcp   0   0  mailhub.3322   mail.mel.aone.ne.smtp   SYN_RCVD
tcp   0   0  mailhub.3320   edunet.edunet.dk.smtp   SYN_RCVD
tcp   0   0  mailhub.1723   kraken.mvnet.wne.smtp   SYN_RCVD
tcp   0   0  mailhub.1709   plover.net.bridg.smtp   CLOSE_WAIT
```

At first, this looked like a classic Denial of Service attack called a SYN Flood or a SYN-ACK attack. To understand these attacks, we have to digress for a moment and talk a little bit about how the TCP/IP protocol works.

Every TCP/IP connection begins with a handshake between the participants. This little dance lets both the initiator and the recipient signal their readiness to enter into a conversation. The first step is taken by the initiating network entity. It sends a SYN (for SYNchronize) packet to the recipient. If the recipient wishes to talk, it will send back a SYN-ACK, an ACKnowledgment of the request, and record that a conversation is about to begin in its pending connection table. The initiator then replies to the SYN-ACK with an ACK packet, confirming the SYN-ACK was heard. The recipient hears the ACK, removes the entry from its pending table, and away they go.

At least, that's what should happen. In a SYN Flood situation, a nogoodnik will send a flood of SYN packets to a machine, often with spoofed source addresses. The unsuspecting machine will send SYN-ACKs to the spoofed source addresses and open an entry in its pending communication table for each SYN packet it has received. These bogus connection entries will stay in the pending table until the OS ages them out using some default timeout value. If enough packets are sent, the pending communication table will fill up and no legitimate connection attempts will succeed. This leads to symptoms like those I was experiencing at the time, and similar *netstat* output.

The one anomaly in the *netstat* output that made me question this diagnosis was the variety of hosts represented in the table. It was possible that someone had a program with superb spoofing capabilities, but you usually expect to see many connections from a smaller set of bogus hosts. Many of these hosts also seemed perfectly legitimate. Further clouding the situation was the result of a few connectivity tests I ran. Sometimes I could *ping* or *traceroute* to a randomly selected host listed in my *netstat* output, sometimes I couldn't. I needed more data. I needed to get a better grasp on the connectivity to these remote hosts. That's where Perl came in.

Because I was writing code under the gun, I wrote a very simple script that relied on the output of two other external network programs to handle the hard parts of the task. Let me show you that version, and then we'll use this task as a springboard for some more advanced programming.

The task in this case boiled down to one question: could I reach the hosts that appeared to be trying to connect to me? To find out which hosts were trying to contact my machine, I turned to a program called *clog* written by Brian Mitchell, found at *ftp://coast.cs.purdue.edu/pub/mirrors/ftp.saturn.net/clog*. *clog* uses the Unix *libpcap* library from Lawrence Berkeley National Laboratory's Network Research Group to sniff the network for TCP connection requests, i.e., SYN packets. This is the same library used by the seminal network monitoring program *tcpdump*. Found at *ftp://ftp.ee.lbl.gov/libpcap.tar.Z*, *libpcap* works for Linux machines as well. A *libpcap* port for NT/2000 can be found at *http://netgroup-serv. polito.it/windump/* or *http://www.ntop.org/libpcap.html*, but I have yet to see one for MacOS.

clog reports SYN packets like this:

```
Mar 02 11:21|192.168.1.51|1074|192.168.1.104|113
Mar 02 11:21|192.168.1.51|1094|192.168.1.104|23
```

The output above shows two connection requests from 192.168.1.51 to 192.168.1. 104. The first was an attempt to connect to port 113 (ident), the second to port 23 (telnet).

With *clog* I was able to learn which hosts were attempting connections to me. And now I needed to know whether I could also reach them. That task was left to a program called *fping* by Roland J. Schemers III. *fping*, which can be found at *http://www.stanford.edu/~schemers/docs/fping/fping.html*, is a fast and fancy *ping* program for testing network connectivity on Unix and variants. Putting these external commands together, we get this little Perl program:

```
$clogex   = "/usr/local/bin/clog";       # location/switches for clog
$fpingex  = "/usr/local/bin/fping -r1";   # location/switches for fping

$localnet = "192.168.1";                  # local network prefix

open CLOG, "$clogex|" or die "Unable to run clog:$!\n";
```

```
while(<CLOG>){
    ($date,$orighost,$origport,$desthost,$destport) = split(/\|/);
    next if ($orighost =~ /^$localnet/);
    next if (exists $cache{$orighost});
    print `$fpingex $orighost`;
    $cache{$orighost}=1;
}
```

This program runs the *clog* command and reads its output *ad infinitum*. Since our internal network connectivity wasn't suspect, each originating host is checked against our local network's addressing prefix. Traffic from our local network is ignored.

Like our last SNMP example, we perform some rudimentary caching. To be a good net citizen we want to avoid hammering outside machines with multiple *ping* packets, so we keep track of every host we've already queried. The *–r1* flag to *fping* is used to restrict the number of times *fping* will retry a host (the default is three retries).

This program has to be run with elevated privileges, since both *clog* and *fping* need privileged access to the computer's network interface. This program printed output like this:

```
199.174.175.99 is unreachable
128.148.157.143 is unreachable
204.241.60.5 is alive
199.2.26.116 is unreachable
199.172.62.5 is unreachable
130.111.39.100 is alive
207.70.7.25 is unreachable
198.214.63.11 is alive
129.186.1.10 is alive
```

Clearly something fishy was going on here. Why would half of the sites be reachable, and the other half unreachable? Before we answer that question, let's look at what we could do to improve this program. A first step would be to remove the external program dependencies. Learning how to sniff the network and send *ping* packets from Perl could open up a whole range of possibilities. Let's take care of removing the easy dependency first.

The `Net::Ping` module by Russell Mosemann, found in the Perl distribution, can help us with testing connectivity to network hosts. `Net::Ping` allows us to send three different flavors of *ping* packets and check for a return response: ICMP, TCP, and UDP. Internet Control Message Protocol (ICMP) echo packets are "*ping* classic," the kind of packet sent by the vast majority of the command-line *ping* programs. This particular packet flavor has two disadvantages:

1. Like our previous *clog/fping* code, any `Net::Ping` scripts using ICMP need to be run with elevated privileges.

2. Perl on MacOS does not currently support ICMP. This may be remedied in the future, but you should be aware of this portability constraint.

The other two choices for Net::Ping packets are TCP and UDP. Both of these choices send packets to a remote machine's *echo* service port. Using these two options gains you portability, but you may find them less reliable than ICMP. ICMP is built into all standard TCP/IP stacks, but all machines may not be running the echo service. As a result, unless ICMP is deliberately filtered, you are more likely to receive a response to an ICMP packet than to the other types.

Net::Ping uses the standard object-oriented programming model, so the first step is the creation of a new *ping* object instance:

```
use Net::Ping;
$p = new Net::Ping("icmp");
```

Using this object is simple:

```
if ($p->ping("host")){
    print "ping succeeded.\n";
else{
    print "ping failed\n";
}
```

Now let's dig into the hard part of our initial script, the network sniffing handled by *clog*. Unfortunately, at this point we may need to let our MacOS readers off the bus. The Perl code we are about to explore is tied to the *libpcap* library we mentioned earlier, so using it on anything but a Unix variant may be dicey or impossible.

The first step is to build *libpcap* on your machine. I recommend you also build *tcpdump* as well. Like our use of the UCD-SNMP command-line utilities earlier, *tcpdump* can be used to explore *libpcap* functionality before coding Perl or to double-check that code.

With *libpcap* built, it is easy to build the Net::Pcap module, originally by Peter Lister and later completely rewritten by Tim Potter. This module gives full access to the power of *libpcap*. Let's see how we can use it to find SYN packets, à la *clog*.

Our code begins by querying the machine for an available/sniffable network interface and the settings for that interface:

```
use Net::Pcap;

# find the sniffable network device
$dev = Net::Pcap::lookupdev(\$err) ;
die "can't find suitable device: $err\n" unless $dev;

# figure out the network number and mask of that device
die "can't figure out net info for dev:$err\n"
  if (Net::Pcap::lookupnet($dev,\$netnum,\$netmask,\$err));
```

Most of the *libpcap* functions use the C convention of returning 0 for success, or −1 for failure, hence the die if ... idiom is used often in Net::Pcap Perl code. The meaning of the arguments fed to each of the functions we'll be using can be found in the *pcap(3)* manual page.

Given the network interface information, we can tell *libpcap* we want to sniff the live network (as opposed to reading packets from a previously saved packet file). Net::Pcap::open_live will hand us back a packet capture descriptor to refer to this session:

```
# open that interface for live capture
$descript = Net::Pcap::open_live($dev,100,1,1000,\$err) ;
die "can't obtain pcap descriptor:$err\n" unless $descript;
```

libpcap gives you the ability to capture all network traffic or a select subset based on filter criteria of your choosing. Its filtering mechanism is very efficient, so it is often best to invoke it up front, rather than sifting through all of the packets via Perl code. In our case, we need to only look at SYN packets.

So what's a SYN packet? To understand that, you need to know a little bit about how TCP packets are put together. Figure 10-2 shows a picture from RFC793 of a TCP packet and its header.

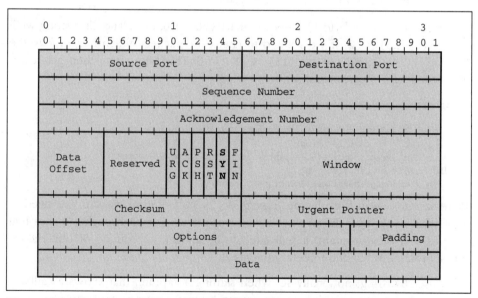

Figure 10-2. Diagram of a TCP packet

A SYN packet, for our purposes, is simply one that has only the SYN flag (highlighted in Figure 10-2) in the packet header set. In order to tell *libpcap* to capture packets like this, we need to specify which byte it should look at in the packet. Each tick mark above is a bit, so let's count bytes. Figure 10-3 shows the same packet with byte numbers.

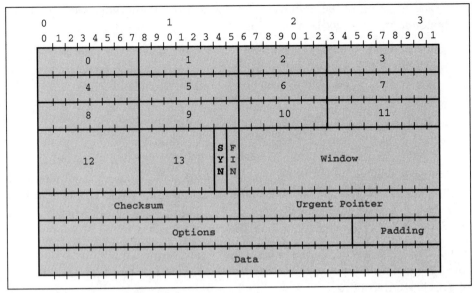

Figure 10-3. Finding the right byte in a TCP packet

We'll need to check if byte 13 is set to binary 00000010, or 2. The filter string we'll need is `tcp[13] = 2`. If we wanted to check for packets which had *at least* the SYN flag set, we could use `tcp[13] & 2 != 0`. This filter string then gets compiled into a *filter program* and set:

```
$prog = "tcp[13] = 2";

# compile and set our "filter program"
die "unable to compile $prog\n"
  if (Net::Pcap::compile($descript ,\$compprog,$prog,0,$netmask)) ;
die "unable to set filter\n"
  if (Net::Pcap::setfilter($descript,$compprog));
```

We're seconds away from letting *libpcap* do its stuff. Before we can, we need to tell it what to do with the packets it retrieves for us. For each packet it sees that matches our filter program, it will execute a callback subroutine of our choice. This subroutine is handed three arguments:

1. A user ID string, optionally set when starting a capture, that allows a callback procedure to distinguish between several open packet capture sessions.

2. A reference to a hash describing the packet header (timestamps, etc.).

3. A copy of the entire packet.

We'll start with a very simple callback subroutine that prints the length of the packet we receive:

```
sub printpacketlength {
  print length($_[2]),"\n";
}
```

With our callback subroutine in place, we begin watching the wire for SYN packets:

```
die "Unable to perform capture:".Net::Pcap::geterr($descript)."\n"
  if (Net::Pcap::loop($descript,-1,\&printpacketlength, ''));

die "Unable to close device nicely\n"
  if (Net::Pcap::close($descript));
```

The second argument of -1 to Net::Pcap::loop() specifies the number of packets we wish to capture before exiting. In this case we've signaled it to capture packets *ad infinitum*.

The code you've just seen captures SYN packets and prints their lengths, but that's not quite where we wanted be when we started this section. We need a program that watches for SYN packets from another network and attempts to ping the originating hosts. We have almost all of the pieces; the only thing we are missing is a way to take the SYN packets we've received and determine their source.

Like our nitty-gritty DNS example in Chapter 5, we'll need to take a raw packet and dissect it. Usually this entails reading the specifications (RFCs) and constructing the necessary unpack() templates. Tim Potter has done this hard work, producing a set of NetPacket modules: NetPacket::Ethernet, NetPacket::IP, NetPacket::TCP, NetPacket::ICMP, and so on. Each of these modules provides two methods: strip() and decode().

strip() simply returns the packet data with that network layer stripped from it. Remember, a TCP/IP packet on an Ethernet network is really just a TCP packet embedded in an IP packet embedded in an Ethernet packet. So if $pkt holds a TCP/IP packet, NetPacket::Ethernet::strip($pkt) would return an IP packet (having stripped off the Ethernet layer). If you needed to get at the TCP portion of $pkt, you could use NetPacket::IP::strip(NetPacket::Ethernet::strip($packet)) to strip off both the IP and Ethernet layers.

decode() takes this one step further. It actually breaks a packet into its component parts and returns an instance of an object that contains all of these parts. For instance:

```
NetPacket::TCP->decode(
    NetPacket::IP::strip(NetPacket::Ethernet::strip($packet)))
```

This returns an object instance with the following fields:

Field Name	Description
src_port	Source TCP port
dest_port	Destination TCP port
Seqnum	TCP sequence number
Acknum	TCP acknowledgment number

Field Name	Description
Hlen	Header length
Reserved	6-bit "reserved" space in the TCP header
Flags	URG, ACK, PSH, RST, SYN, and FIN flags
Winsize	TCP window size
Cksum	TCP checksum
Urg	TCP urgent pointer
Options	Any TCP options in binary form
Data	Encapsulated data (payload) for this packet

These should look familiar to you from Figure 10-2. To get the destination TCP
port for a packet, we can use:

```
$pt = NetPacket::TCP->decode(
        NetPacket::IP::strip(
            NetPacket::Ethernet::strip($packet)))->{dest_port};
```

Let's tie this all together and throw in one more dash of variety. Potter has created
a small wrapper for the Net::Pcap initialization and loop code and released it in
his Net::PcapUtils module. It handles several of the steps we performed, making our code shorter. Here it is in action, along with everything else we've learned
along the way in the last section:

```
use Net::PcapUtils;

use NetPacket::Ethernet;
use NetPacket::IP;

use Net::Ping;

# local network
$localnet = "192.168.1";
# filter string that looks for SYN-only packets not originating from
# local network
$prog = "tcp[13] = 2 and src net not $localnet";

$| = 1; # unbuffer STDIO

# construct the ping object we'll use later
$p = new Net::Ping("icmp");

# and away we go
die "Unable to perform capture:".Net::Pcap::geterr($descript)."\n"
  if (Net::PcapUtils::open_live(\&grab_ip_and_ping, FILTER => $prog));

# find the source IP address of a packet, and ping it (once per run)
sub grab_ip_and_ping{
    my ($arg,$hdr,$pkt) = @_ ;
```

```
# get the source IP adrress
$src_ip = NetPacket::IP->decode(
             NetPacket::Ethernet::strip($pkt))->{src_ip};

print "$src_ip is ".(($p->ping($src_ip)) ?
                    "alive" : "unreachable")."\n"
   unless $cache{$src_ip}++;
}
```

Now that we've achieved our goal of writing a program completely in Perl that would have helped diagnose my server problem (albeit using some modules that are Perl wrappers around C code), let me tell you the end of the story.

On Sunday morning, the central support group outside of my department discovered an error in their router configuration. A student in one of the dorms had installed Linux on his machine and misconfigured the network routing daemon. This machine was broadcasting to the rest of the university that it was a default route to the Internet. The misconfigured router that fed our department was happy to listen to this broadcast and promptly changed its routing table to add a second route to the rest of the universe. Packets would come to us from the outside world, and this router dutifully doled out our response packets evenly between both destinations. This "a packet for the real router to the Internet, a packet for the student's machine, a packet for the real router, a packet for the student's machine..." distribution created an asymmetric routing situation. Once the bogus route was cleared and filters put in place to prevent it from returning, our life returned to normal. I won't tell you what happened to the student who caused the problem.

In this section, you have now seen one diagnostic application of the `Net::Pcap`, `Net::PcapUtils`, and `NetPacket::*` family of modules. Don't stop there! These modules give you the flexibility to construct a whole variety of programs that can help you debug network problems or actively watch your wire for danger.

Preventing Suspicious Activities

The very last attribute of a night watchman that we will consider is an eye towards prevention. This is the voice that says "You know, you shouldn't leave those fresh-baked pies on the window sill to cool."

We're going to conclude this chapter with an example that, when properly deployed, could positively impact a single machine, or an entire computing infrastructure. As a symbolic gesture to close this book, we'll build our own module instead of showing you how to make use of other people's.

The goal I have in mind is the prevention, or at least reduction, of bad passwords. Good security mechanisms have been thwarted by the selection of bad passwords since the dawn of time. Oog's password to get back into the clan's cave was probably "oog." Nowadays, the situation is exacerbated by the widespread availability of sophisticated password cracking programs like *John the Ripper* by Solar Designer, *L0phtCrack* by Mudge and Weld Pond, and Alec Muffett's *Crack*.

The only way to prevent the vulnerability in your systems these programs expose is to avoid bad passwords in the first place. You need to help your users choose and retain hard-to-crack passwords. One way to do this on Unix machines (though the code could easily be ported to NT or MacOS) is to use *libcrack*, also by Alec Muffett. In the process of writing *Crack*, Muffett did the system administration community a great service by taking some of the methods used in *Crack* and distilling them to a single password-checking library written in C.

This library has exactly one function for its user interface: `FascistCheck()`. `FascistCheck()` takes two arguments: a string to check and the full pathname prefix of the dictionary file created when installing *libcrack*. It returns either NULL if the string would be a "safe" password, or an explanatory piece of text, e.g., "is a dictionary word," if it is vulnerable to cracking. It would be extremely handy to be able to use this functionality as part of any Perl program that sets or changes a password,* so let's look at how we would build a module that would incorporate this function. This foray will require a very brief peek at some C code, but I promise it will be quick and painless.

Our first step is to build the *libcrack* package at *http://www.users.dircon.co.uk/ ~crypto/*. The process detailed in the distribution is straightforward. Let me offer two hints:

- The larger the dictionary you can build, the better. A good source of wordlists to be included in that dictionary is *ftp://ftp.ox.ac.uk/pub/wordlists*. The build process requires a significant amount of temporary disk space (for the *sort* process in *utils/mkdict*), so plan accordingly.

- Be sure to build *libcrack* with the same development tools you built Perl. For instance, if you used *gcc* to compile Perl, be sure to use *gcc* for the *libcrack* build process as well. This is true of all modules that need to link in additional C libraries.

Once we have the C library *libcrack.a* built, we need to pick a method for calling the `FascistCheck()` function in that library from within Perl. There are two popular methods for creating this sort of binding, XS and SWIG. We'll be using XS because it is easy to use for simple jobs and all of the necessary tools ship with

---

* A similar example where *libcrack* has been put to good use is *npasswd* (found at *http://www.utexas.edu/ cc/unix/software/npasswd/*), Clyde Hoover's superb replacement for the Unix changing program *passwd*.

the Perl distribution. For an in depth comparison of the two methods, see *Advanced Perl Programming* by Sriram Srinivasan (O'Reilly).

The easiest way to begin with XS is to use the *h2xs* program to create a proto-module for you:

```
$ h2xs -A -n Cracklib
Writing Cracklib/Cracklib.pm
Writing Cracklib/Cracklib.xs
Writing Cracklib/Makefile.PL
Writing Cracklib/test.pl
Writing Cracklib/Changes
Writing Cracklib/MANIFEST
```

Table 10-2 describes the files created by this command.

Table 10-2. Files Created by h2xs -A -n Cracklib

Filename	Description
Cracklib/Cracklib.pm	Prototype Perl stub and documentation
Cracklib/Cracklib.xs	C code glue
Cracklib/Makefile.PL	Makefile-generating Perl code
Cracklib/test.pl	Prototype test code
Cracklib/Changes	Version documentation
Cracklib/MANIFEST	List of files shipped with module

We only need to change two of these files to get the functionality we seek. Let's take on the hardest part first: the C code glue. Here's how the function is defined in the *libcrack* documentation:

```
char *FascistCheck(char *pw, char *dictpath);
```

In our *Cracklib/Cracklib.xs* glue file, we repeat this definition:

```
PROTOTYPES: ENABLE

char *
FascistCheck(pw,dictpath)
        char *pw
        char *dictpath
```

The **PROTOTYPES** directive will create Perl prototypes for the functions in our glue file. This isn't an issue for the code we're writing, but we include the directive to stifle a warning message in the build process.

Right after the function definition, we describe how it's called and what it returns:

```
CODE:
RETVAL = (char *)FascistCheck(pw,dictpath);
OUTPUT:
RETVAL
```

RETVAL is the actual glue here. It represents the transfer point between the C code and the Perl interpreter. Here we tell Perl that it should receive a string of characters returned from the **FascistCheck()** C library function and make that available as the return value (i.e., **OUTPUT**) of the Perl **Cracklib::FascistCheck()** function. That's all the C code we'll need to touch.

The other file we need to modify needs only a single line changed. We need to add another argument to the **WriteMakefile()** call in *Makefile.PL* to be sure Perl can find the *libcrack.a* file. Here's that new line in context:

```
'LIBS'     => [''],    # e.g., '-lm'
'MYEXTLIB' => '/usr/local/lib/libcrack$(LIB_EXT)' # location of cracklib
'DEFINE'   => '',      # e.g., '-DHAVE_SOMETHING'
```

That's the bare minimum we need to do to make this module work. If we type:

```
perl Makefile.PL
make
make install
```

we could begin to use our new module like this:

```
use Cracklib;
use Term::ReadKey;     # for reading of password
$dictpath = "/usr/local/etc/cracklib/pw_dict";

print "Please enter a password: ";
ReadMode 2;              # turn off echo
chomp($pw = ReadLine);# read password
ReadMode 0;             # return tty to prev state
print "\n";

$result = Cracklib::FascistCheck($pw,$dictpath);
if (defined $result){
    print "That is not a valid password because $result.\n";
}
else {
    print "That password is peachy, thanks!\n";
}
```

Don't skip right to using the module yet. Let's make this a professional-grade module before we install it.

First, add a script to test that the module is working correctly. This script needs to call our function with some known values and report back in a very specific way if it received the correct known responses. At the start of our tests, we need to print a range of test numbers. For example, if we were going to provide 10 tests, we would first print `1..10`. Then, for every test we perform, we need to print either "ok" or "not ok" and the test number. The standard Perl module building code will then interpret this output and present the user with a nice summary of the test results.

h2xs was kind enough to provide a sample test script we can modify. Let's make a *t* directory (the standard default directory for a module test suite) and rename *test.pl* to *t/cracklib.t*. Here's some code we can tag on to the end of *t/cracklib.t* to perform a set of tests:

```
# location of our cracklib dictionary files
$dictpath = "/usr/local/etc/pw_dict";

# test strings and their known cracklib responses
%test =
   ("happy"        => "it is too short",
    "a"            => "it's WAY too short",
    "asdfasdf"     => "it does not contain enough DIFFERENT characters",
    "minicomputer" => "it is based on a dictionary word",
    "1ftm2tgr3fts" => "");

# Cycle through all of the keys in our mapping, checking to see if
# cracklib returns the expected response. If it does, print "ok",
# otherwise print "not ok"
$testnum = 2;
foreach $pw (keys %test){
    my ($result) = Cracklib::FascistCheck($pw,$dictpath);
    if ((defined $result and $result eq $test{$pw}) or
        (!defined $result and $test{$pw} eq "")){
        print "ok ",$testnum++,"\n";
    }
    else {
        print "not ok ",$testnum++,"\n";
    }
}
```

There are six tests being made (the previous five from the `%test` hash and a module load test), so we need to change the line in *t/cracklib.t* that says:

```
BEGIN { $| = 1; print "1..1\n"; }
```

to:

```
BEGIN { $| = 1; print "1..6\n"; }
```

Now, we can type *make test* and *Makefile* will run the test code to check that our module is working properly.

A test script is certainly important, but our script won't be nearly respectable if we omit this crucial component: documentation. Take some time and flesh out the stub information in the *Cracklib.pm* and *Changes* files. It is also a good idea to add a *README* or *INSTALL* file describing how to build the module, where to get the component parts like *libcrack*, example code, etc. These new files and the earlier renaming of the *test.pl* file should be noted in the *MANIFEST* file to keep the generic module-building code happy.

Finally, install your module everywhere in your infrastructure. Sprinkle calls to `Cracklib::FascistCheck()` everywhere you need to set or change passwords. As the number of bad passwords diminishes in your environment, so shall the night watchman smile kindly upon you.

Module Information for This Chapter

Module	CPAN ID	Version
`Getopt::Std` (ships with Perl)		1.01
`Digest::MD5`	GAAS	2.09
`Net::DNS`	MFUHR	0.12
`FreezeThaw`	ILYAZ	0.3
`File::Find` (ships with Perl)		
`Net::SNMP`	DTOWN	3.01
`SNMP`	GSM	3.10
`Net::Ping` (ships with Perl)	RMOSE	2.02
`Net::Pcap`	TIMPOTTER	0.03
`Net::PcapUtils`	TIMPOTTER	0.01
`NetPacket`	TIMPOTTER	0.01
`Term::ReadKey`	KJALB	2.14

References for More Information

Change Detection Tools

http://www.securityfocus.com is one of the best security-related sites on the Net. In addition to being home to some of the top security-related mailing lists, this site also has a superb free tools library. Many *tripwire*-like tools can be found in the "auditing, file integrity" portion of this library.

MacPerl:Power and Ease, by Vicki Brown and Chris Nandor (Prime Time Freeware, 1998). This book plus the *perlport* manual page were the major sources for the `stat()` information table in the first section of this chapter.

RFC1321:The MD5 Message-Digest Algorithm, R. Rivest, 1992.

http://www.tripwire.com/tripwire used to be the canonical free tool for filesystem change detection. It has since been commercialized, but the older free versions are still available.

SNMP

There are approximately 60 active RFCs with SNMP in their titles (and about 100 total which mention SNMP). Here are just the RFCs we reference in this chapter or in Appendix E.

RFC1157:A Simple Network Management Protocol (SNMP), J. Case, M. Fedor, M. Schoffstall, and J. Davin, 1990.

RFC1213:Management Information Base for Network Management of TCP/IP-based internets:MIB-II, K. McCloghrie and M. Rose, 1991.

RFC1493:Definitions of Managed Objects for Bridges, E. Decker, P. Langille, A. Rijsinghani, and K. McCloghrie, 1993.

RFC1573:Evolution of the Interfaces Group of MIB-II, K. McCloghrie and F. Kastenholz, 1994.

RFC1905:Protocol Operations for Version 2 of the Simple Network Management Protocol (SNMPv2), J. Case, K. McCloghrie, M. Rose, and S. Waldbusser, 1996.

RFC1907:Management Information Base for Version 2 of the Simple Network Management Protocol (SNMPv2), J. Case, K. McCloghrie, M. Rose, and S. Waldbusser, 1996.

RFC2011:SNMPv2 Management Information Base for the Internet Protocol using SMIv2, K. McCloghrie, 1996.

RFC2012:SNMPv2 Management Information Base for the Transmission Control Protocol using SMIv2, K. McCloghrie, 1996.

RFC2013:SNMPv2 Management Information Base for the User Datagram Protocol using SMIv2, K. McCloghrie, 1996.

RFC2274:User-based Security Model (USM) for version 3 of the Simple Network Management Protocol (SNMPv3), U. Blumenthal and B. Wijnen, 1998.

RFC2275:View-based Access Control Model (VACM) for the Simple Network Management Protocol (SNMP), B. Wijnen, R. Presuhn, and K. McCloghrie, 1998.

RFC2578:Structure of Management Information Version 2 (SMIv2), K. McCloghrie, D. Perkins, and J. Schoenwaelder, 1999.

Here are some good general SNMP resources:

http://ucd-snmp.ucdavis.edu is the home of the UCD-SNMP project.

http://www.cisco.com/public/sw-center/netmgmt/cmtk/mibs.shtml is the location of Cisco's MIB files. Other vendors have similar sites.

http://www.snmpinfo.com is the home of the company SNMPinfo and David Perkins (an SNMP guru who actively posts to *comp.protocols.snmp*, and one of the authors of *Understanding SNMP MIBs*).

http://www.ibr.cs.tu-bs.de/ietf/snmpv3/ is an excellent resource on Version 3 of SNMP.

http://www.mrtg.org and *http://www.munitions.com/~jra/cricket/* are the homes of find Multi Router Traffic Grapher (MRTG) and its descendant Cricket (written in Perl!), two good examples of how SNMP can be used to do long-term monitoring of devices.

Understanding SNMP MIBs, by David Perkins and Evan McGinnis (Prentice-Hall, 1996).

http://www.snmp.org is the home of the company SNMP Research. The "SNMP Framework" section of their site has some good references, including the *comp.protocols.snmp* FAQ.

Other Resources

Advanced Perl Programming, by Sriram Srinivasan (O'Reilly, 1997) has a good section on the creation of Perl modules.

http://www.bb4.com and *http://www.kernel.org/software/mon/* are the homes of BigBrother and Mon, two good examples of packages that provide a general framework for monitoring real-time events (as opposed to the historical monitoring frameworks provided by MRTG and Cricket).

http://www.tcpdump.org is the home of *libpcap* and *tcpdump*.

RFC793:Transmission Control Protocol, J. Postel, 1981.

The Five-Minute
RCS Tutorial

This quick tutorial will teach you everything you need to know about how to use Revision Control System (RCS) for system administration. RCS has considerably more functionality than we'll discuss here, so be sure to take a look at the manual pages and the reference at the end of this appendix if you plan to use it heavily.

RCS functions like a car rental agency. Only one person at a time can actually rent a particular car and drive it off the lot. A new car can only be rented after the agency has added it to their pool. Customers can browse the list of cars (and their features) at any time, but if two people want to rent the same car, the second must wait for the car to be returned to the lot before renting it. Finally, car rental agencies inspect cars very carefully after they have been returned and record any changes to the car during the rental. All of these properties hold true for RCS as well.

In RCS, a file is like a car. If you wish to keep track of a file using RCS (i.e., add it to the rental lot) you "check it in" for the first time:

```
$ ci -u filename
```

ci stands for "check in," and the $-u$ tells RCS to leave the file in place during the check-in. When a file is checked in (i.e., made available for rental), RCS does one of two things to remind the user that the file is under RCS's control:

1. Deletes the original file, leaving only the RCS archive file behind. This archive file is usually called *filename,v* and is either kept in the same directory as the original file or in a subdirectory called *RCS* (if the user creates it).

2. If $-u$ is used as we showed above, it checks the file out again, leaving the permissions on the file to be "read-only."

To modify a file under RCS's control (i.e., rent a car), you first need to "check-out" that file:

```
$ co -l filename
```

The **-l** switch tells RCS to "strictly lock" that file (i.e., do not allow any other user to check out the file at the same time). Other switches that are commonly used with *co* are:

- *-r<revision number>:* to check out an older revision of a file.
- *-p:* to print a past revision to the screen without actually checking it out.

Once you are done modifying a file, you need to check it back in using the same command we used above to put the file under RCS in the first place (*ci -u filename*). The check-in process stores any changes made to this file in a space-efficient manner.

Each time a file that has been modified is checked in, it is given a new revision number. At check-in time, RCS will prompt you for a comment to be placed in the change log it automatically keeps for each file. This log and the listing of the current person who has checked out a file can be viewed using *rlog filename*.

If someone neglects to check their changes to a particular file back into RCS (e.g., they've gone home for the day and you have a real need to change the file yourself), you can break their lock using *rcs-u filename*. This command will prompt for a break-lock message that is mailed to the person who owns the lock.

After breaking the lock, you should check to see how the current copy differs from the RCS archive revision. *rcsdiff filename* will show you this information. If you wish to preserve these changes, check the file in (with an appropriate change-log comment), and then check it back out again before working on it. *rcsdiff*, like our *co* example above, can also take a *-r<revision number>* flag to allow you to compare two past revisions.

Table A-1 lists some command RCS operations and their command lines.

Table A-1. Common RCS Operations

RCS Operation	Command Line
Initial check-in of file (leaving file active in filesystem)	*ci -u filename*
Check out with lock	*co -l filename*
Check in and unlock (leaving file active in filesystem)	*ci -u filename*
Display version *x.y* of a file	*co -px.y filename*
Undo to version *x.y* (overwrites file active in filesystem with the specified revision)	*co -rx.y filename*
Diff file active in filesystem and last revision	*rcsdiff filename*

Table A-1. Common RCS Operations (continued)

RCS Operation	Command Line
Diff versions *x.y* and *x.z*	*rcsdiff -rx.y -rx.z filename*
View log of checkins	*rlog filename*
Break an RCS lock held by another person on a file	*rcs -u filename*

Believe it or not, this is really all you need to get started using RCS. Once you start using it for system administration, you'll find it pays off handsomely.

References for More Information

ftp://ftp.gnu.org/pub/gnu/rcs has the latest source code for the RCS package.

Applying RCS and SCCS: From Source Control to Project Control, by Don Bolinger and Tan Bronson (O'Reilly, 1995).

http://www.sourcegear.com/CVS is where to go if you find you need features not found in RCS. The next step up is the very popular Concurrent Versions System (CVS). This is its main distribution point.

B

The Ten-Minute LDAP Tutorial

The Lightweight Directory Access Protocol (LDAP) is one of the pre-eminent directory services deployed in the world today. Over time, system administrators are likely to find themselves dealing with LDAP servers and clients in a number of contexts. This tutorial will give you an introduction to the LDAP nomenclature and concepts you'll need when using the material in Chapter 6, *Directory Services*.

The action in LDAP takes place around a data structure known as an *entry*. Figure B-1 is a picture to keep in mind as we look at an entry's component parts.

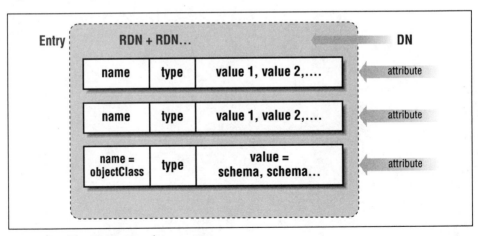

Figure B-1. The LDAP entry data structure

An entry has a set of named component parts called *attributes* that hold the data for that entry. To use database terms, they are like the fields in a database record. In Chapter 6 we'll use Perl to keep a list of machines in an LDAP directory. Each machine entry will have attributes like name, model, location, owner, etc.

Besides its name, an attribute consists of a *type* and a set of *values* that conform to that type. If you are storing employee information, your entry might have a phone attribute that has a type of telephoneNumber. The values of this attribute might be that employee's phone numbers. A type also has a *syntax* that dictates what kind of data can be used (strings, numbers, etc.), how it is sorted, and how it is used in a search (is it case-sensitive?).

Each entry has a special attribute called *objectClass*. *objectClass* contains multiple values that, when combined with server and user settings, dictate which attributes must and may exist in that particular entry.

Let's look a little closer at the *objectClass* attribute for a moment because it illustrates some of the important qualities of LDAP and allows us to pick off the rest of the jargon we haven't seen yet. If we consider the *objectClass* attribute, we notice the following:

LDAP is object-oriented

Each of the values of an *objectClass* attribute is a name of an object class. These classes either define the set of attributes that can or must be in an entry, or expand on the definitions inherited from another class.

Here's an example: an *objectClass* in an entry may contain the string residentialPerson. RFC2256, which has the daunting title of "A Summary of the X.500(96) User Schema for use with LDAPv3," defines the residentialPerson object class like this:

```
residentialPerson
    ( 2.5.6.10 NAME 'residentialPerson' SUP person STRUCTURAL MUST l
      MAY ( businessCategory $ x121Address $ registeredAddress $
      destinationIndicator $ preferredDeliveryMethod $ telexNumber $
      teletexTerminalIdentifier $ telephoneNumber $
      internationaliSDNNumber $
      facsimileTelephoneNumber $ preferredDeliveryMethod $ street $
      postOfficeBox $ postalCode $ postalAddress $
      physicalDeliveryOfficeName $ st $ l ) )
```

This definition says that an entry of object class residentialPerson must have an l attribute (short for locality) and may have a whole other set of attributes (registeredAddress, postOfficeBox, etc.). The key part of the specification is the SUP person string. It says that the superior class (the one that residentialPerson inherits *its* attributes from) is the person object class. That definition looks like this:

```
person
    ( 2.5.6.6 NAME 'person' SUP top STRUCTURAL MUST ( sn $ cn )
      MAY ( userPassword $ telephoneNumber $ seeAlso $ description ) )
```

So an entry with object class residentialPerson must have sn (surname), cn (common name), and l (locality) attributes and may have the other attributes listed in the MAY sections of these two RFC excerpts. We also know that person is the top of the object hierarchy for residentialPerson since its superior class is the special abstract class top.

In most cases, you can get away with using the pre-defined standard object classes. If you need to construct entries with attributes not found in an existing object class, it is usually good form to locate the closest existing object class and build upon it, like residentialPerson, builds upon person above.

LDAP has its origins in the database world

A second quality we see in *objectClass* is LDAP's database roots. A collection of object classes that specify attributes for the entries in an LDAP server is called a *schema*. The RFC we quoted above is one example of an LDAP schema specification. We won't be addressing the considerable issues surrounding schema in this book. Like database design, schema design can be a book topic in itself, but you should at least be familiar with the term "schema" because it will pop up later.

LDAP is not limited to storing information in strict tree structures

One final note about *objectClass* to help us move from our examination of a single entry to the larger picture: our previous object class example specified top at the top of the object hierarchy, but there's another quasi-superclass worth mentioning: alias. If alias is specified, then this entry is actually an alias for another entry (specified by the aliasedObjectName attribute in that entry). LDAP strongly encourages hierarchical tree structures, but it doesn't demand them. It's important to keep this flexibility in mind when you code to avoid making incorrect assumptions about the data hierarchy on a server.

LDAP Data Organization

So far we've been focused on a single entry, but there's very little call for a directory that contains only one entry. When we expand our focus and consider a directory populated with many entries, we are immediately faced with the question that began this chapter: How do you find anything?

The stuff we've discussed so far all falls under what the LDAP specification calls its "information model." This is the part that sets the rules for how information is represented. But for the answer to our question we need to look to LDAP's "naming model," which dictates how information is organized.

If you look at Figure B-1, you can see we've discussed all of the parts of an entry except for its name. Each entry has a name, known as its *Distinguished Name* (DN). The DN consists of a string of *Relative Distinguished Names* (RDNs). We'll return to DNs in a moment, but first let's concentrate on the RDN building blocks.

An RDN is composed of one or several attribute name-value pairs. For example: cn=Jay Sekora (where cn stands for "common name") could be an RDN. The attribute name is cn and the value is Jay Sekora.

Neither the LDAP nor the X.500 specifications dictate which attributes should be used to form an RDN. They do require RDNs to be unique at each level in a directory hierarchy. This restriction exists because LDAP has no inherent notion of "the third entry in the fourth branch of a directory tree" so it must rely on unique names at each level to distinguish between individual entries at that level. Let's see how this restriction plays out in practice.

Take, for instance, another example RDN: cn=Robert Smith. This is probably not a good RDN choice, since there is likely to be more than one Robert Smith in an organization of even moderate size. If you have a large number of people in your organization and your LDAP hierarchy is relatively flat, name collisions like this are to be expected. A better entry would combine two attributes, perhaps cn=Robert Smith + l=Boston. (Attributes in RDNs are combined with a plus sign.)

Our revised RDN, which appends a locality attribute, still has problems. We may have postponed a name clash, but we haven't eliminated the possibility. Furthermore, if Smith moves to some other facility, we'll have to change both the RDN for the entry *and* the location attribute in the entry. Perhaps the best RDN we could use would be one with a unique and immutable user ID for this person. For example, we could use that person's email address so the RDN would be uid=rsmith. This example should give you a taste of the decisions involved in the world of schemas.

Astute readers will notice that we're not really expanding our focus; we're still puttering around with a single entry. The RDN discussion was a prelude to this; here's the real jump: entries live in a tree-like* structure known as a *Directory Information Tree* (DIT) or just *directory tree*. The latter is probably the preferred term to use, because in X.500 nomenclature DIT usually refers to a single universal tree, similar to the global DNS hierarchy or the Management Information Base (MIB) we'll be seeing later when we discuss SNMP.

Let's bring DNs back into the picture. Each entry in a directory tree can be located by its Distinguished Name. A DN is composed of an entry's RDN followed by all of the RDNs (separated by commas or semi-colons) found as you walk your way back up the tree towards the root entry. If we follow the arrows in Figure B-2 and accumulate RDNs as we go, we'll construct DNs for each highlighted entry.

---

* It is called *tree-like* rather than just *tree* because the alias object class we mentioned earlier allows you create a directory structure that is not strictly a tree (at least from a computer-science, directed-acyclic-graph perspective).

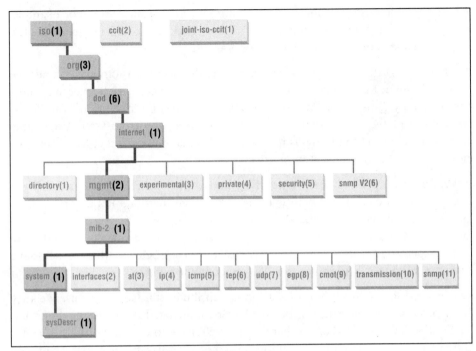

Figure B-2. Walking back up the tree to produce a DN

In the first picture, our DN would be:

```
cn=Robert Smith, l=main campus, ou=CCS, o=Hogwarts School, c=US
```

In the second, it is:

```
uid=rsmith, ou=systems, ou=people, dc=ccs, dc=hogwarts, dc=edu
```

ou is short for organizational unit, o is short for organization, dc stands for "domain component" à la DNS, and c is for country (Sesame Street notwithstanding).

An analogy is often made between DNs and absolute pathnames in a filesystem, but DNs are more like postal addresses because they have a "most specific component first" ordering. In a postal address like:

> Pat Hinds
> 288 St. Bucky Avenue
> Anywhere, MA 02104
> USA

you start off with the most specific object (the person) and get more vague from there, eventually winding up at the least specific component (the country or planet). So too it goes with DNs. You can see this ordering in our DN examples.

The very top of the directory tree is known as the directory's *suffix*, since it is the end portion of every DN in that directory tree. Suffixes are important when constructing a hierarchical infrastructure using multiple delegated LDAP servers. Using an LDAPv3 concept known as a *referral*, it is possible to place an entry in the directory tree that essentially says, "for all entries with this suffix, go ask that server instead." Referrals are specified using an *LDAP URL*, which look similar to your run-of-the-mill web URL except they reference a particular DN or other LDAP-specific information. Here's an example from RFC2255, the RFC that specifies the LDAP URL format:

```
ldap://ldap.itd.umich.edu/o=University%20of%20Michigan,c=US?postalAddress
```

The Eight-Minute XML Tutorial

One of the most impressive features of XML (eXtensible Markup Language) is how little you need to know to get started. This appendix gives you some of the key pieces of information. For more information, see one of the many books being released on the topic or the references at the end of Chapter 3, *User Accounts*.

XML Is a Markup Language

Thanks to the ubiquity of XML's older and stodgier cousin, HTML, almost everyone is familiar with the notion of a markup language. Like HTML, XML consists of plain text interspersed with little bits of special descriptive or instructive text. HTML has a rigid definition for which bits of markup text, called *tags*, are allowed, while XML allows you to make up your own.

XML provides a range of expression far beyond that of HTML. We see an example of this expression in Chapter 3, but here's another simple example that should be easy to read even without any prior XML experience:

```
<machine>
  <name> quidditch </name>
  <department> Software Sorcery </department>
  <room> 129A </room>
  <owner> Harry Potter </owner>
  <ipaddress> 192.168.1.13 </ipaddress>
</machine>
```

XML Is Picky

Despite XML's flexibility, it is pickier in places than HTML. There are syntax and grammar rules that your data must follow. These rules are set down rather tersely in the XML specification found at *http://www.w3.org/TR/1998/REC-xml-19980210*.

Rather than poring through the official spec, I recommend you seek out one of the annotated versions, like Tim Bray's version at *http://www.xml.com*, or Robert Ducharme's book *XML: The Annotated Specification* (Prentice Hall). The former is online and free; the latter has many good examples of actual XML code.

Here are two of the XML rules that tend to trip up people who know HTML:

1. If you begin something, you must end it. In the above example we started a machine listing with `<machine>` and finished it with `</machine>`. Leaving off the ending tag would not have been acceptable XML.

   In HTML, tags like `<img src="picture.jpg">` are legally allowed to stand by themselves. Not so in XML; this would have to be written either as:

   ```
   <img src="picture.jpg"> </img>
   ```

   or:

   ```
   <img src="picture.jpg" />
   ```

   The extra slash at the end of this last tag lets the XML parser know that this single tag serves as both its own start and end tag. Data and its surrounding start and end tags is called an *element*.

2. Start tags and end tags must mirror themselves exactly. Mixing case in not allowed. If your start tag is `<MaChINe>`, your end tag must be `</MaChINe>`, and cannot be `</MACHine>` or any other case combination. HTML is much more forgiving in this regard.

These are two of the general rules in the XML specification. But sometimes you want to define your own rules for an XML parser to enforce. By "enforce" we mean "complain vociferously" or "stop parsing" while reading the XML data. If we use our previous machine database XML snippet as an example, one additional rule we might to enforce is "all `<machine>` entries must contain a `<name>` and an `<ipaddress>` element." You may also wish to restrict the contents of an element to a set of specific values like "YES" or "NO."

How these rules get defined is less straightforward than the other material we'll cover because there are several complimentary and competitive proposals for a definition "language" afloat at the moment. XML will eventually be self-defining (i.e., the document itself or something linked into the document describes its structure).

The current XML specification uses a DTD (Document Type Definition), the SGML standby. Here's an example piece of XML code from the XML specification that has its definition code at the beginning of the document itself:

```
<?xml version="1.0" encoding="UTF-8" ?>
<!DOCTYPE greeting [
  <!ELEMENT greeting (#PCDATA)>
]>
<greeting>Hello, world!</greeting>
```

The first line of this example specifies the version of XML in use and the character encoding (Unicode) for the document. The next three lines define the types of data in this document. This is followed by the actual document content (the `<greeting>` element) in the final line of the example.

If we wanted to define how the `<machine>` XML code at the beginning of this appendix should be validated, we could place something like this at the beginning of the file:

```
<?xml version="1.0" encoding="UTF-8" ?>
<!DOCTYPE machines [
  <!ELEMENT machine (name,department,room,owner,ipaddress)>
  <!ELEMENT name        (#PCDATA)>
  <!ELEMENT department  (#PCDATA)>
  <!ELEMENT room        (#PCDATA)>
  <!ELEMENT owner       (#PCDATA)>
  <!ELEMENT ipaddress   (#PCDATA)>
]>
```

This definition requires that a machine element consist of **name**, **department**, **room**, **owner**, and **ipaddress** elements (in this specific order). Each of those elements is described as being **PCDATA** (see the "Leftovers" section at the end of this appendix).

Another popular set of proposals that are not yet specifications recommend using data descriptions called *schemas* for DTD-like purposes. Schemas are themselves written in XML code. Here's an example of schema code that uses the Microsoft implementation of the XML-data proposal found at *http://www.w3.org/TR/1998/ NOTE-XML-data/*:

```
<?XML version='1.0' ?>
<schema id='MachineSchema'
        xmlns="urn:schemas-microsoft-com:xml-data"
        xmlns:dt="urn:schemas-microsoft-com:datatypes">

<!-- define our element types (they are all just strings/PCDATA) -->
    <elementType id="name">
        <string/>
    </elementType>
    <elementType id="department">
        <string/>
    </elementType>
    <elementType id="room">
      <string/>
    </elementType>
    <elementType id="owner">
        <string/>
    </elementType>
    <elementType id="ipaddress">
        <string/>
    </elementType>
```

```
<!-- now define our actual machine element -->
<elementType id="Machine" content="CLOSED">
    <element type="#name"        occurs="REQUIRED"/>
    <element type="#department"  occurs="REQUIRED"/>
    <element type="#room"        occurs="REQUIRED"/>
    <element type="#owner"       occurs="REQUIRED"/>
    <element type="#ipaddress"   occurs="REQUIRED"/>
</elementType>
</schema>
```

XML schema technology is (as of this writing) still very much in the discussion phase in the standards process. XML-data, which we used in the above example, is just one of the proposals in front of the Working Group studying this issue. Because the technology moves fast, I recommend paying careful attention to the most current standards (found at *http://www.w3.org*) and your software's level of compliance with them.

Both the mature DTD and fledgling schema mechanisms can get complicated quickly, so we're going to leave further discussion of them to the books that are dedicated to XML/SGML.

Two Key XML Terms

You can't go very far in XML without learning these two important terms. XML data is said to be *well-formed* if it follows all of the XML syntax and grammar rules (matching tags, etc.). Often a simple check for well-formed data can help spot typos in XML files. That's already an advantage when the data you are dealing with holds configuration information like the machine database excerpted above.

XML data is said to be *valid* if it conforms to the rules we've set down in one of the data definition mechanisms mentioned earlier. For instance, if your data file conforms to its DTD, it is valid XML data.

Valid data by definition is well-formed, but the converse does not have to be true. It is possible to have perfectly wonderful XML data that does not have an associated DTD or schema. If it parses properly, it is well-formed, but not valid.

Leftovers

Here are three terms that appear throughout the XML literature and may stymie the XML beginner:

Attribute

The descriptions of an element that are part of the initial start tag. To reuse a previous example, in `<img src="picture.jpg" />`, `src="picture.jpg"` is an attribute for this element. There is some controversy in the XML world about when to use the contents of an element and when to use attributes. The best set of guidelines on this particular issue can be found at *http://www.oasis-open.org/ cover/elementsAndAttrs.html.*

CDATA

The term CDATA (Character Data) is used in two contexts. Most of the time it refers to everything in an XML document that is not markup (tags, etc). The second context involves *CDATA sections*. A CDATA section is declared to indicate that an XML parser should leave that section of data alone even if it contains text that could be construed as markup.

PCDATA

Tim Bray's annotation of the XML specification (mentioned earlier) gives the following definition:

The string PCDATA itself stands for "Parsed Character Data." It is another inheritance from SGML; in this usage, "parsed" means that the XML processor will read this text looking for markup signaled by < and & characters.

You can think of this as data composed of CDATA and potentially some markup. Most XML data falls into this classification.

XML has a bit of a learning curve. This small tutorial should help you get started.

D

The Fifteen-Minute SQL Tutorial

Relational databases can be an excellent tool for system administration. A relational database is accessed and administered using Structured Query Language (SQL) statements. As a result, it is a good idea for system administrators to learn at least the basics of SQL. The goal of this appendix is not to make you a full-time database programmer or even a real database administrator; that takes years of work and considerable expertise. However, we can look at enough SQL so you can begin to fake it. You may not be able to speak the language, but you'll at least get the gist if someone speaks it at you, and you'll know enough to go deeper into the subject if you need to. In Chapter 7, *SQL Database Administration*, we'll use these basic building blocks extensively when we integrate SQL and Perl.

SQL is a command language for performing operations on databases and their component parts. Tables are the component parts you'll deal with most often. Their column and row structure makes them look a great deal like spreadsheets, but the resemblance is only surface-level. Table elements are not used to represent relationships to other elements—that is, table elements don't hold formulas, they just hold data. Most SQL statements are devoted to working with the data in these rows and columns, allowing the user to add, delete, select, sort, and relate it between tables.

Let's go over some of the operators offered by SQL. If you want to experiment with the operators we'll be discussing, you'll need access to an SQL database. You may already have access to a server purchased from Oracle, Sybase, Informix, IBM, Microsoft, etc. If not, an excellent open source database called MySQL can be downloaded from *http://www.mysql.org*.

For this appendix, we'll be using mostly generic SQL, though each database server has its own SQL quirks. SQL statements particular to a specific database implementation will be noted.

The SQL code that follows will be shown using the capitalization standard found in most SQL books. This standard capitalizes all reserved words in a statement.

Most of the example SQL code in this appendix will use a table that mirrors the flat-file machine database we saw in Chapter 5, *TCP/IP Name Services*. As a quick refresher, Table D-1 shows how that data looks in table form.

Table D-1. Our Machine Database

name	ipaddr	aliases	owner	dept	bldg	room	manuf	model
shimmer	192.168.1.11	shim shimmy shimmy-doodles	David Davis	soft-ware	main	309	Sun	Ultra60
bendir	192.168.1.3	ben ben-doodles	Cindy Col-trane	IT	west	143	Apple	7500/100
sander	192.168.1.55	sandy micky mickydoo	Alex Rollins	IT	main	1101	Inter-graph	TD-325
sulawesi	192.168.1.12	sula sulee	Ellen Monk	design	main	1116	Apple	G3

Creating/Deleting Databases and Tables

In the beginning, the server will be empty and void of objects useful to us. Let's create our database:

```
CREATE DATABASE sysadm ON userdev=10 LOG ON userlog=5
GO
```

This SQL statement creates a 10MB database on the device **userdev** with a 5MB log file on the **userlog** device. This statement is Sybase/Microsoft SQL Server-specific, since database creation (when performed at all) takes place in different ways on different servers.

The **GO** command is used with interactive database clients to indicate that the preceding SQL statement should be executed. It is not an SQL statement itself. In the following examples, we'll assume that GO will be typed after each individual SQL statement if you are using one of these clients. We'll also be using the SQL commenting convention of "--" for comments in the SQL code.

To remove this database, we can use the **DROP** command:

```
DROP DATABASE sysadm
```

Now let's actually create an empty table to hold the information shown in Table D-1.

```
USE sysadm
-- Last reminder: need to type GO here (if you are using an interactive
-- client) before entering next statement
CREATE TABLE hosts (
  name     character(30)     NOT NULL,
  ipaddr   character(15)     NOT NULL,
  aliases  character(50)     NULL,
  owner    character(40)     NULL,
  dept     character(15)     NULL,
  bldg     character(10)     NULL,
  room     character(4)      NULL,
  manuf    character(10)     NULL,
  model    character(10)     NULL
)
```

First we indicate which database (*sysadm*) we wish to use. The USE statement only takes effect if it is run separately before any other commands are executed, hence it gets its own GO statement.

Then we create a table by specifying the name, datatype/length, and the NULL/NOT NULL settings for each column. Let's talk a little bit about datatypes.

It is possible to hold several different types of data in a database table, including numbers, dates, text, and even images and other binary data. Table columns are created to hold a certain kind of data. Our needs are modest, so this table is composed of a set of columns that hold simple strings of **characters**. SQL also allows you to create user-defined aliases for datatypes like **ip_address** or **employee_id**. User-defined datatypes are used in table creation to keep table structures readable and data formats consistent between columns across multiple tables.

The last set of parameters of our previous command declares a column to be mandatory or optional. If this parameter is set to NOT NULL, a row cannot be added to the table if it lacks data in this column. In our example, we need a machine name and IP address for a machine record to be useful to us, so we declare those fields NOT NULL. All the rest are optional (though highly desirable). There are other constraints besides NULL/NOT NULL that can be applied to a column for data consistency. For instance, one could ensure that two machines are not named the same thing by changing:

```
name     character(30)     NOT NULL,
```

to:

```
name     character(30)     NOT NULL CONSTRAINT unique_name UNIQUE,
```

We use `unique_name` as the name of this particular constraint. Naming your constraints make the error messages generated by constraint violations more useful. See your server documentation for other constraints that can be applied to a table.

Deleting entire tables from a database is considerably simpler than creating them:

```
USE sysadm
DROP TABLE hosts
```

Inserting Data into a Table

Now that we have an empty table, let's look at two ways to add new data. Here's the first form:

```
USE sysadm
INSERT hosts
   VALUES (
      'shimmer',
      '192.168.1.11',
      'shim shimmy shimmydoodles',
      'David Davis',
      'Software',
      'Main',
      '309',
      'Sun',
      'Ultra60'
   )
```

The first line tells the server we are going to work with objects in the *sysadm* database. The second line selects the *hosts* table and adds a row, one column at a time. This version of the *INSERT* command is used to add a complete row to the table (i.e., one with all columns filled in). To create a new row with a partial record we can specify the columns to fill, like so:

```
USE sysadm
INSERT hosts (name,ipaddr,owner)
   VALUES (
      'bendir',
      '192.168.1.3',
      'Cindy Coltrane'
   )
```

The `INSERT` command will fail if we try to insert a row does not have all of the required (`NOT NULL`) columns.

`INSERT` can also be used to add data from one table to another; we'll see this usage later. For the rest of our examples, assume that we've fully populated the *hosts* table using the first form of `INSERT`.

Querying Information

As an administrator, the SQL command you'll probably use the most often is SELECT. SELECT is used to query information from a server. Before we talk about this command, a quick disclaimer: SELECT is a gateway into a whole wing of the SQL language. We're only going to demonstrate some of its simpler forms. There is an art to constructing good queries (and designing databases so they can be queried well), but more in-depth coverage like this is best found in books entirely devoted to SQL and databases.

The simplest SELECT form is used mostly for retrieving server and connection-specific information. With this form, you do not specify a data source. Here are two examples:

```
-- both of these are database vendor specific
SELECT @@SERVERNAME

SELECT VERSION();
```

The first statement returns the name of the server from a Sybase or MS-SQL server; the second returns the current version number of a MySQL server.

Retrieving All of the Rows in a Table

To get at all of the data in our hosts table, use this SQL code:

```
USE sysadm
SELECT * FROM hosts
```

This returns all of the rows and columns in the same column order as our table was created:

```
name       ipaddr       aliases                      owner              dept
bldg   room manuf       model
---------  ------------ ---------------------------- ------------------ -------- ---
---  ---- ---------- ---------
shimmer    192.168.1.11  shim shimmy shimmydoodles   David Davis        Software
Main  309  Sun          Ultra60
bendir     192.168.1.3   ben bendoodles              Cindy Coltrane     IT
West  143  Apple        7500/100
sander     192.168.1.55  sandy micky mickydoo        Alex Rollins       IT
Main  1101 Intergraph TD-325
sulawesi   192.168.1.12  sula su-lee                 Ellen Monk         Design
Main  1116 Apple        G3
```

If we want to see specific columns, we just need to specify them by name:

```
USE sysadm
SELECT name,ipaddr FROM hosts
```

When we specify the columns by name they are returned in the order we specify them, independent of the order used when creating the table. For instance, to see IP addresses per building:

```
USE sysadm
SELECT bldg,ipaddr FROM hosts
```

This returns:

```
bldg        ipaddr
----------  ---------------
Main        192.168.1.11
West        192.168.1.3
Main        192.168.1.55
Main        192.168.1.12
```

Retrieving a Subset of the Rows in a Table

Databases wouldn't be very interesting if you couldn't retrieve a subset of your data. In SQL, we use the **SELECT** command and add a **WHERE** clause containing a conditional:

```
USE sysadm
SELECT * FROM hosts WHERE bldg="Main"
```

This shows:

```
name       ipaddr         aliases                      owner              dept
bldg    room manuf      model
---------  ------------   ----------------------------  -----------------  -------- ---
--- ---- ---------- ---------
shimmer    192.168.1.11   shim shimmy shimmydoodles     David Davis        Software
Main 309 Sun          Ultra60
sander     192.168.1.55   sandy micky mickydoo          Alex Rollins       IT
Main 1101 Intergraph TD-325
sulawesi   192.168.1.12   sula su-lee                   Ellen Monk         Design
Main 1116 Apple        G3
```

The set of available conditional operators for **WHERE** clauses are the standard programming fare:

```
=      >      >=      <       <=       <>
```

Unlike Perl, SQL does not have separate string and numeric comparison operators.

Conditional operators can be combined with **AND/OR** and negated with **NOT**. We can test for an empty column using **IS NULL** or non-empty with **IS NOT NULL**. For instance, this SQL code will show all of the machines without owners listed in our table:

```
USE sysadm
SELECT name FROM hosts WHERE owner IS NULL
```

If you want to find all of the rows that have a column whose contents is one of several specified values, you can use the IN operator to specify a list:

```
USE sysadm
SELECT name FROM hosts WHERE dept IN ('IT', 'Software')
```

This shows all of the machines in use in either the IT or software departments. SQL will also allow you to return rows that match a certain range of values (most useful with numeric or date values) with the BETWEEN operator. Here's an example that shows all of the machines in the main building on the tenth floor:

```
USE sysadm
SELECT name FROM hosts
   WHERE (bldg = 'Main') AND
         (room BETWEEN '1000' AND '1999')
```

Finally, the WHERE clause can be used with LIKE to choose rows using weak pattern matching (in comparison to Perl's regular expressions). For instance, this will select all of the machines that have the string "doodles" somewhere in their aliases:

```
USE sysadm
SELECT name FROM hosts WHERE aliases LIKE '%doodles%'
```

Table D-2 lists the supported LIKE wildcards.

Table D-2. LIKE Wildcards

Wildcard	Meaning	Closest Perl Regexp Equivalent
%	Zero or more characters	.*
_	A single character	.
[]	A single character that is one of a specified set or range	[]

Some database servers have added extensions to SQL to allow for regular expression use in SELECTs. For instance, MySQL offers the REGEXP operator for use with SELECT. REGEXP doesn't have all the power of Perl's regular expression engine, but it offers a substantial increase in flexibility over the standard SQL wildcards.

Simple Manipulation of Data Returned by Queries

Two useful clauses for a SELECT statement are DISTINCT and ORDER BY. The first allows us to eliminate duplicate records returned by a query. If we want a list of all of the distinct manufacturers represented in our hosts table, we could use DISTINCT:

```
USE sysadm
SELECT DISTINCT manuf FROM hosts
```

If we want to see our data returned in a sorted order, we can use ORDER BY:

```
USE sysadm
SELECT name,ipaddr,dept,owner FROM hosts ORDER BY dept
```

SQL has several operators that can be used to modify the output returned by a query. They allow you to change column names, do summary and intra/intercolumn calculations, reformat how fields are displayed, perform subqueries, and a whole host of other things. Please see an SQL book for more detail on SELECT's many clause operators.

Adding the Query Results to Another Table

A new table containing the results of a query can be created on the fly by using an INTO clause on some SQL servers:

```
USE sysadm
SELECT name,ipaddr INTO itmachines FROM hosts WHERE dept = 'IT'
```

This statement works just like those we've seen previously, except the results of the query are added to another table called *itmachines*. With some servers, this table is created on the fly if it does not exist. You can think of this operator clause as the equivalent of the ">" operator in most Unix and NT command-line shells.

Some database servers (like MySQL) do not support SELECT INTO; they require the use of an *INSERT* command to perform this action. Other servers such as MS-SQL and Sybase require a special flag be set on a database before SELECT INTO can be used within that database, or the command will fail.

Changing Table Information

Our working knowledge of the SELECT command comes into play with other commands as well. For instance, the INSERT command we saw earlier can also take a SELECT clause. This allows us to insert query information into an existing table. If our software department were to merge with IT, we could add their machines to the *itmachines* table:

```
USE sysadm
INSERT itmachines
  SELECT name,ipaddr FROM hosts
  WHERE dept = 'Software'
```

If we want to change any of the rows in our table, we can use the UPDATE command. For example, if all of the departments in the company moved into a single facility called Central, we can change the name of the building in all rows like so:

```
USE sysadm
UPDATE hosts
   SET bldg = 'Central'
```

It's more likely that we'll need to change only certain rows in a table. For that task, we use the handy WHERE clause we saw when discussing the SELECT operator:

```
USE sysadm
UPDATE hosts
   SET dept = 'Development'
   WHERE dept = 'Software'
```

That changed the name of the Software department to Development. This moves the machine called *bendir* to our Main building:

```
USE sysadm
UPDATE hosts
   SET bldg = 'Main'
   WHERE name = 'bendir'
```

If we wanted to remove a row or set of rows from a table instead of updating them, we can use the DELETE command:

```
USE sysadm
DELETE hosts
   WHERE bldg = 'East'
```

There's no way to undo a straight DELETE operation, so be careful.

Relating Tables to Each Other

Relational databases offer many ways to forge connections between the data in two or more tables. This process is known as "joining" the tables. Joins can get complex quickly, given the number of query possibilities involved and the fine control the programmer has over the data that is returned. If you are interested in this level of detail, your best bet is to seek out a book devoted to SQL.

Here is one example of a join in action. For this example we'll use another table called *contracts,* which contains information on the maintenance contracts for each of our machines. That table is shown in Table D-3.

Table D-3. Our Contracts Table

name	servicevendor	startdate	enddate
bendir	Dec	09-09-1995	06-01-1998
sander	Intergraph	03-14-1998	03-14-1999

Table D-3. Our Contracts Table (continued)

name	servicevendor	startdate	enddate
shimmer	Sun	12-12-1998	12-12-2000
sulawesi	Apple	11-01-1995	11-01-1998

Here's one way to relate our hosts table to the contracts table using a join:

```
USE sysadm
SELECT name,servicevendor,enddate
  FROM contracts, hosts
  WHERE contracts.name = hosts.name
```

The easiest way to understand this code is to read it from the middle out. `FROM contracts, hosts` tells the server that we wish to relate the *contracts* and *hosts* tables. `ON contracts.name = hosts.name` says we will match a row in *contracts* to a row in *hosts* based on the contents of the `name` field in each table. Finally, the `SELECT...` line specifies the columns we wish to appear in our output.

SQL Stragglers

Before we close this tutorial section, there are a few more advanced SQL topics you may encounter in your travels.

Views

Some SQL servers allow you to create different *views* of a table. Views are like magic permanent `SELECT` queries. Once you create a view using a special `SELECT` query, the results of your query stick around and behave like their own table. Views can be queried like any other table. Modifications to a view, with a few restrictions, are propagated back to the original table or tables.

Note I said *tables*. Here's where the magic of views comes in: a view on a table can be created that consists of a join between that table and another. This view behaves as one large virtual table. Changes to this view are propagated back to the original tables that are part of the join that created the view.

A view can also be created with a new column consisting of calculations performed between other columns in that table, almost like a spreadsheet. Views are useful for more mundane purposes also, like query simplification (i.e., may be able to select fewer columns) and data restructuring (i.e., table users sees a view of the data that doesn't change, even if other columns in the underlying table structure are modified).

Here's a view creation example that demonstrates query simplification:

```
USE sysadm
CREATE VIEW ipaddr_view AS SELECT name, ipaddr FROM hosts
```

Now we can use a very simple query to get back just the information we need:

```
USE sysadm
SELECT * FROM ipaddr_view
```

The result of this query is:

```
name                               ipaddr
------------------------------     ---------------
shimmer                            192.168.1.11
bendir                             192.168.1.3
sander                             192.168.1.55
sulawesi                           192.168.1.12
```

Like tables, views are dropped using a form of the DROP command:

```
USE sysadm
DROP VIEW ipaddr_view
```

Cursors

In all of the queries we've seen above, we've asked the server to hand us back all of the results once the query has completed. Sometimes it is preferable to receive the answer to a query one line at a time. This is most often the case when embedding SQL queries in other programs. If your query returns tens of thousands of lines, chances are pretty good that you'll want to process the results one line at a time, rather than storing them all in memory for later use. Most SQL programming in Perl uses this line-at-a-time method. Here's a small native-SQL program that demonstrates cursor use on a Sybase or MS-SQL Server:

```
USE sysadm
-- declare our variables
DECLARE @hostname character(30)
DECLARE @ip character(15)

-- declare our cursor
DECLARE hosts_curs CURSOR FOR SELECT name,ipaddr FROM hosts

-- open this cursor
OPEN hosts_curs

-- iterate over table, fetching rows one at a time,
-- until we receive an error
FETCH hosts_curs INTO @hostname,@ip
WHILE (@@fetch_status = 0)
  BEGIN
     PRINT "----"
     PRINT @hostname
     PRINT @ip
     FETCH hosts_curs INTO @hostname,@ip
  END

-- close the cursor (not strictly necessary when followed
-- by a DEALLOCATE)
```

```
CLOSE hosts_curs

-- undefine cursor def
DEALLOCATE hosts_curs
```

This produces the following output:

```
----
shimmer
192.168.1.11
----
bendir
192.168.1.3
----
sander
192.168.1.55
----
sulawesi
192.168.1.12
```

Stored Procedures

Most database systems allow you to upload SQL code to the server where it is stored in an optimized, post-parsed form for faster execution. These uploads are known as *stored procedures*. Stored procedures are often a critical component of SQL for administrators because large parts of server administration for some servers rely on them. For example, to change the owner of the *sysadm* database in Sybase, you might do this:

```
USE sysadm
sp_changedbowner "jay"
```

See Chapter 7 for examples of calling stored procedures. Now that you've seen the basics of SQL, you're ready to tackle Chapter 7.

The Twenty-Minute SNMP Tutorial

The Simple Network Management Protocol (SNMP) is the ubiquitous protocol used to manage devices on a network. Unfortunately, as we metioned at the beginning of Chapter 10, *Security and Network Monitoring*, SNMP is not a particularly simple protocol (despite its name). This longish tutorial will give you the information you need to get started with Version 1 of SNMP.

SNMP is predicated on the notion that you have a management station that polls an SNMP agent running on a remote device for information. The agent can also be instructed to signal the management station if an important condition arises (like a counter exceeding a threshold). When we programmed in Perl in Chapter 10, *Security and Network Monitoring*, we essentially acted as a management station, polling the SNMP agents on other network devices.

We're going to concentrate on Version 1 of SNMP. There have been seven versions of the protocol (SNMPv1, SNMPsec, SNMPv2p, SNMPv2c, SNMPv2u, SNMPv2* and SNMPv3) proposed. v1 is the only one that has been widely implemented and deployed, though v3 is expected to eventually ascend thanks to its superior security architecture.

Perl and SNMP both have simple data types. Perl uses a scalar as its base type. Lists and hashes are just collections of scalars in Perl. In SNMP, you also work with scalar *variables*. SNMP variables can hold one of four primitive types: integers, strings, object identifiers (more on this in a moment), or null values. And just like Perl, in SNMP a set of related variables can be grouped together to form larger structures (most often *tables*). This is where their similarity ends.

Perl and SNMP diverge radically when we come to the subject of variable names. In Perl, you can, given a few restrictions, name your variables anything you'd like. SNMP variable names are considerably more restrictive. All SNMP variables exist

within a virtual hierarchical storage structure known as the Management Information Base (MIB). All valid variable names are defined within this framework. The
MIB, now at version MIB-II, defines a tree structure for all of the objects (and their
names) that can be managed via SNMP.

In some ways the MIB is similar to a filesystem. Instead of organizing files, the
MIB logically organizes management information in a hierarchical tree-like structure. Each node in this tree has a short text string, called a *label*, and an accompanying number that represents its position at that level in the tree. To give you a
sense of how this works, let's go find the SNMP variable in the MIB used to hold a
system's description of itself. Bear with me; we have a bit of a tree walking (eight
levels' worth) to get there.

Figure E-1 shows a picture of the top of the MIB tree.

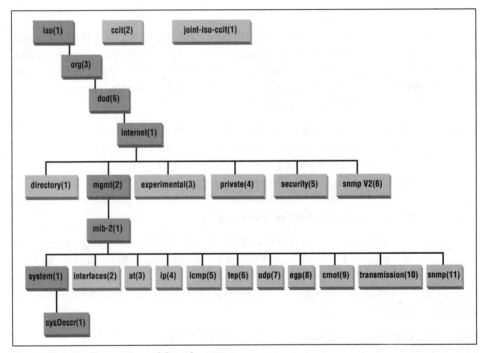

Figure E-1. Finding sysDescr(1) in the MIB

The top of the tree consists of standards organizations: `iso(1)`, `ccitt(2)`,
`joint-iso-ccitt(3)`. Under the `iso(1)` node, there is a node called `org(3)` for
other organizations. Under this node is `dod(6)`, for the Department of Defense.
Under that node is `internet(1)`, a subtree for the Internet community.

Here's where things start to get interesting. The Internet Activities Board has
assigned the subtrees listed in Table E-1 under `internet(1)`.

Table E-1. Subtrees of the internet(1) Node

Subtree	Description
directory(1)	OSI directory
mgmt(2)	RFC standard objects
experimental(3)	Internet experiments
private(4)	Vendor-specific
security(5)	Security
snmpV2(6)	SNMP internals

Because we're interested in using SNMP for device management, we will want to take the mgmt(2) branch, The first node under mgmt(2) is the MIB itself (this is almost recursive). Since there is only one MIB, the only node under mgmt(2) is mib-2(1).

The real meat (or tofu) of the MIB begins at this level in the tree. We find the first set of branches, called object groups, that hold the variables we'll want to query:

```
system(1)
interfaces(2)
at(3)
ip(4)
icmp(5)
tcp(6)
udp(7)
egp(8)
cmot(9)
transmission(10)
snmp(11)
```

Remember, we're hunting for the "system description" SNMP variable, so the system(1) group is the logical place to look. The first node in that tree is sysDescr(1). We've located the object we need.

Why bother with all of this tree-walking stuff? This trip provides us with sysDescr(1)'s Object Identifier. The Object Identifier, or OID, is just the dotted set of the numbers from each label of the tree we encountered on our way to this object. Figure E-2 shows this graphically.

So the OID for the Internet tree is 1.3.6.1, the OID for the system object group is 1.3.6.1.2.1.1, and the OID for the sysDescr object is 1.3.6.1.2.1.1.1.

When we want to actually use this OID in practice, we'll need to tack on another number to get the value of this variable. We will need to append a .0, representing the first (and only, since a device cannot have more than one description) *instance* of this object.

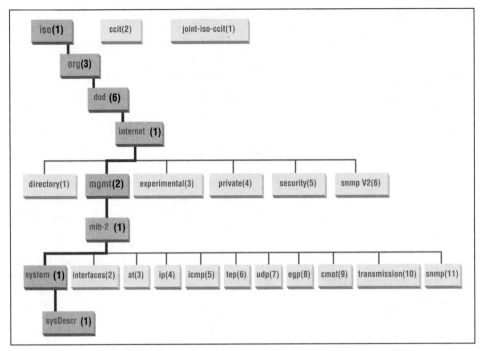

Figure E-2. Finding the OID for our desired object

In fact, let's do that; let's use this OID in a sneak preview of SNMP in action. In this appendix we'll be using the command-line tools from the UCD-SNMP package for demonstration purposes. The UCD-SNMP package that can be found at *http://ucd-snmp.ucdavis.edu/* is an excellent free SNMPv1 and v3 implementation. We're using this particular SNMP implementation because one of the Perl modules links to its library, but any other client that can send an SNMP request will do just as nicely. Once you're familiar with command-line SNMP utilities, making the jump to the Perl equivalents is easy.

The UCD-SNMP command-line tools require us to prepend a dot if we wish to specify an OID/variable name starting at the root of the tree. Otherwise the OID/ variable name is assumed to begin at the top of the `mib-2` tree. Here are two ways we might query the machine *solarisbox* for its systems description:

```
$ snmpget solarisbox public .1.3.6.1.2.1.1.1.0
$ snmpget solarisbox public .iso.org.dod.internet.mgmt.mib-2.system.sysDescr.0
```

These lines both yield:

```
system.sysDescr.0 = Sun SNMP Agent, Ultra-1
```

Back to the theory. It is important to remember that the P in SNMP stands for *Protocol*. SNMP itself is just the protocol for the communication between entities in a management infrastructure. The operations, or "protocol data units" (PDUs), are meant to be *simple*. Here are the PDUs you'll see most often, especially when programming in Perl:[*]

get-request

> `get-request` is the workhorse of the PDU family. `get-request` is used to poll an SNMP entity for the value of some SNMP variable. Many people live their whole SNMP lives using nothing but this operation.

get-next-request

> `get-next-request` is just like `get-request`, except it returns the item in the MIB just *after* the specified item (the "first lexicographic successor" in RFC terms). This operation comes into play most often when you are attempting to find all of the items in a logical table object. For instance, you might send a set of repeated `get-next-request`s to query for each line of a workstation's ARP table. We'll see an example of this in practice in a moment.

set-request

> `set-request` does just what you would anticipate; it attempts to change the value of an SNMP variable. This is the operation used to change the configuration of an SNMP-capable device.

trap/snmpV2-trap

> `trap` is the SNMPv1 name, and `snmpV2-trap` is the SNMPv2/3 name. Traps are beyond the scope of this book, but in essence they allow you to ask an SNMP-capable box to signal its management entity about an event (like a reboot, or a counter threshold being reached) without being explicitly polled.

response

> `response` is the PDU used to carry the response back from any of the other PDUs. It can be used to reply to a `get-request`, signal if a `set-request` succeeded, and so on. You rarely reference this PDU explicitly when programming, since most SNMP libraries, programs, and Perl modules automatically handle SNMP response receipt. Still, it is important to understand not just how requests are made, but also how they are answered.

If you've never dealt with SNMP before, a natural reaction to the above list might be "That's it? Get, set, tell me when something happens, that's all it can do?" But *simple*, as SNMP's creators realized early on, is not the opposite of *powerful*. If the manufacturer of an SNMP device chooses her or his variables well, there's little that cannot be done with the protocol. The classic example from the RFCs is the rebooting of an SNMP-capable device. There may be no "reboot-request" PDU, but a manufacturer could easily implement this operation by using an SNMP trigger

---

[*] The canonical list of PDUs is found in RFC1905 for SNMPv2 and v3, which builds upon the PDUs in SNMPv1's RFC1157. The RFC list isn't much bigger than the PDUs cited here, so you're not missing much.

variable to hold the number of seconds before a reboot. When this variable is changed via `set-request`, a reboot of the device could be initiated in the specified amount of time.

Given this power, what sort of security is in place to keep anyone with an SNMP client from rebooting your machine? In earlier versions of the protocol, the protection mechanism was pretty puny. In fact, some people have taken to expanding the acronym as "Security Not My Problem" because of SNMPv1's poor authentication mechanism. To explain the *who*, *what*, and *how* of this protection mechanism, we have to drag out some nomenclature, so bear with me.

SNMPv1 and SNMPv2C allow you to define administrative relationships between SNMP entities called *communities*. Communities are a way of grouping SNMP agents that have similar access restrictions with the management entities that meet those restrictions. All entities that are in a community share the same *community name*. To prove you are part of a community, you just have to know the name of that community. That is the *who can access?* part of the scheme.

For the "what can they access?" part, RFC1157 calls the parts of a MIB applicable to a particular network entity an *SNMP MIB view*. For instance, an SNMP-capable toaster* would not provide all of the same SNMP configuration variables as that of an SNMP-capable router.

Each object in a MIB is defined as being accessible `read-only`, `read-write`, or `none`. This is known as that object's *SNMP access mode*. If we put an SNMP MIB view and an SNMP access mode together, we get an *SNMP community profile* that describes the type of access available to the applicable variables in the MIB by a particular community.

Now we bring the *who* and the *what* parts together and we have an *SNMP access policy* that describes what kind of access members of a particular community offer each other.

How does this all work in real life? You configure your router or your workstation to be in at least two communities, one controlling read, the other controlling read-write access. People often refer to these communities as the `public` and the `private` communities, named after popular default names for these communities. For instance, on a Cisco router you might include this as part of the configuration:

```
! set the read-only community name to MyPublicCommunityName
snmp-server community MyPublicCommunityName RO

! set the read-write community name to MyPrivateCommunityName
snmp-server community MyPrivateCommunityName RW
```

---

* There's an SNMP-capable Coke machine (information on it is available at *http://www.nixu.fi/limu*), so it isn't all that farfetched.

On a Solaris machine, you might include this in the */etc/snmp/conf/snmpd.conf* file:

```
read-community  MyPublicCommunityName
write-community MyPrivateCommunityName
```

SNMP queries to either of these devices would have to use the `MyPublicCommunityName` community name to gain access to read-only variables or the `MyPrivateCommunityName` community names to change read-write variables on those devices. The community name is then functioning as a pseudo-password to gain SNMP access to a device. This is a poor security scheme. Not only is the community name passed in clear text in every SNMP packet, but it is trying to protect access using "security by obscurity."

Later versions of SNMP, Version 3 in particular, added significantly better security to the protocol. RFC2274 and RFC2275 define a User Security Model (USM) and a View-Based Access Control (VACM) Model. USM provides crypto-based protection for authentication and encryption of messages. VACM offers a comprehensive access control mechanism for MIB objects. These mechanisms are still relatively new and unimplemented (for instance, only one of the available Perl modules supports it, and this support is very new). We won't be discussing these mechanisms here, but it is probably worth your while to peruse the RFCs since v3 is increasing in popularity.

SNMP in Practice

Now that you've received a healthy dose of SNMP theory, let's do something practical with this knowledge. You've already seen how to query a machine's system description (remember the sneak preview earlier). Now let's look at two more examples: querying the system uptime and the IP routing table.

Until now, you just had to take my word for the location and name of an SNMP variable in the MIB. We need to change that, since the first step in querying information via SNMP is a process I call "MIB groveling:"

Step 1

Find the right MIB document. If you are looking for a device-independent setting that could be found on any generic SNMP device, you will probably find it in RFC1213.* If you need vendor-specific variable names, e.g., the variable that holds "the color of a blinky-light on the front panel of a specific ATM switch," you will need to contact the vendor of the switch and request a copy of their *MIB module*. I'm being pedantic about the terms here because it is not uncommon to hear people incorrectly say, "I need the MIB for that device."

---

* RFC1213 is marginally updated by RFC2011, RFC2012, and RFC2013. RFC1907 adds additional SNMPv2 items to the MIB.

There is only one MIB in the world; everything else fits somewhere in that structure (usually off of the `private(4)` branch).

Step 2

Search through MIB descriptions until you find the SNMP variable(s) you need.

To make this second step easier for you, let me help decode the format.

MIB descriptions aren't all that scary once you get used to them. They look like one long set of variable declarations similar to those you would find in source code. This is no coincidence because they *are* variable declarations. If a vendor has been responsible in the construction of its module, that module will be heavily commented like any good source code file.

MIB information is written in a subset of Abstract Syntax Notation One (ASN.1), an Open Systems Interconnection (OSI) standard notation. A description of this subset and other details of the data descriptions for SNMP are found in RFCs called Structure for Management Information (SMI) RFCs. These accompany the RFCs that define the SNMP protocol and the current MIB. For instance, the latest (as of this writing) SNMP protocol definition can be found in RFC1905, the latest base MIB manipulated by this protocol is in RFC1907, and the SMI for this MIB is in RFC2578. I bring this to your attention because it is not uncommon to have to flip between several documents when looking for specifics on an SNMP subject.

Let's use this knowledge to address the first task at hand: finding the system uptime of a machine via SNMP. This information is fairly generic, so there's a good chance we can find the SNMP variable we need in RFC1213. A quick search for "uptime" in RFC1213 yields this snippet of ASN.1:

```
sysUpTime OBJECT-TYPE
              SYNTAX   TimeTicks
              ACCESS   read-only
              STATUS   mandatory
              DESCRIPTION
                      "The time (in hundredths of a second) since the
                      network management portion of the system was last
                      re-initialized."
              ::= { system 3 }
```

Let's take this definition apart line by line:

sysUpTime OBJECT-TYPE

This defines the object called `sysUpTime`.

SYNTAX TimeTicks

This object is of the type `TimeTicks`. Object types are specified in the SMI we mentioned a moment ago.

ACCESS read-only

This object can only be read via SNMP (i.e., `get-request`); it cannot be changed (i.e., `set-request`).

STATUS mandatory

This object must be implemented in any SNMP agent.

DESCRIPTION...

This is a textual description of the object. Always read this field carefully. In this definition, there's a surprise in store for us. `sysUpTime` only shows the amount of time that has elapsed since "the network management portion of the system was last re-initialized." This means we're only going to be able to tell a system's uptime since its SNMP agent was last started. This is almost always the same as when the system itself last started, but if you spot an anomaly, this could be the reason.

::= { system 3 }

Here's where this object fits in the MIB tree. The `sysUpTime` object is the third branch off of the system object group tree. This information also gives you part of the Object Identifier should you need it later.

If we wanted to query this variable on the machine *solarisbox* in the read-only community, we could use the following UCD-SNMP tool command line:

```
$ snmpget solarisbox MyPublicCommunityName system.sysUpTime.0
```

This returns:

```
system.sysUpTime.0 = Timeticks: (5126167) 14:14:21.67
```

The agent was last initialized fourteen hours ago.

The examples in this appendix assume our SNMP agents have been configured to allow requests from the querying host. In general, if you can restrict SNMP access to a certain subset of "trusted" hosts, you should.

"Need to know" is an excellent security principle to follow. It is good practice to restrict the network services provided by each machine and device. If you do not need to provide a network service, turn it off. If you do need to provide it, restrict the access to only the devices that "need to know."

Time for our second and more advanced SNMP example: dumping the contents of a device's IP routing table. The complexity in this example comes from the need to treat a collection of scalar data as a single logical table. We'll have to invoke the `get-next-request` PDU to pull this off. Our first step towards this goal is to look for a MIB definition of the IP routing table. Searching for "route" in RFC1213, we eventually find this definition:

```
-- The IP routing table contains an entry for each route
-- presently known to this entity.
ipRouteTable OBJECT-TYPE
    SYNTAX   SEQUENCE OF IpRouteEntry
    ACCESS   not-accessible
    STATUS   mandatory
    DESCRIPTION
            "This entity's IP Routing table."
    ::= { ip 21 }
```

This doesn't look much different from the definition we took apart just a moment ago. The differences are in the **ACCESS** and **SYNTAX** lines. The **ACCESS** line is a tip-off that this object is just a structural placeholder representing the whole table, and not a real variable that can be queried. The **SYNTAX** line tells us this is a table consisting of a set of **IpRouteEntry** objects. Let's look at the beginning of the **IpRouteEntry** definition:

```
ipRouteEntry OBJECT-TYPE
    SYNTAX   IpRouteEntry
    ACCESS   not-accessible
    STATUS   mandatory
    DESCRIPTION
            "A route to a particular destination."
    INDEX    { ipRouteDest }
    ::= { ipRouteTable 1 }
```

The **ACCESS** line says we've found another placeholder—the placeholder for each of the rows in our table. But this placeholder also has something to tell us. It indicates that we'll be able to access each row by using an index object, the **ipRouteDest** object of each row.

If these multiple definition levels throw you, it may help to relate this to Perl. Pretend we're dealing with a Perl hash of lists structure. The hash key for the row would be the **ipRouteDest** variable. The value for this hash would then be a reference to a list containing the other elements in that row (i.e., the rest of the route entry).

The **ipRouteEntry** definition continues as follows:

```
ipRouteEntry ::=
    SEQUENCE {
        ipRouteDest
            IpAddress,
        ipRouteIfIndex
            INTEGER,
        ipRouteMetric1
            INTEGER,
        ipRouteMetric2
            INTEGER,
```

```
            ipRouteMetric3
                INTEGER,
            ipRouteMetric4
                INTEGER,
            ipRouteNextHop
                IpAddress,
            ipRouteType
                INTEGER,
            ipRouteProto
                INTEGER,
            ipRouteAge
                INTEGER,
            ipRouteMask
                IpAddress,
            ipRouteMetric5
                INTEGER,
            ipRouteInfo
                OBJECT IDENTIFIER
        }
```

Now you can see the elements that make up each row of the table. The MIB continues by describing those elements. Here are the first two definitions for these elements:

```
ipRouteDest OBJECT-TYPE
      SYNTAX  IpAddress
      ACCESS  read-write
      STATUS  mandatory
      DESCRIPTION
              "The destination IP address of this route. An
              entry with a value of 0.0.0.0 is considered a
              default route. Multiple routes to a single
              destination can appear in the table, but access to
              such multiple entries is dependent on the table-
              access mechanisms defined by the network
              management protocol in use."
      ::= { ipRouteEntry 1 }

ipRouteIfIndex OBJECT-TYPE
      SYNTAX  INTEGER
      ACCESS  read-write
      STATUS  mandatory
      DESCRIPTION
              "The index value which uniquely identifies the
              local interface through which the next hop of this
              route should be reached. The interface identified
              by a particular value of this index is the same
              interface as identified by the same value of
              ifIndex."
      ::= { ipRouteEntry 2 }
```

Figure E-3 shows a picture of the `ipRouteTable` part of the MIB to help summarize all of this information.

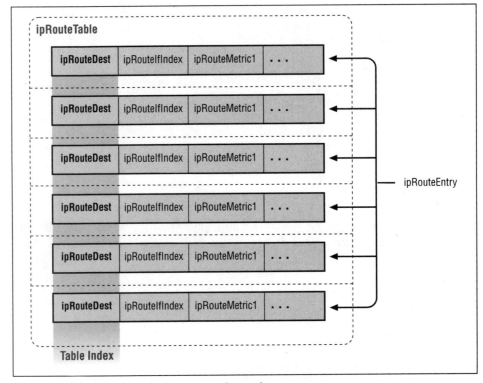

Figure E-3. The ipRouteTable structure and its index

Once you understand this part of the MIB, the next step is querying the information. This is a process known as "table traversal." Most SNMP packages have a command-line utility called something like *snmptable* or *snmp-tbl* that will perform this process for you, but they might not offer the granularity of control you need. For instance, you may not want a dump of the whole routing table; you may just want a list of all of the `ipRouteNextHop`s. On top of this, some of the Perl SNMP packages do not have tree-walking routines. For all of these reasons, it is worth knowing how to perform this process by hand.

To make this process easier to understand, I'll show you up front the information we're eventually going to be receiving from the device. This will let you see how each step of the process adds another row to the table data we'll collect. If I log into a sample machine (as opposed to using SNMP to query it remotely) and type *netstat −nr* to dump the IP routing table, the output might look like this:

```
default          192.168.1.1      UGS      0     215345   tu0
127.0.0.1        127.0.0.1        UH       8     5404381  lo0
192.168.1/24     192.168.1.189    U        15    9222638  tu0
```

This shows the default internal loopback and local network routes, respectively.

Now let's see how we go about obtaining a subset of this information via the UCD-SNMP command-line utilities. For this example, we're only going to concern ourselves with the first two columns of the output above (route destination and next hop address). We make an initial request for the first instance of those two variables in the table. Everything in bold type is one long command line and is only printed here on separate lines for legibility:

```
$ snmpgetnext computer public ip.ipRouteTable.ipRouteEntry.ipRouteDest
ip.ipRouteTable.ipRouteEntry.ipRouteNextHop
ip.ipRouteTable.ipRouteEntry.ipRouteDest.0.0.0.0 = IpAddress: 0.0.0.0
ip.ipRouteTable.ipRouteEntry.ipRouteNextHop.0.0.0.0 = IpAddress: 192.168.1.1
```

There are two parts of this response we need to pay attention to. The first is the actual data, the information returned after the equals sign. `0.0.0.0` means "default route," so the information returned corresponded to the first line of the routing table output above. The second important part of the response is the `.0.0.0.0` tacked on to the variable names above. This is the index for the `ipRouteEntry` entry representing the table row.

Now that we have the first row, we can make another `get-next-request` call, this time using the index. A `get-next-request` always returns the *next* item in a MIB, so we feed it the index of the row we just received so we can get back the next row after it:

```
$ snmpgetnext gold public ip.ipRouteTable.ipRouteEntry.ipRouteDest.0.0.0.0
ip.ipRouteTable.ipRouteEntry.ipRouteNextHop.0.0.0.0
ip.ipRouteTable.ipRouteEntry.ipRouteDest.127.0.0.1 = IpAddress: 127.0.0.1
ip.ipRouteTable.ipRouteEntry.ipRouteNextHop.127.0.0.1 = IpAddress: 127.0.0.1
```

You can probably guess the next step. We issue another `get-next-request` using the `127.0.0.1` part (the index) of the `ip.ipRouteTable.ipRouteEntry.ipRouteDest.127.0.0.1` response:

```
$ snmpgetnext gold public ip.ipRouteTable.ipRouteEntry.ipRouteDest.127.0.0.1
ip.ipRouteTable.ipRouteEntry.ipRouteNextHop.127.0.0.1
ip.ipRouteTable.ipRouteEntry.ipRouteDest.192.168.1 = IpAddress: 192.168.1.0
ip.ipRouteTable.ipRouteEntry.ipRouteNextHop.192.168.11.0 = IpAddress: 192.168.1.
189
```

Looking at the sample *netstat* output above, you can see we've achieved our goal and dumped all of the rows of the IP routing table. How would we know this if we had dispensed with the dramatic irony and hadn't seen the *netstat* output ahead of time? Under normal circumstances we would have to proceed as usual and continue querying:

```
$ snmpgetnext gold public ip.ipRouteTable.ipRouteEntry.ipRouteDest.192.168.1.0
ip.ipRouteTable.ipRouteEntry.ipRouteNextHop.192.168.1.0
ip.ipRouteTable.ipRouteEntry.ipRouteIfIndex.0.0.0.0 = 1
ip.ipRouteTable.ipRouteEntry.ipRouteType.0.0.0.0 = indirect(4)
```

Whoops, the response did not match the request! We asked for `ipRouteDest` and `ipRouteNextHop` but got back `ipRouteIfIndex` and `ipRouteType`. We've fallen off the edge of the `ipRouteTable` table. The SNMP `get-next-request` PDU has done its sworn duty and returned the "first lexicographic successor" in the MIB for each of the objects in our request. Looking back at the definition of `ipRouteEntry` in the excerpt from RFC1213 above, we can see that `ipRouteIfIndex(2)` follows `ipRouteDest(1)`, and `ipRouteType(8)` does indeed follow `ipRouteNextHop(7)`.

The answer to the question we asked a moment ago, "How do you know when you are done querying for the contents of a table?" is "When you notice you've fallen off the edge of that table." Programmatically, this translates into checking that the same string or OID prefix you requested is returned in the answer to your query. For instance, you might make sure that all responses to a query about `ipRouteDest` contained either `ip.ipRouteTable.ipRouteEntry.ipRouteDest` or `1.3.6.1.2.1.4.21.1.1`.

Now that you have the basics of SNMP under your belt, you may want to turn to Chapter 10 to see how we can use it from Perl. You should also check out the references at the end of Chapter 10 for more information on SNMP.

Index

About the Author

David N. Blank-Edelman is the Director of Technology at the Northeastern University College of Computer Science. He has spent the last 14 years of his life as a system/network administrator in large multiplatform environments, including Brandeis University, Cambridge Technology Group, and the MIT Media Laboratory. David N. Blank-Edelman has served as Senior Technical Editor for *The Perl Journal* and has written many magazine articles on world music. In his spare time, he studies *mbira*, a traditional Shona instrument from Zimbabwe.

Colophon

Our look is the result of reader comments, our own experimentation, and feedback from distribution channels. Distinctive covers complement our distinctive approach to technical topics, breathing personality and life into potentially dry subjects.

The animal on the cover of *Perl for System Administration* is a sea otter. North American sea otters make their homes along the Pacific coast, near the kelp beds containing the shellfish that make up the majority of their diet. Sea otters can be found in great numbers in Alaska, and on beaches as far south as California.

Sea otters are agile and intelligent mammals, and are known to make ingenious use of tools. Floating on their backs, they hold a shellfish such as a mussel or abalone on their bellies, and use a rock to break the shell.

Intensely social, sea otters gather to float in groups called rafts. They are excellent swimmers, propelling themselves swiftly through the water with their flipper-like, webbed back paws. Their thick fur provides them with efficient insulation in the water. At times, their existence has been threatened as they have been mercilessly hunted to near extinction for their fur.

Colleen Gorman was the production editor and copyeditor for *Perl for System Administration*. Jane Ellin was the proofreader. Mary Sheehan and Emily Quill provided quality control. Molly Shangraw, Maeve O'Meara, Gabe Weiss, Mary Sheehan, and Darren Kelly provided production support. Nancy Crumpton wrote the index.

Hanna Dyer designed the cover of this book, based on a series design by Edie Freedman. The cover image is an original illustration created by Lorrie LeJeune. Emma Colby produced the cover layout with QuarkXPress 3.32 using Adobe's ITC Garamond font.

Alicia Cech and David Futato designed the interior layout based on a series design by Nancy Priest. Mike Sierra and David Futato implemented the design in FrameMaker 5.5.6. The text and heading fonts are ITC Garamond Light and Garamond Book. The illustrations that appear in the book were produced by Robert Romano and Rhon Porter using Macromedia FreeHand 8 and Adobe Photoshop 5. This colophon was written by Colleen Gorman.

Whenever possible, our books use RepKover™, a durable and flexible lay-flat binding. If the page count exceeds RepKover's limit, perfect binding is used.

How to stay in touch with O'Reilly

1. Visit Our Award-Winning Web Site

http://www.oreilly.com/

★ "Top 100 Sites on the Web" —*PC Magazine*
★ "Top 5% Web sites" —*Point Communications*
★ "3-Star site" —*The McKinley Group*

Our web site contains a library of comprehensive product information (including book excerpts and tables of contents), downloadable software, background articles, interviews with technology leaders, links to relevant sites, book cover art, and more. File us in your Bookmarks or Hotlist!

2. Join Our Email Mailing Lists

New Product Releases

To receive automatic email with brief descriptions of all new O'Reilly products as they are released, send email to:
listproc@online.oreilly.com
Put the following information in the first line of your message (*not* in the Subject field):
subscribe oreilly-news

O'Reilly Events

If you'd also like us to send information about trade show events, special promotions, and other O'Reilly events, send email to:
listproc@online.oreilly.com
Put the following information in the first line of your message (*not* in the Subject field):
subscribe oreilly-events

3. Get Examples from Our Books via FTP

There are two ways to access an archive of example files from our books:

Regular FTP

- ftp to:
  ftp.oreilly.com
  (login: anonymous
  password: your email address)
- Point your web browser to:
  ftp://ftp.oreilly.com/

FTPMAIL

- Send an email message to:
  ftpmail@online.oreilly.com
  (Write "help" in the message body)

4. Contact Us via Email

order@oreilly.com
To place a book or software order online. Good for North American and international customers.

subscriptions@oreilly.com
To place an order for any of our newsletters or periodicals.

books@oreilly.com
General questions about any of our books.

software@oreilly.com
For general questions and product information about our software. Check out O'Reilly Software Online at **http://software.oreilly.com/** for software and technical support information. Registered O'Reilly software users send your questions to: **website-support@oreilly.com**

cs@oreilly.com
For answers to problems regarding your order or our products.

booktech@oreilly.com
For book content technical questions or corrections.

proposals@oreilly.com
To submit new book or software proposals to our editors and product managers.

international@oreilly.com
For information about our international distributors or translation queries. For a list of our distributors outside of North America check out:
http://www.oreilly.com/www/order/country.html

5. Work with Us

Check out our website for current employment opportunites:
www.jobs@oreilly.com
Click on "Work with Us"

O'Reilly & Associates, Inc.
101 Morris Street, Sebastopol, CA 95472 USA
TEL   707-829-0515 or 800-998-9938
      (6am to 5pm PST)
FAX   707-829-0104

O'REILLY®

International Distributors

UK, EUROPE, MIDDLE EAST AND AFRICA (EXCEPT FRANCE, GERMANY, AUSTRIA, SWITZERLAND, LUXEMBOURG, LIECHTENSTEIN, AND EASTERN EUROPE)

INQUIRIES
O'Reilly UK Limited
4 Castle Street
Farnham
Surrey, GU9 7HS
United Kingdom
Telephone: 44-1252-711776
Fax: 44-1252-734211
Email: information@oreilly.co.uk

ORDERS
Wiley Distribution Services Ltd.
1 Oldlands Way
Bognor Regis
West Sussex PO22 9SA
United Kingdom
Telephone: 44-1243-779777
Fax: 44-1243-820250
Email: cs-books@wiley.co.uk

FRANCE

INQUIRIES
Éditions O'Reilly
18 rue Séguier
75006 Paris, France
Tel: 33-1-40-51-52-30
Fax: 33-1-40-51-52-31
Email: france@editions-oreilly.fr

ORDERS
GEODIF
61, Bd Saint-Germain
75240 Paris Cedex 05, France
Tel: 33-1-44-41-46-16 (French books)
Tel: 33-1-44-41-11-87 (English books)
Fax: 33-1-44-41-11-44
Email: distribution@eyrolles.com

GERMANY, SWITZERLAND, AUSTRIA, EASTERN EUROPE, LUXEMBOURG, AND LIECHTENSTEIN

INQUIRIES & ORDERS
O'Reilly Verlag
Balthasarstr. 81
D-50670 Köln
Germany
Telephone: 49-221-973160-91
Fax: 49-221-973160-8
Email: anfragen@oreilly.de (inquiries)
Email: order@oreilly.de (orders)

CANADA (FRENCH LANGUAGE BOOKS)

Les Éditions Flammarion ltée
375, Avenue Laurier Ouest
Montréal (Québec) H2V 2K3
Tel: 00-1-514-277-8807
Fax: 00-1-514-278-2085
Email: info@flammarion.qc.ca

HONG KONG

City Discount Subscription Service, Ltd.
Unit D, 3rd Floor, Yan's Tower
27 Wong Chuk Hang Road
Aberdeen, Hong Kong
Tel: 852-2580-3539
Fax: 852-2580-6463
Email: citydis@ppn.com.hk

KOREA

Hanbit Media, Inc.
Chungmu Bldg. 201
Yonnam-dong 568-33
Mapo-gu
Seoul, Korea
Tel: 822-325-0397
Fax: 822-325-9697
Email: hant93@chollian.dacom.co.kr

PHILIPPINES

Global Publishing
G/F Benavides Garden
1186 Benavides Street
Manila, Philippines
Tel: 632-254-8949/637-252-2582
Fax: 632-734-5060/632-252-2733
Email: globalp@pacific.net.ph

TAIWAN

O'Reilly Taiwan
No. 3, Lane 131
Hang-Chow South Road
Section 1, Taipei, Taiwan
Tel: 886-2-23968990
Fax: 886-2-23968916
Email: taiwan@oreilly.com

CHINA

O'Reilly Beijing
Room 2410
160, FuXingMenNeiDaJie
XiCheng District
Beijing, China PR 100031
Tel: 86-10-66412305
Fax: 86-10-86631007
Email: beijing@oreilly.com

INDIA

Computer Bookshop (India) Pvt. Ltd.
190 Dr. D.N. Road, Fort
Bombay 400 001 India
Tel: 91-22-207-0989
Fax: 91-22-262-3551
Email: cbsbom@giasbm01.vsnl.net.in

JAPAN

O'Reilly Japan, Inc.
Yotsuya Y's Building
7 Banch 6, Honshio-cho
Shinjuku-ku
Tokyo 160-0003 Japan
Tel: 81-3-3356-5227
Fax: 81-3-3356-5261
Email: japan@oreilly.com

ALL OTHER ASIAN COUNTRIES

O'Reilly & Associates, Inc.
101 Morris Street
Sebastopol, CA 95472 USA
Tel: 707-829-0515
Fax: 707-829-0104
Email: order@oreilly.com

AUSTRALIA

Woodslane Pty., Ltd.
7/5 Vuko Place
Warriewood NSW 2102
Australia
Tel: 61-2-9970-5111
Fax: 61-2-9970-5002
Email: info@woodslane.com.au

NEW ZEALAND

Woodslane New Zealand, Ltd.
21 Cooks Street (P.O. Box 575)
Waganui, New Zealand
Tel: 64-6-347-6543
Fax: 64-6-345-4840
Email: info@woodslane.com.au

LATIN AMERICA

McGraw-Hill Interamericana
Editores, S.A. de C.V.
Cedro No. 512
Col. Atlampa
06450, Mexico, D.F.
Tel: 52-5-547-6777
Fax: 52-5-547-3336
Email: mcgraw-hill@infosel.net.mx

O'REILLY®